Stalinist Perpetrators on Trial

Stalinist Perpetrators on Trial

Scenes from the Great Terror in Soviet Ukraine

LYNNE VIOLA

OXFORD
UNIVERSITY PRESS

OXFORD
UNIVERSITY PRESS

Oxford University Press is a department of the University of Oxford. It furthers
the University's objective of excellence in research, scholarship, and education
by publishing worldwide. Oxford is a registered trade mark of Oxford University
Press in the UK and certain other countries.

Published in the United States of America by Oxford University Press
198 Madison Avenue, New York, NY 10016, United States of America.

Library of Congress Cataloging-in-Publication Data
Names: Viola, Lynne, author.
Title: Stalinist perpetrators on trial : scenes from the Great Terror in Soviet Ukraine / Lynne Viola.
Description: New York : Oxford University Press, 2017. | Includes bibliographical references and index.
Identifiers: LCCN 2017006386 (print) | LCCN 2017008661 (ebook) |
ISBN 9780190674168 (hardcover : alk. paper) | ISBN 9780190674175 (Updf) |
ISBN 9780190674182 (Epub)
Subjects: LCSH: Trials (Political crimes and offenses)—Ukraine | Trials (Political crimes and
offenses)—Soviet Union. | Political purges—Soviet Union. | Political purges—Ukraine. | Political
persecution—Ukraine. | Ukraine—History—1921–1944. | Soviet Union—History—1925–1953.
Classification: LCC KKY40.P64 V56 2017 (print) | LCC KKY40.P64 (ebook) |
DDC 345.47/023109477—dc23
LC record available at https://lccn.loc.gov/2017006386

9 8 7 6 5 4 3 2 1

Printed by Edwards Brothers Malloy, United States of America

Contents

Chronology

1 December 1934	Kirov assassination
1 December 1934	Law of December 1 (simplifying legal measures)
28 February 1936	A. I. Uspenskii appointed deputy chief of Western Siberian NKVD
17–18 July 1936	Spanish Civil War begins
19–23 August 1936	First Moscow Show Trial ("Trotskyite–Zinovievite Terrorist Centre")
26 September 1936	N. I. Ezhov appointed NKVD commissar. Former NKVD commissar G. G. Iagoda dismissed from post and appointed commissar of communications. Arrested 28 March 1937. Sentenced to death on 15 March 1938
23–30 January 1937	Second Moscow Show Trial ("Antisoviet Trotskyite Centre")
16 March 1937	Uspenskii appointed chief of Orenburg regional NKVD
11 May 1937	NKVD Ukraine commissar V. A. Balitskii dismissed. Arrested on 7 July 1937. Sentenced to death on 27 November 1937
11 June 1937	Convictions of Tukhachevskii and other generals (arrested in May)
14 June 1937	I. M. Leplevskii appointed commissar of NKVD Ukraine
17 June 1937	NKVD request to use extrajudicial troika in Western Siberia
23–29 June 1937	Central Committee of the Communist Party Plenum (Ezhov "sketched an all-embracing conspiracy against Stalin" implicating regional party organizations as well as NKVD, military, etc.)
28 June 1937	Politburo decree on uncovering a "counterrevolutionary organization of exiled kulaks" in Western Siberia

16 July 1937	NKVD conference in Moscow with regional NKVD organizations on NKVD Order 00447. Regional leaders bring plans for 00447. In second half of July regional NKVD leaders hold conferences locally for town and district NKVD cadres
17 July 1937	Ezhov awarded Order of Lenin
23 July 1937	Conference of NKVD Ukraine on NKVD Order 00447
25 July 1937	NKVD Order 00439 on repression of Germans suspected of espionage
28 July 1937	Conference of NKVD Ukraine on NKVD Order 00447
30 July 1937	NKVD Order 00447
3 August 1937	Conference of NKVD Ukraine on NKVD Order 00447
7 August 1937	Vyshinskii telegram to all procurators on no longer needing procurator's sanction for arrests
11 August 1937	NKVD Order 00485 on the Polish Operation (followed by other orders on national operations of other nationalities in August and September)
22 August 1937	NKVD circular on foreigners living in the USSR, indicating overwhelming majority of them are spies
September 1937	Uspenskii called to Moscow by Ezhov, met with Stalin, was about to be arrested, but impressed Stalin
20 December 1937	Twentieth anniversary celebrations of Cheka
21 December 1937	Leplevskii orders regional NKVD chiefs to force work of troikas
28 December 1937	NKVD Ukraine demands arrest of "antisoviet Zionist activists"
January 1938	Uspenskii in Moscow at session of Supreme Soviet: Ezhov tells him he will go to Ukraine
11–20 January 1938	Central Committee of Communist Party Plenum. Condemns mistakes in Communist Party purges
18 January 1938	Frinovskii directive to increase repression of Socialist Revolutionaries (SRs)
24–25 January 1938	NKVD conference in Moscow with NKVD regional chiefs
25 January 1938	Commissar of NKVD Ukraine, Leplevskii, dismissed. Arrested 26 April 1938. Executed 28 July 1938
25 January 1938	Uspenskii becomes commissar of NKVD Ukraine
27 January 1938	Khrushchev becomes first secretary of Communist Party of Ukraine, replacing Kosior
31 January 1938	Politburo decree extends Operation 00447 to 15 March 1938

1 February 1938	NKVD Operation 00447 coming to end in most places, but not in Ukraine or Far East
2 February 1938	Ezhov telegram to all NKVD regional chiefs in Ukraine—to carry on with mass operations until April 15
11–19 February 1938	Ezhov visit to Kiev
14 February 1938	Frinovskii directive on repression of Mensheviks and anarchists
17 February 1938	Ezhov leads conference of NKVD leaders in Ukraine, with Khrushchev in attendance
17/23 February 1938	Politburo increases limits in Operation 00447 in Ukraine by 30,000
21 February 1938	Uspenskii order to all Ukrainian regional NKVDs—on repression in defense factories (both social aliens and nationals)
22 February 1938	Vyshinskii to Molotov about 1937 complaints regarding repressions
end February 1938 (to early March)	Ezhov condemns preparations and implementation of mass operations in Ukraine
26 February 1938 (and March 3)	Many NKVD regional chiefs in Ukraine changed
28 February 1938	Uspenskii gives order to regional NKVDs to begin operation to destroy the "Petliurist underground"
2 March 1938	NKVD regional chiefs of Ukraine in Kiev for conference
2–13 March 1938	Third Moscow Show Trial ("Antisoviet Bloc of Rightists and Trotskyites")
12–14 March 1938	*Anschluss*
25 March 1938	NKVD conference in Kiev
8 April 1938	Ezhov retains his position as NKVD commissar and receives additional appointment as commissar of water transport
17 April 1938	Vyshinskii circular to check mistakes in Operation 00447 only in individual cases. Otherwise to tell relatives decisions are final
May 1938	Vyshinskii convenes meeting of procurators. Participants discuss "groundless prosecution" and other problems in mass operations. (22 May: Belorussian procurator criticizes former Belorussian Communist Party and procurator for groundless arrests of rural activists, leading to unrest)
21 May 1938	NKVD order to remove criminal and déclassé elements from large industrial towns

26 May 1938	Politburo decree confirming new NKVD appointments, including Dolgushev as chief of Kiev regional NKVD
5 June 1938	NKVD Ukraine report on "antisoviet manifestations in connection with preparations for elections to the Supreme Soviet of Ukraine"
12–13 June 1938	Liushkov (head of NKVD in Far East) flees
13–18 June 1938	14th Congress of Communist Party Ukraine; Dolgushev elected member of Central Committee of Communist Party Ukraine (declines, elected to plenum of Kiev regional committee of Communist Party)
July 1938	NKVD resident in Spain, Aleksandr Orlov defects
July 1938	Uspenskii trips to Dnepropetrovsk and Donbas (Grabar' sent ahead to Zaporozh'e)
12 July 1938	Uspenskii leads NKVD operational meeting in Dnepropetrovsk
22 August 1938	L. P. Beriia appointed deputy to Ezhov
15 September 1938	Abolition of album method for national operations
23 September 1938	Ezhov letter to Stalin, admitting to a series of failures
30 September 1938	Munich agreement
8 October 1938	Formation of Politburo commission to work on 17 November directive curtailing mass operations
14 November 1938	Uspenskii flees Kiev
14 November 1938	Central Committee directive about inspection by Communist Party organizations of leading operatives of NKVD USSR (to complete by 1 January)
17 November 1938	Directive on halting mass operations
19 November 1938	Politburo reviews "allegations by the head of the NKVD bureau in Ivanovo," V. P. Zhuravlev (denunciations of Ezhov)
24 November 1938	Politburo decree accepting Ezhov's resignation
25 November 1938	Stalin coded telegram to leaders of all party organizations on problematic situation in NKVD (re: Zhuravlev and other signals to which Ezhov did not react)
25 November 1938	Beriia replaces Ezhov, becoming NKVD commissar
26 November 1938	Beriia condemns groundless mass arrests
26 November 1938	Beriia Order 00762 on implementation of directive of 17 November 1938
14 December 1938	Kiev regional NKVD Communist Party meeting
22 December 1938	Beriia to NKVD organs—unimplemented troika sentences no longer have any force; direct to court

28 December 1938 · Directive of NKVD and Procurator USSR on reexamination of troika decisions in light of complaints of victims

end December 1938 · Report of deputy commissar of NKVD Ukraine A. Z. Kobulov to Beriia on implementation of 17 November 1938 directive in Ukraine

3 January 1939 · Stalin note to Vyshinskii on the possibility of organizing open trials of NKVD operatives

3 January 1939 · Report by RSFSR Procurator Volin to Vyshinskii on illegal troika decisions

8 January 1939 · Politburo decision on NKVD in Ukraine (leads to series of dismissals of NKVD regional chiefs)

10 January 1939 · Stalin's coded telegram to all Communist Party secretaries, NKVD chiefs on the issue of torture in the practice of the NKVD

26 January 1939 · Vyshinskii note to Stalin on acquainting procuracy workers with his coded telegram of 10 January 1939

27 January 1939 · Stalin sends same to Communist Party secretaries on familiarizing them with 10 January coded telegram

5 February 1939 · Beriia letter complaining regional courts blocking work of NKVD because of complaints about torture on part of arrested—leads to Stalin's telegram of 14 February on torture (again) to acquaint procurators with his telegram of 10 January

10 February 1939 · Beriia note to Stalin complaining about incorrect understandings in implementation of directive of 17 November 1938

14 February 1939 · Stalin sends note to Communist Party secretaries (again) to acquaint them with coded telegram from 10 January

20 February 1939 · NKVD Order 00156 on measures for the fulfillment of the 17 November 1938 directive

21 February 1939 · Special communications of Beriia, Vyshinskii, and N. M. Rychkov to Stalin on course of fulfilling directive of 17 November 1938 (notes poor control from Procuracy, large quantity of unfinished cases, gulf between number of court workers and demands of work; calls for increasing number of procuracy workers observing NKVD organs by 1,100 people. Declares it inadmissible to return cases to NKVD from courts for further investigation

10–21 March 1939 · 18th Congress of the Central Committee of the Communist Party

10 April 1939	Ezhov arrested
15 April 1939	Uspenskii arrested
14 June 1939	Note from Ulrikh, chair of Military Collegium, to Stalin and Molotov, writing that majority of condemned are denying confessions, referring to "difficult conditions of investigations"
23 August 1939	Soviet–Nazi Pact signed
January 1940	Uspenskii executed
February 1940	Ezhov executed
22 June 1941	Germany invades the Soviet Union
7 December 1941	Beriia request to Stalin for permission to liberate 1,610 NKVD cadres punished earlier for violations of socialist legality and to release them to fight in the war

A Note on Usage

I HAVE USED the Library of Congress transliteration system for Russian and a modified Library of Congress transliteration system for Ukrainian in this work.

The words of perpetrators feature heavily in this book and closely adhere to the original documentation. The official language employed by the NKVD in Ukraine at this time was Russian. Therefore I have used Russian for geographic place names rather than making use of current place names. Kyiv therefore appears as Kiev; Moldova is written as Moldavia.

Because the text draws so heavily on the words of perpetrators, I would ask the reader to assume quotation marks around contentious language. The reader will also notice that quotations do not include certain words identified in the documents only as curse words or with ellipses. This choice was not mine, but rather that of the author (or typist) of the original document.

Some of the perpetrators in the pages that follow appear in multiple chapters. Some served as plenipotentiaries from higher levels of NKVD administration, but others are lower- and middle-level NKVD actors who moved frequently from one position to another during these years.

Glossary

agentura: Networks of NKVD secret agents and informers

aktiv: Activists; the most politically active segment of an organization or group

All-Union: Federal level of the Soviet Union

Article 54: Charge for counterrevolutionary crimes in the Ukrainian criminal code, equivalent to Article 58 in the Russian criminal code

Article 206-17: Charges for violations of socialist legality, malfeasance, crimes of office in the Ukrainian criminal code, equivalent to Article 193-17 in the Russian criminal code

Bund: Prerevolutionary League of Jewish Workers in Russia and Poland, founded in 1897

byvshie liudi: Literally, former people (*ci-devant*, from the French Revolution); used to refer to prerevolutionary economic and political elites, including lesser elites like former gendarmes and village elders

CC VKP (b): Central Committee of the All-Union Communist Party (Bolshevik)

Cheka (VChK, or Vserossiiskaia Chrezvychainaia Komissiia): All-Russian Extraordinary Commission (the state security police from 1917 to 1922; superseded by the GPU)

Chekist: Member of the Cheka

dekulakization: Shorthand for the process of the "liquidation of the kulaks as a class"—the expropriation, deportation, and, in some cases, execution of peasants labeled as kulaks that accompanied wholesale collectivization in the early 1930s

dvoika: Two-person panels, charged with sentencing in the national operations, to be confirmed in Moscow

extraordinary measures: The extralegal measures employed in grain requisitioning in the late 1920s

First Five-Year Plan: The transformative plan of 1928–1932 that included rapid industrialization and wholesale collectivization

FSB: See TsA FSB

FZU: Factory apprenticeship school

GARF (Gosudarstvennyi arkhiv Rossiiskoi Federatsii): State Archive of the Russian Federation

gastrolery: Touring actors

gorotdel: City department

GPU: See OGPU

Gosplan (Gosudarstvennaia planovaia komissiia): State Planning Commission

Greens: Largely anarchistic forces, initially Red Army deserters, fighting on the peasantry's behalf during the civil war

GULAG (Glavnoe upravlenie ispravitel'no-trudovykh lagerei): Chief administration of corrective labor camps

interdistrict operational group: NKVD operational group during the Great Terror that united a series of districts [*raions*] within each region [*oblast'*]

Kadets: Constitutional Democratic Party, a prerevolutionary political party that emerged from the 1905 Revolution, outlawed on 28 November 1917

KGB (Komitet gosudarstvennoi bezopasnosti): Committee of State Security, from 1954

kharakteristika: Certificate or document providing a political and social profile of an individual

Komsomol (Kommunisticheskii soiuz molodezhi): Communist Youth League

krai: Territory

kulak: Literally a "fist"; a prosperous peasant who exploits hired labor; often used as a term of political opprobrium against opponents of the collective farm and other state policies (see dekulakization)

kulak operation: See NKVD Order 00447

lichnye dela: Personnel files

maroderstvo: Pillaging or looting.

MVD (Ministerstvo vnutrennykh del): Ministry of Internal Affairs (the secret or political police from 1946; superseded by the KGB [Komitet gosudarstvennoi bezopasnosti] in 1954)

Mensheviks: The non-Leninist wing of the Russian Social Democratic Party that emerged after the 1903 schism of the Russian Social Democratic Party; its nemesis, the Bolsheviks, also formed at this time

militsia: Regular police forces

militsioner: Regular police personnel

nachal'nik: Boss

Narkom: Shorthand for People's Commissar

nekul'turnost': Uncultured, crude

NEP (Novaia ekonomicheskaia politika): New Economic Policy of the 1920s

NKVD (Narodnyi komissariat vnutrennykh del): People's Commissariat of Internal Affairs (the state security police from 1934; later the MVD)

NKVD Order 00447: Major mass operation of state repression, inaugurated by the decree of 30 July 1937, aimed against former "kulaks," recidivist criminals, and other "antisoviet" and "socially dangerous" elements

oblast': Region

obvinitel'noe zakliuchenie: Indictment

OGPU (Ob"edinennoe gosudarstvennoe politicheskoe upravlenie): Unified State Political Administration (the state security police from 1922 to 1934; superseded by the NKVD)

okrug: County

ONU (Otdel naima i uvol'neniia): Hiring and firing departments within factories, with an NKVD operative serving in the role of deputy head

Osoboe soveshchanie: Highest Sentencing Board of the NKVD

otdel: Department

otdelenie: Sector

Pale of Settlement: The territories of the Russian Empire where Jews were permitted to live

Petliura: Ukrainian nationalist and civil war leader who led Ukraine's struggle for independence after the 1917 Revolution

Petliurists: Supposed or real followers of Petliura, civil war leader in Ukraine

Politburo: Political Bureau of the All-Union Communist Party (Bolshevik)

Politotdel: Political Department

Procuracy: Legal agency responsible for the conduct of prosecutions and the supervision of legality

Procurator: Legal official responsible for the conduct of prosecutions and the supervision of legality

PSZ (Protokol sudebnogo zadedaniia): Stenographic records of court hearings

raion: District

RO NKVD: Raion or district branch of the NKVD

Right Opposition: The last semipublic opposition to Stalin, led by N. I. Bukharin and A. I. Rykov; the Right Opposition crystallized around the issue of extraordinary measures in grain requisitioning in the late 1920s

RSFSR (Rossiiskaia Sovetskaia Federativnaia Sotsialisticheskaia Respublika): Russian Soviet Federated Socialist Republic

SBU (*Haluzevyi derzhavnyi arkhiv Sluzhbyi bezpeky Ukrainy*): Branch State Archive of the Security Police of Ukraine

sel'sovet: A village soviet or council

shatnye **witnesses:** "Official" witnesses

sledchasti: NKVD Investigation Departments

sledstvennye dela: Investigative files

Socialist Revolutionary (SR): Member of prerevolutionary political party representing the peasantry

soviet: A council or administrative unit, found on various regional levels, from village (rural soviet) and city levels to district, provincial, and central levels

Sovnarkom (Sovet narodnykh komissarov): Council of People's Commissars

Special Departments: Special departments within factories that included an NKVD operative as deputy head

spetspereselentsy or *spetsposelentsy*: Special settlers (official nomenclature from 1930 to 1933 and again after 1944; otherwise labor settlers)

spetsposelka or *spetsposelenie*: Special settlement or village

spetsproverka: Special NKVD inspection or report

spravka: Official certificate, usually testifying to an individual's political and social status

stoiki: Prolonged, forced standing

Torgsin: A chain of state stores (1930–1936) that sold food and goods to foreigners and Soviet citizens (from June 1931) in exchange for foreign currency, gold, silver, platinum, diamonds, and other precious stones and metals

troika: A committee consisting of three individuals, most often used in this book to refer to the important NKVD extrajudicial panels that issued sentences in mass operations of repression and including the head of the NKVD, party committee, and procuracy at the specific regional level

TsA FSB (Tsentral'nyi arkhiv Federal'noi sluzhby bezopasnosti): Central Archive of the Federal Security Bureau (successor institution to the Cheka–OGPU–NKVD–MVD–KGB)

TSD: A reference to the published series *Tragediia Sovetskoi derevni: Kollektivizatsiia i raskulachivanie. Dokumenty i materialy, 1927–1939* (*The Tragedy of the Soviet Countryside: Collectivization and Dekulakization. Documents and Materials, 1927–1939*), 5 vols. (Moscow, 1999–2006), eds. V. P. Danilov, R. T. Manning, L. Viola

TsIK (Tsentral'nyi ispolnitel'nyi komitet): Central Executive Committee

USSR: Union of Soviet Socialist Republics

uchet: NKVD surveillance registration system

upravlenie: Administration

VTsIK (Vserossiiskii tsentral'nyi ispolnitel'nyi komitet): All-Russian Central Executive Committee (of Soviets)

vydvizhentsy: "Socially pure" workers and peasants who were sent to schools of higher education or promoted directly within the Communist Party and government administration

Whites: The main adversaries of the Bolsheviks (Reds) in the civil war, representing the forces of the old regime

zakliuchenie: See *obvinitel'noe zakliuchenie*

zapal: Shorthand for distribution of goods following an execution

Zionism: Jewish movement committed largely to the emigration of Jews from the Russian Empire to what would become Israel; the prerevolutionary Poalei Zion Party, founded in 1906, represented a part of this movement

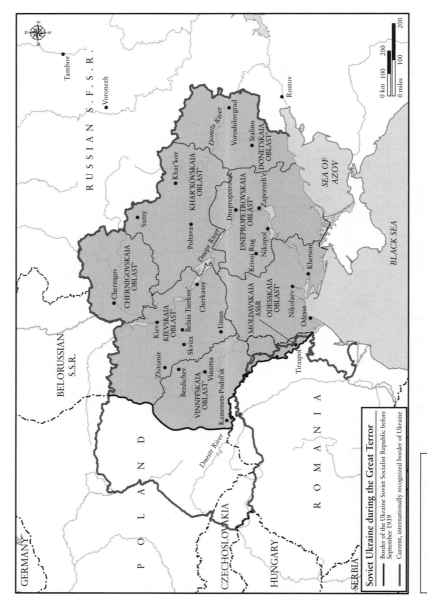

Soviet Ukraine during the Great Terror

— Border of the Ukraine Soviet Socialist Republic before
September 1939

— Current, internationally recognized border of Ukraine

See following page for detail.

Oblasts in the Ukrainian SSR

Khar'kovskaia oblast' (Khar'kov)
Poltavskaia oblast' (formed 22 September 1937) as an administrative division within Khar'kovskaia oblast') (Poltava)

Kievskaia oblast' (Kiev)
Zhitomirskaia oblast' (formed 22 September 1937 as an administrative division within Kievskaia oblast') (Zhitomir)

Vinnitskaia oblast' (Vinnitsa)
Kamenets-Podol'skaia oblast' (formed 22 September 1937 as administrative division within Vinnitskaia oblast')
(Kamenets-Podol'sk)

Donetskaia oblast' (Donetsk)
Stalinskaia oblast' (formed 3 June 1938 as administrative division of Donetskaia oblast') (Stalino)
Voroshilovgradskaia oblast' (formed 3 June 1938 as administrative division of Donetskaia oblast') (Voroshilovgrad)

Odesskaia oblast' (Odessa)
Nikolaevskaia oblast' (formed 22 June 1937 as administrative division within Odesskaia oblast') (Nikolaev)

Dnepropetrovskaia oblast' (Dnepropetrovsk)

Chernigovskaia oblast' (Chernigov)

Moldavskaia ASSR (Tiraspol)

Introduction

A Chekist has only two paths—advancement or prison.

—I.V. STALIN

ALEKSEI ROMANOVICH DOLGUSHEV was arrested on 18 January 1939, in the waning days of Stalin's Great Terror.[1] Born in 1902 in Tambov, Russia, to a working-class family, Dolgushev began working in a factory at the age of 13, after just five years of schooling. A beneficiary of the October 1917 Revolution, he joined the Red Guard in the "struggle against banditry" and, later, the Red Army. In 1929, he became a member of the Communist Party of the Soviet Union. In the 1930s, his work took him to dizzying heights of success, abruptly halted by his arrest. Subject to months of interrogation, Dolgushev struggled to defend his innocence. He claimed that enemies had slandered him and that he was never an enemy of Soviet power. He spoke of his pristine social and political background, arguing that "there is nothing socially alien about me, I am myself a worker, my father was a worker and party member; my brothers are all Communists." His arguments were futile. He was declared guilty and sentenced to death.

Ivan Stepanovich Drushliak was arrested in April 1939, shortly after Dolgushev. Born in 1913 in Kupiansk, Ukraine, to Ukrainian parents, Drushliak was a product of the October Revolution. At 15, he joined the Komsomol, the Communist Party's youth wing, and, three years later, the Communist Party. He graduated from a factory apprenticeship school as one among tens of thousands of young workers educated and promoted as a result of Stalin's First Five-Year Plan Revolution.[2] Moving to Khar'kov, he began work in a factory and soon became the secretary of the Komsomol organization there. Like Dolgushev, his career took off in the 1930s, eventually landing him a plum position in Kiev, the capital of the Ukrainian Soviet Socialist Republic. His arrest put an end to his upward mobility. His colleagues were surprised by this news because he had consistently received stellar work evaluations describing him as "an energetic and promising worker," as "disciplined, politically well developed, and seasoned as a Communist." He was said to be "assiduous" in his work, even a model worker. Drushliak strenuously proclaimed his innocence, adamantly telling his interrogator, "I do not admit my guilt since I committed no crime." He attributed the charges against him to "slander" on the part of envious rivals. He insisted that he had always worked "honestly and faithfully." All the same, Drushliak was pronounced guilty and sentenced to death.

Samuil Moiseevich Abramovich, born in 1903 in Khar'kov, was the son of a Jewish tailor. He too had climbed to the height of his career, taking advantage of both Stalin's First Five-Year Plan promotions of workers and newfound opportunities for Jews in the Soviet Union following the 1917 Revolution. He was arrested and subjected to brutal treatment at the hands of his interrogator. Shocked by his experience, he later remembered thinking that he had somehow "fallen into the hands of fascists." His interrogator called him a "Red Guard scoundrel" and threatened to turn him into a "piece of meat" if he did not confess. Abramovich fought back, telling his interrogator that he was innocent and loyal to the "party of Lenin." His interrogator shot back, "We know that you are dedicated to the party of Lenin, but you betrayed the party of Stalin." It was impossible to win this contest. Abramovich was declared guilty and sentenced to imprisonment in the Gulag, the Soviet regime's notorious system of labor camps.

Vasilii Romanovich Grabar' was arrested on 4 December 1938. Born in 1908 in Odessa to a Ukrainian father and a Russian mother, Grabar' had no more than seven years of schooling. He began work in his late teens, serving in a series of positions in his rural soviet (or village council). He later moved into a variety of other posts, before landing an important position in Kiev. He joined the Communist Party in 1932. After his arrest, he was beaten terribly by his interrogators. Yet he fought back against most of the accusations and admitted only to certain personality faults in his dealings with underlings, such as tactlessness, coarseness, and the use of foul language. He insisted on his innocence, declaring, "I was not and will not be an enemy of the people. I loved my motherland and will continue to love it. . . . I am still young and have only begun to live and therefore I ask you to see me as a living human being." His pleas were to no avail. He was declared guilty and executed on 25 December 1940.[3]

These are but a few of the hundreds of thousands of people who experienced the repression of Stalin's Great Terror. Yet they were not victims, at least not in the usual sense of the term. On the contrary, they were perpetrators, members of the Soviet internal security police, the NKVD,[4] who themselves had worked as interrogators, jailers, and executioners during the darkest days of the terror. Together, they were responsible for countless false arrests, unjust imprisonments under deplorable conditions, the torture of prisoners, and executions. That they too met the same fate that had claimed their victims was testament neither to some abstract concept of justice for the real victims nor, least of all, a change of heart on the part of Stalin, who, after all, bore the main responsibility for the tragedy of the Great Terror. Yet it was they, along with several thousands of their co-workers, who would pay for the terror. Although their arrests may not have provided much of a sense of relief or justice to their surviving victims, their experience left a rich documentary trail, allowing for a deep look into the inner workings of the Great Terror and the largely uncharted terrain of the Stalinist perpetrator.

THE 1930S WERE years of mass repression in the Soviet Union. From 1930 to 1939, close to 725,000 people were executed, over 1.5 million were interned in prisons and labor camps, and well over 2 million people were forcibly exiled to "special" or "labor settlements" in the far hinterlands of the Soviet Union. The statistical high points of mass repression occurred in the early 1930s, during the forced collectivization of agriculture, the "elimination of the kulak as a class," and the consequent famine, and again in 1937–1938 during the Great Terror.[5]

The Great Terror was a hallmark of Stalinism. It was both an elite and a mass terror. Before the partial opening of archives in the early 1990s following the fall of the Soviet Union, scholars assumed that the Great Terror was primarily a repressive action aimed against Soviet elites—members of the Communist Party, the Soviet government, and the intelligentsia—that affected ordinary people only by chance or association with elite victims of the terror (such as administrative staff or domestics).[6] Now it is clear that the overwhelming majority of victims of the Great Terror were ordinary people, mainly peasants, caught up in two large mass operations launched in these years: one against former kulaks, recidivist criminals, and other "antisoviet" and "socially dangerous" elements (NKVD Order 00447), and the other against a series of non-Russian nationalities.[7]

Since the fall of the Soviet Union, scholars inside and outside the former Union of Soviet Socialist Republics (USSR) have been exploring the dynamics and scope of the Great Terror, examining its prehistory, mechanisms, and local and social dimensions.[8] Among the most contentious issues has been the degree to which Stalin exerted control over the implementation of the terror. Whereas some have argued that the terror was a closely controlled mass operation, others have highlighted its local dimensions, conflicts between center and periphery, and societal input.[9] Although this issue may never be determined conclusively, it is clear at least that when Stalin called for an end to what he labeled "defects" and "distortions" of socialist legality in November 1938, the machinery of terror came to a grinding halt.

Stalin reversed gears at this time and aimed the terror at the NKVD itself, in what was in effect a "purge of the purgers." He was a master of the practice of scapegoating at times of radical policy reversal. In March 1930, he dramatically, if only temporarily, called a halt to the campaign to collectivize Soviet agriculture, claiming lower-level Communist Party cadres and rural Soviet government officials had become "dizzy from success" and blaming them for what he labeled "excesses" in the violent campaign against the peasantry. In November 1938, he did something very similar, calling a halt to the mass operations of the Great Terror and scapegoating members of the NKVD, mainly investigators and interrogators, and a series of other officials connected to the terror campaign.[10] If in collectivization, the beneficiaries and audience for the scapegoating campaign were by and large the peasantry, the case is less clear in 1938 and subsequent years. Although there were public aspects to the scapegoating in the Soviet press, the trials of NKVD operatives (in the main, NKVD investigators and interrogators) that ensued were secret and not open to the public. Still, they sent an important signal, both to the NKVD and to the Communist Party.[11] The trials allowed Stalin to rein in the NKVD and to announce to the Communist Party, especially its newly reinstated members and those who had suffered arrest and imprisonment, an end to illegalities, caused by NKVD commissar Nikolai Ezhov and his underlings—not Stalin.

The result of this purge of NKVD operatives was the removal in 1939 of 7,372 people (or 22% of the general operative cadres of the NKVD). Of these, 66% were fired for government crimes, counterrevolutionary activity, and other compromising activity. Cadres from the central apparatus of the NKVD SSSR accounted for 695 of these dismissals. From the 5 heads of the main administration of the central apparatus of the NKVD, 4 were replaced; of 5 deputies and assistant bosses of the main administration, 4 were replaced; of 31 heads of operative departments, 28 were changed; of 72 deputies and assistant bosses of operative departments, 69. From a total of 6,174 leading operative cadres, 3,830 (or 62%) were replaced. In Moscow Province, over half of all heads of NKVD district departments were arrested. At the same time, 14,506 new people were brought in to the NKVD in 1939, constituting 45.1% of all operative workers.[12] In 1939 alone, 937 NKVD operatives were arrested across the Soviet Union, some receiving lengthy penal sentences or even execution, most receiving only symbolic punishment followed by release to the fronts of the Second World War.[13]

THE CAPSTONE OF the purge of the purgers was a series of secret, closed trials of individuals and groups of NKVD operatives that took place between 1939 and 1942. Dolgushev, Drushliak, Abramovich, and Grabar', among many others, would stand trial at this time for the crimes of the Stalinist regime. The trials were aimed, by and large, at Ezhov's clientele network. In Ukraine, the primary targets of the arrests were clients of the Ukrainian republican NKVD boss, A. I. Uspenskii, who in turn was appointed by Ezhov.[14] These tended to be NKVD operative officers—the chiefs of the republican, *oblast'* [regional], and *raion* [district] NKVD offices along with chiefs of key departments [*otdely*] within these offices, usually investigators and interrogators engaged most directly with the *kulak* and national operations. In some cases, operatives purged after November 1938 had less important positions or were members of the militia, or regular police; in these cases, such individuals could be candidates for repression based on any number of factors, including an outsized personality or outsider status, an especially egregious act of misconduct or serious technical violation of procedure, or internal NKVD office politics, including grudges. There were repeated purges of the NKVD during the course of the Great Terror, but none quite like that of the purge of the purgers. If earlier arrests of NKVD cadres were classified as treason, counterrevolution, Trotskyism, and the like, this last series of arrests fell largely under the heading of violations of socialist legality or law during the implementation of the Great Terror and resulted, most often of all, in charges related to abuse of office.[15]

These trials were not a Soviet version of the Nuremberg trials of World War II German war criminals; nor do they resemble the many other trials of war criminals, perpetrators of genocide, and participants in repressive regimes that have dotted the landscape of the late twentieth and early twenty-first centuries. Yet they had something in common with these other dramatic confrontations. The Nuremberg trials opened a window onto the world of the Nazi perpetrator.[16] Similarly, the information yielded in the South African Truth and Reconciliation Commission, the Hague trials of war criminals from the former Yugoslavia, and a series of other perpetrator trials have allowed the world to peer behind the official facades of secrecy that left perpetrators in the shadows of history.

The secret trials of Soviet NKVD operatives at the end of the Great Terror likewise provide a glimpse behind the curtains of the terror, at the lower- and middle-level NKVD cadres who carried out Stalin's murderous policies—in the main, investigator–interrogators. However, these were not trials for the public. They were neither open court trials in the Nuremberg style nor the kind of show trials usually associated with the Stalin regime, such as the ones conducted to try the leading luminaries of the October Revolution, people like Zinoviev, Kamenev, and Bukharin.

In Ukraine, the trials of NKVD operatives continued for several years, at least one trial occurring as late as 1942 in wartime evacuation in the Urals. Here, at a minimum, 665 NKVD cadres were arrested between 1936 and 1938 for a range of offenses; at least 151 of them were arrested specifically for violations of socialist legality.[17] Their trials were held under the jurisdiction of Military Tribunals behind closed doors. The Military Tribunals existed outside the regular Soviet criminal and civil courts and were used for various purposes, most importantly for trials of military and NKVD personnel. They could also be used for civilians in cases of treason.[18] Although most transcripts of such trials outside Ukraine remain classified, the trials occurred everywhere. The trial transcripts demonstrate that the Military Tribunals followed procedure, offering these defendants far more rights than their victims ever had, in spite of the absence of the kinds of adversarial mechanisms present in jurisprudence in the "bourgeois" West. Moreover, the transcripts present frank, often disturbing, testimony that illuminates not only aspects of the individual perpetrator's motivations, but also the terror on the ground in precise and painful detail. Defendants had a right to call witnesses and a very few even had the right to make use of defense attorneys; and all exercised their rights to interrupt—often frequently—the testimony of witnesses, including victims, in spontaneous and at times lengthy interjections. The defendants also had the right to a "last word."

The trials of these NKVD operatives, along with the preceding interrogations, written confessions, and witness and expert testimony, generated volume upon volume of documentation. These documents are a unique source for exploring the machinery of terror and the behavior and mentality of NKVD perpetrators. They illuminate some of the darkest recesses of Stalinist repression—most notably, the interrogation room, the prison cells, and the places of execution—thereby shedding new light on what is arguably the most vital of all topics of Soviet history, Stalin's Great Terror.[19]

The archival records of these trials lay submerged in the bowels of the KGB archives through the Soviet period. Even after the fall of the Soviet Union, access to these kinds of files is mostly impossible, given the restrictive nature of the now FSB archives in Moscow.[20] The security police archives of some former Soviet republics in places like Ukraine and Georgia have recently allowed scholars to work with these files, thus opening new lines of inquiry into the Great Terror and its practitioners. However, the files on Uspenskii, the head of the NKVD in Ukraine, and certain other leading NKVD cadres from this former Soviet republic are still under lock and key in Moscow.

The research for this book derives from the security police archives of Ukraine, which, after the Euro–Maidan Revolution, has followed a remarkably liberal and democratic approach to access despite limited resources and personnel. The documents, which form the centerpiece of this work, constitute one of the relatively few sources accessible for a study of lower- and middle-level NKVD cadres. The investigative files [*sledstvennye dela*] of individuals and groups tried in the wake of the Great Terror remarkably contain stenographic records of the interrogations of the accused, written confessions and autobiographical materials (sometimes numbering in the hundreds of pages), witness and expert testimony (from victims, NKVD colleagues, NKVD secretaries and jailers, and prison doctors), victim autopsy reports, letters and petitions for clemency (to Stalin, Ezhov, Khrushchev, Beriia, and the like), summary indictments, the verbatim trial transcripts, and sentencing and appeal information. Combined with other types of documentation, like the personnel files [*lichnye dela*] of arrested NKVD cadres and the stenographic records of NKVD party organizations at various regional levels, these documents are an invaluable source of information.

These files are not easy to read. They are full of graphic depictions of violence, including sexual sadism and the filthy work of executions. Equally important, they are overlaid with all the biases and falsifications typical of Soviet sources. The fact that the NKVD operatives on trial almost without exception denied their guilt, while simultaneously admitting to the most vile acts, makes them plausible sources of information.[21] At the same time, an exploration and appreciation of the biases as well as the falsifications of these files is essential to understanding the mentality of the times in which these perpetrators lived.

These files are, of course, very partial and select portraits of the perpetrators. Although they contain victim testimony, it is too constrained and brief to constitute the necessary counterpart to the perpetrators' words. Perpetrator testimony is full of self-justifications centered around fear, obedience, and belief. At the same time, the trials adhered strictly to Soviet law (such as it was); they were correct in procedure and frank and open in discussion. Although some of the defendants had themselves been tortured, they retracted their earlier false confessions by the time of their trials and fought vigorously for their innocence.[22]

THIS BOOK DOES not pretend to present a comprehensive portrait of the Great Terror in Ukraine or of NKVD perpetrators. Instead, it presents a series of scenes from within the whirlwind of the terror based on investigative cases mainly, though not exclusively, from Kiev Oblast', the region or province surrounding the capital of Ukraine. The cases chosen are from a number of specific and varied settings, including a rural district, an interdistrict operational sector, an industrial city, and the regional capital of Kiev. Each details the terror on different administrative levels of the NKVD. Two cases follow the actions of specific perpetrators elsewhere—one in Khar'kov and one in Zaporozh'e—as they moved from one area to another, but ultimately back to Kiev. Most of the action takes place in 1938, when Ukraine experienced a new surge of repression, unprecedented in scale.

This series of microhistories essentially opens a curtain on the backstage of the Great Terror—the internal mechanisms of the terror, its language and euphemisms, and the illogical logic of the terror's master plot. The construction of each story circles around the perpetrator, examining the indictment, exploring different points of view in the testimony of victims and co-workers, and then turning to the perpetrator himself.[23] The voices of witnesses and defendants alike are used to capture the radical texture of the times. The stories are necessarily and sometimes frustratingly incomplete. The centerpiece of each case is the trial, which featured NKVD perpetrators fighting for their lives, speaking remarkably candidly about their work and seeking to explain and justify their actions, now deemed criminal, by reference to the usual panoply of perpetrator self-justifications: orders from above, fear of superiors, belief in their mission, ignorance, and pride. Along the way, the specific contexts in which these NKVD cadres worked is described, as well as an attempt made to assess questions of perpetrator agency within a framework set by Stalin and, to the misfortune of the perpetrators, subject to sudden and arbitrary reversal.

The stories that emerge in these pages may be considered representative of the actions and mentality of NKVD operatives in the Soviet Union.[24] At the same time, Ukraine was distinctive in its geography and population. Its position as a borderland, with a multiethnic population, served, in Stalin's eyes, to transform Ukraine into one of the most dangerous territories of the country, where "internal enemies" were supposedly in league with "external enemies," in this case, just across the border. Additionally, the specter of Ukrainian nationalism, real and imagined, loomed large as a threat to Soviet security. It is, in part, this context that, especially in 1938, conditioned the actions of the NKVD. However, Ukraine's cadre of NKVD operatives, as one interrogator phrased it, "changed like a kaleidoscope," with new cadres coming in from the Russian Republic and multitudes of local Communists and Komsomols (young Communists) mobilized to take part in the mass operations.[25] This cadre kaleidoscope, which also occurred elsewhere, brought in not only cadres from the outside, but served to destabilize the NKVD itself and to intensify the chaos of the terror, especially in 1938.

To raise the question of the perpetrator is neither to establish a paper court of history nor to condone or rationalize the perpetrators' deadly behavior. Historian Marc Bloch noted that the "satanic enemy of true history" is "the mania of judgment."[26] This book does not attempt to prosecute these men. At the same time, it is essential to emphasize, as historian Christopher Browning puts it, that "explaining is not excusing; understanding is not forgiving."[27] More fully comprehending the perpetrator may ultimately increase our understanding of the dynamics of state violence. The question of why individuals, in this case members of the NKVD, acted as they did in the implementation of state repression against officially labeled enemies, mainly innocent people, is a central question in ongoing efforts to fathom the mass violence of the Stalin era.[28]

1

The Incomplete Civil War and the Great Terror

The distinction between "one of us" and "not one of us" (or "alien elements," to use the phrase then current) went back to the Civil War with its iron law of "Who [will beat] whom?"
—NADEZHDA MANDELSTAM

1937 was necessary. Bear in mind that after the Revolution we slashed right and left; we scored victories, but tattered enemies of various stripes survived, and as we were faced by the growing danger of fascist aggression, they might have united. Thanks to 1937 there was no fifth column in our country during the war.
—V. M. MOLOTOV

THE SOVIET UNION was in the grip of a never-ending civil war in the years from the Revolution of 1917 to the Great Terror, and perhaps beyond.[1] This was not an ordinary civil war. It was instead a series of radical reverberations, no less lethal, of the original armed conflagration of 1918 to 1920, the period associated with civil war. It was a contrived civil war, mainly one-sided, periodically revived and manipulated by the Stalinist regime during phases of radical and violent transformation.

The profound ruptures of the 1917 Revolution, which played out on the battlefields of the 1918–1920 civil war, did not disappear in subsequent years. The list of enemies of the Revolution remained fairly consistent, if anything paradoxically expanding rather than contracting.[2] Each crisis introduced new enemies into the political lexicon as well as expanding the definitions of old enemies. The old enemies of the Revolution—the Whites, landlords, factory owners, *kulaks* (supposedly wealthier peasants), clergy, and non-Bolshevik political parties—were augmented by the addition of newly coined enemies from among the Soviet elite (members of the Communist Party, the Soviet government, the military), non-Russian (mainly diaspora) ethnicities, and the ever-growing categories of the socially alien and the socially danger-ous. Although most of the old contingent of enemies shrank over the years, marginalized and largely harmless, Stalin claimed that these and the new enemies would become more dangerous and more numerous as the "victory of socialism" neared.[3] For Stalin, the civil war had never ended. This was the (il)logic of a repressive dictatorship and an incomplete civil war.

Stalinist repression in the 1930s was largely prophylactic, a series of pre-emptive strikes against potential enemies.[4] The aftermath of civil war combined with the fierce intraparty struggles in the Communist Party in the 1920s, the upheavals of the First Five-Year Plan, the collectivization of Soviet agriculture, and the famine to form in the Stalinist mindset a dangerous internal environment. The internal enemy, moreover, did not act alone according to Stalinist logic, but in cooperation with the forces of the "capitalist encirclement" that had held the Soviet Union in a political vise after 1917. In the context of the increasingly dangerous international situation of the mid-1930s, following the rise of fascism in Europe, an increasingly revanchist Germany, and an expansionist Japan, Stalin and his cohort of radical Communists feared the emergence of a Fifth Column of "internal enemies" within the Soviet Union who would aid the "external enemy" in the event of war. The Great Terror of 1937–1938, as the Russian historian Oleg Khlevniuk argues, was a preemptive strike against this inherently dangerous, mostly theoretical, and as-yet-inert Fifth Column.[5] Neither its timing nor its horrendous scale can be fully comprehended outside the context of the specter of war.[6]

The Great Terror would be a purge, a cleansing of the entire nation in preparation for war. In a letter to Stalin from 10 December 1937, the condemned and imprisoned Nikolai Bukharin, once, in the words of Lenin, "the favorite of all the party," wrote:

> I have formed, more or less the following conception of what is going on in our country:
>
> There is something *great and bold about the political idea* of a general purge. It is a) connected with the prewar situation and b) connected with the transition to democracy. This purge encompasses 1) the guilty; 2) persons under suspicion; and 3) persons potentially under suspicion.[7]

Although his words about the "the great and bold" nature of the political idea of the purge, as well as the "transition to democracy," may be downplayed given either his tragically beleaguered position or lingering elements of his own Stalinist mindset, Bukharin captured the essence of the Great Terror. The incomplete civil war, enhanced by the mass repression of collectivization, cut a huge swath across the political, social, and ethnic fabric of the Soviet Union. Through the Great Terror, Stalin sought to complete the Revolution, the civil war, by eliminating all real, suspect, and potential enemies.

ROBERT CONQUEST FIRST coined the term Great Terror in his classic 1968 book on Stalin's repression in the second half of the 1930s. Conquest documented the history of Stalin's elite terror—the decimation of the Communist Party, Soviet state, military, Comintern, and Soviet scientific and cultural intelligentsia. Like most of his generation, he viewed the terror as the key mechanism by which Stalin "established himself as unchallenged dictator."[8]

Understanding of the Great Terror expanded as the Soviet archives began to yield some of the secrets that Conquest saw as so distinctive to this terrible bloodletting.[9] In 1992, the trade union newspaper *Trud* published NKVD Order 00447 on the so-called kulak mass operation.[10] This order came as a revelation, for the first time illuminating the full scope of the terror and its impact beyond Soviet elites. Within a short time, the NKVD orders for the so-called national operations appeared as well. These two operations showed that the largest numbers of victims of the Great Terror were common people, mainly peasants and a range of non-Russian suspect ethnicities, many of them also of peasant background.[11]

The mass operations demonstrated a striking continuity with the repressive campaigns against the kulak during collectivization. The violence of the First Five-Year Plan had served as the first and perhaps formative experience in state repression under Stalin, reigniting the ethos of civil war and shaping police practices. Many of the organizational structures and policies of the mass operations were derived from this first Stalinist terror and its aftermath, as were the categorization of enemies, social and ethnic, that populated both campaigns. The regular police clearly played a key role in the social purging of urban and other areas as the Stalinist state sought to order its society in the wake of the socioeconomic transformations and massive population movements, voluntary and coerced, of the First Five-Year Plan. These social policing techniques carried over directly to the mass operations of the Great Terror. Like the civil war before it, collectivization divided the world into sharp binaries of friend and enemy, revolution and counterrevolution, fascism and communism, stoking the fires of social and political hatreds and shaping the mindset and practices of a generation of Communists and Chekists.[12]

The mass operations came largely in the wake of the elite purge, spreading the terror far and wide through the vast territories of the Soviet Union. Mass operation 00447, dated 30 July 1937, was titled "the operation to repress former kulaks, criminals, and antisoviet elements." Although this operation has come to be known in the literature as the "kulak operation," this is a misnomer. The kulak or former kulak figured prominently in this operation, but was not the sole sociopolitical category subsumed. Nor should the figure of the kulak be confused with an objective socioeconomic category. The kulak was mostly a political construct, defined oxymoronically as a "capitalist peasant" during collectivization and, later, by earlier repression in exile or in the labor camps, so-called biological factors, such as a parent or grandparent who was a kulak or other socioeconomic enemy, and largely subjective political criteria, including participation in anticollectivization protests or a tendency to critique aspects of the Soviet regime.[13]

In addition to the kulak, mass operation 00447 included as targets of repression former members of "antisoviet" political parties, a series of old regime elites falling under the category of *byvshie liudi* (or former people, such as tsarist officials, gendarmes, village elders, and clergy), fugitives from repression, and a range of recidivist petty criminals. These already-elastic categories would expand according to regional specificities that led to additional enemy categories. Mass operation 00447 also included "the most hostile and active participants" of "cossack white-guard insurrectionary organizations, fascist, terrorist, and espionage-diversionary formations," thus allowing a slide, in practice, into the terrain of the national operations.[14]

Following a month of preparations, including canvassing of lower-level NKVD organs on the numbers of "antisoviet elements" in their domains and a 16 July 1937 meeting of regional NKVD representatives in Moscow, the All-Union NKVD compiled a set of control figures for the number of people to be arrested in the course of mass operation 00447.[15] The total numbers of planned arrests was 268,950, divided between a first, "most dangerous" category (75,950) and a second, "less dangerous" category (193,000). First-category subjects were to be executed by shooting; second-category subjects were to be confined in the Gulag for periods of eight to ten years.[16] With some exceptions, the operation was set to begin on 5 August 1937, beginning with the arrest of first-category subjects, and to end in four months.[17]

Each republic, territory [*krai*], and region [*oblast'*] was to be divided into NKVD operational sectors, generally uniting a series of districts. Within the operational sector, an operational brigade led by an NKVD leader assumed responsibilities for compiling arrest lists and carrying out arrests. The arrest lists were to be assembled on the basis of the NKVD's existing files of suspicious people. The operational groups were permitted to draw in soldiers or regular police to assist them, depending on local conditions.[18]

NKVD investigations of arrested suspects were to occur "quickly" and "in simplified order," with an eye to establishing the "criminal connections" of those arrested.[19] On completion of the investigation, the accused were sent on to an extrajudicial *troika*, generally consisting of the leaders of the relevant republic or regional NKVD, Communist Party committee, and Procuracy.[20] The troika passed judgment on the accused, sentencing them either to time in the Gulag or death.[21] An NKVD memo of 8 August 1937 ordered the troikas not to announce death sentences to those assigned to the first category, most likely as a precaution against unrest at the time of execution.[22] The troikas generally worked at night without the accused. They also worked at great speed. One troika in Leningrad condemned 658 Solovetskii Island prisoners in one night; another, in Omsk, "reviewed" fifty to sixty cases per hour.[23]

The number of arrests quickly surged beyond the NKVD's initial control figures, reaching as many as 555,641 by the end of December 1937.[24] Although the original NKVD order strictly forbade any lower NKVD organ from independently increasing its arrest numbers, it did allow these organs to petition for larger numbers, and Stalin and the Politburo seldom refused.[25] The deadline for the completion of mass operation 00447, moreover, was repeatedly extended, first to 10 December 1937, then to 1 January 1938, and finally to 15 March 1938.[26] After that last date, with the exception of Ukraine, the capital cities, and certain key penal regions such as Siberia, the kulak operation gave way to the national operations.[27]

The national operations largely followed suit. After the confirmation of the kulak operation, at the end of July 1937, the NKVD produced a series of operational orders against specific ethnicities—Poles, Germans, Finns, Latvians, Estonians, Greeks, Romanians, Chinese, and others. On paper, none of these orders called for targeting an entire ethnicity, but for the arrests of national "elements" supposedly engaged in espionage. In fact, at their worst, the national operations swept up thousands based only on ethnic indicators.[28] To take the Polish Operation (00485), for example, candidates for arrest included all those who could be said to belong, or to have belonged, to the Polish Military Organization (POV); this was a largely nonexistent organization within the Soviet Union at this time that was said to have infiltrated the Polish Communist Party, the Red Army, the NKVD, and other institutions. Also targeted were Polish prisoners of war (POWs) from the 1920 Soviet–Polish war, Polish political émigrés, former members of a series of Polish political parties, and the most active local "antisoviet and nationalist elements" from territories with Polish populations.[29] At times of want, however, anyone with a Polish or Polish-sounding name could be arrested.

The Poles suffered the heaviest losses (105,485), followed by the Germans (75,331).[30] As a rule, most nationalities targeted represented diaspora nations, which, in Stalin's eyes, raised the risk of dual loyalty, particularly in the vulnerable border zones where these populations often lived. Some of these same groups had also been repressed during the collectivization and dekulakization campaigns of the early 1930s.[31] At the same time, as historian Peter Holquist has noted, many of "the preconditions and tools for operating on the social body through techniques of violence long predated the Bolshevik regime." This dynamic was most evident in the ways in which ethnicity increasingly became a marker of group suspicions and group loyalties.[32]

The primary administrative difference between the kulak and the national operations was that, instead of the troika, a *dvoika*, or two-man team consisting of the heads of the relevant regional NKVD and Communist Party organs, sat in judgment, condemning individuals and groups either to the first or second category of punishment. After judgment, the dvoika's lists were sent to Moscow for confirmation.[33] The other singularity of the national operations, especially the Polish Operation, was that they were far deadlier than 00447, with an imprisonment-to-execution ratio of one to three, versus that of one to one for 00447.[34] Initially, the national operations were to be completed within three months; the deadline was subsequently and repeatedly altered, with a final date set for 1 August 1938 in most regions.[35] In practice, the kulak and the national operations overlapped temporally and could share similar targets; in Ukraine, in 1938, the implementation of the two operations often lacked clear demarcations, with categories of enemies shifted among different NKVD departments.

The number of arrests for both operations skyrocketed far beyond the original control figures. In the Soviet Union as a whole, by 1 July 1938, roughly 1,420,711 people had been arrested; of these, 699,929 were apprehended in the course of the kulak operation, including 376,207 "former kulaks," 121,963 recidivist criminals, and 201,860 "miscellaneous counterrevolutionary elements." The totals for both operations listed some 522,774 "former kulaks," 191,384 byvshie liudi, 168,286 "elements" without a defined occupation, 45,009 clergy, and 229,957 white-collar employees; from these, a "mere" 99,188 were Communist Party members and 15,088 were members of the Komsomol.[36] From the 681,692 executions of the Great Terror, some 90% were caught up in these mass operations.[37] In Ukraine, at a minimum, 267,579 people were arrested and 122,237 of them executed in 1937 and 1938.[38]

The original control figures issued by the All-Union NKVD surged as initial plans were fulfilled and overfulfilled, and republican and regional NKVD organs besieged Moscow to petition for ever higher numbers. The master narrative of the Great Terror was expansive; it could accommodate any number of enemies, including the innocent among them. The brutal political culture of the times was captured in the slogan "when the forest is cut, the chips will fly."[39] What this slogan meant in practice was that if ten arrested innocents yielded one guilty person, it was a justifiable sacrifice to lose all ten. Celebrated NKVD interrogators earned the title of "chopper" [*kolun*].[40] The country, after all, was, to paraphrase a Ukrainian NKVD official, "in war times now."[41] The Fifth Column had to be destroyed before the actual war began. The country was to be cleansed of all political, social, economic, national, and even so-called biological enemies.

Soviet law, moreover, was enabled for terror. As a rule, law or legal constraints had never been a hindrance for the Soviet regime. The concept of revolutionary or socialist legality arose as a counterbalance to what Soviet legal authorities considered "bourgeois law" during the course of the civil war. Alongside carefully worded criminal codes and rules of procedure, not entirely unlike those in the "bourgeois" world, socialist legality allowed great scope for subjective, revolutionary interpretations of the law. At the same time, the NKVD order on the kulak operation clearly called for a "speedy" and "simplified" procedure to be employed in the investigations of arrested suspects.[42]

This simplification of procedure stemmed in part from the law of 1 December 1934, which came about as a reaction to the assassination of Leningrad Communist Party leader S. M. Kirov. According to Peter Solomon, the leading western expert on Soviet law,

> a new law had empowered the police to use in cases of terrorism a drastically simplified procedure that gave the accused a mere twenty-four hours to acquaint himself with charges and evidence, provided for an *in camera* hearing without defense counsel, disallowed cassation appeals, and authorized immediate implementation of the death penalty.[43]

By 1937, this simplified procedure was extended to "the common political charges of the time, wrecking and sabotage."[44] On 7 August 1937, A. Ia. Vyshinskii, the All-Union Procurator, dispatched telegrams to all procurators indicating that a procurator's sanction was no longer necessary for arrest.[45]

Within this legal world of simplified procedures, the confession of the accused became the centerpiece of guilt; in most cases, it served as the only evidence of guilt. According to Solomon, Vyshinskii had devised a "theory of evidence that downgraded the importance of 'objective proofs' and gave special weight to confessions, especially in cases of counterrevolutionary crimes."[46] The centrality of confessions served as both an enabling feature of the terror as well as a surrogate for real evidence. It opened the way to manipulation and massive violations. In 1937, arrests, historians agree, occurred largely on the basis of *uchet*—the NKVD's record catalog of "suspicious elements," a catalog kept in every regional NKVD office since the 1920s.[47] Historians also agree, however, that by 1938, the subjects on file were largely exhausted in most places, thereby leading to far more arbitrary arrests in 1938 as NKVD operatives at times simply arrested according to ethnic or biological criteria, unrelated to any objective notion of crime.[48] If pressed for evidence, which was infrequent before November 1938, NKVD officers in the field made use of official [*shtatnye*] witnesses—largely local officials ordered to comply by supplying false evidence or handing over blank, stamped documents. The NKVD was unable through most of the Great Terror to use its extensive network of agents and informers because so many of these had been caught up themselves in the mass arrests.[49]

The result of the privileging of confessions was the extensive use of torture to force individuals to admit to what in most cases were fabricated and often mind-boggling charges. The extreme time pressures and scale of the mass operations, along with the objective of creating large group cases, especially in 1938, in which the "naming of names" (denunciation) was an essential part of a confession, made torture the most effective means for providing the kinds of numbers of arrests and convictions that each higher rung of the NKVD ladder demanded of that below it. Enhanced methods of interrogation ranged widely from threats and humiliation to physical violence. Although many victims resisted self-incrimination through false confession, most were unable to hold out in the face of relentless psychological and physical pressure.

There is no extant written order on the use of torture, though it is clear that torture had been permitted by the Central Committee of the Communist Party from 1937.[50] Stalin said as much in a coded telegram to the Communist Party on 10 January 1939.[51] Instructions on the use of torture came down from the very top of the NKVD, either orally or through what some NKVD operatives called *gastrolery* [touring actors], visiting NKVD plenipotentiaries, often high ranking, who literally instructed lower NKVD organs on the use of torture by example.[52] In Ukraine, NKVD first deputy M. P. Frinovskii and Ukrainian Republican NKVD head I. M. Leplevskii traveled through the countryside on exactly this mission.[53] Ukrainian NKVD officials, later condemned for their use of torture, argued that permission to apply what the

NKVD called "physical measures" required each time the "sanction" of the head of the NKVD organ or department within the organ. It is clear though that, in practice, torture was applied without sanctions in many places, becoming the basic means for moving the seemingly endless victims of the mass operations from arrest to conviction.

Arrest numbers also rose as a result of "socialist competition" among NKVD organs. Almost immediately after the orders on mass operations were issued, regional NKVD leaders began to compete for higher figures, larger numbers of arrests and convictions, all for recognition or gain from higher authorities. Such competitions recalled the regional Communist Party's "race for numbers" during the collectivization campaigns of 1930. In the case of the mass operations, such competition occurred from top to bottom in the NKVD as operatives vied to carry out more arrests, obtain larger numbers of confessions, and liquidate the most enemies.[54]

In some regions, enemy categories changed in accordance with local conditions. In practice, this could mean larger or smaller numbers of specific ethnic groups or the inclusion of new groups, depending on region. It could also mean, for example in Ukraine, the inclusion of new, regionally specific categories such as "Ukrainian bourgeois nationalists." In some cases, city NKVD organs, as in Moscow, made use of the mass operations in order to rid their city of undesirables—homeless people, beggars, prostitutes, and petty criminals.[55]

There is no doubt that the dynamics and expansion of the Great Terror depended on actions, laws, and decrees coming from the top—from Stalin and his NKVD lieutenants. However, Stalin was not the sole perpetrator of the Great Terror. Despite being purged itself, the Communist Party and Soviet state were at the same time agents of terror, participating in the implementation of the mass operations, its planning, and key organizational forms. And there was, by necessity, mass social participation in the Great Terror as well as huge areas of gray. Stalin provided the tools, sent out his plenipotentiaries, and depended on a small army of people who would carry out the implementation of the terror. Stalin opened a floodgate of repression, and it is within this flood that the NKVD operated, allowing it immense institutional and individual agency.

AT ELABORATE TWENTIETH-ANNIVERSARY celebrations in December 1937, the NKVD laid claim to the revolutionary heritage of the Cheka, the Extraordinary Commission to Combat Counterrevolution, Sabotage, and Speculation. Founded in late 1917 by Feliks ("Iron") Dzerzhinskii to spearhead the Red Terror of the Revolution, the Cheka's hallowed reputation was made up of equal parts fear and sanctity. The Soviet security police styled itself as a special institution, dedicated to the salvation of the Revolution and the Soviet order amid an internal and external world of enemies. Chekists, as they were called ever after, were expected to be selfless, morally pure ascetics. The security police was an institution veiled in murder, mystery, and myth. By the time of its twentieth anniversary, the NKVD had achieved a cult-like status in the pantheon of the Revolution, with immense power, second only to Stalin and the Politburo.[56]

The NKVD served as the primary institution of terror. As an All-Union, or federal, commissariat, the NKVD, established in 1934, was nominally under the jurisdiction of Sovnarkom (the Council of People's Commissars), the cabinet of the Soviet government. It was the Communist Party's ruling body, the Politburo, however, that formally authorized the actions of the NKVD. However, in 1937 and 1938, during the mass operations, Stalin controlled and directed the NKVD both in the broad contours of policy and in specific operational policies.[57]

Nikolai Ezhov (1895–1940) was the People's Commissar of the NKVD during the Great Terror. Appointed to his position in September 1936, Ezhov led the NKVD until November 1938, during which time Stalin granted him enormous power. By the time of the December 1937 anniversary celebrations, Ezhov held a cult-like status and was widely and obsequiously celebrated in the main Communist Party newspaper, *Pravda*.[58] Ezhov's name is inextricably linked to the Great Terror, which was labeled afterward the Ezhovshchina, or time of Ezhov. In fact, Stalinshchina is a far more accurate label for the terror, given that Ezhov's power and fate rested in Stalin's hands.

By 1937, the NKVD was an extremely powerful institution with control not only of the Soviet security police, but also of the regular police, fire brigades, the administration and guarding of the Gulag, and the internal security troops of the NKVD. The NKVD had an estimated high of 366,000 employees by the time of the Great Terror.[59] This huge number, however, is deceiving. In fact, the operational workers, that is, the investigators and interrogators who carried out the mass operations, were far fewer in number. Russian historians N. G. Okhotin and A. B. Roginskii estimate that there were some 25,000 NKVD operational officers as of 1 March 1937.[60] This number grew in the course of the mass operations as NKVD organs took on more and more workers to try to keep pace. According to Siberian scholar Aleksei Tepliakov, there were some 32,000 operational workers in 1939, and this number may have increased to as many as 46,000 by January 1940.[61]

The territorial-administrative grasp of the NKVD was still formidable. Directed from Moscow by the All-Union NKVD, headed by Ezhov and powerful lieutenants Frinovskii (the architect of the mass operations), L. N. Bel'skii, and others, each Soviet republic within the All-Union structure, with the exception of the Russian Republic, had a republican-level NKVD organ, with jurisdiction over regional and district organs. Each NKVD administration [*upravlenie*] was divided into departments [*otdely*] and, within departments, sectors [*otdelenie*]. Although the functions of the departments and names changed frequently in the course of 1937 and 1938 and all operational workers were involved to one extent or another in the terror, the Third Department (in charge of counterespionage) and the Fourth Department (in charge of secret-political operations) were key to the mass operations, respectively in charge of the national operations and the kulak operation. Each administration was led by a *nachal'nik*, or boss, assisted by the heads of the various departments and sectors. NKVD offices varied widely in size, with the largest numbers of operational workers present in the central, republic, and regional offices of the NKVD; the district offices generally had only one or two officers, assisted by the understaffed offices of the regular police. To make up for staff shortages, which became extreme at this time, Moscow and the republican NKVDs made use of an extensive network of plenipotentiaries, whom the NKVD mobilized, military style, from higher to lower NKVD organs to serve as troubleshooters, to spur on arrests and convictions, and to ensure there were no liberals among their colleagues.[62]

During the Great Terror, the NKVD was responsible for the compilation of arrest lists, searches, arrests, interrogations, and executions. It also tended, by default of power and fear, to be the dominant force on the extrajudicial troikas that held power of life and death over its prisoners. Yet despite its immense power, the organization was in permanent flux in 1937 and 1938. The NKVD never had enough operatives to handle the immense numbers of prisoners filtered through the mass operations. To take just the example of Ukraine, by the end of January 1938, there were 95,000 prisoners in prisons intended to hold no more than 24,000.[63] The NKVD had no choice but to expand its cadre of personnel in the very course of the operations. Students from the NKVD preparatory schools were mobilized to help staff the NKVD organs. The NKVD also made use of extensive auxiliaries directly in arrests, interrogations, and executions—a motley crew of semiliterate policemen, NKVD couriers, chauffeurs, accountants, firemen, postal workers, and others.[64]

At the same time, the institution of the NKVD underwent a series of purges as leaders fell and their "tails," or clientele networks, fell with them. In Ukraine, there were at least two purges of the NKVD before the final rout of November 1938—following the fall of earlier NKVD commissars V. A. Balitskii (1892–1937) and I. M. Leplevskii (1896–1938), who fell in May 1937 and January 1938, respectively, before the appointment to this position of A. I. Uspenskii (1902–1940). These purges within the NKVD differed from the post–November 1938 purge of the purgers. In these earlier purges, NKVD operatives were generally accused of Trotskyism, espionage, or counterrevolutionary activities, whereas after November 1938, below the All-Union level, NKVD operatives were more likely to be charged with violations of socialist legality, charges that could still have deadly consequences. At the All-Union and occasionally at the republic levels of the NKVD, charges against leaders could be those of counterrevolution and treason.[65]

The NKVD was far from a monolithic organization during the Great Terror; indeed it underwent a demographic shift in these years. As endemic transfers, mobilizations of new cadres, and purges escalated within its ranks, the age and social profile of leading operatives changed. The NKVD became younger, with most rank-and-file workers in their thirties, more plebeian and less educated, with larger numbers of operatives with working-class or peasant social origins. By the end of the Great Terror, a relatively small number had served in the NKVD from the time of the Revolution and civil war, declining from some 71% in 1934 to only 5% by July 1939. That meant that for many NKVD operatives nationwide, their formative experience was no longer the civil war, but more likely collectivization, dekulakization, and the famine. In Ukraine, this decline was less drastic; some 44.8% of NKVD operatives in Ukraine entered the Cheka during the civil war, and an additional 25.6% entered in 1921. The national profile of NKVD operatives also changed: The percentage of Jews in the NKVD as a whole fell from a high of 38.54% in 1934 to 3.92% in early 1939. In Ukraine, the percentage of Jews within the NKVD was about 20% by 1938, and declined further after the fall of Uspenskii. Here, the percentage of Ukrainian operatives increased somewhat, from about 5% in 1934 to 19% by early 1939, whereas Russians remained the dominant force in both the NKVD as a whole and in the Ukrainian NKVD.[66]

The cumulative effect of these changes had a huge impact on the NKVD. In Ukraine, for instance, at NKVD party meetings at various regional levels in late 1938 and early 1939 when it became possible to speak openly and critically for a short time, NKVD operatives regularly complained about how difficult the mass operations were for them. Most complaints were not about the suffering of victims. The operatives complained relentlessly about their hard lot—the grueling nighttime hours, the huge caseloads, and their living and working conditions. Because of the frequent transfers of NKVD personnel, many complained of inadequate housing, frequently living in their offices, hotels, and rented hovels, far from their families in the housing-short Soviet Union. They complained about long lines in the cafeterias and about access to goods, especially clothing. Most rank-and-file NKVD operatives lived little better than the average Soviet worker, in relative poverty. In the meantime, new cadres, younger or recently mobilized from the regular police, complained of inexperience in interrogation work, while older NKVD workers described an all-pervasive fear and mistrust among colleagues.[67]

At the same time, the culture of the NKVD remained unchanged. In her memoirs, Nadezhda Mandelstam wrote that the reigning ethos in the NKVD was "Give us a man, and we will make a case."[68] NKVD workers themselves frequently cited the delusion that if someone was arrested, he must be guilty. It was, moreover, considered a matter of shame and weakness to release a prisoner because of a failure to obtain a confession. Given the relentless pressure from above, the endless demands to name names (to denounce others) to create artificial group cases, and the perverse centrality of confessions to convictions, the use of torture became all but inevitable. How else was it possible to extract confessions of often fanciful and outrageous acts from prisoners intent on claiming their innocence? As one NKVD operative put it, "physical measures of influence"—the leading euphemism for torture—worked "splendidly" in the rapid extraction of confessions.[69] It could not have been otherwise, given the scale of the operation and the NKVD's culture and habits of extrajudicial practice. The main means of obtaining confessions were falsification and torture. To paraphrase a policeman drawn into the mass operations, there were "interrogators of the pen" and "interrogators of the fist."[70]

Stalin was well aware of the procedures of the Great Terror, having sanctioned most and tolerated the rest. These procedures served his aims well, allowing a breakthrough in the purge of the nation. At some point, however, criticism from the Procuracy (office of the public prosecutor, approximately) and countless citizen letter writers began to wear down the machinery of terror.[71] Moreover, it is clear that it was impossible to maintain the highest levels of secrecy around the mass operations. The clothing of executed prisoners began to turn up in town markets and bazaars. In some areas, the wives of the arrested began to protest, at times publicly.[72] Moreover, countless Soviet citizens outside the NKVD participated in some aspect of the terror, including the official witnesses in apartment buildings who formally observed NKVD searches, the washerwomen in the prisons, the cemetery workers who ran the gravesites, the doctors who were called in to attend, all too infrequently, badly beaten prisoners, the railroad workers who transported prisoners to the Gulag, and, according to the NKVD, factory workers, who, in some areas, witnessed the decimation of their ranks. And if Nadezhda Mandelstam can be believed, "In small towns such news spread quickly, since landladies could never resist telling their neighbors about the arrest of a lodger."[73]

From at least January 1938, various party and soviet organs, especially the Procurator's office, began to issue warnings on mass violations of socialist legality. November 1938 marked the beginning of the end of the Great Terror. On 14 November, Stalin ordered the first secretaries of all regional, territorial, and republic-level Communist Party committees to systematically report on problems in the work of the NKVD organs.[74] On 17 November 1938, the state and party leadership issued a directive titled "On arrests, procurator supervision and carrying out investigations." This directive would serve to rein in the NKVD, put a halt to mass operations, and abolish the extrajudicial troikas.[75] It would also lead to the arrest and trials of hundreds of NKVD operatives.

The November retreat served as a tactical ploy for Stalin. While celebrating and taking credit for the "successes" of the purge, he could blame all failings on the NKVD. Already in August 1938, Stalin had appointed L. P. Beriia (1899–1953) to serve as Ezhov's deputy, making clear that Ezhov's days were numbered. After Ezhov submitted his resignation, which was accepted by the Politburo on 24 November 1938, Beriia took over as People's Commissar of the NKVD, leading the purge of the purgers. Beriia soon placed his emissary, A. Z. Kobulov (1905–1955), at the head of the NKVD in Ukraine, replacing the disgraced Uspenskii.[76] Ezhov was arrested in April 1939 and executed in February 1940. "His people"—indeed, Stalin's scapegoats—found themselves facing trial from 1939 into the war years.

Stalin's seeming about-face was actually nothing of the sort. As in the collectivization campaign when the key players, Communists and Soviet activists, were charged with "dizziness from success," the NKVD had succeeded, in Stalin's mind, in making a breakthrough in the purge of the country. At that point, it became a zero-sum game for Stalin as he faced the inevitable pushback from this onslaught of terror. Language changed accordingly. Instead of the howling rampages against enemies, the talk turned to victims, especially if they were Communists, and the excesses of the NKVD. This phenomenon of radical offensive followed by retreat was an intrinsic part of Stalinist mass repression. Given the size of the Soviet Union and its relatively weak administrative infrastructure, massive mobilizations, rule by plenipotentiaries, and extreme methods allowed for breakthrough. That was one side of the coin. The other side was the logic and language of retreat, "democracy," and croc- odile tears for select victims abused because of violations of legality. Stalin could move between these extremes and remain largely unscathed. The tim- ing of the retreat, moreover, was not coincidental. As historian David Shearer writes, "the timing may very well have been linked to the Munich conference that September, in which Britain, France and other western powers consented to Adolph Hitler's demands for the partition of Czechoslovakia."[77]

The Great Terror represented a heady brew of extreme violence, ideologi- cal intransigence, and political hatreds. It was superimposed on the Soviet Union's incomplete civil war, with all of its political, social, and ethnic cleav- ages. Nowhere was this cauldron of violence quite as heady as in Ukraine, where all the issues and contrivances of the incomplete civil war would be on display.

THE SOVIET REPUBLIC of Ukraine was among the deadliest zones of terror during the mass operations. The terror struck everywhere, but consumed the largest numbers of victims in the capital cities of Moscow and Leningrad, zones of Gulag incarceration in the Urals and Siberia, and the western bor- derlands of Belorussia and Ukraine. Given its geographical expanse and population, the largest numbers of victims, almost 700,000, were from the Russian Republic; Ukraine, however, came in second among the Soviet republics with a recorded 253,051 victims by 1 July 1938.[78] The numbers of ethnic Ukrainians among all victims were 189,410, second only to the num- ber of Russians at 657,799. Moreover, among the next four largest numbers of ethnicities victimized—Poles (105,485), Germans (75,331), Belorussians (58,702), and Jews (30,000)—three out of the four resided overwhelmingly in the Ukrainian Republic.[79]

Ukraine was a borderland, with a mixed ethnic population and a large agrarian population. Its borderland status, with ethnic Ukrainians and Poles on either side of the Soviet–Polish borders, spelled danger to Stalin who saw spies, especially Polish and German, everywhere and feared the force, largely suppressed, of Ukrainian nationalism. Stalin viewed Ukraine not only as an entryway and rich agricultural area for potential invaders, but also as a land whose population could have multiple ethnic and national loyalties across borders. Stalin also disdained and feared Ukrainian bourgeois nationalism, real and imagined.

In addition to its reputedly dangerous mixed ethnic population, Ukraine, in Stalin's eyes, had large numbers of what the Soviet regime called remnants or leftovers from the civil war and the Soviet–Polish war of 1919–1920: byvshie liudi, veterans of the anti-Bolshevik white and green sides of the civil war, and members of anti-Bolshevik political parties, especially Ukrainian nationalists, Socialist Revolutionaries, Zionists, and Bundists. These remnants were largely a legacy of the civil war. Collectivization, dekulakization, and famine added newer legacies. Stalin had treated Ukraine brutally in these years, forcibly deporting close to 64,000 peasant families labeled as kulaks in 1930 and 1931, and leaving, minimally, more than 4 million to die of starvation in the aftermath of collectivization.[80] The kulak label was always contrived and politically subjective, but a spell in the special settlements or labor camps of the Gulag made the status official. To make matters worse, Stalin distrusted and disdained the peasantry, especially in Ukraine, making for a very thin line separating a peasant or collective farmer from the kulak status. Most of the ethnicities represented as targets in the national operations, moreover, had experienced earlier repression and displacements not just during collectivization and the first half of the 1930s, but during the First World War, thus indicating a continuing dynamic of violence and distrust of non-Russian populations that went beyond ideology.[81]

In Ukraine, former enemies (those still alive) abounded, but in status only; they were certainly not an imminent danger to the regime. The NKVD's system of filing, however, listed them all: It was clear to the NKVD who fought when, where, and for whom in the civil war, who was arrested for anticollectivization protests, who was a runaway or fugitive kulak, and who had committed criminal acts. Increasingly, as the terror raged on, it also became clear that the biological approach (as some NKVD operatives called it) was in play, leading to arrests based on the social, economic, political, or citizenship status of parents, grandparents, and even siblings. Although the Communist Party Central Committee would condemn the biological approach as "having nothing in common with Marxism" in 1939 at its Eighteenth Congress, this approach had served as a staple in Soviet repressive politics, especially at the local level, dating back at least to the time of the civil war.[82]

When a new stage of terror began in Ukraine in February 1938, Ezhov extended the Ukrainian purge categories further. He called for a thorough purge of the cities and the border zones, especially emphasizing the arrest of remnants from the civil war and Ukrainian nationalist groups. In addition to the Polish, German, and other national operations, Ezhov broadened the cast of the already-amorphous antikulak operation 00447 to include a host of former civil war opponents, political bandits, members of antisoviet peasant uprisings, former Whites, special settlers from border zones, POWs from the Polish Army, Red Army veterans who had been POWs and did not return immediately, tsarist Army veterans who had been in German and Austrian POW camps, individuals connected to foreign embassies, former employees of foreign firms, former members of Ukrainian nationalist groups, clergy, Socialist Revolutionaries, Kadets, Mensheviks, Zionists, Bundists, anarchists, former tsarist policemen, factory owners, and landowners. Ezhov ordered a full-scale purge of all past, present, and potential enemies of Soviet power who might serve as part of a Fifth Column in the case of the inevitable future war.[83] Ezhov insisted further that the NKVD go after the "big shots" among the antisoviet and counterrevolutionary organizations and that they arrest not individuals but entire groups and organizations of the supposed anti-soviet underground.[84] When the soon-to-be-former head of the Chernigov regional NKVD asked what to do with invalids and elderly people who fell among the arrested, Ezhov spat back at him, "Ekh, you are a Chekist! Take them all to the woods and shoot them."[85]

Elsewhere, with certain key exceptions, mass operation 00447 was wind-ing down and giving way to the national operations. In Ukraine, in February 1938, Stalin granted Ezhov permission to arrest an additional 30,000 "kulak and miscellaneous antisoviet elements," the largest increase anywhere.[86] Although the NKVD in Ukraine had arrested some 183,343 people by 15 January 1938, Ezhov argued that the repression of 1937 had failed to strike the "leaders, organizers, and active participants" of Ukraine's "kulak insurrection-ary, Ukrainian nationalist, white guard, and spy base." The peculiarities of the civil war in Ukraine, according to Ezhov, had left strong contingents of ene-mies both from the First World War and the civil war, all working in combi-nation with the foreign agents of capitalist encirclement.[87] Ezhov's first move was to install a new NKVD leader in Ukraine and a new, younger generation of NKVD leading operatives in the Ukrainian NKVD's territorial apparatus.

The escalation of the terror in Ukraine was inaugurated by a major shake-up of both the Communist Party and the NKVD. At the end of January 1938, N. S. Khrushchev became the first secretary of the Communist Party of Ukraine. He replaced S. V. Kosior, who was put to work in Moscow until his arrest in May 1938 and execution in February 1939.[88] The new commissar of the Ukrainian republican-level NKVD was A. I. Uspenskii, an experienced NKVD leader who most recently had served as the head of the Orenburg NKVD in the Russian Republic.[89] He replaced Leplevskii, who was moved into the central apparatus of the NKVD in Moscow until his arrest in April 1938 and execution in July.[90] On 25 January 1938, Uspenskii became the new head of the Ukrainian NKVD. A day later, he traveled with Khrushchev to

Kiev. Ezhov would join them there from 11 to 19 February. Together they would reignite the terror in Ukraine.[91]

Uspenskii immediately declared that "Moscow had already uncovered a large national underground in Ukraine."[92] This meant, according to Ezhov and Uspenskii, that the NKVD of Ukraine was seriously behind in its work. Uspenskii's first step was to purge the NKVD, mainly of former Ukrainian NKVD Commissar Leplevskii's "people," who included large numbers of Jewish NKVD operatives. Purged NKVD operatives were then either transferred to punishment positions in the Gulag or arrested and charged with an array of counterrevolutionary crimes.[93] Uspenskii replaced much of the republican and regional NKVD leadership with new cadres, many from the NKVD in Russia.

The new cadres were called *vydvizhentsy*, former workers in the main who experienced rapid career advancement in the 1930s, along with tens of thousands of other supposedly socially pure workers and peasants who were sent to schools of higher education or promoted in Communist Party and government administration.[94] Most had experienced the civil war only as teenagers, too young to serve in the Red Army. Some took part in the repressive campaigns of the collectivization era, working in forced grain requisitioning, deportations of peasant families, and the repression of peasant activities deemed to be antisoviet; others entered the NKVD later in the 1930s. All were products of the Soviet system. Regardless of the time of their entry into the security police, the ethos of the incomplete civil war and its reverberations in the collectivization period remained defining influences on their mentality, behavior, and actions.[95]

After November 1938, Stalin would cast these NKVD operatives in Ukraine and elsewhere as criminals, as officials who had violated socialist legality in the performance of their duties. Simultaneously, he put a very temporary spotlight on the victims of the terror, particularly Communist Party members, Soviet government officials, and sometimes even NKVD operatives arrested earlier. The reason for this was not, as some Russian historians claim, that the NKVD was engaged in a war with the Communist Party during the Great Terror.[96] Although there is no question that many Communists were victimized, the Communist Party—from Stalin and the Politburo down to the regional party committees—fully shared the guilt.[97] Moreover, most NKVD operatives were themselves Communist Party members, following the dictates, first and foremost, of the highest Communist Party offices in the land. Rather, Stalin's retreat served in part to address the perception, incorrect as it was, that the Communist Party was, in a sense, both most victimized and most culpable. By responding to the grievances of selected Communists, a fraction of the whole, and calling on the party to take the lead in investigating the NKVD, Stalin was able both to demonstrate his continued trust in the party and, to some extent, relegitimize a battered party in the eyes of the Soviet population.

Furthermore, the November 1938 retreat had set off an avalanche within the overcrowded prisons. Those whose cases had not been finalized by November 1938 were fortunate in receiving something like a reprieve. Troika sentences that had not yet been implemented were dismissed, and these cases were redirected to the regular courts. At the same time, thousands recanted their confessions at this time. When (and if) their tormenters were tried, it was from among these victims that the state would elicit testimony at trials and select individuals for the role of "signalers," or whistleblowers, of violations, which in some cases they may have been.[98] After the November retreat, 77,000 Communists were reinstated in the party and as many as 110,000 prisoners were freed.[99] All this is not to suggest that the victims had the final say. Only a relatively small number of all victims experienced this reprieve. The reinstatements and releases were a largely symbolic gesture, a gift from Stalin to the Communist Party. Most victims were not Communists.

The trials of NKVD operatives in Ukraine suggest that most of these men—and so far only the cases of male NKVD operatives have surfaced—more or less understood that they were being scapegoated and resented the fact. Consequently, most denied very little, admitting to an array of horrors. At the same time, they proclaimed their innocence, admitting their newly labeled crimes but justifying their actions by reference to higher orders in addition to a panoply of perpetrator justifications, ranging from belief, pride, and ignorance to fear and military obedience. Most of the NKVD personnel in the pages to follow did believe unquestionably in the Communist Party and the NKVD, as well as more abstractly in the existence of a Fifth Column. Their testimony is littered with references to war, Germany, Jews, and the Gestapo. Many, however, expressed doubts, professing to have questioned the reality of individual cases, to have understood that what they were doing or—after the fact—what they had done was wrong. Others continued to believe in enemies. Stalin appears very infrequently in their statements.

The ferocity of the Great Terror in Ukraine was distinctive. The mushrooming of enemy categories in 1938 and the push to create large group cases, along with repeated extensions of mass operation deadlines and repeated increases in arrest control figures, also played key roles in the scope and scale of terror in Ukraine. At the same time, grassroots practices of the terror in Ukraine likely differed little from those elsewhere in the Soviet Union.

Ukraine's perpetrators of the Great Terror worked within a larger culture of NKVD violence shaped by the incomplete civil war, as well as the distinctive features characterizing terror in Ukraine, all of which facilitated, permitted, and sanctioned a wide range of criminal activity performed by an equally wide range of individual actors. Oleg Khlevniuk argues that, "Just because the center controlled the operations that made up the Great Terror (and other similar operations) does not mean, however, that 'elemental factors' and local initiative did not play a role in shaping them."[100] Stalin, in fact, granted enormous, often plenipotentiary, powers to the NKVD, opening up a wide field of action in which operatives could work "creatively" and, for a period of time, with few restraints.[101] These operatives, moreover, were not simply automatons fulfilling orders from above, cogs in the machinery of terror. Each had a distinct personality and voice, each was an individual with a role to play and a degree of agency, however constrained, in helping to enact the Great Terror.

2

A Taste for Terror

We are all guilty ... in the first place, I am guilty as head of the regional administration.
-A. R. DOLGUSHEV, *head of the Kiev regional NKVD*

These violations occurred in every department, in every sector, among all [NKVD] workers and there is nothing to some comrades imagining themselves in the role of "Jesus"
and saying—I didn't beat, I had a directive, etc. Everyone obtained confessions in the
same way.
-I. N. KLEIMAN, *deputy head of Third Department of the Kiev NKVD*

ALEKSEI ROMANOVICH DOLGUSHEV stood at the head of the Kiev regional
NKVD. An Uspenskii appointment, he held the office for a mere five months.
During this time, he held power over life and death in the dominions of the
Kiev region. After his arrest, Dolgushev accepted overall responsibility for the
violations of socialist legality that occurred within the Kiev region, including those of many of the perpetrators portrayed in the following pages.[1] Still,
he insisted that he was neither a traitor nor a criminal, and he claimed that
he had done everything that "an honest person" could do given "the circumstances of the time."[2]

Dolgushev was one of the new NKVD *vydvizhentsy* in Ukraine. He was
born in 1902 to a Russian working-class family in Tambov, Russia. He completed five years of schooling, after which he began his life as a factory worker
at the age of 13. When the Revolution came, he joined the Red Guard and took
part in the "struggle against banditry" in Tambov during the civil war, a struggle between the Red Army and the Antonov peasant movement. He served
in the Red Army from 1924 to 1929 and was a member of the Komsomol. In
1929, he joined the Communist Party, following in the footsteps of his father,
sister, and two brothers. In 1930, he began work in the OGPU, the prede-
cessor of the NKVD. By 1932, he was working in that capacity in Ukraine,
where he no doubt witnessed the raging famine. He served as deputy head of
the Fifth Department of the Ukrainian NKVD from 1934 to 1937, becoming

director of the First Department after receiving the Order of the Red Star on the occasion of the security police's twentieth anniversary. That promotion occurred on the recommendation of Uspenskii, as did Dolgushev's promotion to the head of the Kiev regional NKVD in June 1938.[3]

Dolgushev was arrested on 18 January 1939 and interrogated on and off for eight months. He was tried three times by the Military Tribunal of the NKVD before the charges stuck.[4] In his first trial before a closed court (10–13 August 1940), he was accused of participation in an NKVD antisoviet conspiracy led by the newly designated enemy of the people, Uspenskii. He was also charged with violating socialist legality, the more common charge levied against NKVD officials in this wave of arrests.[5] Only the second charge held, and he was sentenced to seven years in a labor camp under the Ukrainian criminal code Article 206-17 (A).[6] Following a protest by the procurators of both the Kiev military district and of the USSR, the Soviet Supreme Court's Military Collegium overturned the sentence on 22 November 1940, calling for a new trial.[7] The second trial (24–27 February 1941) featured similar charges and a similar outcome, but with a slightly longer sentence of ten years in a labor camp.[8] The Supreme Court of the USSR overturned this sentence too, arguing that it was "too light."[9] The third trial took place in Sverdlovsk on 20–21 May 1942, when Kiev had already been overrun by the Germans. This trial resulted in a death sentence for Dolgushev.[10]

DOLGUSHEV FIRST ENCOUNTERED Ezhov and Uspenskii at a drunken orgy of a party in Kiev on the last night before Ezhov's return to Moscow. This party would serve as a key piece of "evidence" of "conspiracy" once Ezhov, Uspenskii, and Dolgushev fell at the end of 1938. Dolgushev attended with some of the other vydvizhentsy who would lead the next stage of the terror in Ukraine. He claimed that they were there only because they had recently been awarded medals. They sat in their dress uniforms in awe of the more senior NKVD officers in Ezhov's and Uspenskii's entourages.[11]

Before leaving Moscow for Kiev, Ezhov held a meeting with his entourage in his Lubianka office. G. M. Kobyzev, who accompanied Ezhov to Kiev, where he would work first in the republican NKVD cadre department and then as head of the Khar'kov NKVD (20 May 1938–15 January 1939), later, under interrogation, recalled the conversation in Ezhov's office.[12] Frinovskii, Ezhov's first deputy and a key organizer of the mass operations, was also there, as were several other new appointees destined for the Ukrainian NKVD.[13] According to Kobyzev, Ezhov asked his company if any of them spoke Ukrainian, knowing full well that the official bureaucratic language in Kiev at that time was Russian. When no one answered affirmatively, he said, "How then will we communicate in Ukraine?" Frinovskii laughed and answered, "But come on, there is not one Ukrainian there, they are all Jews." Ezhov smiled and said, "We will get rid of them all."[14]

When they arrived in Kiev, Ezhov sent Kobyzev to work in the cadre department compiling data on the NKVD staff. When Ezhov saw the data, he exclaimed, "This is not a Ukrainian apparatus, it is Birobidzhan," referring to Stalin's invented Soviet Jewish "homeland" in the Soviet Far East.[15] Later under testimony, Frinovskii confirmed the spirit of Kobyzev's recollections, adding that after Ezhov's return to Moscow, he quipped: "When I went to Ukraine, they told me that many Jews worked there. But they deceived me— only Jews worked there."[16] While still in Kiev, on 13 February according to Kobyzev, Ezhov told Ukrainian NKVD workers that "in the apparatus of the NKVD Ukraine there are very few Ukrainians. The apparatus is very contaminated." Kobyzev said that Ezhov believed that "Zionist agents" worked in the NKVD in Ukraine.[17]

According to the Ukrainian researcher Vadym Zolotar'ov, "there is reason to believe that the Ukrainian Narkom [People's Commissar Uspenskii] understood the words of the All-Union Narkom [Ezhov] as a signal for an attack on Jewish Chekists."[18] I. A. Zhabrev, the head of the Kamenets-Podol'sk NKVD from 26 February to 17 November 1938, later said that Uspenskii actually issued a directive to remove Jews from the NKVD, supposedly following orders from Ezhov. Zhabrev claimed that other regional NKVD heads also received this order.[19] Yet it is far from clear that there was such an order to purge Jews from the NKVD or that an order was even necessary, as a number of mainly Jewish Chekists would argue in December 1938 meetings of the Kiev NKVD party collective.[20] What is clear is that many Jewish Chekists would be purged under Uspenskii and that Dolgushev would be accused of sharing the blame. Andrei Ivanovich Egorov, the former head of the Chernigov regional NKVD now under arrest, also claimed that Uspenskii promoted "a clearly hostile line on the expulsion of NKVD Jewish cadres" as well as writing that Uspenskii additionally directed his operatives to "look at individuals with a large party tenure [stazh]," suggesting a distrust toward "old Bolsheviks."[21]

Ezhov certainly initiated the early 1938 purge of the Ukrainian NKVD. Anecdotal material suggests that he loathed Leplevskii, a Jew and head of the Ukrainian NKVD prior to Uspenskii's arrival. Ezhov recruited Uspenskii because, according to one source, "the party had lost trust" in Leplevskii.[22] In January, Ezhov called Uspenskii in for a chat while the latter was in Moscow for a session of the Supreme Soviet of the USSR. Uspenskii later recalled under testimony, "Ezhov suddenly called me. I went to his office. Ezhov was quite drunk. Ezhov said to me, 'well, you are going to Ukraine.'"[23] Earlier, in November 1937, he had warned Uspenskii that, "if you think you can just sit in Orenburg for five years, you are mistaken. You will soon be called to more responsible work."[24]

Leplevskii's removal left "his people" defenseless and subject to a wholesale purge. Leplevskii was eventually accused not only of conspiring to overthrow the Soviet Union, but also of being a former member of the Bund, the pre-revolutionary Jewish socialist workers' organization. His clientele network in Ukraine would similarly be faulted with the facts of their social, economic, or political past in what some later called with disgust the biological approach.[25] The precise mix of antisemitism and biological sins in the purge of the Ukrainian NKVD in the first months of 1938 is not clear, but the percentage of Jews in the NKVD did decline fairly drastically at this time in Ukraine and throughout the Soviet Union, from 38.54% in 1934 to 3.92% in January 1939.[26] In Ukraine, only between 15 February and 5 April 1938, Uspenskii would dismiss 558 Chekists, arresting 154 of them.[27] Although Uspenskii was very likely antisemitic, he was in fact no fonder of Ukrainians, claiming at one point that 75% to 80% of them were "bourgeois nationalists."[28]

Dolgushev, the new head of the Kiev regional NKVD, would later vehemently deny that he too was antisemitic.[29] He would, however, recall very clearly Ezhov's party and the radical turn the terror in Ukraine took after Ezhov's visit and Uspenskii's appointment as commissar. Dolgushev recalled Ezhov extolling the NKVD operatives at the banquet and drunkenly toasting them: "let's drink to the oper," meaning the lower- and middle-ranking Chekists dispersed through the territorial apparatus of the NKVD.[30] He announced that they needed to promote these "opers" to serve as leaders of the Ukrainian territorial NKVD administrations.[31] According to Dolgushev, Ezhov looked out at the young operatives and said, "As I look at them, these splendid people, *real Russians*, I can read their faces."[32] Ezhov was totally drunk at the party, not unusual for the commissar. He would be dragged out, dead drunk, by his arms.[33] In the days and weeks after the party, Uspenskii would begin to promote these "real Russians" into leadership positions throughout the Ukrainian NKVD. Some of the former regional leaders returned to Moscow with Ezhov and Leplevskii to work, temporarily, in the central NKVD office; others found themselves behind bars or transferred to operational work within the Gulag, a special punishment for Chekists that fell just short of arrest.[34]

Uspenskii met with his new regional leaders in Kiev at a series of confer-
ences in late February and early March. The atmosphere was already charged
from Ezhov's visit. Ezhov had rallied his troops to a frenzy. He radically
expanded the mass operations, increasing the categories of enemies and calling for a thorough purge of the cities and the border zones, especially emphasizing the arrest of individuals who were euphemistically called remnants or
leftovers from the civil war and Ukrainian nationalist groups.[35] Uspenskii
would basically repeat Ezhov's commands, declaring that "Moscow had
already uncovered a large nationalist underground in Ukraine."[36] Uspenskii
then acquainted his lieutenants with a detailed diagram of the so-called
nationalist underground, highlighting Poles and supposed Ukrainian
nationalists, and, in a sense, merging the *kulak* and national operations in
Ukraine.[37]

With his marching papers in order both as head of the Kiev regional
NKVD and as chair of the infamous troika, which sentenced all those arrested,
Dolgushev set out to do battle with the enemy. He later claimed—and several witnesses confirmed this—that he did not want to take the position of
head of the Kiev regional NKVD.[38] The chief of the Kiev NKVD prison,
I. G. Nagornyi, even recalled later that Dolgushev was extremely agitated by
the appointment and said, "there you can break your head," a most prophetic
comment.[39] All the same, Dolgushev set to work, following the instructions of Uspenskii, who told him "to force the work of the troika . . . and
to push more people through it."[40] From 1 January to 1 July 1938, alone, the
NKVD would arrest 17,515 "enemies" in Kiev region, most of whom (10,946)
would be executed, according to minimal figures.[41] Dolgushev would also be
responsible for the region's seven interdistrict command units, each of which
controlled what happened in the districts of Kiev region.[42] In this capacity,
Dolgushev would initially be linked to cases in the towns of Skvira and Uman
(see Chapters 4 and 5), though these charges, like the charge of antisemitism,
would not hold. Dolgushev's criminal case sheds light on antisemitism within
the NKVD as well as the rules and practices of interrogation, torture, and
the workings of the troika. His fate illustrates that of many of the NKVD's
vydvizhentsy.

THE CHIEF ACCUSATION against Dolgushev was his alleged participation in
an antisoviet conspiracy with Uspenskii, Leplevskii, and others. In the course
of three trials, Dolgushev successfully pointed out the errors, contradictions,
and downright lies behind this charge. When he was first interrogated, on
20 January 1939, he "categorically denied" any part in Uspenskii's "hostile

work."[43] By 15 June 1939, under torture, he admitted to everything at his interrogation, including participation in Uspenskii's plot.[44]

In the meantime, Uspenskii, imprisoned, was telling tales in Moscow.[45] He claimed that he personally recruited Dolgushev because the latter was close to Leplevskii. He told his interrogators that Ezhov agreed that they could "use" Dolgushev. Rambling on, Uspenskii "confessed" that he had told Dolgushev about Ezhov's plans to seize power in the Soviet Union and that Dolgushev had agreed to support these plans.[46] The NKVD then transported Dolgushev to Moscow for a confrontation with Uspenskii that took place on 20 July from 11:00 p.m. to 2:21 a.m. At the confrontation, Uspenskii repeated his earlier claims about Dolgushev. Surprising the interrogator, Dolgushev suddenly denied everything.[47] When he returned to Ukraine, Dolgushev again reversed himself, admitting to participation in Uspenskii's cabal in renewed interrogations on 19 August 1939. He explained that his sudden change of heart during the confrontation with Uspenskii in Moscow was due to his fear of admitting his crimes.[48]

Then, in a long handwritten confession dated 16 October 1939, Dolgushev once again changed his story, for the last time. He wrote that, after four to five months in prison, he finally succumbed under "physical measures of influence [*fizicheskie mery vozdeistviia*]"—the standard euphemism for torture—and "admitted" to participation in Uspenskii's conspiracy. He wrote that he had been "forced to slander himself and others" and that Uspenskii's confession was a lie.[49] From this point on, including at all three trials, Dolgushev adamantly denied participation in the nonexistent conspiracy, consistently proclaiming his innocence. His claim of innocence in this regard was backed up by none other than Ezhov, who, under interrogation on 31 January 1940, claimed that he had not met Dolgushev and never had a conversation with Uspenskii about him.[50] A. P. Radzivilovskii, who was the former deputy head of the Ukrainian NKVD during Ezhov's visit and soon after transferred to work in the central NKVD apparatus just prior to his own arrest and execution, also denied that Dolgushev was involved in any sort of antisoviet activity. He called Uspenskii a liar.[51]

The accusations of conspiracy and indeed treason were clearly a fantasy. Less fanciful were the charges against Dolgushev related to his work as chair of the Kiev regional troika, which served as the clearinghouse for the final sentencing of the victims of the so-called antikulak operation. Dolgushev was charged with illegally sentencing to death through the troika a series of highly qualified specialists (engineers, doctors, professors) and NKVD officials in the fall of 1938. According to his interrogator, these actions directly violated

Beriia's circular from 21 September 1938, which explicitly forbid the troika from sentencing these individuals.[52] Here, Dolgushev would be less successful in dodging the charges, even though it remained a fairly common practice earlier for the troika to issue death penalties for these categories of people. In regard to the sentencing of NKVD cadres, Dolgushev presented a rather convoluted story of seeking permission from Uspenskii, who then supposedly sent him to A. D. Slavin, the deputy head of the Second Department of NKVD Ukraine, who in turn, Dolgushev claimed, told him only NKVD employees without a rank could be thus sentenced. Then he claimed to have confirmed Slavin's conclusion with Uspenskii by telephone.[53] At his first trial, Dolgushev blamed Uspenskii directly for the decision to use the troika in these cases.[54] At his second trial, he told the court that when he approached Uspenskii for permission, the latter told him to decide for himself. When Dolgushev demurred, Uspenskii sent him to Slavin.[55] At his third trial, he basically admitted that such cases went through the troika, that he knew about Beriia's circular, but that only NKVD cadres without rank were so sentenced.[56]

Dolgushev also discussed the working of the troika in an attempt to explain the difficulties of accuracy during the sentencing process. First, he explained that the troika leaders had only a simplified agenda with a short summary of the essence of the charges for each defendant. Second, the troika depended on the accuracy of the presenter, or interrogator, who reported on the case. Third, Dolgushev admitted that "as a rule" they did not examine the actual raw criminal files of the defendants.[57] One of his subordinates, department head L. N. Treshkov, told the court that Dolgushev falsified documents at the troika, crossing out the position of engineers and writing that they were without a defined occupation. Dolgushev parried, saying that he did this only because the person in question had not worked in a year and he therefore considered him to be without a defined occupation.[58] It is likely that Dolgushev was guilty as charged; at the same time, his defense was based on the culture of oral communication within the NKVD and his own requirement to follow higher orders. Both claims were an accurate reflection on the NKVD's work culture and would be repeated by many other NKVD cadres charged at this time. In addition, the sheer workload of the troikas precluded any attempt at accuracy, however unlikely.

Dolgushev faced another charge that would in the end simply disappear. This was the charge of antisemitism in the Uspenskii-era purge of NKVD cadres. These accusations against Dolgushev first arose at the highly charged meeting of the Kiev regional NKVD party collective on the eve of Dolgushev's arrest, which was convened between 14 and 16 December 1938 to discuss the 17 November 1938 directive rolling back the mass operations.[59] The meeting was lively, with a host of charges flying back and forth between colleagues. One of the most important issues animating the gathering was the explosive charge of antisemitism and rumored orders from above to purge the NKVD of Jews. Most said the orders came from Uspenskii, who was widely believed to be antisemitic; others pointed to Ezhov and the All-Union NKVD as the source of these supposed orders.[60]

Accusations of antisemitism were based on hearsay as well as on concrete cases of the expulsion of Jews from the NKVD at this time. One delegate to the meeting, for example, stated quite adamantly, "I want to say that the harmful line of Uspenskii in relation to the persecution of Jews among us was and is a fact." He claimed that the issue of antisemitism in the Ukrainian NKVD was well known: "They talk about antisemitism everywhere, in the club, in the cafeteria, in the buffet, but not at party meetings."[61] Another delegate claimed to have heard that Zhabrev, the head of the Kamenets-Podol'sk NKVD, was driving out Jews.[62] The same Zhabrev claimed that he had received a directive from Uspenskii to purge Jews from the NKVD and that Uspenskii had told him the order came from the All-Union NKVD—in other words, from Ezhov.[63] M. M. Tsirul'nitskii, who worked in the Kiev regional NKVD Third Department, also referred to conversations about such an order around the Kiev regional NKVD administration. He said that he considered that "this line" was indeed implemented and, although there seemed to be no concrete written order, he warned the delegates that "where there is smoke there is fire."[64] I. N. Kleiman, deputy head of the Third Department of the Kiev regional NKVD, stated that Uspenskii used "different sauces" to destroy NKVD cadres in Ukraine, but that undoubtedly antisemitism was one of the sauces.[65] NKVD worker Radomskii went so far as to compare the situation of Jews in Germany with that of Jews in the NKVD, noting, however, that the difference was that the issue was hidden within the Soviet Union.[66]

Dolgushev denied these charges, though at times he seemed to admit that antisemitism did in fact occur in practice. Frequent interruptions by angry colleagues at times forced his hand in this regard. In general, however, he claimed never to have received such orders and never to have issued any kind of antisemitic directives.[67] Instead, he referred to an operational meeting held in Kiev when Ezhov was in town, where the question of the contamination of the Ukrainian NKVD was discussed, meaning the supposedly murky social backgrounds of many of the NKVD operatives. Apparently, claims were made about the Ukrainian NKVD being closed off to outsiders, which may have been a veiled antisemitic reference to some purported Jewish cliques under Leplevskii.[68] At the same time, Dolgushev said he thought it would be a good idea to move people around, to bring in "Sidorov" from Orel and send him to Odessa, while sending "Ivanov" from Odessa to Orel. This, he said, would represent "a fresh situation, new people."[69] Transfers of cadres were indeed endemic at this time within the NKVD. However, at the party meeting, he said he now understood that "in the conditions of Ukraine," this policy might be viewed otherwise and used by enemies.[70] He did not budge from his position on the need to purge the NKVD, given that "we have here still daughters of priests, a not small number of traders . . . and people whose nearest relatives have been executed."[71] What he was referring to was the compromising material from NKVD cadres' personnel files, in which they listed their relatives, their parents' occupations, relatives who had emigrated or, by virtue of the geographic arrangements that accompanied the end of the First World War, simply ended up in another country. Responding to specific charges of antisemitism in relation to his refusal to appoint one Khodorkovskii to serve as the head of a district-level NKVD department, Dolgushev said it had nothing to do with his Jewish nationality, but instead was based on the fact that Khodorkovskii and his wife were both the offspring of traders. According to Dolgushev, the background of the head of a district NKVD department must be "crystal clear."[72] Yet, by these standards, most of the Jews in the Ukrainian NKVD would have been purged, given the traditional occupational profile of pre-revolutionary Jews in trade, commerce, and artisanal crafts.

Dolgushev defended himself further at the party meeting by acknowledging that "we have a second extreme," a distrust for people coming into the Ukrainian NKVD from Voronezh, Samara, Gor'kii—in other words, from Russia. As far as gathering compromising materials on cadres, this was perhaps, according to Dolgushev, "overinsurance" on the part of the cadre department, which naturally was just following orders as well as trying to protect itself.[73] The charge of antisemitism would all but disappear at the trials—with the exception of a reference to Dolgushev saying, "we don't need people from the Podol'" in the organs, a reference to the NKVD offspring of Jewish tradesmen from the Kiev city center.[74] Lest the issue of antisemitism within the NKVD seem a provincial matter, it is worth pointing out that these concerns arose at a time when the proportion of Jews in the NKVD as a whole and especially in Ukraine was plummeting, as well as at a time when thousands of Jews completely outside the NKVD were being arrested in mass operations under the pretext that they were "Zionists" or "Bundists."[75]

Antisemitism, though, was the least of Dolgushev's worries and certainly not a subject whose semiofficial existence could be admitted more generally. The main accusation against NKVD cadres generally and Dolgushev specifically at this time was the umbrella accusation of violations against socialist legality. At both the party gathering and at the trials, Dolgushev faced an array of charges revolving around this blanket accusation and including groundless arrests, the widespread use of torture in interrogations, the overreliance on "confessions," and crude behavior [*grubost'*]. According to O. M. Berman at the Kiev regional NKVD party meeting, Dolgushev intimidated his subordinates with curses and threats of arrests. Other delegates backed him up.[76] Dolgushev admitted to *grubost'*, saying "undoubtedly, there were such elements."[77] And, of course, Dolgushev recalled that Uspenskii's style of work was "screams and curses" [*okrik i mat*] and said everyone at the NKVD knew this.[78] Dolgushev was correct: The style of the NKVD in the days of terror (and before and beyond) was to yell, to harangue, to curse, and to threaten.

Needless to say, the victims of the NKVD received far worse. Most of the delegates at the Kiev regional NKVD party meeting, including Dolgushev, agreed that "methods of physical influence" were widely used in the extraction of confessions. Of equal importance, confessions had become the primary and often only evidence to prove a victim's "guilt," especially in the new group cases demanded by Ezhov and Uspenskii. Given the fantastical nature of the charges of the times, it could not have been otherwise. The scenarios of counterrevolution in Ukraine came down from above—from Ezhov and Uspenskii, at times literally drawn and outlined in specific, hierarchical detail. Charges of counterrevolution, espionage, membership in a host of antisoviet parties, or simply a socially suspect family background were pinned on tens of thousands of innocent people. Many victims initially denied the charges, but in the end torture could produce virtually any confession the NKVD desired. The issue of torture, its legal mandate, is important in the cases against NKVD interrogators. Although no written evidence is extant on central directives regarding "physical methods," Stalin later justified the use of torture in a coded telegram of 10 January 1939, addressed to secretaries of regional and national party committees and to the NKVD leadership. He wrote that the Central Committee of the Communist Party had permitted the use of physical measures from 1937. He wrote that "such measures" give results, but should be used as "exceptions" and only in relation to "obvious enemies of the people" who refuse to confess. He did admit that these measures had been abused by "enemies" within the NKVD, but noted that the use of torture was routine in the practices of foreign intelligence services and therefore justified in its use in the Soviet Union.[79]

The evidence in the case against Dolgushev and others suggests that actual lower-level directives on torture were largely oral, spread by example, and may or may not have required a sanction on a case-by-case basis from a superior NKVD head, his deputy, or the head of the specific department in which a defendant was charged. In any case, Dolgushev always argued that the use of torture was fully in place long before his appointment to head the Kiev regional NKVD.

One of the final accusations against Dolgushev was the creation of a special room for the torture of prisoners. At the second trial, Kleiman attempted to blame Dolgushev for the creation of a special room in the town of Uman.[80] The Uman case in fact came up repeatedly in Dolgushev's interrogations and in the first two trials, but was eventually dropped and tried as a separate case. Among the reasons the Uman case did not stick to Dolgushev may be that he admitted to authorizing the use of force there, as well as calling into question Uman's special room.[81] Here, Dolgushev admitted something that could otherwise only have been guessed at. He said, "The room about which Kleiman spoke actually existed in all NKVD offices, this was legal. These were small rooms, the doors were padded with felt, the walls were not covered, and there was a divan [in the room]. . . ." He then contradicted himself, adding that he had no idea whether there was a special order about the organization of such rooms.[82]

The reliance on confessions and torture meant that the NKVD neglected other types of evidence. The November 1938 directive curtailing mass operations castigated the NKVD for its unprofessional investigation techniques— despite the fact that such techniques came from above. Investigators, it was claimed, had ceased to use the services of its agents in the field, its secret informants, not least because most of the agents were arrested during the mass operations. The NKVD was also assailed for its misuse of witnesses. So-called official [shtatnye] witnesses were used repeatedly. Most were officials, but listed as rank-and-file workers or collective farm workers in the official witness statements. Many were simply told or forced to sign false statements. At the Kiev regional NKVD party meeting in Kiev, Karafelov stated, "How we selected witnesses in the cases was simply shameful. We discredited ourselves. We had the confession of the arrested and no other documents. . . . That's when the search for witnesses began. We went all over in the town, the party organizations, the factories . . . [making use of] the chairmen of factory committees, the heads of [factory] special sections [spetschasti]."[83]

Although Dolgushev said little about these practices, the issue would arise in other cases.

All of these practices were inevitable given an NKVD institutional culture in which, in the words of Dolgushev, "[it was] considered shameful when someone under arrest was released" and "once you arrest someone, it means he is guilty."[84] Moreover, time and again, NKVD officials claimed that they were forced, under the threat of arrest, to deliver signed confessions. If fear was not enough of an incentive, they were also a part of a hierarchical military organization in which orders were never to be questioned. At the December NKVD party meeting in Kiev, NKVD operatives spoke repeatedly about these issues to the point that Kleiman stood up and said, "These violations occurred in every department, in every sector, among all [NKVD] workers, and there is nothing to some comrades imagining themselves in the role of 'Jesus' and saying—I didn't beat, I had a directive, etc. Everyone beat. Everyone obtained confessions in the same way."[85]

Kleiman was very likely correct, although it is doubtful that Jesus came into the picture. Everyone was guilty. Yet, at the same time, orders came from above—from one's immediate superior, from the Kiev regional NKVD, the republican NKVD, or Ezhov and Stalin in Moscow. NKVD interrogators worked within a closed system in which, whether through fear, obedience, belief, or sadism, they dutifully fulfilled orders—in this case, obtaining signatures on confessions. Still, individuals bear responsibility for their actions. Although Dolgushev adamantly refused to admit participation in any counterrevolutionary conspiracy, he admitted his responsibility, such as it was, for most of the charges of violating socialist legality.

DOLGUSHEV'S NKVD COLLEAGUES played a key role in his trials. Unlike many other perpetrator trials at this time, where victims, NKVD office staff, prison guards, and doctors were among the witnesses, most witnesses (both those of the Military Tribunal and those of Dolgushev) in this case were Dolgushev's NKVD superiors or subordinates. Some of them were still at liberty; others were pulled from their own prison cells to testify. Overall, Dolgushev probably had more friends than foes among them, possibly testifying to his modest attempts to follow procedures in circumstances that depended on their very abrogation, possibly a result of group allegiances.

Prison commandant Nagornyi, who remembered Dolgushev's reluctance to assume his position as Kiev regional NKVD head, recalled that Dolgushev "always actively spoke up at party meetings, was in the vanguard, was sociable with his colleagues, was not conceited."[86] Nikolai Ivanovich Emel'ianov, formerly head of the Economic Department of the Kiev regional NKVD and subsequently in the reserves, said, "Dolgushev was strict and demanding at work. I did not receive illegal orders from him; on the contrary, he even forbid [us] to carry out the orders of the Narkomat [People's Commissariat] on exiling the families of the repressed if there was no sanction from the procurator."[87] Andrei Grigor'evich Nazarenko, the convicted former head of the Ukrainian republic NKVD Special Department, said, "Dolgushev exercised authority among his colleagues and I do not know of any criminal actions on his side."[88] Even the regional procurator, Simon L'vovich Kolesnikov, a not-unprejudiced witness, defended Dolgushev, with whom he sat in judgment on the troika. He said, "I noticed no violations of socialist legality. . . . On the contrary, I recall that when doubts arose and I suggested [the need for] further investigation, Dolgushev agreed with me."[89]

Dolgushev's colleagues also denied that he was close to enemy of the people Uspenskii or involved in any sort of counterrevolutionary conspiracy. Despite Uspenskii's colorful confessions and claims to have recruited Dolgushev into his nefarious activities, both Ezhov and Radzivilovskii, Uspenskii's erstwhile fellow conspirators, had denied any such recruitment, with Radzivilovskii calling Uspenskii a liar.[90] Andrei Ivanovich Egorov, the former head of the Chernigov regional NKVD, another vydvizhenets behind bars, told the court that Uspenskii's confession about Dolgushev was a lie.[91] Egorov also recalled Uspenskii's rough treatment of Dolgushev when, at an NKVD operational meeting, the former accused the latter of "piecework" in his approach to mass operations and of neglecting the "big cases" (i.e., the organizations and their leaders).[92] Prison commandant Nagornyi said he did not know if Dolgushev and Uspenskii were close, but believed that Uspenskii held Dolgushev in low regard, recalling an episode in which Uspenskii castigated Dolgushev soundly in his presence.[93] Others remembered Uspenskii and Dolgushev sparring over the compilation of data on arrests required by Moscow. A. G. Nazarenko, a highly placed official in the republican NKVD, who recalled Uspenskii cursing Dolgushev over the telephone, said Uspenskii was displeased with Dolgushev over the issue of "reconstituting" the statistics on the socioeconomic status of the victims. Uspenskii claimed Dolgushev had too many *byvshie liudi* among his victims and ordered him to substitute "Mensheviks and others" for byvshie liudi. When Dolgushev objected, Uspenskii referred to some order or other from above.[94] Even Slavin, who disagreed with Dolgushev over the troika treatment of specialists and NKVD operatives, recalled Uspenskii telling Dolgushev, "you discredit the work of the organs" and "you cannot put collective farmers and workers in the graph" of arrested victims—lest the official story of a purge of socially alien enemies be in doubt.[95]

Although some colleagues noted Dolgushev's differences with Uspenskii over the issue of correctly identifying the socioeconomic status of the victims of the mass operations in their paperwork for Moscow, some colleagues frankly pointed out Dolgushev's "errors" in his work on the troika, violating directives against trying specialists of high qualifications and NKVD officers there. This surely was a catch-22 for Dolgushev as many other NKVD officials had been trying precisely these categories of officials from the start.[96] Yet timing was everything in 1938, and it seems clear that Dolgushev erred in this regard, with or without the assent of Uspenskii. Solomon Abramovich Al'tzitser, the former head of the Special Department of the Kiev regional NKVD, said that Dolgushev allowed specialists to go before the troika under the pretext that "on the day of arrest, they did not work according to their specialty."[97] Kleiman charged Dolgushev with altering occupations on tens of [troika] agendas, which listed in the most abbreviated form biographical data on the accused.[98] L. N. Treshkov, an associate of Dolgushev in the NKVD earlier, noted cases in which Dolgushev "falsified" documents at troika meetings, crossing out occupations and substituting other lesser occupations (like bookkeeper) or penning "without defined occupation" on the documents.[99] Only Kolesnikov, the regional procurator, said otherwise, but then again he was complicit in the workings of the troika.[100]

Dolgushev's deputy, L. M. Pavlychev, generally backed Dolgushev's version of events. He was appointed deputy head of the Kiev regional NKVD at the end of July 1938 and continued in this position until October. He claimed that Uspenskii had told him that "the situation there [in the Kiev regional NKVD] is difficult, that there are many arrestees, and it is necessary to help relieve the NKVD in its investigations and unload prisoners from the jail," thus acknowledging the difficult conditions confronting Dolgushev in Kiev. Pavlychev added that he "did not observe any particular irregularities" at the Kiev regional NKVD, but noted that there were indeed "many arrested" with cases left incomplete and/or resolved according to "simplified" procedures.[101] Nonetheless, he concluded, "I consider that those charged in these cases were tried correctly, and that Uspenskii had confirmed the troika cases of NKVD workers."[102]

Pavlychev is not necessarily to be trusted. He soon found himself under investigation for the murder of a prisoner under interrogation.[103] Still, he is more convincing in his discussion of the use of "physical means of influence" to force confessions for the very reason that he rather clumsily pointed out the contradictions involved in this practice. He told the court that "there were cases of the use of physical measures on those arrested in the [Kiev regional] NKVD, and that signals came to me as well as to Dolgushev." He continued by noting that at operational meetings "Dolgushev forbade the use of force unless he [Dolgushev] was present, and in each case [required] a sanction from him or his deputy." He further stated that sanctions were infrequently issued and only after a formal report on the materials of a case. Still, Pavlychev conceded, "it was difficult to regulate how this order was fulfilled." In the final analysis—whether as simple contradiction or recognition of the underlying contradictions and indeed hypocrisy around the issue of torture—he said, "The application of physical measures, when applied with a sanction, was not an illegal phenomenon given that there was a corresponding order."[104]

Other NKVD witnesses more or less confirmed Pavlychev's testimony about sanctions and the use of violence to extract confessions. Tsirul'nitskii testified to Dolgushev's warnings against the use of force without his sanction, as did Dolgushev's own witness, S. N. Livshits, the head of the Cherkassk district-level NKVD.[105] Treshkov told the court that Dolgushev had indeed warned his subordinates at operational meetings against the use of force without a sanction. At the same time, he testified to Dolgushev's own willingness to use violence when he walked into one of Treshkov's interrogations and struck a prisoner who had refused to confess.[106] Boris Markovich Zalesskii, head of a sector in the Second Department of the Kiev regional NKVD, believed that Dolgushev held overall responsibility at the NKVD. He also said that there were many violations in Kiev, but nonetheless repeated that Dolgushev forbade the use of force without his explicit sanction.[107]

Kleiman admitted that Dolgushev "many times" warned against "physical measures," but, all the same, he said, "The use of physical measures of influence on the accused in the NKVD was systemic."[108] Moisei Grigor'evich Shapiro, who had worked in the Kiev regional NKVD from 1936—a relative old-timer in these circumstances—told the court: "Dolgushev ordered me to walk at night around the interrogation offices to check whether investigators were applying physical measures of influence to the arrested during interrogations. Shekhman excelled in the use of such methods and therefore received a reprimand. On these grounds, an order was issued and all [NKVD] workers were warned against the use of such investigative methods."[109] Vasili Ivanovich Burakov acknowledged the existence of this order but said that, in his opinion, "the order was for show given that there was also an order to beat."[110] Burakov's words more or less substantiate those of Shapiro. Shapiro, however, offered other evidence that is equally compelling. He told the court that someone, presumably a superior, phoned Dolgushev to say that the screams of prisoners could be heard on the street. Dolgushev sent Shapiro outside to check. When Shapiro reported that he heard nothing, Dolgushev angrily accused him of what Shapiro called *panibratstvo*, of covering up for his friends, thereby seeming to suggest that he was indeed concerned about what was going on in his interrogators' offices, even if it was only a matter of noise reaching the streets.[111]

K. D. Kupyrin, the former head of the First Department and current deputy head of the Kiev regional NKVD Investigation Department, succinctly characterized the work of the Kiev NKVD. He said, "At that time not one prisoner was held according to the observation of established procedural norms and there were wholesale violations in relation to all. I reported this to no one since it was obvious to everyone, including the Procurator and Moscow."[112] Kupyrin clearly knew not only that the "violations" were systemic, but that everyone knew about their ubiquitous existence. After all, it was not illegal to use force. Because this issue of sanctions appears so regularly in the self-defense of NKVD officials, it is likely that sanctions were indeed required from the head of the regional NKVD, his deputy, or the heads of departments. At the same time, with or without sanctions, violence in the extraction of confessions occurred at all times and everywhere, and few interrogators did not make use of it.

Apart from the charges of treason and troika malfeasance, most of Dolgushev's violations were frustratingly general, involving groundless arrests, violations of procedure, and convictions of innocent people. There were, however, three incidents of a far more specific nature used in the accusations against Dolgushev. The first concerned the horrendous conduct of the mass operations in Uman. Boris Naumovich Neiman, who had worked in Uman, was a key witness there. He was brought in first to testify about Dolgushev's relations to the Uman events. He said that Dolgushev was well informed about what happened and had even witnessed beatings there.[113] Kleiman talked about a "special room" set up in Uman for torture.[114] Pavlychev said Dolgushev was suspicious about some sort of sham [*lipa*] in nearby Belaia Tserkov', which was under the operational control of the Uman interdistrict group.[115] Dolgushev admitted to issuing sanctions for the use of force in Uman, but only against two or three "political bandits." Responding to Kleiman's charges about a special torture room, Dolgushev bluntly responded that such rooms "existed in all the [regional-level] NKVDs."[116] Whatever the exact nature of Dolgushev's involvement in Uman, these charges all but disappeared, and the Uman case was tried separately.[117]

The second incident of a more concrete charge against Dolgushev involved the torture of Tsapenko, identified as the former chairman of the Kiev regional NKVD party collective. Zalesskii discussed this case, noting that "there was material on Tsapenko, but he refused to confess." Zalesskii continued: "I personally saw how Dolgushev applied to him measures of [physical] influence." Dolgushev disputed this charge, arguing that he in fact had not given Tsapenko's interrogator, Lapsker, his sanction. Instead, he decided to talk to Tsapenko himself. Dolgushev then warned Tsapenko that he would beat him if he refused to confess. According to Doglushev, this warning was enough to persuade Tsapenko to confess.[118]

Dolgushev also attempted to fend off a third charge concerning the death under interrogation of the former NKVD officer, Mozheiko. The Mozheiko case was clearly a kind of cause célèbre for many of his former colleagues. Already, at the December 1938 meeting of the Kiev NKVD party collective, delegates aggressively went after one of Mozheiko's interrogators, Stroilov, as he spoke about the violations in the arrest of NKVD workers. Audience members interrupted his speech with shouts of "talk about Mozheiko." Stroilov attempted with some success to sidestep the issue by instead talking about Mozheiko's less than satisfying biological past. He said that Mozheiko was the son of a trader; his wife's father had even been a large-scale trader. Moreover, according to Stroilov, Mozheiko was born in Latvia and served in the tsarist army in World War I. He became a Soviet citizen only in 1935, claiming at various times to be Belorussian, Latvian, or even Russian, none of which was unusual in these borderland zones at that time.[119] Mozheiko was well known to be seriously ill with tuberculosis. He died under interrogation at the hands of Stroilov and Pavlychev. Pavlychev claimed that he was aware of Mozheiko's frail health, but that he had a sanction to use force and had consulted with Dolgushev in advance. According to Pavlychev, Dolgushev warned him that Mozheiko was ill and that Pavlychev must not "overdo" it with him. Pavlychev claimed that he "only" struck Mozheiko two or three times on the head. When he finished, Mozheiko sat at the interrogation table, wheezing and unable to talk. He died the next day.[120] The prison doctor falsely attributed his death to tuberculosis. Dolgushev denied giving his sanction and maintained to the end that his only guilt was in not thoroughly researching how Mozheiko died.[121]

In the end, Dolgushev would be charged with "not preventing" the death of Mozheiko.[122] This curious charge stuck through all three trials, whereas the charges concerning Uman and Tsapenko were dropped. The charges of anti-semitism simply fell away, perhaps in part given the proximity in time between the first two trials and the Nazi–Soviet Pact. At the same time, Dolgushev continued to face charges of treason and violations of socialist legality. His pretrial depositions (once he denied his initial confessions extracted through torture) and his testimony at the trials remained fairly consistent (apart from the issue of troika sentencing). As head of the Kiev regional NKVD, he acknowledged overall responsibility, while contesting many of the specific charges. His colleagues backed him up in most but not all instances, leaving the impression that Dolgushev may have tried to mitigate the worst of the violations of socialist legality.

IT IS IMPOSSIBLE to know for sure if Dolgushev and his NKVD colleagues were telling the truth. Still, it is instructive to return to Dolgushev himself— to his speeches at the December Kiev regional NKVD party meeting, his interrogations and confessions, and his courtroom testimony—to see how he attempted to defend himself against accusations of treason and violations of socialist legality.

Dolgushev repeatedly stated that the use of physical measures of influence had become a "system" in the work of the NKVD. Signed confessions were tantamount to a conviction within the context of the simplified procedures of the Great Terror. Investigators no longer investigated—the system of relying on agents and informers had collapsed, partly as a result of the widespread arrest of agents and informers; witnesses were pressed to incriminate others by force, intimidation, or supposed duty; and many of the arrested either had no compromising material in their personnel files or material that testified only to family connections (the biological approach) with the socially or politically impure, to relatives abroad, or to grandfathers involved in trade or other now-forbidden commercial occupations. Simplified procedures had been sanctioned by no less than chief USSR Procurator Vyshinskii at the start of mass operations, and orders on torture appear to have been largely oral. At the same time, the sheer quantity of arrests, the unrelenting pressure to obtain confessions and additional denunciations for group cases, and the endless threatening orders from above made it all but inevitable that NKVD cadres, never known for respecting legality in the first place, would engage in mass acts of violence against the accused, who were deemed enemies of the people from the moment of arrest.

Dolgushev noted that when he first assumed his position as head of the Kiev regional NKVD, there were around 5,000 people under arrest at the Kiev regional NKVD, all imprisoned by way of violations of legal norms.[123] The March operation against "White counterrevolutionaries" netted in one night 500 or 600 people for whom there was "no sort of concrete material." By June, over 2,000 people still sat in these prisons and not a single one— over the course of three to four months—had been interrogated because of the sheer scale of arrests.[124] At the same time, Dolgushev was under constant pressure from Uspenskii to produce more arrests, especially arrests of entire groups of enemies, and more confessions. According to Dolgushev, every meeting with Uspenskii was the same, with the latter cursing him and saying, "You are doing nothing. You have nothing."[125] When, at an operative meeting, Dolgushev asked Uspenskii what to do if the accused denied his confession, Uspenskii yelled at him: "You don't understand anything! How can you be the head of the [regional] NKVD?"[126]

Dolgushev attempted to defend himself by arguing, correctly, that the system of beatings had been in force before he began his work as head of the Kiev regional NKVD. As early as May 1937, before the announcement of mass operations but during the purge of Communist Party and government elites, Leplevskii had apparently overseen the mass expansion of and/or return to the use of widespread violence that colored NKVD practices during campaigns of repression.[127] Dolgushev witnessed how this practice was reinforced from above. He told his interrogators and the court that L. N. Bel'skii, at the time deputy commissar of the All-Union NKVD, arrived in Kiev from Moscow sometime in 1937 to "teach" the practice of torture by word and by example. At a meeting of NKVD operatives in Kiev, Bel'skii "gave a clear directive" regarding torture, telling subordinates that, whether spy or counterrevolutionary, "all the same [the enemy] will be shot" and that during interrogation it was necessary "to give it to him [the enemy] in the snout."[128] Dolgushev observed how the practice of physical methods moved from the All-Union to Ukrainian republican NKVD and then down to the regional NKVDs, interdistrict groups, and the district levels of the NKVD, becoming "systemic." Dolgushev "concluded that this [torture] was not a local phenomenon but a defined system of investigation."[129]

At the December meeting of the Kiev regional NKVD party collective, Dolgushev boldly stated, "We are all guilty in this [the use of torture], in the first place, I am guilty as head of the regional administration."[130] "Everyone," he continued, accepted this practice and everyone beat.[131] He claimed there and in his court testimony that he had attempted from the very start to try to control and regulate this practice, warning his subordinates "at every operational meeting, in conversations with each department head . . . not to touch [the accused]" and, in each case, to obtain his sanction or the sanction of his deputy before using force to extract confessions. He also talked about how his colleagues had developed an unhealthy "taste for torture," considering it the primary means and end of interrogations. After all, he stated, people in the NKVD "considered it shameful" to let anyone go according to the reasoning that "only the guilty are arrested."[132]

Dolgushev was a rare exception among NKVD cadres arrested at this time.[133] He not only took general responsibility for violating socialist legality as regional NKVD head, but also openly acknowledged that the practice of torture in extracting confessions was ubiquitous and based on orders from above. This is not to excuse the NKVD cadres who certainly were not newcomers to enhanced methods of interrogation; nor is it to deny that the implementation of the terror demanded the recruitment of literally thousands of new cadres mobilized from the party and Komsomol who would claim their own innocence by arguing that they did not know better, had not been trained properly, or were simply obeying orders.[134] It is also not to negate the complaints of NKVD workers like Ia. E. Rotshtein, who, while never denying the use of torture, talked about their grueling work—the long all-night sessions of NKVD interrogators, lasting into the mornings and taking place every day for months and months without a break.[135] Rather, the combination of brutal orders from above and terrible conditions on the ground only served to accentuate the worst of practices. And Dolgushev knew this.

What Dolgushev refused to admit was any charge of treason in connection to his supposed part in the mythical Ezhov–Uspenskii NKVD conspiracy to topple the Soviet Union. He repeatedly insisted that he was not "Uspenskii's man," but rather that he was "Khrushchev's vydvizhenets," having served in Khrushchev's personal guard (when he was head of the NKVD Ukraine First Department). He took pains to tell the court about his numerous clashes with Uspenskii and Uspenskii's disrespectful treatment of him, which his colleagues generally backed up.[136] In the recantation of his confession and in his court testimony, he revealed that it was only the use of torture that forced him initially to admit to a guilt he later denied.[137]

Dolgushev believed that the use of torture in the extraction of confessions had become systemic and that Chekists had developed a "taste" for violence in the interrogation room. Unlike other NKVD operatives under arrest, he did not evince any particular belief that the enemies were real. This lack of belief—or perhaps cynicism or retrospective awareness of the truth—is significant, but it is difficult, if not impossible, to delve further into Dolgushev's mindset. A singularly important and relatively rare document, however, may allow for a glimpse beyond Dolgushev's own words.

Iakov Alekseevich Kozlov was with Dolgushev in cell number 43 in the late spring and early summer of 1939. He was an informer, planted to draw out Dolgushev in conversation in the hope of self-incrimination. Kozlov submitted two statements, on 9 May and 15 June 1939, to Dolgushev's interrogator, O. M. Tverdokhlebenko, and was also depositioned by Tverdokhlebenko on 13 May 1939.[138] His words are no more to be trusted than Dolgushev's. It is not possible to assess their overall credibility, and some of what he says carries the whiff of the predominant plot line of the times. Yet his comments are worth exploring—if not as a direct conduit to Dolgushev's thinking, then as a reflection of ideas circulating within the prison cells and closed culture of the NKVD.

One might reasonably expect an informer to dwell on the official constructs of enemies and counterrevolutionaries, in this case, on Dolgushev's ties to Uspenskii. Kozlov did attempt to draw out Dolgushev on the subjects of Uspenskii and the concocted NKVD plot against the Soviet Union, but with limited success. Dolgushev was not naive, and, if Kozlov is to be trusted, Dolgushev warned him to be careful about what he said and told him that a microphone was planted in the cell. Still, according to Kozlov, Dolgushev talked about Uspenskii:

> Dolgushev told me that you think that Uspenskii is an enemy, but Uspenskii is not an enemy, he knows Chekist work well, destroyed enemies, and when he saw that they began to arrest those Chekists who destroyed enemies, he decided to take off and save himself. It seems Uspenskii knew still before the appointment of Beriia as Narkom NKVD SSSR that Beriia would become the Narkom. And therefore, that meant that all of the leadership would be in the hands of Georgians and they would suppress the *nachal'niki* [heads of NKVDs] as is happening at present. The people who occupy responsible posts in the NKVD organs would be removed. They would use any material against them in order to put these people in prison and replace them with Georgians. All of those who were awarded medals were also put in prison, but then this is how they earned their medals. . . . You know, they are fools, the best Chekists sit in prison. Uspenskii pulled together around himself the best Chekists and [A. Z.] Kobulov [Beriia's emissary in Ukraine] is now destroying them in order to strengthen his own authority.[139]

Although this "declaration" may have been drawn from whole cloth, still it provides a sense of the understanding at the time that "Georgians"—"Beriia's people"—were replacing "Uspenskii's people" in responsible NKVD posts. This was hardly the stuff of counterrevolution, but it did seem to show that Dolgushev, or at the very least Kozlov, believed that Uspenskii was a victim of the struggle between competing NKVD networks.

More important, Kozlov's depiction of Dolgushev portrays a former Chekist who understood that he and his cohort had become scapegoats in the Great Terror. Kozlov quotes Dolgushev as saying:

> You think Uspenskii is an enemy, no, I now understand that the CC VKP (b) [Central Commitee of the Communist Party], fearing international talk, decided to destroy us because we know that the CC must answer for all the shortcomings in work. Now they can say that they are not guilty, the Chekists are guilty. You see the CC, having seen that Hitler was destroying Jews because we shot many Germans, immediately decided to imprison us.[140]

Kozlov's Dolgushev, then, betrays an understanding of Stalin's mechanism of repression. He understands how different cohorts or networks operated within the NKVD, manipulated by Stalin, and how Stalin made use of scapegoating techniques to reverse the mass operations. At the same time, he was keenly aware of the international situation.

The Dolgushev of Kozlov's pen also was convinced that he would be destroyed. When Kozlov attempted to suggest to Dolgushev that everything would turn out fine in the end, the latter reportedly responded, "You are stupid if you think they arrested us by mistake, they arrested us to destroy us."[141] Moreover, he continued, they could make anyone denounce him. According to Kozlov, Dolgushev was quite clear that anyone could be made to say anything to denounce anyone, to admit to anything.[142] Kozlov said that Dolgushev even denied the guilt of the Red Army leadership, claiming they were repressed "only because they were against Voroshilov, a talentless commander." Dolgushev reportedly believed that the Central Committee was at fault in the "mistakes in the repression of the population" and in order "to raise its authority within the country and abroad" (because of the repression of national minorities), the Central Committee had blamed the NKVD and carried out arrests among the "best Chekists," particularly in Ukraine where Uspenskii had mobilized around himself the "best Chekists:" "Thus, the CC VKP (b) in this way destroyed living witnesses who knew about the mistakes committed by the CC VKP (b)."[143]

This was dramatic testimony. Rightfully blaming the Central Committee was as subversive as a concocted alliance and conspiracy with Uspenskii, if not more so. Dolgushev, according to Kozlov, also knew rather accurately what happened to the enemies who received Gulag sentences. He told Kozlov that they were exiled so that they could work in construction and build canals. Dolgushev also purportedly compared these poor souls with the exiles of tsarist times, talking about the horrid conditions and poor chances of survival in the Gulag.[144]

If any of Kozlov's testimony was correct, Dolgushev had a very clear sense of the causes, conduct, and consequences of the Great Terror. Yet Kozlov's character was largely undermined at Dolgushev's trial. Prison commandant Nagornyi considered Kozlov's behavior in prison abnormal and said he was even sent to a psychiatric hospital. E. B. Belen'kii, who at one time shared the cell with Kozlov and Dolgushev, also claimed that Kozlov was not normal.[145] Either way, Kozlov's testimony was more than the court wanted to hear and certainly went far beyond any of Dolgushev's other statements in interrogation or at his trials. In any case, Dolgushev denied all of Kozlov's claims in his formal testimony.[146]

Dolgushev had three chances to address the court. In addition to his opening remarks and interjections throughout the trials, Dolgushev had the right to a last word, the right to present a final speech in his own defense. All three concluding speeches were basically consistent. He very carefully went over the facts of his case, pointing out the contradictions, inaccuracies, and downright lies. He insisted that he warned his subordinates against the use of physical measures, groundless arrests, and other violations of procedure. He claimed, "I did everything that an honest person could do." He admitted to sanctioning the use of beatings but maintained that he did this not more than fifteen times. He admitted that the regional NKVD had a special room for torture, but added that these existed everywhere. He denied sanctioning the beating of Mozheiko, but admitted the use of his fists on occasion.[147] At his second trial, he ended his speech with the following words:

> Enemies slandered me. I was never an enemy and did not lead any kind of hostile work. I myself am from a socially near [proletarian] family, all my brothers are Communists. I was brought up by the party and Soviet power and did not have a basis or reason to join the enemy. Enemies conspired against me, and this is my misfortune, but [there was] no crime.[148]

At the end of his final trial, held after Germany invaded the Soviet Union, Dolgushev asked the court to take into account that he was a "young vydvizenets promoted to leading work in the circumstances of that time. I could not suddenly change and correct the illegal methods of investigation that had been established." He continued: "I am not an enemy, not a traitor, there is nothing socially alien about me, I am myself a worker, my father was a worker and party member; my brothers are all Communists and one has already died at the front of the fatherland war." He pleaded with the court to send him to the front, noting that he had worked honorably during his time in the Gulag awaiting trial.[149]

Dolgushev's first two sentences were overturned. His third trial occurred during wartime in Sverdlovsk in the Urals on 20–21 May 1942. This time the court sentenced Dolgushev to death.[150] The verdict was upheld, but once again the Supreme Court intervened, substituting a ten-year Gulag sentence for execution on the basis of Dolgushev's character.[151] Dolgushev served his term in the Gulag and died quietly in 1973. The post-Soviet Ukrainian state turned down a relative's request to overturn his conviction on 4 June 1997.[152]

AS HEAD OF the Kiev regional NKVD, Dolgushev accepted responsibility for the "violations of socialist legality" that occurred in Kiev and throughout the region on his watch. At the same time, he insisted that he had committed no crime against the state, but rather had done everything that "an honest person" could do given "the circumstances of that time." Athough there is scant reference to ideology and belief and no mention of Stalin in his criminal file, Dolgushev consistently declared his loyalty to the Communist Party and Soviet power, while still betraying elements of doubt and cynicism about his work in the regional NKVD.

Dolgushev was both a scapegoat for the Great Terror and a victim of NKVD clientele practices, falling along with Uspenskii and many other Uspenskii-appointed vydvizhentsy in the Ukrainian NKVD. Given his position, Dolgushev was well placed to serve as a witness to the policies and practices of the terror, albeit from a perspective within the NKVD, from the perspective of the perpetrator. His case illuminates the interactions between center and periphery by highlighting the centrality, however self-serving, of "orders from above" conveyed in writing, orally, or by example. This issue of obeying higher orders is central in the continuing discussions among arrested NKVD operatives of the issue of sanctions permitting the use of physical means of influence, of torture in short. Yet such obedience constituted a slippery slope that could end only with Stalin. Because blaming Stalin was all but impossible, blame was generally projected little further than to the next rung of authority on the NKVD hierarchy.

Dolgushev's case also highlights some of the great fictions of the Great Terror. Most important, it shows how Ezhov and then Uspenskii brought the plot of the terror—the counterrevolution in all its manifestations with its threatening Fifth Column—from center to periphery. To prove the fiction of the terror, the NKVD had to provide a vast panoply of enemies who, once arrested, had to confess according to established tropes. Because the charges were fictitious, NKVD operatives had little choice but to extract confessions through force and to create witness testimony through manipulation and threat. The "circumstances of that time," as Dolgushev put it, add yet another layer of understanding to the terror's realities. The very compression of the terror dictated from above to achieve the most horrendous quantitative results in the shortest period of time, along with the frequent transfer and arrests of NKVD personnel including Jewish NKVD operatives, the pressure and fear that accompanied their actions, the endless hours of work, the demands for constant reports and data, the overcrowding of prisons, and the threatening calls and visits from above, created the worst possible conditions for the victims of the Great Terror. These conditions served as the context in which many of the NKVD operatives worked and led to the development of "a taste for torture" as well as allowing, indeed enabling, local conditions to play a role in the overall trajectory of the terror.

3

Vania the Terrible

I ask the court to take into account that I was in operative work only from December 1936 and before that was in technical work. The time when I was in operative work was the same time that the leadership's directive about the use of physical measures in investigations was in force. I was trained to consider that if the NKVD organs arrested a person, then he was an enemy and he must confess his enemy activity. I did not use physical methods in the investigations of the arrested without the sanction of the leadership. They told me that there was a party directive on the application of physical methods of investigation. I am not an enemy. I am dedicated to the core to Soviet power. I am young and want to live. I ask you to spare my life.

—I. S. DRUSHLIAK, *former NKVD investigator*

ON 15 JANUARY 1940, 27-year-old NKVD investigator Ivan Stepanovich Drushliak was sentenced to be shot.[1] The Military Tribunal of the NKVD Forces of Kiev County [*okrug*] charged him with violating Article 206-17, (B), of the Ukrainian criminal code. Drushliak had abused his office, fabricated confessions, and crudely violated socialist legality in carrying out interrogations in the course of the Great Terror of 1937–1938, first in Khar'kov and then in Kiev.[2]

Drushliak—or Vania, as he was known—began his work in the NKVD in 1935 at the age of 22. When the mass operations began, the NKVD mobilized him to work as an investigator–interrogator in the Khar'kov regional NKVD, first as an assistant operative-plenipotentiary [*operupolnomochennyi*] and then as assistant head of a sector [*otdelenie*] of the Fourth Department [*otdel*]. In spring 1938, he moved up to the republic-level NKVD in Kiev, continuing his work in investigations and interrogations, and eventually attaining the position of assistant head of sector of the Fourth Department. By April 1939, Drushliak was under arrest, awaiting interrogation and trial.[3]

Drushliak was a typical *vydvizhenets*, whose rapid career rise in the 1930s reached its peak in 1938 with the appointment of Uspenskii as head of the NKVD in Ukraine. His fate paralleled that of Dolgushev. From his work in 1937 to his final sentence in 1940, his case sheds additional light on the question of sanctions in relation to torture, as well as illuminating issues of obedience to orders from above, belief in his mission, and, likely, elements of sadism.

WHO WAS DRUSHLIAK? He was Ukrainian by nationality, born in Kupiansk in Ukraine in 1913. That meant he was both relatively local and extremely young when he became an NKVD investigator at the end of 1936. He had worked for the NKVD from 1935 in Khar'kov until his transfer to Kiev in 1938. He had been in the Komsomol from 1928 and the Communist Party from 1931. After completing technical studies in a factory apprenticeship school, he was a factory Komsomol secretary in Khar'kov until joining or being recruited into the internal security police. Drushliak was married, with two children. There is conflicting information on whether he came from a working-class or a peasant background. There were dark suggestions in his personnel file that his father had been a village elder and a member of the right-wing, antisemitic Union of Russian People before the Revolution.[4] Drushliak, of course, denied such accusations, but in all likelihood his father had been a peasant.

His first positions in operative work were as assistant special plenipotentiary and then assistant head of a sector of the Fourth Department of the Khar'kov regional NKVD. As such, he led investigations, in particular of participants of so-called counterrevolutionary Ukrainian nationalist organizations, but also of Trotskyists and Zionists, including some of his former NKVD colleagues. The evaluation in his personnel file was sterling. It read (in part): "An energetic and promising worker, he individually worked up and led the investigation of a counterrevolutionary Trotskyist organization in the Tiniavka Factory . . . in investigative work, he was persistent and knew investigative work. . . . He is disciplined, politically well developed, and seasoned as a Communist."[5] In their depositions and at the trial, his colleagues in the Khar'kov NKVD remembered how Drushliak was held up as a model for others. Iakov Efimovich Rotshtein worked in the Economic Department of the regional NKVD in Khar'kov when Drushliak's trial was underway. He had started in the NKVD as a party worker in the Communications Department of the Khar'kov NKVD. At the height of the Great Terror, in late 1937 or early 1938, like legions of others, he was mobilized into work in the Investigation Department and began to lead interrogations, first under Drushliak's tutelage. Rotshtein told the investigator, "I was not interested in his [Drushliak's] 'successes,' his art became the property of all the workers at the Khar'kov NKVD. They talked about Drushliak not only at operative meetings and meetings of our group, but at meetings of the entire party collective, describing him as a worker with promise." Rotshtein continued, "In 1937, there was a banquet to celebrate the [twentieth] anniversary of the Cheka. The former head of the Khar'kov NKVD, Reikhman, embraced Drushliak, proposed a toast to him as the best of the best and the most progressive young worker, followed by an exchange of kisses."[6]

Drushliak was "assiduous," according to Nikolai Nesterovich Kriukov, a department head in the NKVD in Khar'kov at the time of the trial. Like Rotshtein, Kriukov told of how Drushliak was praised at meetings of the department. The head of the Khar'kov NKVD, L. I. Reikhman, as well as head of the Fourth Department (and later head of the Khar'kov NKVD), A. M. Simkhovich, and deputy head of the Khar'kov NKVD, F. S. Fedorov-Berkov, described him as one of the best investigators who routinely produced six to seven confessions per night. Even Drushliak's immediate boss, S. D. Kaluzhskii, with whom Drushliak would be at cross-purposes during the trial, told the court that Drushliak was a "good worker."[7]

Moisei Evseevich Gokhberg, a seasoned NKVD man, accused of "liberalism" during the Great Terror, had known Drushliak since 1936. Asked at the end of his deposition what more he could say about Drushliak, he replied, "We Jews [*zhidy*] got on well with him. By nature, he is a nice fellow and a good comrade.... A few times, as a much older person, I warned him that his methods of interrogation were illegal and that in the end they would punish him severely. However, Drushliak paid no attention to my warning since he was then under the influence of the former leadership of the department, Simkhovich and Fedorov, and also the former head of the regional NKVD administration, Reikhman, who not only did not stop Drushliak from beating prisoners but, on the contrary, in all ways encouraged him ... always setting him up as an example to others."[8]

Drushliak was a man of ambition, according to Boris Aleksandrovich Polishchuk, a former NKVD worker who had been arrested during the Great Terror. He told the investigator: "The leadership of the department always set him up as a model, as a young growing worker ... he was expected to receive a medal and, when he didn't, he literally stopped working. The bosses enlisted Babushkin [then Polishchuk's cellmate and former NKVD worker] to talk to Drushliak (they were friends) and he convinced him that Communists do not work because of awards."[9]

Semen Borisovich Ratner came up in the NKVD from the district level. Because he was new and had no experience with "big cases," he was initially assigned to assist Drushliak. In the beginning, he was impressed: "I had the idea that Drushliak was the boss, since he would stop by [at the other] offices of investigators, interfering in their questioning of people. They all said Drushliak was a model worker. They put him forth as an example to others. When I began to lead my own investigations, Drushliak stopped by one time when I was questioning someone and asked how the prisoner was behaving, which meant—had the prisoner confessed or not. Initially, when I didn't know and thought that Drushliak was the boss, I told him how the prisoner was behaving. If I said the prisoner behaved badly, that is didn't confess, then Drushliak cursed the prisoner, struck him, and spit in his face." Later, or so Ratner claimed, he always said that the prisoner was behaving well.[10]

Semen Il'ich Gol'dshtein, another NKVD worker in Khar'kov, knew Drushliak from their Komsomol days in the mid-1930s. He too remembered how at operative meetings "it was always understood that Drushliak was the best investigator and [could] produce each night from 8 to 10 and more confessions." He then added that he and his colleagues believed that Reikhman simply failed to carefully analyze Drushliak's work, "for we all knew that Drushliak, meeting no obstacle from the leadership, used physical methods of influence." When at operative meetings others were accused of liberalism, Drushliak would be held up as an example, "but for us it was understood that to obtain such a large number of confessions, Drushliak made use of physical methods of influence" and, he added, more than the others.[11]

With the exception of Drushliak's immediate former boss, Kaluzhskii, who did not know which way the political winds were blowing until the end of the trial when he himself was placed under investigation, Drushliak's colleagues did not hesitate to describe the various manifestations of his "art" as an interrogator. From their statements and testimony, moreover, it is abundantly clear that they discussed this art continuously in these years; "top secret" held no water in the back offices of the Khar'kov NKVD. Investigator Rotshtein said that Drushliak "was looked upon in general as a sadist."[12] Kriukov described Drushliak storming into his office in "sadistic ecstasy."[13] At a closed regional NKVD party meeting in January 1939, one Mordukhovich called Drushliak a "regular sadist." He went on to say that he currently worked in Drushliak's old office "where to this day the walls are all broken from Drushliak hammering them with prisoners' heads."[14] Boris Konstantinovich Frei, before his own arrest as head of one of the Khar'kov NKVD's departments, remembered seeing traces of blood on the walls of Drushliak's office.[15]

Rotshtein also talked about conducting joint investigations in three capital punishment cases. He said, "Drushliak always used the same measures of physical persuasion, that is, he would assume the pose of a boxer and fire off blows with his fists to the stomach, with a truncheon, spit in prisoners' faces, mouth, make the prisoner bend down and beat him on his ribs. . . . He took them by the chest and back and head and beat the prisoners against the wall." Rotshtein claimed that he had "tried to stop Drushliak during the beatings of prisoners, but for this received threats and insults reported to the former head of the Fourth Department, Simkhovich, that I was 'disturbing' his [Drushliak's] 'work.'"[16]

According to Gokhberg, Drushliak walked from office to office with a large truncheon he called "Rando," used to beat prisoners. Gokhberg went on to say that he "often had to go to Drushliak's office with a question and observed in the course of several minutes his work with the accused, whom he literally persecuted, beating them up with his hands, legs, stick, spitting in their face and breaking a chair on their backs."[17] According to Polishchuk, another former NKVD colleague in his cell spoke of how Drushliak "brutally beat people with an especially large club, which [this colleague] dubbed the 'staff of Ivan the Terrible.'"[18]

Drushliak's tutelage was "outrageous," recalled Aleksei Konstantinovich Egupov, who worked under Drushliak and later became an operative pleni-potentiary of the Second Department of the Khar'kov NKVD. He knew of one young NKVD worker who actually refused to work with Drushliak. Egupov recalled interrogating one man whom he found to be innocent. Drushliak said about this prisoner: "he is a bit (curse word) [*sic*] enemy, and participated in a counterrevolutionary organization, beat a confession out of him." When Drushliak found out about Egupov's conclusion of innocence, he was enraged and told Egupov "ironically" that he "doesn't know how to conduct an interrogation." Egupov complained of Drushliak's methods, saying that they were not in the spirit of the Communist Party [*nepartiinye*], to which Drushliak told him to be more modest and learn to toady to the leadership. Later, at the trial, Drushliak would claim that Egupov had a score to settle with him, because he had told the leadership that Egupov was a loafer. Egupov also described in some detail Drushliak's methods:

During Drushliak's interrogations of prisoners at the NKVD build-ing, I observed the following methods of physical influence, applied systematically: [he] forced prisoners to stoop, after which he struck them in the ribs, boxed their ears, hit them in the head, kneed them in the stomach, beat them on the bones of their feet, spit in the faces of prisoners, forced them to imitate the voices of animals. Besides this, he often threw at the prisoners paperweights and other office materials.

Drushliak himself, while conducting these interrogations, went into a frenzy, striking the glass on the table with his fists.[19]

According to investigator Moisei Samoilovich Gorokhovskii, who was head of a sector in the republican-level Ukrainian NKVD, but first encountered Drushliak in Khar'kov, Drushliak was considered so good at what he did that his superiors transferred prisoners who refused to confess to their interrogators to Drushliak. Once, later in Kiev, Gorokhovskii had to interrogate several people who had been arrested as a result of Drushliak's work. He could not confirm Drushliak's evidence, decided these *kulaks* were actually just regular collective farmers, and told the head of the department that he would not interrogate them. Drushliak took over and in two to three days had full confessions.[20]

Semen Shaevich Shatnyi remembered that Drushliak was always called Vania. He once entered Drushliak's office to find there an acquaintance, a former Chekist, Levchuk, under interrogation. Levchuk pleaded with Shatnyi and said he was innocent—"You know that I am a Jew, survived several pogroms . . . and now some hooligan of an investigator accuses me of being in a Ukrainian nationalist organization." Then he showed Shatnyi the wounds from Drushliak's beating. Shatnyi simply behaved indifferently to his former acquaintance. Later, at the trial, Shatnyi described the rather disturbing scene of Drushliak's office: "Drushliak's office presented itself as something unimaginable. Everything was thrown around and in disorder. There was a terrible smell in the room . . . on the left side there were holes in the wall that were bespattered with blood." Drushliak interjected, with some indignation, saying, "My office was a good one, it was organized not bad." In response, Shatnyi reaffirmed, "In general, Drushliak's office presented itself as something terrible." [21]

There was no question, as one peasant prison guard put it, that there was more noise from Drushliak's office "than from the others."[22] However, Drushliak was certainly not alone in the use of force. Polishchuk said his cellmate had told him that "'beating' was a general phenomenon in Khar'kov as a method of questioning." Polishchuk also told the investigators that "in a moment of frankness," another cellmate, a former friend of Drushliak's, had told him that "'thrashing' of prisoners was a general phenomenon in the Fourth Department" where he had worked earlier.[23] Tikhon Kuz'mich Bessmertnyi, Drushliak's own witness, who had worked in the same investigative unit as Drushliak, told of a case in which literally every investigator of the unit took turns beating a prisoner.[24] Some of the interrogators admitted to the use of force in their work, sometimes with various excuses, other times without. A few were even under arrest. Drushliak told the court that his witnesses—NKVD employees—"slandered me because they themselves used illegal methods of investigation and wanted to put all the blame on me."[25] Perhaps Drushliak was right; perhaps he wasn't. Perhaps his colleagues were afraid themselves or jealous of Drushliak, as he thought. At this point, it might be germane to turn to the "facts" of the case to investigate the specifics of Drushliak's crimes in an effort to contextualize his sadistic behavior.

WHAT HAPPENED IN Khar'kov? There is no simple answer. Drushliak said one thing; the majority of his colleagues said another. But there were other witnesses as well, witnesses no less biased, but in possession of firsthand knowledge. Drushliak's victims, the chatty office staff of the Department, and a series of expert witnesses can help to reconstruct what went on in room 124 at the NKVD. Three of the five main victims of Drushliak's art survived to provide direct testimony.[26]

The first was Lidiia Iosifovna Bodanskaia. At the time of her arrest on the night of 24 October 1937, Bodanskaia was the head of the Art Department of the Khar'kov regional committee of the party. Testifying as a free woman, Bodanskaia had since become the director of the Poltava Philharmonic. On 19 June 1939, she was deposed. The first question was why she admitted to counterrevolutionary activity, when she now denied it. She said:

> This declaration was written at a moment of extreme moral confusion, connected to the difficult questioning expressed in abusive curses, prolonged standing while barking at the lightbulb, spinning in place. It was written under the dictate of Frei in the presence of Drushliak. I slandered myself with this declaration.

According to Bodanskaia, Drushliak subjected her, while she was pregnant, not only to physical abuse but also to humiliation. Perhaps he resented this older woman's education and intelligentsia background. In addition to cursing her, Drushliak threatened to destroy her whole family. He made her stand in the center of the interrogation room and spin, spin until she passed out, after which Drushliak poured water on her and made her start again. Bodanskaia said that a number of NKVD workers came in and saw everything.[27]

Ratner was one of the NKVD workers who witnessed Bodanskaia spinning. He said that Drushliak cursed her when she asked for water. Ratner had come in to relieve Drushliak for a short spell. He claims that he allowed

Bodanskaia to sit down. When Drushliak returned, he screamed at Ratner and cursed him for allowing the prisoner to sit.[28] Although she did not remember Bodanskaia's name, Drushliak's colleague, NKVD investigator Evgeniia Nikolaevna Nechaeva, testified to seeing a prisoner barking like a dog at the lightbulb.[29] Frei, who Bodanskaia said took her statement, was notably silent about the case. Then again, he was under arrest himself.[30]

There is no question that Drushliak exceeded the limits of the grotesque in his torment of Bodanskaia. Fortunately, she lived to testify. It may very well be that her husband's status as a former NKVD man caught the attention of the authorities when they were looking for witnesses.[31] This was likely the case for another of Drushliak's victims, Mosei Vladimirovich Frenkel', a former NKVD worker who found himself rounded up as part of a campaign against so-called Zionists waged in the thick of the Great Terror.

On 17 August 1938, Frenkel' was called out for questioning to Drushliak's office. Drushliak interrogated him all day and into the early morning of the next day, demanding that Frenkel confess to belonging to a Zionist organization. When Frenkel' refused, Drushliak beat him: "He struck me with hard blows with some sort of hard instrument on the back of the head, and [beat me] with a chair leg on my back and other parts of my body." Then one of Drushliak's superiors, Iaroliants, stopped by and told Drushliak to send Frenkel' back to the prison. On parting, Drushliak warned Frenkel', "tomorrow he would come to the prison and I would confess whatever he wanted." The next day, Drushliak beat Frenkel' all day with a chair leg and a rubber hose, and Frenkel' finally submitted. But when Frenkel' saw the typed record of his interrogation, he refused to sign it. Drushliak had "corrected" it—a euphemism for falsification.[32] Drushliak responded by again beating Frenkel'. Frenkel' was so shocked, he said, that he asked Drushliak if something had happened in the Soviet Union (e.g., a fascist coup), to which Drushliak answered, "we are beating old men like you" and spat in his face. Frenkel' immediately dispatched a series of complaints to, stupidly, the head of the NKVD (Ezhov) about what was happening. Drushliak discovered these complaints and said to Frenkel', "the Narkom wrote b—[sic] on your complaint," the final word in the original Russian representing an expletive. Once Frenkel' was freed and rehabilitated, he was listed as an "invalid of the third class" because of Drushliak's beatings.[33]

Drushliak also interrogated L. L. Rokhlin, a professor and senior researcher at the Central Institute of Psychiatry. Rokhlin was accused of belonging to a counterrevolutionary organization. On 27 August 1937, he was called into room 124. Drushliak immediately began to curse him terribly, struck him in the face, and demanded his confession. On the next day, Rokhlin submitted several complaints to Vyshinskii and the regional procurator about what had happened to him. He was then given to another interrogator, Babushkin (Drushliak's friend), in room 136. On the night of 14–15 October, Babushkin called Rokhlin in. There were a number of investigators in the room, and they began to beat him in turns. Finally, they all left, except for Babushkin and Drushliak. Drushliak took his wooden truncheon out and they took turns beating him in the ribs and in the testicles. He remained silent and Drushliak said, "Just look, the Gestapo school is silent." Rokhlin ended up in the hospital from 15 to 29 October, where he continued to write to Vyshinskii and the regional procurator. Then the interrogations began all over again. On the night of 4–5 February 1938, investigator Karasev told him to "stop bombarding" Vyshinskii and others with his complaints. "They all come to me." Still, Rokhlin's case ended up in court, by which time his interrogators were behind bars. After he was freed, Rokhlin wrote to Stalin. At the trial, Babushkin would deny touching Rokhlin, but claimed that Drushliak beat him.[34]

Bodanskaia, Frenkel', and Rokhlin all bore witness to Drushliak's brutality. It is likely that they were allowed to testify because of their NKVD or Communist Party connections and/or their letters to authorities. Another of Drushliak's victims, former NKVD worker Evsei L'vovich Liudmirskii, would also complain of Drushliak's sadism in later years. He wrote in a 1953 application for the restoration of his Communist Party membership that Drushliak told him, "forget forever your [NKVD] connections with us, it is not for that that we arrested you."[35] Two others among Drushliak's many victims never had a chance to speak, so it is necessary to turn to other witnesses to understand what happened to these two men who likely died at Drushliak's hands.

The first of these cases concerns Stepan Bandura, an elderly man who had served in Petliura's ministry, in the Central Rada during the civil war. Drushliak said, "Bandura—this is an ancient man, a fervent nationalist," and naturally for those times, he was accused of participation in a counterrevolutionary Ukrainian nationalist organization.[36] Drushliak's interrogation of Bandura became the talk of the office.

Evgeniia Nechaeva recalled, "One night when I was conducting an interrogation, I heard loud noise in the corridor. I left my office. Across from my room, [they were] leading a prisoner. He was dragged, did not want to go and cried loudly, 'don't take me to him, he will kill me.' Many employees had come out from their offices because of this cry, including Gorokhovskii. I asked Gorokhovskii who was this prisoner, he answered, 'It is Bandura, [they] are taking him to Drushliak and he is afraid that he will kill him.' On the next day, I found out that Bandura was dead." Gorokhovskii had also heard cries while he was interrogating a prisoner and came out to see Bandura crying and begging not to be brought to Drushliak. Investigator Fedorov-Berkov said the same, adding that Simkhovich was there as well.[37]

Lidiia Andrianovna Iakovleva was also there. At the time, she did administrative work in the Fourth Department, but had taken over secretarial duties from Anna Mikhailovna Boiko, who was ill. She said at the trial, "One night I heard a lot of noise. Everyone leaped from their offices, including me and the head of the department and ran to Drushliak's office from where the noise came." When the head of the department, Simkhovich, returned from Drushliak's office, he muttered to her that Drushliak "needed to cease this *fizkul'tura* [sport]." Then Fedorov told everyone to return to their offices and close their doors. Iakovleva later told the whole story to Boiko, who had a story of her own to report. Boiko, as usual, received the autopsy report on Bandura from the morgue and tried to give it to Drushliak. Drushliak refused to take it and suggested she give it to Fedorov, who in turn sent her to Simkhovich, who then sent her back to Fedorov. She carried the report back and forth between Fedorov and Simkhovich several times, but no one would take responsibility. She was also able to tell the court that Drushliak had indeed read the autopsy, which he denied, perhaps unwisely saying, "wouldn't I then have simply destroyed it to hide the crime?"[38]

The autopsy on Bandura took place on 22 February 1938 in the Khar'kov forensic morgue under Dr. L. Sotnikov. His report frankly discussed the many contusions on Bandura's body, the clear signs of hemorrhage, and concluded that Bandura had died as a result of blunt force—most likely, Rando.[39] The very public suffering and death of Stefan Bandura behind the closed doors of the Khar'kov NKVD and prison may have sealed Drushliak's fate. But there was more.

Petr Nikiforovich Tarasov was another of Drushliak's victims. According to Drushliak's criminal file, Tarasov formerly worked at the Central Executive Committee of the Republic of Ukraine and was arrested for belonging to a counterrevolutionary rightist–Trotskyist organization. His acquaintance, one Dubinskii, had provided false testimony on Tarasov while he himself was worked over by Drushliak.[40] Drushliak was charged with the murder of Tarasov. The primary witnesses in this case were a series of prison employees and the prison doctor.

Vasili Filimonovich Benderskii was a prison elder. He said that he knew that Drushliak "regularly from 14 June 1938 to 18 June 1938 inclusively," called out Tarasov for questioning, day and night. He continued: "After 18 June

1938, the arrested Tarasov was no longer called for questioning because he had been beaten to such a degree that he could not walk and laid down all the time in his cell, not able to get up." Benderskii saw that the lower part of Tarasov's body was covered all over with "bruises clotted with blood." He called the doctor, and Tarasov received medical assistance from prison doctor Fraiman, but it was limited to some sort of ointment rubbed into Tarasov's wounds.[41]

David Dmitrievich Kobeniuk, the commandant of Tarnopol prison at the time of the trial, worked in Kiev as assistant to the head of the NKVD's internal prison as well as supervising prisoners in Pechersk. He told the investigators that once, when he was working in Pechersk, they brought in a badly beaten prisoner. Drushliak had interrogated him. It was Tarasov. Kobeniuk immediately brought the case to the attention of the commandant of the prison, Nagornyi. He moved Tarasov to another cell and then to the prison's barbershop, where Drushliak and Iaroliants interrogated him again. Kobeniuk said he did not know what happened, but several days later learned this prisoner had died. Kobeniuk added, significantly for the prosecution, that they always kept a prison register, the arrest book, in which the prison officials jotted down the times at which prisoners were taken and returned and the names of their interrogators. Kobeniuk said that if a prisoner was too weak to sign the book himself, then the officer on duty, Marchenko, made a mark [*skvozniak*] that meant that "the arrested was presented in bad condition."[42] Nikolai Fedorovich Marchenko confirmed this testimony and said that he signed for Tarasov.[43] The arrest book would become an important piece of evidence for the tribunal because Drushliak claimed that another investigator took Tarasov out—something that Kobeniuk claimed simply could not happen.[44] Another guard later told the tribunal that if the time of Tarasov's release to his interrogator was missing, it was because there were so many people arrested and he could not manage to make all the necessary marks. He also stated that a prisoner could not have been called out to Drushliak and then left with another investigator, which Drushliak later claimed.[45]

Kobeniuk testified at the trial that Tarasov died on 26 June. When asked why Drushliak and Iaroliants refused to send Tarasov to the prison hospital, Kobeniuk baldly stated, "In my opinion, they simply did not want the hospital personnel to know about Tarasov's beating." He then suggested that Drushliak and Iaroliants had made Dr. Fraiman declare Tarasov healthy.[46]

Dr. E. E. Fraiman told Drushliak's investigator that Kobeniuk called him in to examine a prisoner—Tarasov—and that he saw that his condition was serious and that he needed to be hospitalized. The doctor asked Tarasov if his heart was healthy, to which Tarasov replied laconically, "It's nothing." He thought that Tarasov had erysipelas (an acute skin infection caused by bacterial infection) and applied an ointment to his rash. Dr. Fraiman, however, was already afraid of Drushliak.

In May 1938, the doctor had attended another of Drushliak's victims. This prisoner, Dobrovol'skii, was in grave condition and Fraiman sent him to the prison hospital. When Drushliak heard, he was enraged. He telephoned the prison and asked Fraiman, in a "state of excitement," what right he had to send his prisoner to the hospital. Fraiman told Drushliak that he had no choice given Dobrovol'skii's condition. Drushliak hung up, but then called several minutes later and asked again what had happened to Dobrovol'skii, to which the doctor again said he was seriously ill. A week later, Drushliak called yet again and repeated to the doctor that he had no right to send his prisoner to the hospital. Drushliak said threateningly that he never should have done that. Fraiman "was already quite upset" when the third call came in.[47] Vania's wrath evidently trumped the Hippocratic Oath.

The final essential testimony came directly from Drushliak's boss, Solomon Davidovich Kaluzhskii. His testimony would be important in establishing whether Drushliak worked on Tarasov alone or with Kaluzhskii. Kaluzhskii had claimed very limited involvement with Tarasov's case. He told the Military Tribunal that Drushliak wanted to use his office because, according to Kaluzhskii, Drushliak's own office was unsuitably situated for the application of what the boss kept calling "sanctions" (in other words, torture), something that curiously had not posed a problem for Drushliak in the past. Almost as soon as he arrived, according to Kaluzhskii, Drushliak began to box Tarasov's ears. Kaluzhskii said that he intervened and told Tarasov to sit down, but that Drushliak spat out, "That's not going to work." Then Drushliak began to apply the "sanction" to Tarasov, resulting in his false confession. Kaluzhskii claimed that the "sanctions were light" and that he had no part in them. He also said that he thought Tarasov was already an ill man— weak, sickly. Kaluzhskii added that he knew of no cases that Drushliak had falsified, "but in that time with Drushliak and with other investigators in connection with overwork, their work with evidence was poorly organized." Kaluzhskii was the sole witness of Drushliak's interrogation of Tarasov.[48]

Tarasov was not autopsied, but simply buried "in the manner" of those executed.[49]

HOW DID DRUSHLIAK defend himself? Unlike his victims, he appears not to have been subject to torture and had the liberty not only to write hundreds of pages of self-justification (in the forms of autobiography, confessions, petitions, and so on), but also to stand up in court, respond to the charges, call his own witnesses, and speak as he pleased. He repeated several times, "I do not admit my guilt since I committed no crime."[50] His defense centered on three basic points: the issue of sanctions or permission to apply "physical methods of influence" (which Drushliak would consistently call sanctions); the issue of whether he used force on Bandura or Tarasov; and the issue of whether he acted alone in these methods of interrogation.

Dolgushev, the head of the Kiev regional NKVD, made it very clear that, at least officially, sanctions from the head of the NKVD, his assistant, or the head of the department in charge of the specific operation were necessary for each and every use of physical measures. He, along with his assistant, Pavlychev, also made it fairly clear that these rules were not always carried out given the "circumstances" of those times. Furthermore, it is clear that actual lower-level directives on torture were most often oral or conveyed by example.[51]

Drushliak told the court, "I never beat anyone without the sanction of the head of the department."[52] He also told Gokhberg, who had negatively questioned his technique, "that a commission from Moscow, workers from the All-Union NKVD came and permitted the application of physical methods of influence."[53] Drushliak was correct in principle about the need to secure higher permission to use torture. Fedorov-Berkov, another of Drushliak's seniors, backed up Drushliak on the all-important issue of obtaining a sanction from the head of the regional administration of the NKVD, but, importantly, he added that, "I almost never was refused." Fedorov-Berkov, who claimed never to have seen any violations on Drushliak's part, also told investigators that, on this question—the use of torture— "the former boss of the regional NKVD Reikhman suggested to investigators to work strongly [*krepko*] with the arrested," which he took to mean to use force.[54] In fact, Drushliak himself claimed that the first beating he saw was at the hands of Reikhman.

Drushliak wrote in one of several confessions that Reikhman, in the presence of Simkhovich, had "accused [me] of liberalism with enemies." At a meeting in Simkhovich's office, he and Reikhman discussed "that the party had given a directive to force enemies with all means possible." Drushliak said that was when he began to use force. Furthermore, he wrote that all operative workers did this in their interrogations and wondered why others were not being prosecuted. Of course, he had been further encouraged by the praise the leaders had bestowed on him at meetings for his prowess in obtaining confessions. He told his investigator that "At the meetings which were then held in the department, they poured shame on the workers of the Fourth Department, Nikitina, Gokhberg, who did not use physical methods of influence, called them *intelligenty* [roughly, intellectuals], unable to work with the arrested, and they set me up as an example to others. And, I, fool, was proud of this."[55]

Drushliak did not deny that he used torture on prisoners. In his early depositions, he in fact seemed anxious to explain to the investigator the "concrete situation" in which sanctions were applied. He first mentioned the case of one prisoner named Miller, whom he had worked over in Kiev. Miller was apparently continuing to carry out "antisoviet work" in the prison, "persuading his cellmates to refuse to confess because Uspenskii had just been arrested and now the weather had changed." One of Drushliak's colleagues had talked with Miller, who boldly stated "that the time has come and passed" in regard to torture. Drushliak knew about this and, with colleagues Voloshin and, most of all, Pavlychev, beat Miller. Drushliak added that they also did this because Miller refused to sign his confession. Later Drushliak even heard that Miller had gone on a hunger strike.[56]

A second case, which Drushliak shared with his interrogator, concerned a prisoner named Vitkovskii. Vitkovskii was questioned, according to Drushliak, at a time when the procurator reviewed all files and spoke to the accused. Vitkovskii had "conducted himself well at the interrogation and did not refuse to sign the confession." Drushliak continued, "I asked the procurator whether he wanted to talk with him then." That evening Vitkovskii suddenly denied his confession and declared that he had told the procurator that he had been beaten and forced to sign. Several days later, Drushliak's colleague procured a sanction, and, at 2:00 a.m., Vitkovskii was called to interrogator Pavlychev's office. He, Drushliak, and another colleague beat him, but nothing changed. Vitkovskii continued to deny his guilt. In this case and in Miller's case, there is more than a suggestion on Drushliak's part that these prisoners' own supposedly hostile actions brought about their beatings.[57] The prisoners, of course, were reacting to the signals of the 17 November 1938 directive reining in the mass operations.[58]

The investigator also asked Drushliak to explain the barking and other animal noises his colleagues heard coming from his office. Simply, perhaps sardonically, Drushliak explained, "In regard to whether I ordered individual prisoners to bark, then I declare the following: in that time, when you walked along the corridor, especially at night, such noises were heard from all sides and from every office."[59] In other words, such were the times.

At the trial, Drushliak was asked to discuss the issue of the beating of for-mer NKVD officer Frenkel'. Drushliak claimed that Frenkel' had already been soundly [*krepko*] beaten by other interrogators by the time he reached him. "During all that time I only gave him two face slaps, and did not beat him brutally as he said."[60]

Drushliak did deny beating Stepan Bandura. He told his interrogator, "Bandura was this sick and old person who died in prison. I interrogated him without using physical measures of influence. He simulated insanity at the interrogation and tried to jump out the window several times. Since I could not work with him, Fedorov—the deputy head of the Fourth Department—told me to send him back to the prison and let him sit for awhile." A little later, Drushliak heard that Bandura had died.[61] The interrogator had uncov-ered a statement by Drushliak on the Bandura case from 18 February 1939 in which Drushliak wrote that he indeed had used force on Bandura on the directive of Simkhovich. Drushliak's response was that he had not been quite clear—the statement was not precise [*netochno*], and he continued to deny beating Bandura.[62] Drushliak never changed his line; at the trial, he contin-ued to deny using force on Bandura, sputtering at one point, "I didn't even touch him with my finger."[63]

Drushliak admitted to beating Tarasov. However, he claimed that his boss Kaluzhskii hit him first and that, moreover, they beat him "lightly." Iaroliants had issued a sanction to Kaluzhskii to permit the "light" beating.[64] Later, when Iaroliants told Drushliak that Tarasov was ill, he added, "You probably gave it to him hard [*krepko*]," to which Drushliak claimed to have responded, "not especially."[65] When news arrived that Tarasov had died, Drushliak claimed Kaluzhskii said, "You did nothing, don't worry."[66] Both Drushliak and Kaluzhskii claimed that Tarasov was already ill, that they could not have been responsible for his death given the light beating. Kaluzhskii, in fact, denied beating Tarasov at all.[67]

In the end, the issue of Drushliak's and/or Kaluzhskii's guilt boiled down to whether another interrogator, presumably Kaluzhskii according to Drushliak, had called out Tarasov for questioning on 17 June and whether Drushliak had forged Tarasov's signature on his confession. Drushliak cate-gorically denied the forgery.[68] In the end, the arrest book offered no definitive truth because the prison guards were so busy at the time, with so many arrests, according to prison guard Vovk, that they could not manage to fill out every-thing. The guards did, however, agree that it would have been unprecedented if another investigator—that is, Kaluzhskii—had taken out Drushliak's prisoner for questioning.[69] All the same, the tribunal ordered an investigation into Kaluzhskii's activities.[70]

All the technicalities did not really matter. In the final analysis, Drushliak was indeed guilty, although he certainly was not alone in the torture of innocent prisoners. Drushliak had gone from model worker to a convicted criminal, sentenced to death. Reading his testimony, one cannot help but notice Drushliak's declining confidence in his answers to the investigator as well as his surprise at the accusation of wrongdoing. According to his investigator, when Drushliak was first called into NKVD headquarters on 8 February 1939, he "refused to give answers put to him, declaring, 'you arrest me, then interrogate me, I will not sign the interrogation records.' "[71] Of course, like all NKVD interrogators, Drushliak had signed a state secrecy act, pledging to maintain complete secrecy about his work, but still there is more than a hint of the model worker's bravado here. The times had changed ahead of Drushliak.

Drushliak did try to justify his actions before his interrogator and at his trial. He still believed—or said he believed—that he was dealing with dangerous enemies in his NKVD office. When asked if he still believed in the guilt of two of his other victims, Drushliak responded, "I believed and believe." When read the testimony of one of these victims about Drushliak beating him "like an animal," Drushliak responded, "This is the slander of the enemy who tried to use the situation to his favor and attain release. I repeat, that I applied no sort of physical methods of influence on Babchenko."[72] In regard to Dobrovol'skii, the prisoner about whom he had a telephone confrontation with the doctor, Drushliak said, "That Dobrovol'skii is an enemy. I do not doubt."[73] As for Tarasov, Drushliak told the court, "I related to Tarasov as to an enemy, like they taught me."[74]

Drushliak was in all probability a true believer. He believed he had worked "honestly and faithfully."[75] As he told the tribunal, "They taught us that it is necessary to relate brutally to the enemy, that it is necessary to force them to surrender to the party and Soviet power."[76] Not only had "they taught us to relate brutally to the enemy, they gave a directive to use on them physical means of interrogation and force them to surrender to Soviet power."[77] Furthermore, Drushliak noted that they worked in a "complex situation" and that he was young and inexperienced when he began work as an investigator. Although he never admitted his guilt, he acknowledged, however begrudgingly, "In this difficult situation, because of my inexperience, I made mistakes."[78]

DRUSHLIAK'S CRIMINAL FILE is full of lies, but, in essence, it is truthful. Setting aside questions of collegial envy, scapegoating, partial truths about applying "sanctions" by other investigators, and possible information sharing ahead of questioning, the file tells the story of how Drushliak conducted himself during the Great Terror, first in Khar'kov and then in Kiev. Although Drushliak seems not to have changed much as his status shifted radically from model worker to state criminal, the times had changed, at least temporarily as Stalin reined in the terror. Drushliak got caught.

Drushliak was too young to have served either in the civil war or collectivization, but he was the product of a Soviet education and had been a Komsomol activist. He was a true believer. He hated the enemy viscerally. He was proud of the praise he received and, according to Kaluzhskii, "suffered the illness of loving to be first."[79] The evidence in this case does not suggest that fear of reprisal motivated him. Rather, he liked what he did. He was original, or creatively sadistic, in his method of interrogations, demonstrating a large degree of agency within the confines of the NKVD's culture of lawlessness.

FOLLOWING AN APPEAL to the Military College of the Supreme Court of the Soviet Union on 11 April 1940, Drushliak's sentence was overturned. The Court decided that, although Drushliak was indeed guilty, his sentence of capital punishment was "not essential" and would be replaced by ten years in a corrective labor camp (without the loss of rights). His later records indicate that he was released during the war to fight on the front and became a war invalid. He was never rehabilitated or granted his pension from the NKVD.[80]

4

Under the Dictation of Fleishman

In general, they sent from Kiev a standard model form, according to which to write indictments. In this form, they indicated the aims and tasks of the counterrevolutionary organization.
—I. I. BABICH, *head of the interdistrict NKVD operational group in Belaia Tserkov'* in 1938

All protocols of interrogations were one and the same tract.... In general, as a rule in all cases, I wrote in the interrogation protocols about the defeatism and antisoviet activities of the arrested.
—M. M. KRIVTSOV, *policeman and NKVD interrogator in Skvira and Belaia Tserkov'*

THE MILITARY TRIBUNAL convened from 3 to 8 August 1940 at the NKVD club in the small city of Skvira, some 120 kilometers from Kiev.[1] Oskar Savel'evich Fleishman and Mikhail Mikhailovich Krivtsov were the defendants, each charged with Article 206-17 of the Ukrainian criminal code, Fleishman with the more serious point "B" and Krivtsov with point "A."[2] Fleishman was the former head of the Skvirskii District NKVD office.[3] Krivtsov worked in the regular police, but had been mobilized to serve as an NKVD investigator–interrogator during the mass operations, a common phenomenon at this time.[4] Both were part of a larger interdistrict NKVD operational group, whose headquarters were located in the town of Belaia Tserkov', roughly halfway between Skvira and Kiev.[5]

The charges against the two were the familiar violations of socialist legality.[6] Both men were charged with the falsification of investigative files and the use of physical methods of influence against arrested suspects. Fleishman was additionally charged with forcing the members of the district's village *aktiv* (e.g., collective farm chairmen, rural soviet secretaries, and village Communists) to provide witness testimony and false information describing the social and political profile of suspects under arrest. In other cases, the charges continued, he simply demanded blank signed and stamped official forms that he personally filled in.[7] The chief and most damning result of these activities was the artificial creation of a counterrevolutionary group of thirty-nine people, five of whom had been put to death by the time the trial began.[8]

Although somewhat less detailed than the cases against Dolgushev and Drushliak, the provenance of this case at the district level makes it particularly interesting. The case demonstrates the trajectory of the contrived master plot of the Great Terror, at the same time illuminating the terror at the lowest level of society, within the much-beleaguered collective farms. Less burdened with contrivances than the other cases, the defense rested on varying combinations of belief, ignorance, and orders from above.

THE CASE OF the "39" was the centerpiece in the accusations against Fleishman and Krivtsov. The two were charged with the arrests of a "series of honest communists and collective farmers" in the summer of 1938.[9] The case originally went directly to the troika for sentencing. The troika sentenced five of the 39 to death, but sent the rest back to the Skvirskii District NKVD. Fleishman then "unsewed" the case—literally (the pages were sewn together into a file) and figuratively—and created a series of new cases based on smaller groups from the original 39 and organized according to the villages where group members lived.[10]

Fleishman and Krivtsov's criminal file contains many of the documents pertaining to the case of the 39, thus permitting a backward glance at the original case. The 39 were caught up in mass operation 00447. The accused, all men, included nine agricultural specialists; seven people from strong *kulak* farms and/or dekulakized families; and ten men with previous criminal convictions, ranging from anticollective farm activities during collectivization to famine-related theft or "sabotage" during the famine. Some fell into multiple categories, and almost all were tainted by accusations of Ukrainian bourgeois nationalism and/or ties to petliurists (members of the anti-Bolshevik army led by Ukrainian nationalist Petliura during the civil war).[11] Fleishman also arrested a group of Skvirskii District schoolteachers who fell outside of the group of 39.[12] The dragnet basically pulled in a combination of technical elites and collective farmers with a suspect past. Fleishman placed the already-arrested Skvirskii District party committee secretary, Fedor Grigor'evich Kokhanenko, at the head of the group of 39 and then linked the group to a larger Ukrainian nationalist operation supposedly led by Vasilenko, already under arrest and said to be the former head of the Kiev regional soviet executive committee.[13]

Thirty-seven of the 39 confessed to the charges leveled against them.[14] Their confessions were extracted forcibly, either through beatings or prolonged periods of standing. The original charge against the group was both exceedingly general yet somehow all-inclusive, and it reflected a Ukrainian version of the master plot of the Great Terror:

> On the assignment of the Ukrainian counterrevolutionary bourgeois nationalist center and through it the participation of the former chair of the Kiev regional [soviet] executive committee, Vasilenko (arrested), was set up a Ukrainian counterrevolutionary nationalist insurrectionary organization led by the former secretary of the Skvirskii District party committee, Kokhanenko (arrested), and subsequently by the boss of the district land department, Zalevskii (arrested), with the aim of overthrowing the socialist system and government of the USSR and resurrecting capitalism and breaking off Ukraine from the USSR and establishing a fascist dictatorship. The organization united antisoviet petliurists and repressed kulak elements with tasks to prepare insurrectionary–diversionary cadres in the event of war against the USSR to raise an uprising in the rear; to carry out harmful activities in agriculture; to create material difficulties in order to stimulate unrest among the masses; to be prepared to destroy food warehouses in the event of war; to draw in new members from kulaks, petliurists, antisoviet elements; to carry out antisoviet propaganda among the population in the aim of discrediting the collective farms and breaking Ukraine from the USSR and orienting Ukraine to the fascist countries of Poland and Germany.[15]

This relentlessly and sullenly repetitive diatribe represented the worst Fifth Column nightmares of the Communist regime, reflecting fears based on the realities of popular protest during the civil war and collectivization, especially in Ukraine, and the tense international situation of the times, but in no way reflected current realities.

The troika and the NKVD special plenipotentiary who later reviewed the case were dismayed by what they considered to be the overly general nature of these charges and the lack of clear evidence.[16] The case against the medical worker Fedor Mikhailovich Iashchenko was the only one with concrete charges. He was accused of making incorrect diagnoses of illnesses and ignoring the unsanitary conditions of the village, thus creating "possibilities" for contagion among children.[17] Anything could be politicized within the context of the Great Terror, including what perhaps were the negligent actions or unpopular personality of the village medic. The remaining cases, however, were completely fanciful, requiring forced confessions and willing or coerced witness testimony. Fleishman would have had to have been far more resourceful, not to mention creative, to present a more specific case within the overall fiction of the Great Terror and the targeting of specific political, economic, and social categories of the population in the mass operation.

Fleishman did try. To bolster the case against the former members of the 39, he sought witness testimony to solidify the confessions.[18] He needed damning information not only about his prisoners' current, vague activities, but, more important, about their social, economic, and political pasts, which virtually determined hostile activities in the Communist worldview. According to the NKVD special plenipotentiary, Fleishman "planted" the fiction of the story of the 39 in his witnesses' testimony. He provided his investigators, mainly simple policemen, with a text and a standard set of questions and answers. He also instructed his investigators to compile witness testimony in such a way that it was to contain not concrete facts but general phrases designed around the master plot. This would also allow Fleishman to make "corrections" in the witnesses' testimony. In most cases, witnesses did not read their testimony, but signed blank papers in advance. Fleishman made use of a set of regular, official witnesses within each village. He and Krivtsov told them they would not be required to appear in court (a common promise made to witnesses at the time) and therefore need not worry about "incorrect testimony" or confronting the accused. Fleishman instructed his investigators to label all witnesses as rank-and-file collective farmers and nonparty.[19]

Fleishman then sent the cases on to the NKVD *Osoboe soveshchanie* (the NKVD's highest sentencing board), where the accused were sentenced to varying lengths of time in the labor camps. Before long, however, many of the accused as well as the witnesses began to retract their confessions and testimony.[20] This was a fairly widespread phenomenon following the November 1938 scaling back of the terror. By November 1939, the NKVD issued a directive to halt the cases against the former members of the 39, particularly singling out district party secretary Kokhanenko, who retracted his confession and told of the "incorrect methods" used during his interrogations. Kokhanenko also reported that he and Fleishman had poor mutual relations and that Fleishman had told an NKVD colleague that he would "ruin" him.[21] On 16 January 1940, the NKVD called for the reexamination of all of Fleishman's cases.[22] Within months, most of the original 39, minus those no longer alive, were freed, and Fleishman and Krivtsov were behind bars.

THE TRIAL TOOK place at the height of a scorching Ukrainian summer in early August 1940. By this time, Fleishman had sat in prison for six to seven months and Krivtsov for four.[23] At the outset of the trial, Fleishman denied all guilt, retracting a partial admission of guilt from his March interrogations, likely made under torture. Krivtsov pleaded guilty.[24]

Fleishman was the first to speak before the tribunal. He was an old NKVD operative, having served in the organs for eighteen years, rising to the level of lieutenant. Born in 1899 in Kielce, a Polish town within the Russian Empire, his family moved to Mogilev-Podol'skii when he was an infant. He came from a working-class family. He had a primary education and was a typesetter by profession. He fought with the Red Army during the Russian civil war and entered the Cheka in 1921. He joined the party in 1931, received a reprimand in 1934 (which was lifted in 1935), and was married with two children.[25] At the beginning of his trial, Fleishman declared that "nothing I did was for mercenary ends. In eighteen years of work in the organs of the NKVD, I never violated revolutionary legality and always honorably carried out my assigned duties."[26]

From Fleishman's testimony and others, it appears that 1937 was a relatively calm year for the NKVD in Skvirskii District. Repression heated up only in 1938, stimulated by deliberate turnover among the leaders of the interdistrict operational group in Belaia Tserkov' and the visits of a series of high-level regional officials. I. M. Pivchikov was the head of the group until sometime in the summer of 1938, when Ivan Ignat'evich Babich arrived. Ivan Babich then served as leader of the group for about one month, during which time the terror steeply escalated. He was followed by Mikhail Mikhailovich Tsirul'nitskii, who ran the group in August, September, and December of 1938.[27]

In his interrogations and in a handwritten confession, Fleishman documented the escalation of the terror and the role he claimed was played by higher-level officials in the summer of 1938. Still under Pivchikov, Fleishman arrested one Nastevich. In his confession, Nastevich literally implicated the entire district's rural officialdom—every collective farm chair, every rural soviet secretary, and many communist and district officials. Fleishman said he told Pivchikov that, according to Nastevich's confessions, he would have to arrest every official in the district. Fleishman also said that he told Pivchikov that they had no compromising evidence on the majority of these people. Pivchikov then told Fleishman to wait for the arrival of Dolgushev, the head of the Kiev regional NKVD, who was scheduled to arrive that evening.[28]

As soon as he arrived, Dolgushev called an operational meeting at which Pivchikov reported that the Belaia Tserkov' interdistrict operational group had uncovered a branch of a Ukrainian insurrectionary organization in Skvirskii District. According to Ivan Babich, Dolgushev called for their "immediate arrest."[29] He mocked Fleishman, telling him, "You will work, Fleishman, or do you think that the operational group will work for you?" Fleishman later claimed that "Dolgushev harshly cursed me and said if there is not a radical change in work then he would be forced to raise the issue of my loyalty to the party."[30] Then Pivchikov intervened, telling Dolgushev that Fleishman said that they would have to arrest the entire district and village aktiv if they followed Nastevich's lead. At that point, Dolgushev changed his tune, hesitating somewhat, and asked Fleishman whether they had compromising evidence for all of the newly accused. Fleishman said they had no compromising material on the majority of suspects.[31] Dolgushev gave Fleishman forty-eight hours to collect the requisite evidence for the cases to proceed. Fleishman then mobilized all of his cadres, sending them out to gather incriminating evidence. Initially, they arrested only seven people, but from these seven, they received additional names, leading to the arrest of the 39. Fleishman claimed that it was Ivan Babich who had the idea to link the 39 to the already-arrested Vasilenko, the former head of the regional Soviet government committee [*ispolkom*] and to make him the group's "leader."[32] The arrest list for the troika would be signed by both Fleishman and Ivan Babich.[33]

Fleishman also claimed that the orders to press for confessions came from above. Sometime after Dolgushev's visit, the head of the Fourth Department of the Kiev regional NKVD arrived with an order to make use of the infamous *stoiki*—the process by which prisoners were forced to stand uninterruptedly, sometimes for days at a time, until they "confessed." The order for forced standing, according to Fleishman, came from Dolgushev.[34] At his trial, Fleishman would claim that Ivan Babich gave the order to use physical force on individual suspects.[35] Fleishman admitted only to striking someone for what he described as "slander" and another person apparently because he was a priest.[36]

Fleishman told the tribunal at his trial that he had closely "studied" the district from early 1937 when he became the head of its NKVD branch. He said that he knew that there were many petliurists and remnants of other "bands" in villages. Following the operational meeting with Dolgushev, Fleishman sent out his investigators, mainly local policemen seconded to the NKVD, to collect witness testimony and the political and social profiles—especially from the past (meaning prerevolutionary times and the civil war)—of the villagers under arrest. He admitted to the tribunal that he told his investigators to write that witnesses were rank-and-file collective farmers and not to indicate that they were in fact party members or other village and collective farm officials; otherwise, however, he claimed that he asked them to obtain "truthful testimonies." He denied that he had used official witnesses—that is, the same select group of witnesses, to testify multiple times. And he claimed that he had no idea that his investigators falsified witness testimony.[37] As far as the actual interrogations of suspects were concerned, Fleishman said that there was "a standard protocol, according to which the interrogator questioned his suspect. I personally gave the interrogators this form of protocol."[38] When he was questioned in March 1940, he also admitted to giving orders to his investigators to include the following in each of their interrogation protocols of the arrested: antisoviet agitation, defeatist agitation, and terrorist manifestations. He then said, "I gave these instructions on the basis of orders from the region."[39] In fact, throughout his trial, he used the excuse that he was following the orders of the various heads of the interdistrict operational group who, he claimed, were really in charge of investigations.[40]

Krivtsov was up next before the tribunal. Like many of his fellow policemen, he was a local. He had been born into a Ukrainian family in a village in the district in 1905. Too young to fight in the civil war, he joined the Red Army in 1923. After he left the army in 1933, he returned to Skvirskii District, working first in a *Politotdel* (Political Department, most probably, in the Skvirskii Machine-Tractor Station [MTS]), and then in a series of other positions before becoming a policeman in April 1937. In September of the same year, he was seconded to work under Fleishman in the district branch of the NKVD. He worked both in Skvira and Belaia Tserkov' until the fall of 1938. He became a member of the Communist Party only in 1938. By October of that year, he had been fired from the regular police on corruption charges. Krivtsov was married with three children.[41]

Krivtsov began his testimony by denying any guilt. He told the tribunal that, prior to his mobilization into the NKVD, he had no experience in investigative work. He said, "In general, I did everything on Fleishman's orders," and he had no idea that he was violating revolutionary legality. His ignorance could only have been based on sheer stupidity or a justified sense that everything was permitted in the brutal culture of those times. He went on to say that Fleishman taught him, along with three other policemen (Romanov, Beregovoi, and Antonets), how to conduct interrogations at one of their operational meetings. Fleishman told them what to write. According to Kritsman, "all interrogation protocols were one and the same tract. . . . In general, as a rule, in all cases, I wrote in the interrogation protocol about the defeatism and antisoviet activities of the arrested."[42]

Krivtsov denied using physical force during interrogations despite accusations from his colleagues. He did freely admit to making suspects stand for prolonged periods of time, but justified this by saying that everyone in the operational team did the same. Moreover, he was under orders from Fleishman to complete his cases "in not more than 40 to 50 minutes." As a seeming corroboration of Fleishman's testimony, he said the arrest of the 39 occurred only after criticism at an operational meeting, "that in Skvira there is nothing," meaning there had been insufficient arrests up to that time. The arrests began directly after this meeting, he said, on the order of Pivchikov, the head of the Belaia Tserkov' interdistrict operative group before Ivan Babich.[43]

Earlier, at his own interrogation, Krivtsov had presented somewhat more detail on some of the practices used in Skvira and Belaia Tserkov'. In particular, he explained to his interrogator how they gathered witness testimony. In the first instance, he claimed "not to remember" falsifying witness testimony; yet all his testimony pointed precisely to falsification. He said that Fleishman ordered them to write the protocols of the witness testimony "in general terms [*ne konkretno*]" and, most of all, to write about antisoviet agitation, agitation against the Supreme Soviet elections, and rumors about the coming war with Germany. This material, according to Krivtsov, had to figure in all witness statements. Further, Fleishman instructed his investigators "that it was necessary preliminarily to select and converse with [members of] the village aktiv and only afterward to question them formally. In cases when a witness did not want to give testimony, they were to find someone else." Fleishman checked each witness statement, making the necessary "corrections."[44]

Krivtsov then moved on to the actual arrests. These were made at night.[45] Fleishman "gave an order to write general, nonspecific [*ne konkretnye*] protocols" when writing up cases for arrest.[46] He would later "correct" them. On one occasion, he cursed Krivtsov "with vulgar words" when the "facts" of a case did not correspond with the suspect's age. Fleishman yelled at Krivtsov: "What? Don't you have a brain?" and then "corrected" the suspect's date of birth.[47] Krivtsov also said that Fleishman had beaten a priest with a ramrod and another victim with his fists.[48] Krivtsov said that everyone was afraid of Fleishman; at the same time, he said that he did not understand that "such methods were incorrect." He explained, "I thought as a member of the party and the organs, Fleishman could not be incorrect." Fleishman had also told him that their directions came from the center and the region. Finally, Krivtsov told his interrogator that he and the other policemen were strictly warned never to talk about these methods of investigation and had to sign a secrecy agreement, a standard practice in the NKVD.[49]

To this point, Fleishman and Krivtsov denied any or almost any personal wrongdoing, attributing their actions to orders from above. Krivtsov had the additional excuse that he lacked experience, not to mention intelligence. At the end of his interrogation, he did volunteer additional testimony, in which he suddenly admitted that he had had doubts about the guilt of a number of the 39 as well as doubts about the methods of interrogation.[50] However, it would be up to their co-workers and superiors, along with a handful of witnesses and a few victims, to complete the story of what happened in Skvirskii District in 1938.

FLEISHMAN AND KRIVTSOV worked closely with three other former policemen from Skvira: Nikolai Alekseevich Romanov, Ivan Mikhailovich Beregovoi, and Avtonom Sidorovich Antonets, the last of whom was originally supposed to stand trial with Fleishman and Krivtsov.[51] Each of them had been mobilized from the regular police to work in mass operations in 1938. None had more than a primary education, if that. Like Krivtsov, they had no prior experience working in interrogations and received no prior training. Antonets told the tribunal that he was sent to Belaia Tserkov' to lead the interrogation of those arrested in Skvirskii District on his second day of work.[52]

They were all afraid of Fleishman. Romanov said, "Fleishman related very crudely to the workers, cursing us with vulgar swear words and threatening arrest and court if we did not fulfill his orders."[53] "Fleishman yelled at everyone," Romanov told the tribunal, "saying, 'what, you are sitting surrounded by bands, counterrevolutionaries, and you do nothing.'"[54]

They all testified to Fleishman's use of physical force in his dealings with the prisoners. Romanov said, "Going by Fleishman's office door, I often heard moans and blows. Besides this, I personally saw how Fleishman beat with a ramrod the arrested Gavva Spiridon while he was lying on the ground. . . . In my presence, he also beat the arrested Korinnyi."[55] Beregovoi admitted that "the beating of prisoners who refused to confess was widely practiced among us in the district branch of the NKVD." He witnessed Fleishman beating confessions out of prisoners and noted one prisoner who was forced to stand continuously for eight days.[56] He told the tribunal that Krivtsov also beat a prisoner.[57] Beregovoi added that Fleishman had arrested a collective farmer–poor peasant with whom Beregovoi had served in the Red Army. Beregovoi said that he knew this man was not a counterrevolutionary and knew at least five others who were also innocent.[58]

Antonets, who said nothing about whether Krivtsov beat anyone, claimed to know of only two cases of prisoners being beaten. He saw Fleishman beat one prisoner "with his fists." And he saw one Grigorevich, presumably a fellow interrogator, beat someone. When Antonets asked Grigorevich about his actions, Grigorevich responded, "There is nothing terrible about this," neatly highlighting the tenor of the times.[59] Another policeman, Fedor Leont'evich Adamchuk, who stood watch over prisoners subject to prolonged standing, remembered Fleishman beating a priest and forcing him to join in.[60]

The collective farmer, Petr Pavlovich Gutsalo, also testified about the violence in Skvira and Belaia Tserkov'. He was arrested in June 1938. Fleishman and Romanov interrogated him, accusing him of belonging to a counterrevolutionary organization. Gutsalo stood his ground, refusing to confess or sign the interrogation protocols. Fleishman then kicked him in the stomach. After that, Fleishman handed him over to a group of six policemen "and ordered them to do with me what they wanted." The six men beat him with the "butt of a rifle, a revolver, and with their hands," then forced him to stand for three days, after which he finally capitulated and signed. Gutsalo said the other people in his cell had also been beaten. He later retracted his confession. He told the tribunal that he had been in his collective farm since its founding in 1929, had received awards for good work, and only fought with Petliura's forces for five days under duress.[61]

Kalistrat Viktorovich Korinnyi was a collective farmer who had been caught up in the group of 39. He told of how Fleishman beat him with the leg of a chair and forced him to stand uninterruptedly when he refused to slander himself. In the end, this simple collective farmer, who had never before been arrested and who fought in the civil war, was forced to incriminate ten innocent people. He said that Fleishman and Krivtsov had also beaten his cellmates. The regional court freed Korinnyi from prison in March 1939.[62]

Fedor Grigor'evich Kokhanenko, the district party secretary in Skvira, testified that Fleishman held a grudge toward him because he had refused Fleishman 2,000 rubles to repair his apartment. Soon after this refusal, at a party meeting, Fleishman accused Kokhanenko of traveling drunk to the villages, corruption, and connections with alien elements. Kokhanenko was arrested in Kiev on 5 June 1937 and subsequently turned into the leader of the 39. He told the tribunal, "I consider that testimony about me given by the arrested was obtained under force" and that the real reason for his arrest was his "bad relations with Fleishman." Fleishman confirmed that he had asked Kokhanenko for money to repair his apartment, but said that when he first came to the district he heard that Kokhanenko was "closely tied to kulak elements." He continued, "I wrote several reports for the the regional NKVD administration [in Kiev] about the leading composition of the district and their links with unreliable elements, in particular I wrote this about Kokhanenko." Kokhanenko then told the court that he received a reprimand for his rude relations with several people and connections with alien elements, but that the reprimand was lifted under appeal. When he received the reprimand, he realized "that Fleishman played in this a role of the first order."[63]

Beregovoi, Antonets, and Romanov testified to the use of standard forms for prisoner interrogations and witness statements, as well as to standard content. Romanov said he regularly rewrote interrogation protocols under Fleishman's dictation.[64] He also said that Fleishman ordered all interrogators to write in their protocols that the prisoner carried out antisoviet agitation and—this was "mandatory"—discussed the defeat of the USSR in war.[65] Romanov continued that if they did not write what Fleishman dictated, Fleishman "screamed at us, saying we were playing into the hands of the enemy."[66] Beregovoi said that Fleishman threatened to arrest him if he did not provide the correct protocols.[67] Antonets added that as far as he knew nothing about conducting an interrogation, he was given a model of a protocol of interrogation and told to question his prisoners according to the standard form.[68]

Ivan Babich, the head of the interdistrict operational group here in the summer of 1938, corroborated the use of a standard pattern, not for the interrogation protocols but for the indictment of the case [obvinitel'noe zakliuchenie], compiled after interrogations and used to present the case and charges before the troika. During the trial, Ivan Babich told the tribunal, "In general, they sent from Kiev a standard model form, according to which to write indictments. In this form, they indicated the aims and tasks of the counter-revolutionary organization and in general if I corrected the introduction to the case summary on the group case [of the 39], I took data from the material of the case."[69] Mikhail Mikhailovich Tsirul'nitskii, who took over as the head of the operational group from Ivan Babich, told the tribunal that he had initially expressed surprise at how quickly Krivtsov interrogated his prisoners. Krivtsov responded that "he only rewrote or wrote under dictation. And some interrogation protocols were simply signed [forged] by Fleishman."[70]

Fleishman was surely dictating charges in Skvira and Belaia Tserkov', but the master plot was from Kiev and Moscow. The fiction of the Great Terror was grafted onto the victims of the mass operations, in the best of cases people with some kind of suspect past, in the worst of cases completely innocent individuals. And everyone was forced to play along—the policemen who had known some of the "enemies" from their youth, as well as the village and collective farm officials and activists who were forced or otherwise influenced to tell lies about their neighbors in their capacity as "witnesses."

WITNESSES PROVIDED TWO types of evidence for the NKVD investigations in Skvira and Belaia Tserkov'. This evidence laid the groundwork for the arrests and interrogations of the 39, although it generally followed rather than preceded the arrests. The first type of document was the *kharakteristika*, a document that provided a political and social profile of the suspects, including information about their activities during the civil war and before the revolution. The second was a *spravka*, which included the witnesses' descriptions of a suspect's antisoviet activities, past and present. In practice, these two types of documents were interchangeable. In almost all cases, the past prevailed over the present in determining a suspect's guilt. It was a matter of not what he did but who he was. The genealogists of the NKVD were particularly interested in a suspect's prerevolutionary past and his political affiliations in the civil war.[71]

Policeman Beregovoi explained: "As a rule, the district branch of the NKVD required from the rural soviet a form about the social past of each of the arrested."[72] As for testimony, he continued, "As a rule, we had permanent official witnesses who testified in multiple cases. Such witnesses gave whatever testimony the interrogator wanted. Generally, in each village, there was a group of witnesses who testified in all cases of [people] arrested from the given village."[73] Beregovoi's colleagues, Romanov and Antonets, corroborated his testimony on the use of official witnesses.[74]

In many cases, perhaps most cases, all the interrogator needed to do was to call in the rural soviet secretary and order him to bring with him official stationery along with the official stamp and press. Beregovoi admitted to this practice, as did the fire warden and former policeman Adamchuk.[75] Romanov told the tribunal that once Fleishman told him, "your protocol [of witness testimony] is worthless, you need another one." Fleishman sent him back to the village two to three times to obtain the "correct" results. Finally, rural soviet secretary Nikolaichuk told Romanov, "I have no time. How about if I just give you a signed blank form and then you can write what you need?"[76] To disguise the fact that he forced village and collective farm officials to serve as witnesses, Fleishman ordered his investigators to describe the witnesses as rank-and-file collective farmers.[77]

The official witnesses followed the script of the Great Terror under the dictation of one or another NKVD investigator. Witnesses testified to antisoviet agitation, conversations about the defeat of the USSR in war, the coming of the fascist order, and so on.[78] Investigator Antonets went so far as to say that they sent witnesses to Belaia Tserkov' to give testimony according to the "standard form," including information on antisoviet conversations, terrorist moods, and the like.[79]

The witnesses themselves also had an opportunity to testify at Fleishman's and Krivtsov's pretrial investigation and, in some cases, even at the trial. Nikolai Luk'ianovich Nikolaichuk, who had given Romanov a signed blank form, was the secretary of a rural soviet and, at the time of his testimony, the head of the Skvirskii MTS. He testified: "I remember that Fleishman called me into the distict-level NKVD two times with my stamp and press in order to provide a certificate for people arrested in [the village of] B. Erchika. Fleishman demanded that I write under his dictation a certificate about the antisoviet activities of these people. However, I refused to do this and wrote about [their] positive activities. Then Fleishman threatened me, declaring that I was defending the enemy. However, I paid no attention to these threats."[80] Although it is unlikely that Nikolaichuk both freely offered Romanov blank forms and stood up to Fleishman, the basic thread of the story is clear.

Another rural soviet secretary, Antonina Nikiforovna Matusevich, a people's judge at the time of her testimony, was also called into the Skvirskii NKVD office in 1938. She told the tribunal, "They called me into the district office of the NKVD and told me to provide a certificate on Tishchenko, where it could be indicated that Tishchenko was an antisoviet individual. I then said that I knew Tishchenko only from the positive side and knew nothing bad about him. After this, they suggested that I give them blank forms with the stamp and press, but I didn't do this. I went home and told my husband that they had demanded blank forms . . . my husband answered to me, 'give them anything they want, if you don't, they'll arrest you.'" So Matusevich returned to the NKVD, where she ran into Beregovoi. She asked him, "can one issue a certificate on Tishchenko if it is not true?" Beregovoi told her to go home, that they no longer needed her. Matusevich added to her testimony: "I knew the Tishchenko family well. They all worked well in the collective farm. Now, Tishchenko leaves behind a family of 8." Tishchenko had been executed.[81]

Andrei Feofanovich Antonik and Domna Mikhailovna Orlova provided witness testimony about Dmitri Ivanovich Ianchuk. Antonik chaired a collective farm. He said he knew nothing about Ianchuk's antisoviet agitation, but that the interrogator Antonets "persuaded me and urged me to sign and I signed." He added that he only knew that when Ianchuk returned from exile in 1934, having most probably been exiled as a kulak in 1930 or 1931, "he worked well in the collective farm, he was the best collective farmer."[82]

Orlova, who was apparently an actual rank-and-file collective farmer, testified that she "had quarreled with Ianchuk's wife and that Ianchuk's children did all sorts of harm in the collective farm," but she said nothing about Ianchuk's antisoviet activities because she knew nothing about this. "I knew Ianchuk worked well in the collective farm." She added, "The investigator did not read me the protocol and I could not sign my testimony since I am completely illiterate and don't know how to write."[83]

Another witness, Andrei Andreevich Dieskul', told the tribunal that Krivtsov did not read the protocol questions to him, but that he signed three blank forms.[84] The witness M. K. Klimas, a rural soviet secretary, admitted that "part of his testimony did not correspond to reality," whereas other witnesses denied their testimony or claimed never to have said what was contained in their interrogation protocols.[85]

The entire district bore witness against Fleishman. His nonlocal status, perhaps his Jewish background, may have contributed to his lack of popularity. At the same time, the entire district was implicated in the Great Terror, whether by force or not.[86] Within the villages of the Soviet Union, the terror was, by necessity, far more public. It was simply not possible to make arrests without the village's knowledge. Furthermore, the machinery of the mass operations required widespread participation beyond the closed corridors of the NKVD. In part, such participation was based on a feeble and perverse show of revolutionary legality that sought to highlight its "evidence" beyond the all-important confession and assumed the aspect of a legal, or, more accurately, administrative fetishism carried to the extreme. In part, the NKVD needed local witnesses who knew the social and political profile of the village for, after all, there were a handful of witnesses—mainly those called by Fleishman—who stuck with their stories about petliurists and former kulaks in the village.[87] Above all, the witnesses—whether coerced or not—played a key role in the elaboration of the fiction of the Great Terror's master plot.

ON THE FACE of it, all roads in this trial lead back to Fleishman and, to a much lesser degree, to Krivtsov. Yet Fleishman also claimed that he was only following orders—the orders of the successive heads of the interdistrict NKVD group, Pivchikov, Ivan Babich, and Tsirul'nitskii, and the head of the Kiev regional NKVD, Dolgushev.

Fleishman told the tribunal that all arrests occurred only on the orders of the regional NKVD.[88] He said that the group of 39 was sent to the troika not by him but by Ivan Babich, something which Babich immediately denied.[89] When the troika returned the case to him, Fleishman claimed that Dolgushev ordered him to "unsew it" (take apart the file) and form new cases based on eight to ten people each, and to direct these cases to the Osoboe Soveshchanie. When Fleishman asked Dolgushev if he should free several of the group's members, Dolgushev said, "do not free even one person."[90] Fleishman also claimed that Ivan Babich had indicated to him that it was permitted to use physical force in interrogations and that the permission to use forced standing came down from the regional NKVD in Kiev.[91]

Fleishman insisted that he had warned his underlings to carefully check the evidence provided by witnesses.[92] He called his own witness—fire inspector Illiarion Iosifovich Levakovskii, who worked in the NKVD in 1938—to back him up on this point.[93] Fleishman admitted to falsifying only one case, the case of an individual named Dement'ev. He said that he did this out of fear that "they" would tie him to Dement'ev, for reasons left unclear, and arrested Dement'ev to "convince" the regional NKVD. He knew the information gathered on Dement'ev was not true.[94]

Still, he held firm in his protestations of innocence. He declared, "I do not admit guilt in the creation of a counterrevolutionary nationalist insurrectionary organization, since all of the arrested confessed"—a rather circular argument. He did admit that he had used "illegal methods in conducting interrogations" and had instructed his subordinates to make use of forced standing. He also admitted to telling his underlings the fictive content of the case, although he added that the interrogators soon learned how to write their protocols on their own. However, he said, "In general, I received orders from the [regional] NKVD to implement everything that occurred in the district-level NKVD."[95]

Fleishman's final statement to the tribunal began on the usual revolutionary autobiographical note, proceeded to his defense, and ended with an appeal for mercy. He said:

> I want first of all to talk about myself. I came from a working-class family. I grew up in poverty and hunger. Already in 1914 I went to work for hire since my father was away in the army.
>
> In 1917, I was among the first to enter the ranks of the Red Guard, and then the Red Army and on 4 January 1921 I was sent to work in the *Osobyi otdel* [Special Department of the internal security police]. Thus I worked uninterruptedly in the organs of the NKVD until 1939. In this time, I had not one reprimand, always honestly relating to my work.
>
> After I was fired from the NKVD organs, I was directed by the party committee to responsible work as the director of the state *Dietfabrika*

in Odessa, where I also worked honestly, and for good results in work, I, together with the factory's collective, was awarded 10,000 rubles.

I didn't think I was committing a crime. Being at the operational meeting, they gave us various orders, how to lead investigations and whom to arrest. If I committed a mistake, then this did not depend on me, but on other circumstances.

I indisputably committed a series of gross mistakes but individual facts are the inventions of the investigators and not my orders.

For seven months, I have been under guard . . . this is for me a big punishment.

I ask that you take into account all circumstances in the determination of my fate.

Dependent upon me are my father and mother and two small children who will remain without any means of existence.

And therefore I again plead for a just sentence.[96]

Krivtsov followed Fleishman to the stand to give his final statement to the tribunal. Initially, Krivtsov had denied all guilt. Over the course of the trial, however, he admitted that he had fabricated several interrogation protocols, but added significantly, that "all this I did only on the orders of Fleishman."[97] His final statement was brief in comparison with Fleishman's. He said, "I request [the tribunal] take into account that I never in my life had to carry out an investigation. Completely not knowing the methods of work and considering the orders of Fleishman to be correct, I see now that I committed a crime. . . . I violated revolutionary legality not because I wanted to, but because they forced me."[98] Krivtsov based his defense on ignorance and orders from above.

The tribunal found both of the defendants guilty. Fleishman was sentenced to eight years in a corrective labor camp. Krivtsov received a lesser sentence of six years. The documents do not say whether they served out their terms or were released to fight in the war, nor is the subsequent fate of Fleishman known. Krivtsov, however, lived long enough to petition for his rehabilitation in the late 1950s. Then, and again in the late 1990s, the courts confirmed the original sentence.[99] The fate of Pivchikov, Ivan Babich, and Tsirul'nitskii is not clear; Dolgushev was arrested in early 1939 and stood trial roughly one week after Fleishman and Krivtsov.[100]

FLEISHMAN AND KRIVTSOV were following orders. There is no doubt about that, nor about the role of senior NKVD officers like Dolgushev in pushing the terror forward. The orders came from Moscow through Kiev. Yet Fleishman in particular certainly believed there were enemies. He not only believed, he knew there were enemies. He had fought in the civil war and knew it still cut a swath through Soviet territory. And he knew, or thought he knew, or lied that he knew who the enemies were. This is not to say that the enemy was real. In almost all cases, the civil war had ended long ago for the defeated; moreover, many men had had no choice regarding which side they served in the civil war, being the objects of forced conscription by all sides. For the victors, however, the civil war remained very real; this was perhaps nowhere more so than in the small and isolated outposts of Soviet power in the countryside like Skvira.

Whether out of fear or vengeance, Stalin and the NKVD leadership also believed in the enemy.[101] In the countryside, people knew who had fought on what side during the civil war and collectivization. The logic of the mass operations was such that it did not matter what former enemies had done in the interval between the end of the civil war and the start of mass operations. When witnesses in the Fleishman case told of neighbors who were good collective farm workers, this did not matter for the NKVD. Their very existence (or survival) remained a threat. Political and social profiles were unchanging in the minds of the executors of the mass operations.

The master narrative of the Great Terror reflected the paranoia of the top leadership. It also captured the fears of a generation of NKVD officials, like Fleishman, who had fought in the civil war and understood enmity. Their fears were not just based on the civil war—indeed many were in territories far from where they fought—but also on their actions in the years following the civil war. Many of these NKVD officials and policemen had served in the violent collectivization and dekulakization campaigns. In Ukraine, they remembered well the famine of 1932–1933. Guilt and memory may have consolidated their fears, thereby helping to shape their actions during the Great Terror. A combination of orders from above, not to mention ignorance, however, were requisite conditioning factors in Skvira, as they would be in Uman, the site of an NKVD interdistrict operational group.

FIGURE 1 A. R. Dolgushev, head of the Kievan regional NKVD. By exclusive permission of the State Branch Archive of the Security Service of Ukraine.

FIGURE 2 A. R. Dolgushev, head of the Kievan regional NKVD. By exclusive permission of the State Branch Archive of the Security Service of Ukraine.

FIGURE 3 L. M. Pavlychev, Dolgushev's assistant and traveling NKVD troubleshooter. By exclusive permission of the State Branch Archive of the Security Service of Ukraine.

FIGURE 4 I. S. Drushliak, NKVD interrogator in Khar'kov and Kiev. By exclusive permission of the State Branch Archive of the Security Service of Ukraine.

FIGURE 5 S. M. Abramovich, prison commandant in Uman. By exclusive permission of the State Branch Archive of the Security Service of Ukraine.

FIGURE 6 S. M. Abramovich, prison commandant in Uman. By exclusive permission of the State Branch Archive of the Security Service of Ukraine.

FIGURE 7 P. A. Korkin, head of the Dnepropetrovsk regional NKVD. By exclusive permission of the State Branch Archive of the Security Service of Ukraine.

FIGURE 8 B. P. Boldin, head of the Zaporozh'e NKVD. By exclusive permission of the State Branch Archive of the Security Service of Ukraine.

FIGURE 9 G. Ia. Dorov, prison commandant in Zaporozh'e. By exclusive permission of the State Branch Archive of the Security Service of Ukraine.

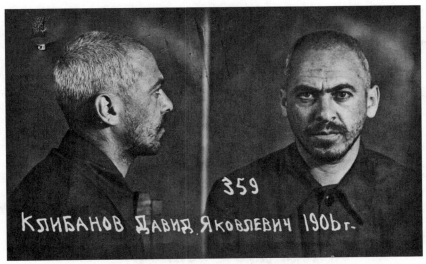

FIGURE 10 D. Ia. Klibanov, head of the Zaporozh'e NKVD Fourth Sector. By exclusive permission of the State Branch Archive of the Security Service of Ukraine.

FIGURE 11 B. L. Linetskii, head of the Zaporozh'e NKVD Third Sector. By exclusive permission of the State Branch Archive of the Security Service of Ukraine.

FIGURE 12 V. Ia. Grabar' as a young NKVD officer. By exclusive permission of the State Branch Archive of the Security Service of Ukraine.

FIGURE 13 V. Ia. Grabar', senior NKVD official in the Ukrainian republican NKVD. By exclusive permission of the State Branch Archive of the Security Service of Ukraine.

FIGURE 14 V. Ia. Grabar' on the eve of his execution. By exclusive permission of the State Branch Archive of the Security Service of Ukraine.

FIGURE 15 M. M. Tul'skii, the NKVD interrogator who worked with Grabar' in Ukrainian Republican NKVD. By exclusive permission of the State Branch Archive of the Security Service of Ukraine.

FIGURE 16 A. I. Uspenskii, commissar of NKVD Ukraine. By exclusive permission of the State Branch Archive of the Security Service of Ukraine.

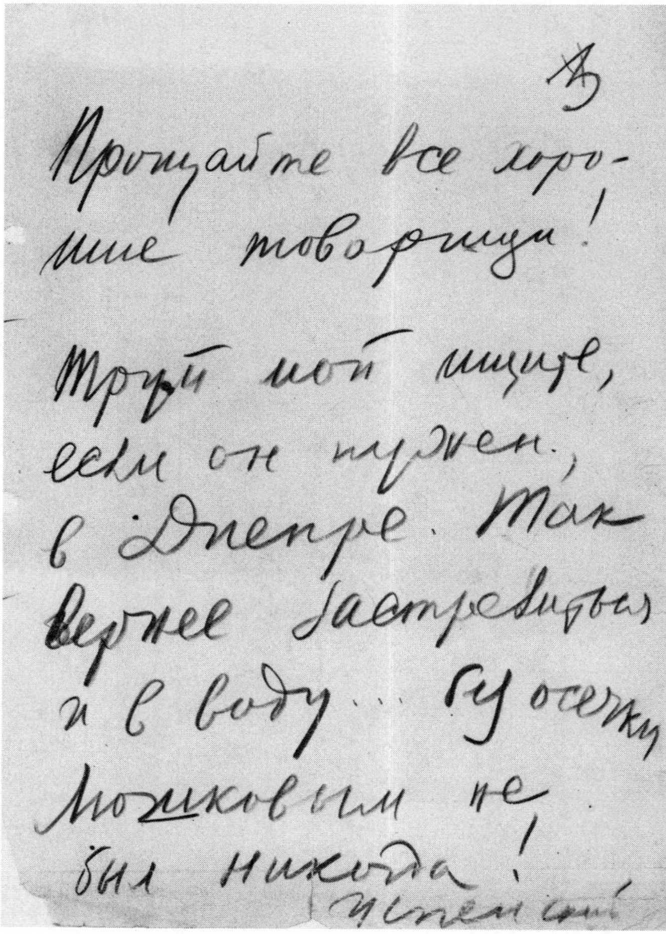
Прощайте все хорошие товарищи!
Труп мой ищите, если он нужен, в Днепре. Так вернее застрелиться и в воду... без осечки.
Мошковым не был никогда!
Успенский

FIGURE 17 Uspenskii's suicide note. By exclusive permission of the State Branch Archive of the Security Service of Ukraine.

5

What Happened in Uman?

Had I actively spoken out against such methods of interrogation ... I would not now be among the living.
—S. I. BORISOV, *former head of the Uman NKVD*

How do I know what happened in room 21? It seems to me that not only I knew about this, but, in my opinion, half the population of Uman also knew about it.
—I. A. MYSHKO, *Uman NKVD interrogator*

A NIGHTMARE UNFOLDED in Uman.[1] The local NKVD organs created a special "laboratory"—room 21—for interrogations, beatings, and forced confessions. Prisoners suffocated to death in the overcrowded holding cells. The chief executioner was said to have hacked out gold teeth from corpses with the barrel of his revolver. The commandant of the local prison was arrested and tried in a closed court hearing for, among other things, the pillaging of corpses. This trial proved inconclusive. It paved the way, however, for two other trials that would feature not only the prison commandant but also the leading lights of the local NKVD. The charges, in both instances, revolved around the violation of socialist legality and malfeasance from within the bowels of the execution chambers.

This case focuses on the activities of an interdistrict operational–investigation group, uniting a series of districts and centered in the town of Uman. Far more complex than some of the earlier cases, it expands from the site of interrogation to the execution chambers. In Uman, there were three trials and six defendants, including several who had been arrested or demoted earlier in the Uspenskii NKVD purges. Their cases were united in the final stage of the purge of the purgers and tried according to the standard charges of violations of socialist legality. Although certainly none of the Uman defendants suffered from liberalism in their conduct of terror, they were united in placing the blame for violations on higher authorities, mainly the regional NKVD in Kiev. Although this was certainly true, the result was that the regional NKVD opened up a spigot that released all the filth of the Uman NKVD's own venality, drunkenness, and violence.

UMAN WAS A sleepy provincial town in central Ukraine, with a mixed population of Ukrainians, Russians, and Jews. It lay some 180 kilometers south of Kiev and was administratively a part of the Kiev region. The local NKVD was housed in a two-story building with twenty rooms and an inner courtyard. The NKVD shared the premises with the local police, who occupied the first floor of the building and took an active part in the terror. The execution chambers were in the cellars, beneath the clubroom. The nearby prison funneled the defendants into the interrogation rooms and the execution site. Built to house 400, at most 450 prisoners, as many as 2,500 people—some said more—were packed into its cells at the height of the terror.[2]

The NKVD building served as headquarters for the mass operations in Uman. What happened within its walls was described many times by defendants, witnesses, and victims. It is instructive, however, to begin with the indictment offered by the Ukrainian republican NKVD on the conclusion of its investigations. The indictment was based on months of interrogations of the defendants and a wide circle of witnesses. It presents a scaled-down and relatively dry encapsulation of events that provides an introduction to the atrocities at Uman.[3]

According to the NKVD indictment, in July 1937, the regional administration of the NKVD in Kiev created in Uman (as elsewhere) an interdistrict operational–investigation group uniting twelve to eighteen districts. After about a month, the regional NKVD leadership appointed Solomon Isaevich Borisov-Lenderman to serve as the head of the interdistrict group. Borisov had been the head of the Uman district NKVD from the fall of 1936. At the same time, the regional leadership appointed Aleksandr Sokratovich Tomin to serve as the head of the Third Section investigation group, responsible for national operations. Tomin would later succeed Borisov after the latter left to take up a position as a Gulag camp director in Komsomol'sk-na-Amure. Tomin would leave Uman to become the deputy head of the Moldavan NKVD in Tiraspol in May 1938. Borisov and Tomin were two of the main defendants in the second and third trials of the Uman NKVD leadership.[4]

The NKVD investigation established that there had been violations of revolutionary legality in Uman. There were groundless arrests, beatings and torture of prisoners to force them to sign confessions, and falsified cases. According to the NKVD indictment,

In order to more quickly receive confessions, in the building of the NKVD in room 21 under the leadership of Borisov and Tomin was organized a so-called "laboratory" led by the former head of the Man'kovskii district militia, G. N. Petrov. The task of this so-called laboratory ... was to obtain from prisoners confessions about their supposed counterrevolutionary activities.... Almost no one did not confess. On the orders of Borisov and Tomin, all the arrested submitted to a preliminary interrogation in room 21. For interrogation, 20 to 30 people were called simultaneously into the room. Before the interrogation, Petrov received from Borisov and Tomin a list of the arrested to be interrogated in which it was indicated what kind of confession this or that arrested was expected to give: who recruited him, to what counterrevolutionary organization, and whom did he recruit in turn. Having announced the charges to the arrested, Petrov asked: "who will write a confession, raise your hand." Some arrested, fearing a beating, signed.... To those arrested who did not wish to give the confession required of them, Petrov, with the repeated participation of Tomin, applied physical measures of influence: They beat, forced [people] to stand uninterruptedly for 10 to 15 days, orchestrated so-called concerts, forced the arrested to beat each other, to sing and to dance, applied the method of the so-called thermometer, inserting a stick under their arm and forcing them to hold it, and then beating them. As a result of all these violations in interrogations, there were mass false, made-up confessions.[5]

Grigorii Nikolaevich Petrov was the main "laboratory assistant" in room 21 and a defendant in the second and third trials.

The NKVD indictment then moved on the second of the two major accusations—the violations of revolutionary legality that took place in the execution chambers. Samuil Moiseevich Abramovich, the commandant of the Uman prison and the third of the main defendants, served as the head of the execution squad, seemingly a common practice for heads of prisons at this time. "With the sanction of Borisov and Tomin" and under the direction of Abramovich,

Looting [*maroderstvo*] occurred, the theft of valuables from the condemned. Abramovich took away and appropriated sums of money belonging to the executed before their execution. Thus was misappropriated 42,485 rubles. On the authority of Borisov and Tomin, Abramovich repeatedly distributed 30 to 40 rubles [each] to the participants of the [execution] brigade. In addition, Tomin many times received large sums of money from Abramovich for his personal use. Valuable properties of the condemned, coats, suits, boots, etc., were appropriated by Abramovich, Shcherbina, and others. Shcherbina especially distinguished himself here. In the presence of Tomin, Abramovich removed gold dental plates, gold teeth, and other dentures from the mouths of the executed.[6]

The final charges were minor in comparison. Leonid Semenovich Shcherbina, mentioned in connection to the execution chamber looting, was accused of entering into intimate relations with the wife of a prisoner, and Tomin was charged with violating search procedures in a Tiraspol prison. Abramovich was additionally charged with violating secrecy rules regarding executions, and the Uman NKVD leaders were charged with the deaths of four prisoners from asphyxiation caused by overcrowding in the cells.[7]

The sixth defendant in the case was the NKVD chauffeur, Nikolai Pavlovich Zudin, who worked mainly in executions. He was also charged with the looting of corpses, taking, according to the official report, "not more than 200 rubles," five pairs of boots, a leather jacket, and three pairs of underwear.[8]

This was, in short, the case against the Uman NKVD. In fact, it was not nearly as cut-and-dried as the official indictment suggested. It took three trials for the charges to stick. The first trial took place in July 1939.[9] Its only defendant was Abramovich, the prison commandant and head executioner. Although Abramovich's guilt seems obvious from the transcripts of the trial, the NKVD Kiev Military Tribunal declined to sentence him, instead attaching his case to a larger case against Tomin, Zudin, and "others."[10] The second trial—against Borisov, Tomin, Abramovich, Petrov, Zudin, and Shcherbina—resulted in sentences for all but Zudin, who was freed. Tomin and Abramovich received three-year sentences, Borisov and Petrov got two years, and Shcherbina received a sentence of one year of noncustodial compulsory labor at his place of work.[11] But the Military Collegium of the Supreme Court of the USSR intervened, overturning the case. The third and final trial resulted in longer sentences for all of the defendants. Borisov received the longest sentence of eight years; Abramovich, six years; Tomin and Petrov, five years; and Shcherbina and Zudin, three years—all to be served in corrective labor camps.[12]

The defendants in the trial convincingly documented the role of not just regional, but republic and All-Union NKVD officials in permitting and facilitating the basic infrastructure for the violations of revolutionary legality that took place in Uman. Although Tomin was initially evasive, particularly in his earliest interrogations, Borisov was frank and forthcoming in his interrogations and trial testimony. Moreover, the witnesses and defendants, including Tomin, backed him up, recalling visits by regional, republic, and All-Union NKVD officials as well as a series of orders and turning points in the developments of the mass operations. It is not that Borisov was not self-serving—he placed the blame for "violations" elsewhere—but he drew a picture of the mass operations in Uman that rings true and provided proof of the regional NKVD's orchestration that the court chose formally to ignore.

BORISOV WAS A long-term NKVD operational worker. Born in 1899 in Kiev, he was the son of a Jewish tailor. He had no more than a few years of schooling and had himself worked as a tailor for hire before the revolution. He joined the Red Army in 1919 and fought for the duration of the Russian civil war. Recruited directly into the Cheka at the end of the civil war, Borisov joined the Communist Party in 1928. From the fall of 1936, he served as head of the NKVD in Uman, where he lived with his wife and teenage son. He left Uman to become the director of a remote labor camp in the Far East in March 1938, most likely as a demotion when Uspenskii came to power in Ukraine, possibly because of his Jewish origins and/or relation to Leplevskii as well as possible financial improprieties. Borisov was arrested there in October 1939.[13]

According to Borisov, it all started in July 1937, the same month that Moscow issued the order for the mass operations. Isai Iakovlevich Babich arrived in Uman that month with orders to create an interdistrict operational–investigation group to lead the struggle with the counterrevolution.[14] Prior to his arrival in Uman, Babich, the son of a Jewish boot maker with a primary education, had served as a top NKVD official in both Kiev and Odessa. On arrival in Uman, he convened an operational assembly of NKVD staff to discuss the tasks ahead. According to Babich, the NKVD's former leader, G. G. Iagoda (1891–1938), had "crushed the initiative of the NKVD" and fostered "liberal relations" in its dealings with enemies. The times, however, had changed. Babich told his audience that the Soviet Union was in a "prewar period" and that it was necessary to eliminate all such liberalism. If need be, he continued, NKVD interrogators should scream, curse, and do everything possible to root out the counterrevolution.[15] The Uman NKVD party organizer, Anton Andronovich Danilov, would later say that the "tone changed" with the arrival of Babich.[16]

Babich had launched the mass operations in Uman. He organized and led the interdistrict group for two months. The group consisted of about seventy people in all, including the heads of the district police and some forty students from the regional security police school in Kiev. In late summer or early fall 1937, Babich was recalled to Kiev. He left Uman with Borisov. Once in Kiev, Nikolai Davydovich Sharov, then head of the Kiev regional NKVD, charged Borisov with leading the interdistrict group in Uman.[17] According to Borisov, Lev Iosifovich Reikhman, then the deputy head of the Kiev regional NKVD, ordered him to force the cases and, if essential, to beat confessions out of the arrested with the agreement of the higher-standing organs.[18] Borisov said, "When I heard this, I was dumbfounded and didn't say a word about this to anyone in Uman."[19]

Before Borisov left Kiev, Sharov told him that he must "work out all unclear issues with Tomin."[20] Tomin was a lieutenant in the NKVD. Born in 1901 in Kiev to a Ukrainian family, Tomin had also fought in the Russian civil war, remaining in the Red Army until 1924. After the war, he graduated from a Communist Institute with what in his words was a higher political education. He joined the security police in 1931. Although he was married with four children, he lived apart from his family. Like many NKVD workers in Uman, he lived in a hotel because of frequent transfers of NKVD personnel and local housing shortages. Tomin had been in Uman from roughly May 1937 and was closely associated with Babich. Although he later denied it, Borisov was sure that Tomin served as the regional NKVD's representative. He led the important Third Section in Uman, the Counterintelligence Department in charge of the "Polish Operations," among others. Borisov called Tomin's section "a filial of the regional NKVD."[21] For Borisov, Tomin was the real head of operations in Uman: "He did what he wanted to do. He came to work when he wanted and left when he considered it convenient for him to leave. Besides that, he interfered literally in all cases" and was frequently in Kiev. Borisov told his interrogator that Tomin was there to force the pace, "to drive me on."[22]

Borisov recalled other instances of outside intervention. One day in December 1937, five or six cars arrived in Uman. He could not believe his eyes as Leplevskii and Frinovskii, two leading NKVD officials from Kiev and Moscow, got out of the cars.[23] According to Borisov, "during the two days they were there, there was complete pandemonium." They observed how the Uman NKVD worked and concluded that "to work like that was not permitted." They then "worked over" a supposed spy and beat him up. "They cursed him with such curses, that I had never heard before in my life," said Borisov, somewhat unconvincingly. In the night, they sat in Borisov's office and told him that he needed "to put the pressure on." Frinovskii said that if noise came from an interrogator's office, that means he is a good interrogator.[24]

Reikhman also paid a visit to Uman. Borisov claimed that Reikhman came because Borisov was unable to obtain a confession from one Dobrokhovskii, a supposedly key figure in an investigation. In Uman, Reikhman called an assembly of NKVD staff and lashed out at Borisov and party organizer Danilov, threatening them both with arrest if they did not turn the pressure on.[25]

Borisov called these NKVD workers who came to Uman from on high *gastrolery*, or touring actors. He claimed that if there were cases of physical pressure, they were a result of the adverse influence of these gastrolery, thus echoing what Dolgushev maintained.[26] Borisov said that he himself had always forbid his workers to use physical force in their work with prisoners. Other witnesses at the trial backed him up in this claim. Even Tomin and Petrov later denied that Borisov had ever issued orders for the beatings.[27]

The volume of work made all but inevitable the use of physical violence. At its height, the terror in Uman netted no fewer than 2,500 prisoners, all of whom were required to complete a certain amount of paperwork, including a signed confession. Sharov had demanded 1,000 arrests for the Polish Operation alone, and Borisov had to phone in daily to the Kiev offices to report on Uman's progress.[28] "Telegrams, telephone calls from Kiev did not give us the possibility to work normally," Borisov remembered.[29] In fact, at one point, Uman NKVD workers went so far as to steal prisoners from another district to fulfill their quotas.[30]

Room 21, or the laboratory as it was known locally, arose to handle the volume of arrests. It was ground zero for the mass production of confessions and existed from roughly November to 5–6 December 1937. Although Borisov said that he didn't organize room 21 and Tomin argued that it arose spontaneously, it seems clear from the evidence that it was Tomin who organized and led the laboratory, perhaps under Sharov's direct influence. However, from the Dolgushev case, it is clear that these special rooms were common at this time. Borisov assigned a number of regular police chiefs to Tomin's section to work as interrogators' assistants because they were semiliterate and unable to handle the paperwork required of regular interrogators. In turn, Tomin assigned some of these police chiefs to supervise room 21 as "lab assistants."[31]

Chief among them was Petrov. Born in 1896 to a working-class Ukrainian family in Donetsk, he was a soldier who had fought first in the tsar's army and then in the Red Army during the Russian civil war. He joined the Communist Party in 1928 when he became a member of the regular police.

By 1935, he was the chief of the Man'kovskii District police and was mobilized to work in mass operations in Uman in August 1937.[32]

Room 21 served to preprocess arrestees by separating out those who immediately or soon after a display of force agreed to confess from those who refused to slander themselves. The room contained a long table, scattered with pencils and standardized forms. There were only enough chairs for some of the arrestees to sit. Petrov would first ask for a show of hands—who is guilty? Those who agreed to be guilty answered a few basic questions and then were redirected to individual interrogators for the full workup. Those who did not confess were subject to humiliation, beatings, and prolonged periods of standing.[33] Petrov prevaricated through the course of his interrogations and the two trials, sometimes saying neither Borisov nor Tomin ordered him to beat prisoners, other times denying that he beat anyone or arguing that he beat but not "systematically." In the end, he admitted beating people, saying, "No one ordered me to beat the arrested, but they said that I had to provide 100 confessions a day."[34]

Borisov admitted that the sole purpose of the laboratory was to extract confessions, with physical force when necessary.[35] He did not deny knowledge of what went on in room 21. He claimed to have expressed surprise to Tomin when he heard that Petrov was producing so many confessions, asking Tomin if there was some sort of "art" to this. Tomin denied that beatings occurred in the laboratory. When Borisov asked Petrov what was going on, Petrov said, "you know, I am a strong man and if I struck someone, I'd kill him. It is enough for me to yell."[36]

Although he claimed that Tomin marginalized him in interrogation work, Borisov appeared to have been a much more active participant in executions. On orders from the regional NKVD, Borisov assembled an execution squad locally. The execution squad consisted of no fewer than seven people at any given time and was assembled from a motley crew of characters, including the NKVD chauffeur, courier, and prison guard, in addition to a series of police chiefs.[37] Borisov appointed prison commandant Abramovich to serve as chief executioner. Like Borisov, Abramovich was the son of a Jewish tailor. Born in 1903 in Khar'kov, he served in the Red Army from 1923 to 1926, entering the security police in 1926. He became a member of the Communist Party in 1930, was married with two children, and had a passion for cars.[38] According to his own testimony, he accepted this onerous position as a "party obligation."[39]

Executions of groups of about forty people took place nightly in the cellars of the NKVD.[40] The execution chambers consisted of three rooms. In the first room, Borisov checked the photo and identification of each person condemned to death. In the second room, Abramovich searched the prisoners, with the understanding that they were going to the baths before being transported to a labor camp. None were aware of their fate until the penultimate moment. In the third room, they were shot.[41] The NKVD chauffeur, Zudin, raced the engine of his car in the courtyard to cover up the sounds of the bullets. After the executions, Zudin and Abramovich each took carloads of corpses, hidden under tarps, to the burial site. [42]

In the beginning, the corpses were buried in their clothes. According to Borisov, there were no instructions on what to do with the money and property of the condemned. When Abramovich warned Borisov that execution squad members were rifling through the pockets of the dead, Borisov first ordered Abramovich to put a halt to this practice. Then, a short time later in Kiev, Borisov asked Sharov what to do with the property of the condemned. Sharov gave Borisov permission to allow the squad members to divide up the property given the "difficulty of this work."[43] After that time, the condemned were forced to undress—"for the baths"—before execution. After the execution, money and goods were divided among the squad members. This practice continued until the wife of a condemned man reported seeing her dead husband's clothes for sale at the local bazaar. Borisov claims to have halted the practice immediately at that point. Not long after, a commission arrived from the regional NKVD's Economic Department, led by one Mishchenko, who ordered that all of the condemned's property be retrieved and destroyed. At that point, Borisov ordered that the stolen goods be buried.[44]

Borisov knew what was happening in Uman, but claimed that Tomin was really in charge. He argued endlessly that he respected revolutionary legality and, with only a few minor exceptions, denied beating anyone. He and others repeatedly noted his warnings against the use of physical force at operational assemblies. In the end, Borisov claimed to have resigned himself to the reality of the mass operations given current circumstances. He said, "Had I actively spoken out against such methods of interrogation . . . I would not now be among the living."[45] He argued that he took "all essential measures to observe revolutionary legality, but in that time I could not take to court one [NKVD] staff member since given the context of the times I would have ended up in court for sabotage."[46]

Surely Borisov was correct in his apprehension. He laid out a neat case for the responsibility of higher officials in creating the conditions for the violations of revolutionary legality in Uman. He denied his guilt through two trials and partially shifted responsibility to Tomin, who, he said, acted as the regional representative. Most of the witnesses backed up his testimony. Yet, despite the detail and precision of Borisov's story, it is not the whole story. Borisov, after all, was demoted to his position in the Gulag in March 1938, supposedly for financial improprieties, a charge that never came up at the trials.[47] By bringing in the testimony of a series of key witnesses, it becomes apparent that "local artistry" combined with higher orders to create the worst possible circumstances in which the mass operations unfolded in Uman.

IN BOTH THEIR pretrial depositions and their court testimony, the witnesses were fairly consistent in acknowledging the widespread violations that occurred in the Uman NKVD, although the NKVD interrogators among them generally denied their own complicity. Many provided additional testimony, supporting Borisov's claims that the regional NKVD created the conditions for the violations. Although few in number, several victims were able to testify to the local artistry of room 21. There was more contention around the issue of looting at the executions, expressed in disagreements, accusations of pressuring witnesses, and lies. Perhaps the ugliest testimony concerned the venality of the execution squad. It is here that it is possible to discern roughly the intersection between higher orders and local NKVD sensibilities.

NKVD party organizer Danilov worked as an operational plenipotentiary in Uman in 1937. He offered some of the most compelling evidence for the key role of the regional NKVD officials in establishing the parameters of the terror in Uman. It was Danilov who testified about how Babich transformed the tone of NKVD practices in Uman.[48] Danilov also provided important testimony backing up Borisov on Reikhman's role in Uman. During the third trial, he told the court:

> At the operational assembly, Reikhman shouted at me, saying I was liberal with prisoners . . . then Reikhman fell upon Borisov in the same way. Reikhman brought me to tears. He cursed and threatened me, saying they'd have to watch me carefully and I was forced to promise that I would change my methods of work.[49]

According to Danilov, after this assembly, it became clear that Tomin "set the tone in work."[50] Danilov also stated that he saw "much worse" in the Kiev regional NKVD than what went on in Uman and, importantly, that there was a "direct order from the regional administration of the NKVD" to beat the arrested.[51] He remembered that Borisov himself did not give sanctions for the use of torture, but had "to telephone the Kiev NKVD administration in order to receive [such] sanctions."[52] Finally, he was emphatic in testifying that Borisov was against the use of force in extracting confessions, but was under terrible pressure from Sharov and Reikhman.[53]

Danilov testified that he had never been in room 21 but heard rumors about its existence and the beatings from other interrogators.[54] He had attended the executions periodically. He recalled the commotion in Borisov's office when they heard that the wife of execution squad member Kravchenko was selling the clothes of the executed at the bazaar. Later, when he brought up the issue with Borisov, the latter told him, "there was some sort of an agreement with the region that it is better to let [squad members] take things than to bury [goods] in the earth given how hellish the work was." He also recalled Abramovich and other executioners complaining about the bad behavior of Shcherbina and his quarrels with Abramovich. In general, though, he had nothing negative to say about Abramovich and said he had never seen him drunk.[55]

Another witness, Boris Naumovich Neiman, backed up most of what Danilov said in regard to Borisov, but had a very different view of Abramovich. Born in 1907, Neiman worked in the Uman NKVD from mid-October to late December 1937, and then again, from 13 March 1938 through April 1939. He had served earlier as an investigator for the Transport Procuracy in Khristinovka. His job in Uman was to write the indictments of cases and then (literally) to sew up the files.[56]

Neiman told the court that, according to hearsay from other NKVD workers, it was Sharov who was responsible for the organization of room 21. Further, regional NKVD officials Rogol', Sharburin, and Reikhman had all visited the laboratory and were well aware of what went on there.[57] Neiman also stated that he recalled Borisov's "categorical prohibition" against beating prisoners.[58] Neiman's testimony on executions was based on his actual presence in the execution rooms, though Abramovich claimed to have thrown Neiman out of the room for fear of ricocheting bullets.[59] Neiman, however, was able to describe the execution procedures. He noted that Borisov's job was to verify the identities of the condemned, to announce that the prisoners were being readied for transport, and then to leave. After Borisov's departure, the condemned went one-by-one to see Abramovich, who took their money and issued them a receipt. After that the prisoners were executed.[60]

Originally, Neiman claimed that he was under the impression that the money of the condemned was given to the government and their possessions buried. Somewhat later, however, he was in Borisov's office when Borisov disciplined the two executioners, Kravchenko and Karpov, for allowing goods from the executions to show up at the bazaar. That is when he claimed to discover that the execution squad members divided up the property of the condemned. Neiman also said he saw Abramovich remove gold teeth from a corpse and claimed to have written up a report on the incident for N. N. Fedorov, who headed up the Kiev regional NKVD from 28 February to 28 March 1938. He added that Abramovich had taken the NKVD uniform coat of one Sobol', a former head of the Monastyrishchenskii District NKVD, after his execution and wore it the next day.[61] Abramovich called Neiman's testimony "fictitious" and claimed that G. P. Sagalaev, the head of the Uman NKVD from August 1938, had conspired with him "to bring down Abramovich."[62] Later, Abramovich claimed that Neiman hated him from the time he expelled him from the execution chambers.[63]

The charge of the removal of gold teeth from corpses came up repeatedly at all three trials. Execution squad member Emil'ian Fedorovich Kravchenko, the Uman prison guard whose wife supposedly sold the clothes at the bazaar, said at the second trial that, "Before execution, the arrested undressed, from which bad clothes were destroyed and Abramovich took the best for himself, partially dividing up the [rest of the] clothes for the brigade's participants." Kravchenko also said he saw Abramovich remove gold teeth.[64] Abramovich retorted that Sagalaev had forced Kravchenko to give this testimony.[65] Execution squad member Petr Mikhailovich Vereshchuk, the Uman NKVD courier, also claimed that Abramovich took the best for himself and removed gold teeth. He then denied that Sagalaev did anything but tell Kravchenko and him to testify, not how to testify.[66] Two other execution squad members who testified only at the first trial, Gregorii Konstantinovich Blinkin and Stepan Nikolaevich Pivanov, each claimed not to have seen Abramovich take gold teeth. Blinkin added that the executions worked like an assembly line, and it seemed to him that "there was not even a minute free in which to remove teeth," to which Kravchenko interjected, "There was time."[67]

The chauffeur Zudin also worked in executions. At the first trial, when he was not a defendant, he claimed that Abramovich took as many as 200 gold teeth. He also charged Abramovich with making him drive sacks of clothes to Abramovich's apartment.[68] At the second and third trials, however, when he was a defendant, Zudin changed his testimony and said he never saw Abramovich take teeth.[69] Zudin claimed that he had been pressured to testify against Abramovich by Sagalaev.[70]

Perhaps more interesting than the issue of the removal of gold teeth was the (im)moral economy that prevailed in the Uman NKVD.[71] A former peasant who had worked in operational investigations in Uman in 1937–1938, Tikhon Semenovich Kalachevskii was depositioned for the trial, most likely the first trial, but never testified. In his deposition, he said that "execution work was difficult and that if participants took things, this was nothing terrible because they deserved it." He claimed to have disapproved of such theft and brought up the problem with both Borisov, who said that the regional NKVD had made it clear to him that this was normal practice, and Danilov, who was apparently upset by these actions. Kalachevskii was personally appalled to see Abramovich wearing Sobol's coat soon after his execution.[72] It was generally believed in the Uman NKVD that execution work was difficult work and that therefore members of the execution squad had a right to take the possessions of the dead.[73]

From Neiman, it is clear that the end of the executions was eagerly awaited. In one of his earliest depositions, Neiman recalled one occasion in December 1937 when the electricity failed during executions. He asked Zudin the chauffeur to take him to the electric station, but Zudin responded, "Later or I'll miss the *zapal*." Zudin explained to Neiman that zapal was shorthand for the distribution of goods that occurred at the end of the executions.[74]

Another contentious issue that arose concerned Tomin's role in the executions and division of looted goods. In his deposition, Tomin claimed to have participated only three times in execution work. He said that Rogol, former head of the regional NKVD Third Section, forbade him to continue in this work because it negatively affected his interrogation work. Nonetheless, Tomin said he continued to stop by the executions for a few minutes at a time.[75] He said, "I personally received not a thing from Abramovich and not a single kopek of money."[76] He did remember what he called "unhealthy conversations" among execution squad members regarding the divisions of goods and their sense, particularly Zudin's, that "they worked much but did not receive."[77] He stuck to these claims throughout both trials.

Zudin told his interrogator that Tomin and Borisov appeared at times at the execution site. However, according to Zudin, when they were there, Abramovich did not force the condemned to undress and did not take anything from them.[78] Neiman said Borisov and Tomin came to the executions and even saw Abramovich remove gold teeth.[79] Abramovich himself claimed at the first trial that Tomin and Danilov received their share of looted property, but changed his story in the second trial, during which he was unable to recall if Tomin received anything.[80] At the end of the first trial, the Military Tribunal arrived at the conclusion that Tomin was aware of Abramovich's crimes and therefore ordered the case expanded.[81] At the conclusion of the second trial, however, the Military Tribunal concluded that there was insufficient evidence of looting at the site of execution.[82] That conclusion likely prompted Moscow to intervene and call for the third trial.

Witnesses also tied Tomin to the deadly overcrowding in the prison that resulted in four deaths. Uman interrogator Ivan Andreevich Myshko recalled "hearing about" the creation of an airless room with lots of prisoners.[83] It is unlikely that Tomin actually created such an intentional death trap. The overcrowding of the prison was common knowledge and had reached crisis proportions.[84] Tomin told the court that he was unable to recall cases of death from overcrowding. Borisov said it was possible that Tomin did not know, but, all the same, attributed the overcrowding to the huge number of cases in Tomin's bailiwick, the Third Section. At the same time, Borisov admitted that he held sole responsibility for this state of affairs as head of the Uman NKVD.[85]

Solomon Naumovich Gol'denstein, the head of the prison's sanitary department, served as the most reliable witness to what happened in the cell in question:

I don't remember when Abramovich called me to the NKVD. When I arrived there, I saw the following picture: 4 to 5 prisoners lying naked, 2 or 3 of them already dead, and 2 undergoing artificial resuscitation. They directed me to the cell where I saw that the arrested there were suffocating from the overheating of air. I treated them medically. One of the suffocated prisoners came to, but as a consequence died of another illness.

He continued to say that he had no information on the four who died of suffocation because they had not been brought to the prison sanitary department, where they normally would have been documented. Further, Gol'denstein said he did not at the time recommend autopsies for those who had suffocated.[86]

Aleksandr Mikhailovich Lebedev was the 47-year-old physician who conducted autopsies on bodies from the Uman prison. Although he had nothing to say specifically on the causes of suffocation, he said that the bodies that came to him had no identification or explanation for the circumstances of death. When Lebedev inquired of Borisov about this omission, Borisov told him that this was "not important" and Lebedev understood not to question further.[87] He knew that some prisoners had been murdered but also knew that it was impossible to write the true reasons for a death. He even said, "It wasn't clear to me what the point of the autopsies was." He feared arrest if he wrote that a murder was a murder and stated, "I am entirely aware that this was a compromise with my conscience. . . ."[88] Dr. Lebedev knew what to do without orders from the region.

The question of orders from above was irrelevant to the victims. Victim testimony in the trials was limited, with the exception of testimony that came from Tomin's time in Tiraspol, where he was deputy head of the Moldavan NKVD after he left Uman. There were, however, survivors from room 21 who testified or wrote complaints to higher authorities. There were also "signalers," generally people working in or with the NKVD who wrote letters to the authorities about the violations in socialist legality.

The first signal of problems came from a student mobilized from the Kiev NKVD school to work in Uman. He sent an anonymous complaint directly to the Communist Party newspaper, *Pravda*. He wrote:

> In school, they taught us to be civil in our relations with people and prisoners and to display Chekist restraint and adroitness. In practice, everything was the opposite and we students were surprised our studies had been in vain and unnecessary. . . . Tomin said that our course knowledge had lagged behind practice, that here you had to change and use physical measures of persuasion in interrogations."[89]

It is not clear whether this signal played any direct role in the trials of the Uman NKVD, but the student's complaint was in the file, and the interrogators who questioned the Uman leaders referred to specific information in the complaint.[90]

There were, however, other signals to the center, complaints from the victims of Uman. Victims wrote to Stalin, the Commission of Soviet Control, the Politburo, the NKVD, and the Ukrainian and All-Union Procurators describing the injustices they experienced. In all, the files contain eight such documents. Former rural soviet chair Danil Alimpievich Delikatnyi (perhaps a pseudonym) wrote to the Commission of Soviet Control from his camp in Perm on 24 May 1939. He claimed that two supposed kulaks had turned the tables on him, denouncing and falsely accusing him and the entire village leadership of belonging to a counterrevolutionary insurgent organization. Delikatnyi was arrested on 15 April 1938 and brought to the Uman NKVD the next day. Once in room 21, he denied the accusations and was forced to stand for five days straight. On the sixth day, Petrov beat him and said if you want to live, you must confess. Petrov told him what to write. He was then, as per procedure, promoted to an individual interrogator who wrote up his confessions and forced him to sign without reading the confession: "I signed, fearing I'd be beaten." He wrote further, "Before this, I could never in my life have imagined that under Soviet power there could occur such events in such conditions."[91]

On 31 January 1939, Evgenii Filippovich Zaionchkovskii wrote to Stalin from his camp in Kareliia. He described what went on in the "infamous room 21." He wrote about beatings of prisoners by other prisoners and the euphemisms of torture in practice: "going to Hitler," "going to Poland," "swinging the kerosene" (euphemisms representing different types of painful and humiliating pressure positions). He told Stalin that mass, groundless arrests occurred in Uman without the permission of the procurator. He specifically mentioned Tomin and Petrov. Zaionchkovskii's brothers also wrote complaints to the Politburo and the Ukrainian Procurator in January.[92]

Ivan Grigor'evich Kondratko wrote to the All-Union NKVD on 4 June 1938 to tell them about his experiences in Uman. The interrogator, Belii, tortured him with what was called the "parachute method," wherein the interrogator placed the victim on the very top of a vertical bench high in the air, forcing him to keep his knees straight so that he fell on his face when the bench was knocked from under him.[93] Avrumberg Moshkovich Kleitman wrote to the Ukrainian Procurator. He wrote, "I was called out 25 times for interrogations and each time they beat me half to death." He refused to sign the confession because he was an "honest citizen." The interrogator, Kriklenko,

> forced me to pray in the Jewish style [po evreiski], giving me two candles to hold and placing a revolver in my mouth. He forced me "to go to Poland" and poured cold water on the back of my head.

Kriklenko threatened his family, in particular his 15-year-old daughter. Kleitman wrote from freedom, but said that he was unable to reconcile himself with the slander and treatment he had received.[94]

The prisoner "Fedia," a math teacher, wrote to his wife, telling her to plead for him in Kiev. He wrote, "With my own eyes, I saw people returning from interrogations black and blue from beatings." One of the main "heroes" [sic] of his story was Petrov. Fedia refused to write lies about himself. He described being in a cell with forty-two people. The cell was "not bigger than our kitchen, without windows with a small opening in the door." After being called out each night (to 6 a.m.) between 20 and 28 July, he finally signed a confession, but remained stricken about lying.[95]

Sidor Viktorovich Kogut served as a witness in both the second and third trials. He was 30 years old and worked in an agricultural cooperative. He arrived in Uman on 24 April 1938 and was brought immediately to the laboratory. There, he saw a drunken Petrov and fifteen to eighteen other prisoners. Petrov struck him in the ear, and when Kogut told him he had no right to do that, Petrov beat him and threw him into a cell. Kogut became deaf as a result of that first blow. He explained the procedure "swinging the kerosene" as prolonged squatting and "going to Hitler" as crawling on all fours. He said that Petrov struck prisoners, including himself, with a stick. Kogut was the only Uman victim to be called to the trial. [96]

Two other victims were questioned but not used in the trials. M. I. Smerchinskii said he was forced to admit to belonging to a counterrevolutionary organization under force. He described his tortures:

I was forced to observe so-called concerts which consisted of prisoners beating each other at the suggestion of the interrogator—they danced and sang. Fomin, Petrov, Tomin, Kuratov led these concerts. I remember the director of the Uman school, Kozak, stood for sixteen days, swelled, and was brutally beaten by Kuratov. I could hear well how in a room full of arrested, elderly Jews called to questioning, they made them sing Jewish songs and dances. The arrested elderly Jew, Shtraus, told me that they forced him to sing and dance.[97]

They also questioned Dmitri Efimovich Dubiniak who had been tortured in room 21 by Petrov. He described the procedures of the laboratory. He recalled Petrov and interrogator Chumak taking turns presiding over the laboratory. He said Chumak was not sober. Dubiniak refused to confess and was eventually freed.[98]

The other victims to testify were women who had experienced Tomin's illegal strip search in Tiraspol. The key witness was Lidiia Iosifovna Pavlik, an economist married to a former NKVD worker in Tiraspol. They were both arrested. She was in a cell with twenty-five other women. On 10 November 1938, Tomin came to the cell with the head of the prison and other NKVD workers. According to Pavlik, the search was conducted in violation of all rules. Tomin made the women undress completely. When some of them protested, he said, "Don't be embarrassed, imagine that you are at the doctor's." Another woman, Liubov' Vladimirovna Statsenko, a bookkeeper from Odessa, also remembered the search. She recalled the prisoner, A. N. Varvaretskaia, the former deputy commissar of Social Services in Moldavia, protesting and refusing to undress in the presence of men. Tomin cursed Varvaretskaia and forced her to remove her brassiere and underwear. Sofiia Moiseevna Pikgol'ts, an imprisoned physician, also remembered Varvaretskaia's protest. She too protested to Tomin, who yelled at her, "What is this crap. You don't want to undress. Take off your shirt." She went on to say, "I stood absolutely naked while the guard Matrena Petrovna Angelusha searched my chest, body, and sex organs." When she refused to allow Angelusha to insert a finger into her, Tomin threatened to throw her in the punishment cell. Angelusha first conveniently forgot about the search, then admitted to it on repeated questioning. She had been a guard since 1932. Along with a more junior guard, Natalia Moiseevna Spogusheva, she confirmed the women's testimony and claimed that strip searches had never occurred in the presence of men before this incident.[99] Tomin later claimed to regret that he had not known the procedures for women's searches.[100]

Tomin's actions in Tiraspol were simply a continuation of the lawlessness that he had engaged in Uman. And the lawlessness did not stop at the gates of the Uman NKVD. Tomin lived in a hotel in town, where he often entertained Abramovich, Shcherbina, and other NKVD officials. According to hotel manager, 24-year-old Elena Aleksandrovna Soboleva, they drank there. She said Abramovich was especially obnoxious, always making demands and finding fault. When she took Abramovich to task for breaking a telephone, he struck her. She subsequently complained to Borisov and lost her job. Soboleva also reported that Shcherbina came to the hotel to sleep with a woman whose husband was under arrest.[101] Sofiia Mefodievna Morozenko lived in one room with this woman and testified that she had told her that Shcherbina wanted her "to take care of him" and that he, in turn, took notes to her husband.[102]

The NKVD's other nighttime activities were probably the reason why interrogator Myshko claimed that the whole town knew what went on in the Uman NKVD.[103] The drunken rowdiness at the local hotel, sales of executed prisoners' clothing at the bazaar, blackmailing women to sleep with them— these were all continuations of the terror in other forms.

HOW DID THE Uman NKVD defendants justify their actions? What does their testimony reveal about their motivations? The first question is easier than the second. The primary justification expressed was what Holocaust historian Raul Hilberg called "the doctrine of superior orders."[104] The defendants and many of the witnesses argued that the regional NKVD, by example and by command, created the conditions for the violations and mistakes of the mass operations in Uman. However, in Uman, there were a series of secondary issues as well: Was Borisov or Tomin in charge? Who knew what and when? How much of an autodidact was Petrov in the laboratory? On the matter of execution crimes, the case revolved around venality, although again it is clear that the regional NKVD, by permitting the execution squad to take money and clothing, facilitated the postmortem atrocities.

Borisov's story is clear. He denied his guilt but did not renounce his responsibility for what happened under his command. Mainly, he claimed that Tomin, as the regional representative, had sidelined him. He said, "I was not in a position to struggle with Tomin because I knew that nothing would come of it for the regional leadership would not react, only leading to more problems right up to arrest and court for breaking 'operational work.'"[105] He claimed that he repeatedly warned his staff against the use of physical force. All his fellow defendants and many witnesses backed him up in this contention, though these claims could very well have been specious and a result of the loyalty of Borisov's own patronage network in Uman. Borisov told the court, "Not one witness could show that I made use of physical methods."[106] In his final words at the second trial, Borisov said, "I am an old operational worker. I have given half my life to the cause of the Revolution. Analyzing the present case and reading the final conclusions, I cannot recognize myself here. The accusations do not correspond to the material of the case."[107] He went on to say:

> I myself am a worker–tailor, my father was also a tailor. From 1914 to 1919, I worked for hire and, in 1919, I escaped the Hetman's mobilization, joined the Red Guard, then the Red Army, as a consequence of which I passed into the organs of the Cheka and worked until the day of my arrest. In the time of my work, I liquidated very many different counterrevolutionary groups and bands. I have been under guard for eight months and have admitted everything. I ask the Tribunal to understand this and to return me to the party and family of workers.[108]

Borisov pleaded for mercy, like all his colleagues. The difference between Borisov and the others was that Borisov knew that the violations of revolutionary legality were indeed violations against the law and admitted this from the outset. He saw everything. He did not justify his actions per se, but explained them as a combination of fear and marginalization. His actions may have been influenced by "compromising material" that the NKVD held on him. In the decree charging Borisov with his crimes, reference was made to a special inspection [*spetsproverka*] conducted on him that indicated that Borisov had relatives in the United States, a deadly charge in 1937 and 1938.[109] His time working as a Gulag boss may also have affected his words and actions. In any case, Borisov served as a prisoner in the Gulag until 1943, when he was sent to the front. He died in 1955.[110]

Tomin was a different case altogether. Like Borisov, he pleaded not guilty in both trials. Unlike Borisov, he refused to admit that anything illegal had occurred in Uman. From the outset of his interrogation, Tomin proved evasive. When asked why he was fired from the NKVD, Tomin claimed ignorance. In answer to questions about the laboratory, he said, "I know nothing about violations." He told his interrogator repeatedly that he gave no orders to extract confessions through torture. He also denied that Borisov was his subordinate.[111] At his first trial, Tomin said,

> I do not understand my guilt. They say that there was an order to appoint me as head of the group, but I myself did not know about this. . . . I came to Uman with Babich in the capacity of a rank-and-file investigator and had poor relations with Babich.[112]

Tomin believed that he acted exclusively according to orders from above, meaning the regional leadership.[113] In both trials, he claimed that he never gave anyone orders to use physical force in interrogations.[114] He even denied seeing anything criminal in room 21 and insisted that he warned others not to beat the arrested.[115] At the same time—and in seeming contradiction—he stated: "At that time any sort of proper relations to the arrested was considered liberal. They [the region] threatened that one could be sent to the cellar for that."[116] According to Tomin, Reikhman "showed how it was necessary to work."[117]

Tomin also minimized his responsibility at the site of executions. He said that he attended executions only a few times and took nothing from the property of the executed. He allowed others to take things because Sharov had granted permission.[118] In regard to the illegal strip search in Tiraspol, Tomin said, "My mistake was that I did not know the order of searches in the women's section [of the prison]."[119] And he simply did not remember that anyone had died in the prison because of asphyxiation caused by overcrowding.[120] His final words to the court at the second trial may provide partial insight into his mindset. He stated,

I am not a criminal. I always strove to dedicate myself to the cause of the party. I was a volunteer in the Red Army. At 18, I took part in the civil war. In all the years of my stay in the party, I had no reprimands and did not stand to the side of active struggle with the enemies of the party. I never committed violations.[121]

Following this fairly standard autobiographical embellishment, he went on to say,

I could not understand the circumstances of 1937. I did not understand then that what happened was criminal. I did not understand its enemy essence. I considered that all these measures must be directed only against the enemy.[122]

In other words, in all probability, Tomin believed in what he was doing. He accepted the truth of 1937. That may explain the rumors that cropped up during the questioning of witnesses that he had attempted suicide.[123] It may also explain why, at the outset of the final trial, he talked about his difficult physical and mental condition.[124] Yet the behavior he displayed in the Tiraspol prison and at the local hotel where the NKVD congregated revealed an arrogance, disdain, and culture of excess that characterized his actions as much as his work in the laboratory. His confidence was such that he repeatedly appealed his case and, in the end, was released to fight in the war.[125] He lived to petition the procurator, unsuccessfully, for rehabilitation in 1977.[126]

By comparison, Petrov was a minor player, a policeman from the backwaters. In his depositions and testimony at the trials, he made much of the fact that he was just a rank-and-file investigator and semiliterate to boot. He told his interrogator that he "now" understood that there were violations in the system.[127] He blamed the violations, repeatedly, on Tomin and, after much hedging, admitted to beating prisoners in the laboratory to force them to confess.[128] However, he admitted nothing more than partial guilt, saying that he only beat individuals and crippled no one.[129] At the second trial, he said, "They did not give me orders to beat the arrested, but said that I had to give one hundred confessions a day. I reported all the time to Tomin and received instructions only from Tomin."[130]

Petrov captured the essence of the problem of 1937–1938. If confessions were the goal rather than actual proof, then there was no recourse but to beat the prisoners, given the numbers involved and the farcical nature of charges.

In that, Petrov was perhaps honest. Yet he showed no remorse or responsibility. Moreover, one of his colleagues not on trial told the court that Petrov was known as a "celebrated chopper [*kolun*]," something that may very well have appealed to his pride.[131] Petrov succeeded in getting record numbers of confessions. He was, in his own words, an "interrogator of the fists."[132] He also testified to the precise types of torture used on the arrested—noting the euphemistic "thermometer," "going to Hitler," "going to Poland," and so on.[133]

In his last words to the court at the second trial, Petrov said,

> Before you stands a peasant laborer–worker–red guard partisan. I struggled my whole life for the establishment of our country. I personally, at Lenin's grave, swore an oath to fight with the enemies of Soviet power, I am a member of the Communist Party from 1918, [and] have not one reprimand. I came to work not with the aim of profit or looting. I swear to prove myself in labor that this is my last lesson."[134]

Like his colleagues, he used the rhetoric of party loyalty in his last words, but only in his last words with which, clearly, he hoped to score ideologically with the Military Tribunal.

Abramovich did the same. He was the only defendant to go through all three trials. He was first arrested on 6 April 1938 (probably in connection with Uspenskii's initial purge of NKVD cadres) and charged with Article 54-6, 7, 10 of the Ukrainian criminal code for his alleged espionage activity. His interrogator told him, "either confess or [we will turn you into a] piece of meat." His interrogator cursed and beat him, at one point calling him "a red guard scoundrel." At that point, Abramovich said he thought he "had fallen into the hands of fascists." When he told the interrogator that he was dedicated to the "party of Lenin," the interrogator shot back, "we know that you are dedicated to the party of Lenin, but you betrayed the party of Stalin." [135]

Abramovich went on a hunger strike. At that point, the deputy head of the regional NKVD took over his case. Abramovich quit his hunger strike and signed a confession. Soon after this, his case was reclassified to Article 206-17 and, on 2 January 1939, he was sent back to Uman. "I considered that the drama of my life was over, but arriving in Uman a new chapter began." His successor as prison commandant, one Stakhurskii, had thrown his wife and children out of their apartment and moved them into one small room.[136] The NKVD confiscated his property, including his beloved car. He approached the new Uman NKVD boss, Sagalaev, who was also in charge of questioning the Uman suspects. Abramovich said Sagalaev was drunk. Abramovich told him that he would write a formal letter of complaint if he did not get his property back. Sagalaev responded, "Write what you want, to whom you want." Abramovich's complaints were to no avail, and then, on 29 March 1939, Uman investigator Ogorodnik called him in to question him about taking gold teeth from prisoners. "I told him that this is not true, that the teeth—they are from my mouth and you can check that with an expert." On 21 May, he was arrested again. He claimed that the arrest was a result of the "provocations" of Zudin (the chauffeur), Kravchenko, and Neiman.[137]

Abramovich claimed that Sagalaev had forced Zudin, Vereshchuk, and Kravchenko to testify against him. He also claimed that Neiman and Sagalaev were friends and that Sagalaev told Shcherbina, "today we take down Abramovich." Zudin, who initially claimed Abramovich had taken 200 teeth, recanted his testimony in the second two trials, saying that he had never seen Abramovich take teeth but had been pressured by Sagalaev. Sagalaev, of course, denied pressuring anyone. Abramovich accused both Zudin and Sagalaev of coveting his car. His car had been taken on the basis of information that Abramovich had obtained it illegally. In one of his petitions, Abramovich said he had saved from 1933 to buy the car. He explained that some men loved women, but he loved cars. He blamed Zudin, Sagalaev, and another Uman NKVD leader, Vasili Korneevich Kozachenko, for taking his car.[138]

In the meantime, Abramovich admitted to looting the corpses—to an extent. That is, he recited the same story told by Borisov about receiving permission from above. He also insisted, against the testimony of other brigade members, that he shared the money and possessions equally among squad members. He denied that he or other execution members drank before or after executions and vehemently denied removing gold teeth from the mouths of executed prisoners.[139]

There is little doubt that Abramovich was venal. According to Petrov, after Abramovich's arrest, Tomin gave an order to secretly remove all valuables from Abramovich's apartment.[140] It is not possible therefore to resolve definitively the issue of the gold teeth; furthermore, the combination of Jews and gold represented one of the oldest tropes of antisemitic lore. However, the Military Tribunal did not charge the Uman NKVD at the second trial with *maroderstvo* [looting].[141] Nonetheless, there were enough accusations charging Abramovich with taking things—a coat for himself, a coat for his wife—to make the charges ring true. That Abramovich had a casual relation to his work seems clear from his visit to Borisov in a blood-smeared coat, when he said, "that son of a bitch got me dirty."[142] The "son of a bitch" was a person whom

Abramovich had just shot. Even Borisov recognized the "unculturedness" [*nekul'turnost'*] of Abramovich's act. Like Tomin, moreover, Abramovich had a reputation, at least at the town's hotel, for carousing with his NKVD colleagues late into the night and, according to the hotel manager, slapping her in the face.[143] He was also charged with violating the state secrecy law. He contended that he did so only within the walls of the prison.[144] Nevertheless, such a violation suggests a certain degree of confidence in his actions. Finally, it may be relevant to note that a special NKVD report on Abramovich cited an NKVD special inspection from 1935 that suggested Abramovich may have been the son of a trader and had had antisoviet conversations.[145] It is not clear if this kind of compromising material played a role in the charges, but Abramovich's biological sins and perhaps his Jewishness played a role in his first arrest. In the end, Abramovich mostly followed orders, but clearly he played a vital role in the venality and atrocities that occurred in Uman.

The final two defendants were the chauffeur, Zudin, and the interrogator and sometimes grave digger, Shcherbina. Nikolai Pavlovich Zudin was born in Moscow in 1912 to a working-class family. He had a primary school education and spent his early years in the Red Army. From 1934, he served as the Uman NKVD chauffeur. He was a member of the Komsomol, married, and the sole supporter of his mother and two sisters.[146] Zudin was a tireless worker, attending to executions almost every night for two months.[147] He lied in his depositions and at the first trial against Abramovich. He later rescinded his testimony regarding Abramovich and the removal of gold teeth from corpses.[148] Several witnesses remembered Zudin arguing over stolen property.[149] He was charged with taking 200 rubles, five pairs of boots, a leather jacket, and three pairs of underwear from the property of the executed.[150] He said that Abramovich took the best for himself.[151] But, in the grand scheme of things, Zudin was a minor player. The Military Tribunal at the second trial even let him go unpunished, although that would not be repeated in the last trial.[152]

Leonid Semenovich Shcherbina, like Zudin, served as a key witness on the subject of theft at the execution site. He was born into a peasant family in 1901. He was a Communist from 1925 and served in the security police from 1930. He had worked in Uman from June 1937.[153] He was accused of quarreling over looted property from the executed. According to Borisov, Shcherbina was "greedy."[154] Shcherbina also slept with the wife of one of his prisoners.[155] He denied these charges, saying that he was married.[156] He claimed that he took money at the executions for the sole purpose—and on the orders of Abramovich—of buying breakfast for the execution squad. Shcherbina claimed that he had been slandered and maintained his innocence through both trials.[157]

The perpetrators of Uman justified their actions largely by reference to orders from above, meaning for the most part the regional NKVD administration in Kiev. Borisov and Tomin also spoke of the consequences of resisting the region's orders, though it is not clear if they meant that they felt fear or, rather, simply recognized which way the winds were blowing in 1937–1938. The role of the regional NKVD was the smoking gun behind the crimes of Uman, though the court chose to ignore it. Actual motivations for perpetrators' actions can never be ascertained beyond a shadow of a doubt. However, it is more than likely that some or all of the Uman defendants believed in their work, unquestioningly following orders. Petrov may additionally have been flattered by the praise that came his way for the "artistry" of the laboratory. Abramovich, Zudin, and Shcherbina were, beyond a doubt, venal. They expected booty from the executions as fair compensation for what they saw as difficult work. Alcohol likely provided a lubricant, both in the laboratory and at the site of executions. In the end, it is fair to say that the Uman NKVD operated in an atmosphere of amorality, arrogance, and untrammeled power.

THE DEFENDANTS IN the Uman trial were in no way unusual. Indeed, they all hailed from humble backgrounds and were "good family men." They had linked their fate to the Revolution, most of them serving in the Red Army during the Russian civil war and entering the security police soon after. They were children of the Revolution, the civil war, and especially the Cheka. They worked in extraordinary circumstances. Yet, for them, much of what they did in 1937 and 1938 became routine, normalized. The practice of terror was their work, and, within the halls of the NKVD, everyone openly discussed what the Soviet state demanded to be kept strictly secret. Violence was their general frame of reference, and the mass operation was their specific field of play.[158] Although terror came from above and, in operational terms, was structured by the regional NKVD, the Uman NKVD were not simply good soldiers. The (im)moral economy of the execution site combined with a laboratory of torture in which lies, euphemisms, and quotas shaped people's fates. On top of that, the sheer overload of work, the constant turnover of personnel, and the motley crew of mobilized workers, including chauffeurs, prison guards, and NKVD couriers, made for a volatile situation. Violence spilled over into the town with rowdy NKVD officers at the local hotel and the clothes of executed prisoners appearing in the bazaar or on the backs of the executioners. In *Golden Harvest,* Jan Tomasz Gross and Irena Grudzinska Gross argue, in reference to the Holocaust in Poland, that "perpetrators were not simply cogs in a machine operating according to preordained rules."[159] In Uman, the perpetrators were also "not simply cogs," but, rather, worked within a larger culture of NKVD violence shaped by war, revolution, and terror that facilitated, permitted, and sanctioned a wide range of criminal activity performed by an equally wide range of individual actors.

An Excursion to Zaporozh'e

Without any exaggeration, I can say that there was not one interrogator who "honestly"
wrote up interrogation records.
—S. A. FRISHKO, *NKVD operative in Zaporozh'e*

ON 8 JULY 1938, V. R. Grabar', a senior official from the Ukrainian republican
NKVD in Kiev, arrived in the industrial city of Zaporozh'e. He led what was
later labeled in the investigative files an assault or storm brigade, replete with
a forced change of leadership for the Zaporozh'e city NKVD and orders from
Uspenskii to arrest 1,000 people. Later, under interrogation, Grabar' said that
some time in June or July 1938, Uspenskii had summoned all regional NKVD
bosses and a series of other NKVD officers to his office in Kiev. He informed
his audience that the Politburo had decided to purge all industrial cities of
antisoviet elements. Uspenskii then sent Grabar' to Zaporozh'e, where, he
said, "spies walked around under the windows" of the city NKVD.[1]

In a few short days of terror, or so it was later claimed, the Zaporozh'e
NKVD was turned on its head. The prison commandant, G. Ia. Dorov,
sometimes called Dorov-Piontashko in the files, claimed that as many as
4,000 prisoners were held in Zaporozh'e in the months between June and
September 1938. The prison was dangerously overcrowded. Cells designed for
four people held anywhere from 30 to 70 people (depending on the source),
while no fewer than 100 prisoners were left in the confined NKVD courtyard for lack of space.[2] According to later reports, confessions were invented
and interrogation protocols were compiled prior to actual interrogations. If
prisoners initially refused to sign the fabricated interrogation protocols and
confessions, they were forced to endure prolonged standing; they were beaten
with a rubber truncheon cut especially for the purpose; or they were encaged
in a tiny airless cell (cell number 8) in the prison's dank cellars.[3] Prisoners
condemned to death were beaten and robbed, their clothes taken to sell at the
local bazaar.[4]

Grabar' was later executed for, among other charges, his part in the Zaporozh'e terror. The newly appointed head of the Zaporozh'e NKVD, Boldin, was arrested in March 1939, but by December 1939, he was declared unfit to stand trial and moved to a psychiatric hospital.[5] Two of his assistants, both heads of sectors, and the prison commandant were arrested at about the same time as their boss and tried in April 1940 for violations of socialist legality.[6]

On the face of it, the Zaporozh'e case bears certain similarities to the case in Uman. Both cases had multiple defendants, including interrogators and the prison commandant; both cases featured a series of violations of socialist legality that encompassed arrests, fabricated cases, torture, and looting at the execution site. Yet the Zaporozh'e case also differed in several fundamental ways. First, Grabar' was accused of playing an outsized role in this case, far exceeding in documentary evidence the role of *gastrolery* in Uman. Second, Zaporozh'e was an important industrial city, making the factory a key site for perpetrators and victims alike. Third, the Zaporozh'e case featured a series of letters sent by an NKVD operative named Frishko. Although these kinds of signals to authorities arrived in Moscow and Kiev in the tens of thousands from everywhere, several key complaints, usually from NKVD cadres or newly released "enemies" from the local elite, were often employed to build cases against NKVD operatives at this time, thus suggesting officially the presence of "honorable" Chekist whistleblowers and martyred Communists coming to the aid of Moscow.[7] Finally, a large part of this case concerned the implementation of the national operations against non-Russian nationalities, an operation, like the purge of industrial cities, with a looming deadline of 1 August 1938.[8]

ZAPOROZH'E SITS ASTRIDE the Dnepr River, some 500 kilometers southeast of Kiev. Home to the Zaporozhian Cossacks from the 1600s to the 1800s and German Mennonite farmers invited to Russia by Catherine the Great in the late eighteenth century, the town, called Aleksandrovsk to 1921, was the site of fierce fighting during the civil war. Starting with the First Five-Year Plan (1928–1932) and through the 1930s, the town of Zaporozh'e developed into a multiethnic city with a population of a quarter of a million people. Its demographic and economic growth was fueled by industrialization and, in particular, the construction of the massive hydroelectric dam, Dneprostroi, just north of the city. At the time of the Great Terror, Zaporozh'e was administratively part of Dnepropetrovsk region.[9]

The Chekists of Dnepropetrovsk region were far from inactive in 1937. They arrested over 17,000 people in a region with a population of 3,721,228, with Ukrainians accounting for some 47% of arrests, Germans 21.5%, and Poles 17.7%.[10] Still, Uspenskii was not satisfied and, under the time pressure of the 1 August 1938 deadline for concluding the national operations and the purge of industrial cities, he insisted on thousands more arrests.[11] P. A. Korkin, the head of the Dnepropetrovsk regional NKVD at this time, admitted to his colleagues at a meeting of his NKVD's party collective on 9–10 January 1939, on the eve of his own arrest, that there had been massive violations in the region in July 1938, particularly in Zaporozh'e, Krivoi Rog, Dneprodzerzhinsk, and Nikopol.[12] By this time, the Ukrainian republican NKVD Investigation Unit had begun its work, under the supervision of the party, resulting in a series of arrests of NKVD officials in these cities in March and April 1939.[13]

According to the indictment signed by the Investigation Unit and sent to Beriia's man Kobulov on 5 July 1939, the leadership of the Zaporozh'e NKVD was charged with "carrying out criminal practices in operational–investigative work, carrying out mass arrests, crudely violating revolutionary legality, and, by way of illegal methods of investigation, creating artificial counterrevolutionary formations." The indicted included Boris Pavlovich Boldin, the head of the Zaporozh'e NKVD; David Iakovlevich Klibanov, the head of the Fourth Sector in charge of cases against supposed Ukrainian nationalists, Zionists, Socialist Revolutionaries, Mensheviks, and former Red Partisans before the last category was transferred to the Third Sector; Boris L'vovich Linetskii, the head of the Third Sector in charge of national operations, among other tasks; and prison commandant Dorov. In all, the NKVD in Zaporozh'e had created operative lists for the arrest of some 882 people. Among those listed were some already on file as individuals under watch [*na uchete*] as well as those with a "social past," referring to past misdeeds or problematic social origins, and national minorities with no compromising materials whatsoever. Dorov was accused of participating directly in the beating of prisoners and the pillaging of corpses.[14]

The indictment claimed that it was the colleagues of the Zaporozh'e NKVD leaders who had "unmasked" their criminal activities. Particularly prominent among the unmaskers was S. A. Frishko, who had been the head of the Vasil'evsk District NKVD office and was mobilized to serve in the Zaporozh'e NKVD in July 1938 at the height of the terror. On 11 August 1938, he wrote a report to Ezhov, accusing the Zaporozh'e NKVD of wholesale falsification and torture. He told Ezhov that about 400 people were arrested in the city between 15 July and 1 August 1938. He charged that these arrests were based on lists prepared by the city's factory special departments and party secretaries. Those under arrest were divided into groups and assigned to an NKVD operative plenipotentiary who was assisted by two to three students or specially mobilized cadres (like Frishko). Each group was assigned a leader of what were invariably labeled spy organizations, numbering from ten to twenty people. The investigators then built up a criminal file according to diagrams of who recruited whom in the spy organization.[15] Once that was accomplished, the investigators created the interrogation records that prisoners subsequently were forced to sign. In the event of refusals to sign and with the sanction of Boldin, Dorov would be called in to beat the accused into guilty submission; in other cases, prisoners were placed in the death trap of cell number 8 to stew in the July heat until they were ready to confess.

Frishko also wrote to Ezhov about the surreal face-to-face encounters, in which prisoners were forced to incriminate other prisoners whom they did not even know. Interrogators, meanwhile, were pressed to turn in five to six signed confessions per day. These procedures led to absurd results. In one case concerning a group of fifty supposed spies arrested as members of the POV (Polish Military Organization), most of whom incidentally were Ukrainian, the spies were accused of publicizing the location of a well-known factory. Frishko wrote that among the arrested, there were many people "from groups socially near to us, absolutely not connected to spies." Poor peasants under arrest were labeled *kulaks*, and most cases were built on completely fabricated evidence.

Frishko claimed in his letter to Ezhov that he had attempted to question these methods with the deputy head of the Third Sector, but was made to understand that he should remain silent. Frishko told Ezhov that he had thought long and hard before making the decision to write his report, admitting that perhaps he was wrong to write. Significantly, he wrote that while innocent people sat in prison, "real enemies" remained at liberty, something that would not be repeated in his later communications. Frishko concluded by saying that "without any exaggeration, I can say that there was not one interrogator who 'honestly' wrote up interrogation records."[16]

Unsurprisingly, Frishko received no response from Ezhov, who, by this time, feared his own demise.[17] Frishko then made the decision—or possibly was influenced to make the decision—to write to Ukrainian Communist Party First Secretary Khrushchev in a letter dated 26 November 1938. In this letter, Frishko was far more political, noting the activities of Korkin and Uspenskii at operational meetings in Dnepropetrovsk and Zaporozh'e. He also told Khrushchev that he had been transferred to lead the Gorodokskii

District NKVD in Kamenets-Podol'sk region. Given that he had sent his letter to Ezhov by way of the special NKVD courier, it is possible that others had read his letter and ordered the transfer, thus providing an additional unspoken motive for his complaint. At the same time, it is significant that this letter was dated just nine days after the all-important 17 November 1938 directive bringing a halt to the mass operations.[18]

At the end of January, Ukrainian republican NKVD officer G. I. Tverdokhlebenko, who appears to have led the investigations into the Zaporozh'e NKVD's activities, questioned Frishko three times. In his depositions, Frishko went into greater detail and, for the first time, mentioned Grabar'. Frishko talked at length about the participation of factory special departments and party secretaries in the composition of arrest lists. He mentioned one factory special department member who was not in the NKVD, who engaged not just in the compilation of arrest lists but in the actual interrogation of prisoners too. He said that both Korkin and the city procurator sanctioned the arrests of everyone listed. Along the lines of his earlier letter, Frishko said that following arrest, the interrogators divided the arrested—numbering, he claimed now, over 800 people—into groups based either on their place of work, in the case of factory employees, or district, in the case of collective farmers. Again, Frishko told of how interrogators invented, in advance of interrogations, charts of counterrevolutionary organizations and interrogation protocols. Thick rubber truncheons were used to elicit false confessions as well as assignment to cell number 8, which generally took no more than a day to "persuade" prisoners to confess. Frishko told Tverdokhlebenko that many of the arrested were misclassified; one supposed member of the Jewish Bund, for example, had no idea what the Bund was. Others gave absurd testimony. One prisoner revealed "spy information" that he had read in the newspaper; another reported on supposed special shops in a factory not his own; and one collective farmer denounced his collective farm brigadier for supposedly recruiting the stable man to find out the exact number of horses in the collective farm. Frishko claimed that other NKVD workers were also troubled by what they were witnessing but were too afraid to speak. Finally, he charged Boldin with relentlessly forcing the pace of interrogations and sanctioning beatings (along with Linetskii), and said that Grabar' himself led mass beatings.[19]

Frishko was also an important witness at the April 1940 trial, where he offered even more detailed testimony, naming perpetrators and victims and specific instances of wrongdoing. Frishko told of interrogating one prisoner who confessed to recruiting nearly all of Zaporozh'e. When Frishko reported this to Boldin, the latter said, "List them—they are all enemies." According to Frishko, Boldin insisted that all the arrested be charged with espionage.[20]

As the case evolved, other NKVD workers, themselves complicit in all probability, came forth or were summoned to testify. Whether by chance or by design, however, Frishko was the star witness. Frishko was a signaler, in this case something like a whistleblower from within the NKVD. He was not alone; many other criminal cases against NKVD operatives at this time involved signals from NKVD workers or from victims. It seems clear that these types of signals were actively employed and manipulated by higher authorities in Kiev and Moscow to serve their purposes in bringing the mass operations to an end and, in some cases, limiting the consequent damage to the NKVD by targeting blame on a "few bad apples."[21] At the same time that higher authorities were exploiting the signals, it is also clear beyond any doubt that literally tens of thousands of signals were arriving in Kiev and Moscow every day from people in all walks of life, appalled by what they heard or saw or attempting to save a relative's life. These signals had to have alarmed the center, especially when they came from industrial cities.

Frishko's testimony demonstrated that the higher authorities were drawing lines of guilt from Boldin, Klibanov, Linetskii, and Dorov to Korkin and Uspenskii, with Grabar' acting as pivot. Although it seems clear that many violations of socialist legality were firmly in place before Grabar' stepped foot in Zaporozh'e, including the existence of cell number 8 and the disposal of over 100 corpses from spring 1938 executions in a cesspool in the courtyard of the NKVD building, it is nevertheless instructive to examine the testimony of other eyewitnesses who detailed the activities of Grabar' and his brigade in July 1938.[22]

NEITHER THE NKVD indictment of 5 July 1939 nor Frishko's original letters mentioned Grabar's role in Zaporozh'e.[23] Yet increasingly as the case developed, Grabar' became the *eminence grise* of the Zaporozh'e terror. Grabar' made a huge impression in Zaporozh'e, and everyone in the NKVD there talked about him. The testimony of two Zaporozh'e NKVD operatives provides a starting place for Grabar's earliest steps there. Both were victims of Grabar's purge of the Zaporozh'e NKVD and therefore beyond a shadow of a doubt prejudiced against him. The first of these two witnesses, Mikhail Grigor'evich Babasev, was deputy head of the Zaporozh'e NKVD from May 1938, having worked earlier in the Second Department of the Dnepropetrovsk regional NKVD. He recalled Grabar' and his entourage arriving in Zaporozh'e on 8 July to prepare for an upcoming visit by Uspenskii and Korkin. Almost immediately, according to Babasev, Grabar' clashed with Vol'skii-Gitler, then the head of the Zaporozh'e NKVD. The issue was whether the NKVD should retain its prisoners locally after arrest or send them on to the regional NKVD in Dnepropetrovsk. Vol'skii wanted to send them on, perhaps according to the justification noted by Boldin[24] that the city NKVD did not have the right to make arrests or perhaps because of the very limited space in the prison. Grabar' was furious, screamed at Vol'skii that this was his "thing" and that things would end badly for him, a less-than-veiled threat. He then stormed out of Vol'skii's office, declaring that he would telephone Uspenskii in Kiev. Ten minutes later, he returned, said that Uspenskii had already left Kiev for Nikolaev, but that Uspenskii's assistant ordered him to hold the prisoners in place until Uspenskii arrived. Vol'skii countered by calling the deputy head of the regional NKVD in Dnepropetrovsk, who backed Vol'skii and ordered the arrested to be sent on to Dnepropetrovsk.[25]

In the midst of this battle of the wills, Babasev, along with Grabar' and other Zaporozh'e NKVD operatives, left for Dnepropetrovsk to attend an NKVD operational meeting that featured the Ukrainian NKVD commissar himself. Babasev remembered that Uspenskii harshly criticized the regional NKVD for its "liberalism" at the meeting. The next day, Uspenskii threw out the old leadership of the Zaporozh'e NKVD, installing in its place Boldin and a new deputy to take Babasev's place. Babasev was flummoxed. He asked Uspenskii what he should do, where he should go. Uspenskii rudely told Babasev to travel with him and the new Zaporozh'e leaders "to show the way" in the lead car. At a roadside stop along the way, Babasev again attempted to learn his fate and approached Uspenskii. According to Babasev, "The Narkom [commissar] answered me angrily, I didn't understand what exactly he said, and [he] left for his car." Arriving in Zaporozh'e, Uspenskii immediately called an operational meeting of the city's NKVD that lasted about thirty to forty minutes. Uspenskii demanded more arrests. Babasev claimed that he "tried to explain to him that we carried out arrests on the basis of carefully checked data and that in the last two months, the city NKVD had uncovered no less than ten to twelve counterrevolutionary organizations deserving serious attention." Regardless of whether Babasev actually said this, he claimed next that Uspenskii interrupted him, told him to shut up and leave. Uspenskii himself left soon after to continue his murderous rounds through the region.[26]

With Uspenskii's departure and the appointment of the new leaders, Babasev said that he was at his wit's end. He approached the Komsomol secretary, Slepovyi, for advice; Slepovyi suggested that he write to Stalin. Ostensibly fearing that Uspenskii's sanction and Grabar's orders to use physical methods of pressure would lead to the creation of fictional cases, but more likely in mortal fear for himself, Babasev wrote to Stalin on 13 July to tell him about Uspenskii's operational meeting and his decision to carry out arrests "to the last particle [*pod metelku*]." In the midst of writing his letter, Grabar' barged into his office and ordered him to travel to the German colony (village) with the new deputy head of the Zaporozh'e NKVD. Babasev departed, leaving his unfinished letter in a desk drawer. When he returned to his office later that day, the letter was gone. He was arrested soon after and sent by special convoy to Kiev. In Kiev, Babasev was tortured; after losing consciousness several times, along with three teeth, during the beatings, Babasev signed a false confession.[27]

Konstantin Alekseevich Brikker was the second witness in the Zaporozh'e NKVD to recall the visit of Grabar'. Brikker had worked in the republican NKVD Cadre Department until January 1938, when he was detailed to work in the NKVD Third Sector in Zaporozh'e. He recalled Grabar's arrival on 8 July. At that time, Linetskii called him into his office and told him that Grabar' had ordered the Third Sector to carry out 300 arrests by the time of Uspenskii's arrival on 12 July. When Brikker had assembled and presented to Linetskii a list of 100 or so people to be arrested, Linetskii told him that he needed 300 people, not 100 people, and that there could be no conversation about "the absence of material"—that is, what passed for evidence. Linetskii then told Brikker that if he failed to find 300 people, it would be up to him, Brikker, to explain why to Grabar'. Brikker managed to add another 30 people to the list on the basis of no more than anonymous denunciations. Some time later, Grabar' demanded to see the personnel files of Zaporozh'e's secret informers. Linetskii made clear to Brikker that Grabar' would arrest any secret informer whose file came his way. Brikker claimed that he then hid a number of files of "good informers" before conveying the remainder to Grabar'. He never found out who from the files was arrested, as he himself was arrested on 14 July.[28]

Brikker believed that he was arrested on orders from Uspenskii based on Grabar's request. When Uspenskii held his operational meeting in Zaporozh'e on 12 July, he told all assembled that there were secondhand traders (*barakhol'shchiki*, a likely euphemism for Jews) in the Zaporozh'e NKVD. He also said, strangely, that he would forgive anyone who had committed a crime among them. Brikker said that everyone remained silent. Uspenskii then turned to Grabar' and said, "name me a *barakhol'shchik*." Grabar' became uncharacteristically flustered and said something to the effect that he would check the files. Uspenskii then turned to Vol'skii with the same demand.

Vol'skii named Brikker. Nonetheless, Brikker blamed Grabar' for his four months in prison.[29]

Although both Babasev and Brikker clearly blamed Grabar' for their troubles and the upsurge in terror in Zaporozh'e, still they were perhaps not in the best position to testify, given their arrests in the midst of Grabar's visit and their justified prejudice. Boldin, the new head of the Zaporozh'e NKVD, was in a better position to offer information on Grabar's visit prior to his departure from Zaporozh'e on 15 July. Unfortunately, he was not much less prejudiced than Babasev and Brikker, and he had a lot more at stake in parrying the blame onto Grabar'.

The newly installed head of the Zaporozh'e NKVD, Boldin, pointed the finger directly at Grabar' in a series of interrogations that continued from February to June 1939. Before his appointment in Zaporozh'e, Boldin (born 1906 in Tambov) worked as head of the First Sector of the Fourth Department in the Dnepropetrovsk regional NKVD. He had worked earlier in the Voronezh regional NKVD, when Korkin served as its head.[30] At the Zaporozh'e NKVD party meeting of 9–10 February 1939, Boldin was labeled "Korkin's tail," meaning he had come to Dnepropetrovsk with Korkin as part of his clientele network.[31] This connection did not bode well, given that Korkin was closely associated with Uspenskii in the accusations that came down from above. Boldin would strenuously deny that he had any relation to Korkin other than professional, only admitting that their wives socialized.[32] Nevertheless, the die was cast, and Boldin was officially Korkin's tail.

Boldin detailed for his interrogators his appointment to Zaporozh'e as well as Grabar's activities there. His observations, unlike those of Babasev and Brikker, begin only on 12 July, when he received his new appointment and traveled, along with Uspenskii and others, to Zaporozh'e. Still in Dnepropetrovsk, he, along with a series of other colleagues, had been called in, one by one, to Korkin's office. Once there, in the presence of Uspenskii, they all received new appointments to various NKVD branches in the industrial cities of the Dnepropetrovsk region. Boldin claimed—like many other new NKVD appointees—that he initially refused the appointment, only to be pressured into accepting it by Korkin and Uspenskii.[33] At the same time, Boldin met his new assistant, Nasonov, an experienced NKVD operative, who would replace Babasev.[34]

Boldin reluctantly admitted his guilt during interrogations, limiting it to overall responsibility for the actions of the Zaporozh'e NKVD by reason of his position at its helm. Whenever possible, he shifted blame to those he had "trusted"—his assistant, Nasonov, Linetskii, Klibanov, and, most of all,

Grabar'. He told his interrogator that "we," meaning either the Zaporozh'e NKVD as a whole or himself in royal mode, "were victims of a hostile provocation which was presented in the name of the party. Now it is clear," he continued, "that all those mass arrests, troikas, and so on have brought me to the bar [of justice]." He charged Uspenskii, Korkin, and Grabar' with using him for their own purposes, saying, "we blindly believed and thought that we were doing the right thing." Not only did he strenuously refuse to say he was an enemy, he insisted that even if they took his party card, his convictions would remain steadfast.[35]

Boldin reserved his main ire for Grabar', whom he called "Uspenskii's stooge." He claimed that Grabar' knew about Uspenskii's orders to arrest 1,000 people in Zaporozh'e before the latter's arrival. Grabar', he continued, had set in place the July terror before Boldin even arrived in the city. Boldin argued that he assumed the actual leadership of the Zaporozh'e NKVD only on 15 July, not coincidentally the day of Grabar's departure.[36] According to Boldin, it was Grabar' who gave the order to use torture on prisoners to extract confessions. Grabar' cultivated torture, Boldin said, walking around to each interrogator's office and teaching by example. Grabar' was even responsible for the introduction of rubber truncheons, a much-dreaded tool of physical influence.[37] All in all, according to Boldin, Grabar' played the most decisive role in the criminal approach to investigations by the city NKVD and repeatedly boasted of his close relation to Uspenskii.[38]

Grabar's primary goal, according to Boldin, was to create large-scale espionage cases, combining as many individual cases as possible. Further, Grabar' divided up prisoners according to enemy classifications in a completely random manner. Naturally, Boldin said, there were innocent people among the arrested. Between 12 and 14 July, Grabar' arrested 500 people and prepared to arrest another 400. Among Grabar's big cases was one that he created with Linetskii through the Third Sector in charge of national operations. This case featured a so-called German fascist organization of some 260 to 280 people. Grabar' insisted on his interrogators eking out at least eight to ten confessions a day. After Grabar' left, the regional NKVD continued to pour on the pressure, with endless, badgering telephone calls demanding numbers.[39]

Grabar' worked primarily through the Zaporozh'e NKVD's Third and Fourth Sectors, led, respectively, by Linetskii and Klibanov. The Third Sector was particularly active in July, given the looming deadline of the national operations on 1 August 1938. According to Boldin, Linetskii coordinated his work with Iakov Vladimirovich Umanskii, who led the Third

Department at the regional NKVD.[40] Boldin said that it was Grabar' who gave the orders for Zaporozh'e NKVD operatives to go out to a series of industrial enterprises to compile arrest lists. At the enterprises, the NKVD operatives worked through the factory special departments and the secretaries of factory party and union committees, demanding that the latter provide the names of anyone with compromising materials. None of this material was subsequently checked, according to Boldin, who claimed to have blindly believed experienced operatives like Nasonov and Linetskii.[41] Boldin said that he believed that the German operation was real, but had doubts about other cases.[42]

On 23 April 1939, Boldin had a face-to-face confrontation with Grabar' in prison. Although Grabar' readily admitted to much of what Boldin charged, they sparred over exact numbers of arrests and over whether Grabar's classification of enemies was falsified. Grabar' also denied cultivating torture, telling the interrogator that Uspenskii gave the order to beat. Grabar' denied several other specific charges, including the decision to use rubber truncheons, which, he claimed, he had told Boldin were in use only in Kiev, rather than ordering him to use them in Zaporozh'e.[43]

In the end, Boldin's partial admission of guilt and his attempts to shift blame to Grabar' and some of his subordinates became redundant. Whether because of a preexisting condition or the months of interrogation, Boldin left the prison for the Pavlov psychiatric hospital, where he was treated in the forensic sector for three months, after which an expert commission declared that Boldin must submit to further psychiatric treatment. On 29 December 1939, his case was removed from the larger case, to be dealt with separately. He was never tried, though, because he died in the psychiatric hospital on 26 January 1942 in German-occupied Kiev.[44] It is likely that Boldin himself was tortured; but, whatever the case may be, his testimony served its purpose in placing blame on Grabar'.

Boldin's would-be fellow defendants would also seek to finger Grabar', as would several other key NKVD witnesses at the trial.[45] Yet the Zaporozh'e NKVD party organization centered its condemnation on Boldin and Linetskii (who also served as party secretary), with Grabar' and his brigade serving merely as background noise in their deliberations. Although there is little doubt that Grabar' was a major player in the Zaporozh'e case, he was far from the only actor to play an important role. Therefore it makes sense at this point to move away from Grabar' and explore the testimony of other witnesses—both perpetrators and victims—regarding the mass operations in Zaporozh'e in July 1938.

THE PRIMARY SITE of mass operations in Zaporozh'e in July 1938 was the city's industrial enterprises. Moscow and Kiev pressed hard for the completion of the purge of industrial cities and the national operations by 1 August. According to the criminal case against the Zaporozh'e NKVD leadership, stepped-up operations began with Grabar's arrival. Working through Linetskii's Third Sector, especially with Linetskii's deputy, Grigorii God'evich Zalevskii, Grabar' and Rovinskii (the brigade member seconded to Zaporozh'e's Third Sector) sent NKVD operatives out in the middle of the night to the city's factories to compile arrest lists.[46] The NKVD operatives worked through the factories' special departments and hiring and firing departments [otdel naima i uvol'neniia or ONU), along with the factories' party and trade union organizations to collect compromising materials on industrial workers and specialists at various enterprises (in much the same way that the NKVD worked, on the district level in rural areas, with rural soviets). Both the special departments and the ONU in the factories were subject to the dual jurisdiction of the NKVD and the factory administration. An NKVD operative typically served as deputy head of these entities.[47]

In the course of mass operations, the NKVD and the factory administration clashed over the damaging loss of skilled workers and specialists in this time of high worker turnover and deficits of skilled personnel. The precise degree of conflict, if and when it existed, is not clear, but was surely muted given the dangers involved in opposing the NKVD. Some, but not all, of these conflicts came to light in Zaporozh'e only after the 17 November 1938 rollback of mass operations. There were some exceptions, however, that suggest a possible troubling social reaction to the terror.

All was not well at the Baronov Defence Factory No. 29. Pavel Vasilevich Filonenko was the secretary of one of the primary party cells of the factory and, after the purge of the Zaporozh'e NKVD, he became the factory's deputy director. In his trial testimony, he recalled that, "once in the night in the summer of 1938, I was summoned to the factory. Simultaneously, all secretaries of the factory's party organizations and members of the party were also called. When we had all assembled, the NKVD worker, Zalevskii, suggested to all of us to provide certificates [spravki] on individuals with compromising materials [in their biographies]. After this, a part of the certificates were compiled into one list, in which Zalevskii suggested to make a political analysis for each individual 'suspected of espionage' or 'suspected of sabotage,' etc. Without completing this work, Zalevskii left in the morning for the NKVD [office], taking with him the list and part of the certificates with individuals not named on the list." Filonenko continued: "There were over 50 people on the list. The majority of them were Communists, the activists among the workers, the leading cadres. Zalevskii had us write *kharakteristiki* [sociopolitical profiles of those] on the list, [and] we all sat and wrote these. There were cases when Zalevskii forced us to rewrite these with more strongly negative characteristics." He claimed that the party secretaries provided compromising material for only three to four people, but that Zalevskii demanded 50 people.[48]

Zakhar Abramovich Semin took up the story from there. Semin worked at the Baronov Factory from November 1937 to September 1939 as a Central Committee party organizer. By the time of the trial in April 1940, he was working in Moscow. In his testimony, he told the court: "In July 1938, I left on a trip to the CC [Central Committee] of the [Communist Party] in Moscow. When I returned, they told me that on the directive of Linetskii from the city [NKVD] office, a list was compiled with 50 to 55 people—workers and engineering–technical staff with compromising materials. I went to Linetskii and asked how this could be. Linetskii answered, 'Keep the list to yourself, you will receive a directive. . . .' The list included the majority of leading workers at the factory. The list was unsigned, but in it all individuals were classified as 'suspected of espionage,' etc. Who had classified them in this way was not established, but a part of the people on the list represented the factory activists, for which we had no compromising materials. I reported this to com[rade] Khrushchev in the presence of the former head of the city NKVD, Boldin. The latter said that this would not happen again and that the material had been compiled in this manner by an inexperienced operative plenipotentiary, Zalevskii—one of Linetskii's workers."[49]

Several NKVD documents from the spring of 1938, including a series of denunciations, surfaced for use at the time of the trial. One such document referred to Semin's purported complaint at a meeting of the factory's ONU about "NKVD interference in factory matters."[50] It seems that at the meeting there was discussion and acrimony about the NKVD's role in hiring and firing. Semin said that "it was necessary to explain the reasons for firing people." The author of the document volunteered that the NKVD had to sanction each new worker hired. This was the reason, reportedly, for Semin's objection to the NKVD's interference. Another report claimed that Semin's "antiparty behavior was leading to discontent [*nedovol'stvo*] among party and nonparty workers." The author of this report then attempted to sully Semin's reputation further by referring to the existence of an off-the-books petty cash fund [*chernaia kassa*] containing some 8,000 rubles which, he claimed, Semin used illegally.[51]

At a 7 July 1938 meeting of the factory's party committee, the director of the Baronov No. 29 Factory, Chernyshev, said the factory's ONU was subject to "dual control." He and others aimed their ire at one Bogdanov, the deputy director of ONU and an NKVD operative.[52] The meeting then produced a directive in which it charged Bogdanov with nepotism in hiring, as well as with groundlessly firing several Communist and Komsomol workers. Issues of corruption and access to deficit goods were also broached. Perhaps most interestingly, the directive enlisted Semin to travel to Moscow to inform Stalin and Ezhov about conditions in the factory.[53]

The Zaporozh'e criminal file also contains a number of denunciations penned by Bogdanov. He wrote about overheard conversations in which Semin purportedly said, in relation to the transfers of party members from town to town, that "it was worse than under serfdom." Another report charged Semin and factory director Chernyshev with interfering in and breaking the purge of the factory's antisoviet and socially foreign elements, claiming that Semin interceded for individual workers and "systematically led antisoviet conversations."[54] All of these reports would lead Boldin and Linetskii, on 2 September 1938, to order "an all-sided check [*proverka*] of Semin" and the gathering of compromising material on him.[55] On the same day, 2 September, Bogdanov penned another denunciation against Chernyshev, complaining of "anarchy" and accidents in the factory.[56] On 6 September, Boldin signed a report on the factory, pointing to Semin's rows [*skloki*], his "hostile politics," and "the spread of unhealthy moods among the factory's workers."[57] On 8 October, Boldin wrote up another report on the factory, accusing its leadership (Chernyshev and Semin) of not fulfilling production plans, breakages, poor living conditions for workers, and so on.[58] Other denunciations of Semin and Chernyshev followed.[59]

Later, during the interrogations of Boldin, it became clear that Semin had complained to him directly about the activities of Zalevskii, who had demanded lists of supposedly compromised workers. Boldin claimed that no one had been arrested from these lists and that he had removed Zalevskii from "servicing" the factory.[60] Whatever the case may be, Zalevskii's actions were not an exception, as is apparent from the testimony of another factory representative, Leonid Iur'evich Mikhailov.

Mikhailov was a Communist Party member and the head of the secret department at the Kommunar Factory. At the trial of the Zaporozh'e NKVD leaders, he testified that "Once in July 1938, the NKVD operative plenipotentiary, Lavrienko, summoned me in the night and asked for a list of people with compromising materials [on them]. According to existing data, I compiled a list of 25 people and gave it to Lavrienko who declared that this was too few and that on Linetskii's order it was necessary to enlarge [the list]. Then with the help of the secretaries of the primary party cells, I compiled a list of 100 people." Linetskii then insisted that he write on the list next to each name accusations of sabotage or espionage. He remembered that they accused a certain Kaizer of espionage simply because he was seen going into an Intourist hotel for foreigners.[61]

At least two Kommunar workers who were on that list survived arrest to testify at the trial. Both were released from prison, one in February and the other in May 1939. Daniil Emel'ianovich Varakuta had worked at the factory as a foreman from 1921. He refused to confess to fabricated charges twice, until Dorov was called in to beat him. After being tortured with the rubber truncheon, he signed the confession.[62] Vasilii Semenovich Shugai, a Communist and a worker at Kommunar since 1908, experienced cell number 8. He also refused to sign a confession of having had some sort of "diversionary intentions" until he was beaten.[63] Other workers testified as well at the trial, telling of beatings by Boldin, Klibanov, and others.[64]

What is perhaps most interesting about these cases is the suggestion of discontent at the factories. The NKVD not only interfered with hiring and firing processes and took away skilled workers and specialists, but it also mobilized seven typists, all women, from the factories to type up interrogations at the NKVD offices.[65] At the Zaporozh'e NKVD party meeting in February 1939, speakers talked about how the hostile activity of the NKVD had called forth "discontent among the masses" [*nedovol'stvo v massakh*].[66] Others hinted that the existence of cell number 8 was "legendary," thereby suggesting that people talked.[67] To make matters worse, the clothes of executed prisoners were turning up, as elsewhere, at local markets.[68]

Although most, but not all, of the NKVD's "harmful activities" occurred in July 1938, there was scant reference to Grabar' by these witnesses. Of course, this was likely because Grabar' remained safely ensconced in the Zaporozh'e NKVD office and was not seen by most victims. Nonetheless, victims and perpetrators alike talked more about the role of Boldin, Linetskii, Klibanov, Dorov, and other local NKVD workers when they recalled the terrible months of terror in Zaporozh'e.

WORK ON THE mass operations in the factories and nearby villages of Zaporozh'e continued within the confines of the Zaporozh'e NKVD building. Although Grabar' never quite leaves the larger picture in July 1938, victims and NKVD operatives alike made serious charges against the key defendants. Among the most serious charges were the falsification of cases, forced confessions, and criminal activities at the site of execution.

The Zaporozh'e NKVD leadership was charged with, among other violations, "the creation of artificial counterrevolutionary formations" "by way of illegal methods of investigation."[69] Ezhov and Uspenskii had initiated this approach as early as February 1938 at the time of Ezhov's visit to Kiev.[70] Grabar' came to Zaporozh'e with the mandate to uncover these formations. The creation of large counterrevolutionary organizations was naturally impressive in the minds of higher NKVD leaders, reflecting both the immense danger of the enemy and the urgent and essential work of the NKVD. These cases, however, were also naturally contrived. Although there is little doubt that former SRs, Mensheviks, Bundists, and Zionists continued to exist and that many different ethnicities were represented in Ukraine, especially at its borders, there is no evidence that any of these groups constituted a real danger. They were simply part of the imaginary, perhaps potential, and definitely feared Fifth Column that both Stalin and Ezhov fought to suppress in the dangerous international environment of the second half of the 1930s.

NKVD operatives in Zaporozh'e testified to the existence of detailed charts and diagrams that displayed the geographical hierarchies among and/or interconnectedness of counterrevolutionary formations in the city and nearby countryside. Efim Donovich Gorodetskii, who worked in investigations in the Zaporozh'e city NKVD for twelve days in July 1938, testified that, in the presence of Linetskii, Boldin's assistant Nasonov drew a diagram outlining the connections between arrested counterrevolutionaries from the region to the district and village levels.[71] Ivan Trofimovich Afanas'ev, another Zaporozh'e NKVD operative, claimed to have seen one such diagram on Linetskii's desk in August 1938.[72] Zaporozh'e NKVD operative Zalevskii also testified to the existence of such diagrams, saying that they came either from Iosif Moiseevich Gendel'man, who worked in the Third Sector, or Linetskii.[73] Gendel'man later denied any knowledge of such diagrams.[74]

The diagrams were deadly, leading to grave accusations of guilt and resulting in entirely fictitious charges against countless people. Daniil Platonovich Platonov, who worked in the Third Sector, said, "The cases were a mess, individual documents were scattered about on the window."[75] Vasilii Sergeevich Kozakov from the Fourth Sector claimed that the Third Sector arrested people in the national operations based exclusively on their ethnicity and "independent of compromising materials." In the Fourth Sector where he worked, he recalled one Vikhman naming a Russian and a Ukrainian as Bund co-conspirators. When Kozakov complained to Linetskii, the latter told him that, "in the given situation, the enemies are uniting and I simply did not understand this."[76] Aleksei Terent'evich Grigor'ev from the Third Sector recalled that it was impossible to pull together the group cases because their supposed participants did not even know each other.[77] Platonov added that "people socially close to us, that is peasants and workers," were purposely misclassified as kulaks to bring quotas up.[78] Other NKVD colleagues also claimed that the "socially near" were misclassified.[79]

During preliminary questioning, Platonov spoke about what he termed "the art of Klibanov." He said, "On orders from Klibanov, I took down required data from the arrested and gave it to him, and he typed up prepared standard protocols [of interrogation]. Fake cases were compiled on the basis of these protocols of interrogation of witnesses who later withdrew their testimony."[80] Gorodetskii said Linetskii "corrected" cases and that the cases he worked on had no corroborating evidence, but were based on self-incrimination and denunciation of others. The denounced would then confirm the guilt of the self-incriminated as well as naming new names.[81] Afanas'ev also said Boldin convened operational meetings where he ordered his interrogators to produce more and more confessions.[82]

Under these circumstances, it was all but inevitable that interrogators resorted to force to extract confessions from mainly innocent people, or, at the least, people innocent of the outrageous charges of those times. That people resisted, that many at first refused to slander themselves, is, in part, attested to by the sheer amount and varieties of torture in effect in 1937 and 1938. In Zaporozh'e, forced standing and beatings, sometimes by rubber truncheon, accompanied internment in the sickening cell number 8. As prison commandant Dorov described it,

> Cell no. 8 had no window and light did not penetrate it. The door, with a small spyhole, opened into the corridor. . . . The cell was meant for no more than four people. It was located in the basement. In the period from June to September 1938 on the orders of . . . Boldin, heads of sectors Linetskii and Klibanov, up to 30 to 40 people were put here.[83]

Later he claimed sixty to seventy people were interned in this cell.[84] Whatever the case may have been, prisoners could hardly move in the cell, leaving most to stand for hours in the heat and sweat of July. An earlier inspection of this cell noted that it could hold six people at most and that the size of the cell was about 2.4 meters wide, 4.8 meters long, and 2.75 meters high.[85]

Boldin told interrogators that the purpose of the cell was to more quickly force confessions out of prisoners. He claimed that the cell existed before he arrived in Zaporozh'e, but that it was Grabar' who "strengthened" the regime of this cell. Boldin claimed that up to thirty people were in the cell at a time. People were held there, he continued, no longer than a day; most held up for five to ten hours before "agreeing" to confess. According to Boldin, he and his assistant, Nasonov, along with Klibanov and Linetskii, had the right to intern prisoners in cell number 8. He said that beatings were minimal on his part because the cell functioned so well in forcing confessions. He also claimed that the Dnepropetrovsk regional NKVD knew about the use of the cell and that such cells "splendidly" helped the interrogators to receive confessions from the arrested.[86]

Klibanov said cell number 8 was used for the Zionist and SR cases. Linetskii, who also used cell number 8 to more quickly extract confessions, said the cell existed before he arrived in Zaporozh'e and that he did not know who first put it to use, but held Nasonov and Boldin responsible. Dorov called attention to the fact that at that time the city NKVD held as many as 4,000 prisoners, with at least 100 held in a courtyard under the open sky. He remembered people fainting in cell number 8 and admitted to one death caused by the lack of ventilation in the cell. Most prisoners sat naked in the cell, given the summer heat.[87] Gorodetskii said, "cell number 8 was a cell where they cooked human bodies."[88] The prisoner, David Moiseevich Gol'dbug, who had worked in the NKVD from 1921 to 1937, said, "The conditions in cell number 8 were terrible. Everyone called it the fat melting [room] because people in it melted, [they] were covered in sweat."[89]

Dr. Dmitrii Mikhailovich Poliakov had worked in the NKVD from 1920. He knew cell number 8 well. In 1938, he testified, he "was called in to the city NKVD office day and night to render aid to prisoners." He noted cases of prisoners fainting in cell number 8 as well as in other cells. "Such illnesses," he continued, "can be explained by the absence of air in the cells and the large crowding of people." He remembered seeing the prisoner Gol'dbug. He suggested to Dorov that they move him to another cell; Dorov responded, "Your job is to heal." Dr. Poliakov said he had no right to improve the condition of the cell. He also said, "I did not report to the procurator about the terrible conditions of the cell because he apparently knew about this himself." He did complain to Boldin, who responded, "Do not interfere in matters that do not concern you." He concluded his testimony by saying:

I could not complain to the city leadership since I saw many of them among the arrested; what happened made a huge impression on me.

Yes, there were times when even I became faint just being at the entry-way to cell number 8. From their stay in cell No. 8, the arrested suffered from swelling of the legs, blisters, bleeding, and infections from open wounds on their feet.[90]

In addition to cell number 8, the interrogator had other means to force confessions out of prisoners. Dorov loomed large in discussions of violence at the Zaporozh'e NKVD. Gorodetskii told Dorov's defense attoney that "Dorov brought horror to the prisoners." He told the court that he "personally saw Dorov twice around prisoners with a truncheon in hand."[91] Afanas'ev also claimed that Dorov beat prisoners more than anyone else.[92] The prison guard, Nikolai Alekseevich Mashchenko, told interrogators that he saw Boldin, Klibanov, Dorov, and others beating prisoners; he admitted that he also took part in beatings from time to time.[93] Gendel'man, who was less than pure himself, said Dorov beat on the orders of Boldin and called Dorov a despot.[94] According to Linetskii, the execution room was known locally as "Dorov's room."[95]

Gol'dbug, the former NKVD operative who found himself under arrest, recalled Dorov beating other prisoners horribly, but said that it was Boldin and Klibanov who beat him.[96] Another victim, Vasilii Nikitovich Sytnikov, a former factory director, told the court that Linetskii did not beat him, but only cursed; he did, however, hear that Klibanov beat prisoners. He also said that Dorov took part in the beatings.[97] Evdokiia Nikolaevna Udovichenko, a former Communist Party District Committee worker, was held prisoner from April to September 1938. She spoke about how Klibanov and others insulted her and forced her to stand until she fainted, and she remembered Boldin threatening her.[98]

Dorov was beater in chief. He admitted this, telling his interrogators that if all else failed, he was called in to beat confessions out of resistant prisoners. Dorov was also executioner in chief. Like Abramovich in Uman, Dorov was in charge of the execution squad. A key accusation against him was looting at the execution site. Although the charges did not approach, in sheer gruesomeness, those leveled against Abramovich, they were sufficiently serious. Dorov was accused of "systematically stealing things and valuables from prisoners during searches in spite of the strict order of the People's Commissar of Internal Affairs USSR that all things belonging to the arrested after 'etap' [execution] work with the first category must be burned in the interests of secrecy."[99]

Dorov explained that still under the former acting head of the Zaporozh'e NKVD, Iankovich, he had been ordered to remove all outer clothing and suits from the executed. He also said that prison guard Sabanskii would search the corpses and gather all the money, which they would then use to pay for breakfast and drinks after a long night of executions. They drank in the same room in which they shot their victims. Dorov explained that when the condemned began to be sentenced without money, Boldin and Korkin promised three rubles for each member of the execution squad to put aside for breakfasts and drinking, but this seems not to have happened.[100] Dorov also said that all clothes taken from executed prisoners were sent to a storeroom and that Iankovich from time to time distributed clothes to him as well as to other members of the squad. However, according to Dorov, Iankovich kept most things for himself.[101]

Z. P. Savichev, who ran the NKVD garage, took part in executions. He claimed that Dorov sold the pillaged clothes at markets in nearby towns and at the barracks of Zaporozh'e, employing prison guard Sabanskii's wife for these purposes.[102] Prison guard M. D. Fil' confirmed Savichev's testimony.[103] The cleaning lady at the Zaporozh'e NKVD, 46-year-old Elizaveta Porfir'evna Volkova, admitted that she accepted an overcoat from Dorov; everything else, she said, she brought to Iankovich's apartment. She claimed not to know if Dorov took anything, but did testify about the drinking that followed executions.[104] Sabanskii, the husband of the trader, showed up at the trial drunk and was thrown out. When he returned, saying, "Yes, I had a little shot this morning," he was not very helpful, instead accusing Volkova of carrying two suitcases of pillaged goods to Dorov's home (which the latter denied).[105] Others testified to receiving clothes from Dorov.[106] I. I. Felosenko served as a guard at the Jewish cemetery, where he dug graves for executed prisoners. He said Dorov gave him a few things, which he then sold from his home at the cemetery.[107]

In the end, looting was not unusual. It happened everywhere as a final insult to the dead. It was testament not only to lawlessness, but also to the (im)moral economy and culture of the NKVD. At one point, Dorov tried to justify the use of pillaged clothes by explaining how dirty the execution squad was after a night of shooting.[108] Most NKVD operatives looked at looting as compensation for "difficult work." Pillaging was a testament to the poverty of the times, even among NKVD workers, who would wear or sell their victims' clothes without remorse.

The Great Terror in Zaporozh'e was likely no worse than elsewhere. As Frishko argued, there was "not one interrogator who 'honestly' wrote up interrogation records."[109] There were also few interrogators who did not resort to the use of torture in their dealings with prisoners. Tragically, this was the logic of the Great Terror, dependent as it was on confessions, the naming of names, and falsified witness statements. The system was generated from above: It would not have occurred without Stalin and Ezhov. Uspenskii, Korkin, and Grabar' were intermediaries, with their own particular styles. Yet the Zaporozh'e NKVD also played a role in the way the terror developed; it is impossible to see its leaders—Boldin, Klibanov, Linetskii, Dorov—as automatons under the control of Moscow and Kiev. By granting plenipotentiary powers, Moscow and Kiev unleashed the Zaporozh'e NKVD leaders in order to push the mass operations as far as possible. There were no real restraints. Yet when Stalin resolved to halt mass operations, it was they who would bear the responsibility for violations of socialist legality.

AS HEAD OF the city's NKVD, Boldin, with equivocation, took responsibility for what happened in Zaporozh'e.[110] He told his interrogators: "I blindly trusted, controlled little, pushed for tempos, convened operational meetings of [NKVD] workers at which I demanded more completed cases, did not pay sufficient attention to the essence, the quality of interrogation of the accused, [and] also did not pay attention to the objectivity of the approach to the accused and to illegal methods in conducting investigations."[111] He added that Uspenskii, Korkin, and Grabar' were responsible for "hostile provocation."[112] At the same time, he insisted that experienced NKVD hands like his assistant Nasonov, Klibanov, and Linetskii "bore responsibility equally with me."[113] He also argued that although his appointment to lead the city NKVD took place on 12 July 1939, Grabar' held de facto control from the time of his arrival on 8 July to his departure on 15 July.[114] Boldin never went to trial. He fell out of the picture by the end of 1939, when he was diagnosed with psychiatric problems, and his death in 1942 ended his case.[115]

This left Klibanov, Linetskii, and Dorov to face trial without their boss. The trial took place in Zaporozh'e from 16 to 20 April 1940. There were thirty witnesses called to testify, all but four of whom appeared before the court. (One of the four was in the Gulag.)[116] Unlike in other trials, these defendants had the benefit of defense attorneys: Klibanov and Linetskii shared a defense attorney, Dunaevskii, whereas Dorov had his own attorney, Starovoitov.[117] As in other trials, the defendants had the right to call their own witnesses. Although Klibanov and Dorov had earlier "admitted" their guilt, Linetskii had never confessed. At the trial, however, they each denied their guilt, stating at the outset of the trial, in almost identical terms, "I do not recognize my guilt."[118] Each then had the opportunity to respond to his accusers at the close of the trial as well as to make a final statement.

The defendants in the Zaporozh'e trial attempted to justify their actions in a variety of ways. Their most common defense was to blame their superiors, Boldin and Grabar' in particular. They blamed others as well, ranging from Nasonov (Boldin's assistant) and other colleagues to Korkin and the regional NKVD all the way up to Uspenskii. At times, they denied specific allegations and contested individual witness testimony, charging others with lying. In other instances, they—especially Linetskii—said they believed that they were dealing with real enemies. Their denials were balanced by partial and grudging admissions of guilt in individual instances in spite of their opening statements.

Dorov's case was the most straightforward. Grigorii Iakovlevich Dorov was born in Berdichev to a Ukrainian working-class family in 1898. Although he never joined the Communist Party, Dorov, who had an elementary education, was a loyal servant of the Revolution. He fought in the Red Army during the Russian civil war and, in 1921 at the war's end, joined what was then the Cheka. From 1930 until his arrest on 8 April 1939, he served as commandant of the Zaporozh'e jail. The only past compromising material in his file was a fifteen-day term in jail in 1923 for accepting a bribe.[119]

Whether because of torture or by design, Dorov readily admitted his guilt under interrogation. He retracted parts of his confession later, in a handwritten missive from December 1939 and at the trial. He testified that cell number 8 (and other basement cells) existed prior to 1938. Conditions in the cell were difficult, he conceded, "but this was not my fault." When Grabar' arrived, Boldin ordered Dorov to cut a three-foot length of rubber for beating prisoners. Dorov told Boldin that rubber was hard to come by, so he used rubber hoses to make a rubber truncheon. He admitted to beating several prisoners, but only on Boldin's orders. He claimed he had refused to beat anyone until Boldin assured him it was the "Narkom's order"—that is, Uspenskii's order. He argued that he did not engage in plundering the corpses of executed prisoners. He gave clothes to members of the execution squad with the permission of Iankovich, the former head of the city NKVD. He somewhat indignantly argued that he had no need of these things and no reason to sell things on the market.[120] His last words at the trial were brief. He told the court, "I worked 9 years as commandant and honestly related to [my] work. My case was falsified by investigator Miklukhin, and two workers, that is, the cleaning lady Volkova and the prison guard Sabanskii, who did not want to give false testimony about me were fired by the NKVD. I am not guilty in these terrible outrages, and therefore I ask for a just sentence."[121]

Dorov's attorney attempted to mitigate the charges against his client, inter-rupting witnesses with questions and prompting Dorov at key points. His main goals were to stress that the worst of the violations coincided with Grabar's visit and that Dorov always acted according to the orders of his superiors. His final statement at the trial was "Dorov is guilty but he deserves mercy."[122]

The other two defendants were Klibanov and Linetskii. Each served as head of a sector in the Zaporozh'e NKVD. Klibanov led the Fourth Sector in charge of the expanded kulak operation, and Linetskii led the Third Sector in charge of national operations. Both men stressed the centrality of Grabar's visit in accelerating the violations. Linetskii also pointed to Boldin and Nasonov as well as noting the role of the regional NKVD in Dnepropetrovsk.[123] Both Klibanov and Linetskii defended their positions during interrogation, pre-senting detailed responses about operational work, lines of authority, and vio-lations of socialist legality in Zaporozh'e.

David Iakovlevich Klibanov was born in Dnepropetrovsk to a Jewish white-collar family in 1906. He received a secondary education and com-pleted courses at a technical institute. He worked as an engine mechanic until 1931, joining the Communist Party in 1930. In 1931, he began work in the security organs, working in the Zaporozh'e city NKVD from June 1934. He led the Fourth Sector unofficially from fall 1937 and then formally from February to August 1938 before going on to work in his last position before his arrest on 18 March 1939 as acting head of the Ninth Department at the Dnepropetrovsk regional NKVD. The records indicate that he was married, and he received a wristwatch in 1938 as a reward for his NKVD service.[124]

As head of the Fourth Sector of the Zaporozh'e NKVD, Klibanov pre-sided over cases falling under—very broadly—the expanded kulak opera-tion: Ukrainian nationalist counterrevolutionaries, Zionists, SRs, and Mensheviks.[125] During his interrogations, he admitted that illegal practices against prisoners began well before the arrival of Grabar', already in the time of Boldin's predecessors, Iankovich and Vol'skii.[126] He also detailed the important leadership role that the Dnepropetrovsk regional NKVD played in determining actions in Zaporozh'e. According to Klibanov, it was the regional NKVD that ordered the creation of cases against both Zionists and the SRs.[127] He spoke, for example, about the arrival of Zdunis, the head of the regional NKVD's Fourth Department, who played a similar role to Grabar', intervening and radicalizing the work of Klibanov's sector.[128] Moreover, according to Klibanov, it was Korkin, the head of the regional NKVD, who ordered the use of physical methods against prisoners who would not confess and it was the successive heads of the Zaporozh'e NKVD, beginning with Iankovich, who sanctioned the beatings.[129]

Klibanov admitted to falsifying cases. He told his interrogator that "part [of the interrogation records] were actually compiled in the absence of the arrested," though, supposedly, based on handwritten notes that interrogators took during preliminary conversations with prisoners.[130] In one case, he recalled, he wrote up a prisoner's interrogation records "under the dictation of Vol'skii."[131] Further, the materials they used against the SRs and the Mensheviks came from 1924 and 1925.[132] He admitted to beating prisoners but claimed that cell number 8 worked better in forcing confessions.[133] He seemed to believe that these methods were necessary given the scale of the operation and the strict timelines established from above.[134]

Although, according to Klibanov's interrogations, the terror was in full swing before the arrival of Grabar's brigade, at the trial he claimed that mass arrests in fact began when the brigade arrived.[135] David Isaakovich Vaisbarg, a member of the brigade, was detailed to work in Klibanov's Fourth Sector. Klibanov maintained that Vaisbarg essentially took over control of the sector.[136] Klibanov told his interrogator that Grabar' and Vaisbarg insisted that individuals with socially alien pasts—for example, priests, gendarmes, "big" kulaks—were to be arrested even in the absence of compromising material.[137] To cover their tracks, they used the "formula" that these individuals had "antisoviet moods" or were "circulating antisoviet rumors."[138] Klibanov added that Grabar' employed the same approach in the national operations, telling the Zaporozh'e NKVD that Uspenskii had said that "the majority of Germans and Poles were enemies," thus justifying mass arbitrary arrests according to ethnicity alone.[139]

The interrogator prodded Klibanov to answer questions about whether he believed in the reality of the cases. Klibanov said that he did not believe the case against the Zionists was real, but, at the time, believed that other cases were real.[140] At the trial, his defense attorney asked why he had not objected to the outrages occurring in Zaporozh'e. He responded, "I believed and could not not have believed in the authority of Uspenskii."[141] In other words, he had little choice not only to follow orders, but also to believe what he was told. In his final statement at the trial, he admitted that he had made mistakes but attributed them to his belief in the leadership. He also strongly denied that he was a careerist—a reference to the closing argument of the Military Procurator. He concluded by asking "to be treated justly." His defense attorney asked the court to keep in mind the centrality of Grabar's visit to the mass violations in Zaporozh'e, as well as Klibanov's illness. In his final words,

Klibanov said, "I am sick with tuberculosis. Therefore a long imprisonment for me will all the same result in death."[142]

Linetskii was far more stubborn in his interactions with his interrogators and in his court testimony. Boris L'vovich Linetskii was born in Odessa to a white-collar Jewish family in 1906. He joined the Communist Party in 1931 and worked as a weaver until 1932, after which he entered the services of the security police. Until his transfer to Zaporozh'e, he worked at the Dnepropetrovsk regional NKVD, first as an operational plenipotentiary and then as assistant head of the Third Section of the Third Department. From May 1938 until his arrest on 18 March 1939, he was in charge of the national operations in Zaporozh'e and simultaneously served as the secretary of the city NKVD's party committee. Linetskii had had only an elementary education. The records indicate he was married, and he was rewarded with a bicycle in 1937 for his services in the NKVD.[143]

Linetskii's Third Sector was responsible for the largest number of arrests in Zaporozh'e in the summer of 1938.[144] This was, at least in part, a consequence of the time limits placed on the completion of the national operations. There is no indication that Linetskii alone was responsible for this volume of arrests. In fact, the NKVD in Dnepropetrovsk closely supervised the operation. According to Boldin, for example, the regional NKVD through one Rusimovich worked closely on the German case with the Zaporozh'e Third Sector.[145] Umanskii, the head of the regional NKVD Third Department, also played his part, calling Zaporozh'e daily to cajole his subordinates in the Third Sector into accelerating arrests and confessions.[146] The arrival of Grabar' and his brigade brought further pressures from the outside. Brigade member Rovinskii was attached to Linetskii's sector and, like Grabar', immediately began to exert his authority.[147] Nonetheless, Linetskii had sufficient power, as Third Sector head and Communist Party committee secretary, to play, as he did, an enormous role in the conduct of mass operations.

Linetskii's confrontation with his interrogator was a contest of wills, with Linetskii stubbornly denying or nuancing the accusations thrown at him. When, on 8 April 1939, the interrogator began by stating that Linetskii, in concert with Boldin, Klibanov, and others, had "engaged in hostile activity," "discrediting Soviet punitive policies in the eyes of workers," Linetskii spat back: "I never engaged in any kind of criminally harmful work. At that time, I considered the methods used in the operational–investigative work absolutely correct and believed that the party required it."[148] Interestingly, this forthright defendant differed from the Linetskii who, on 10 February

1939, was confronted by members of the Zaporozh'e Communist Party collective. There, under heavy criticism, Linetskii said, "Why did this happen? I honestly said at the party committee that I was afraid, since I had received a warning from Uspenskii."[149] Later, he admitted his guilt; at the same time, he blamed Grabar', saying that "conversations in the city [NKVD] were such that if you talked about any of this, they would make you into a spy and shoot you."[150] He also said that the Communist Party District Committee did not assume leadership and "should also recognize its guilt."[151] The party meeting concluded by expelling Linetskii (and Boldin) from the party and dissolving the Zaporozh'e NKVD party committee.[152]

Linetskii immediately changed his tune after his arrest, denying almost all of the interrogator's accusations. He claimed that his sector did not falsify cases, or, in any case, he was not aware of any falsifications.[153] He said that he believed in the guilt of the arrested, never doubting their confessions.[154] He acknowledged the occasional use of cell number 8, but said it was in existence before he arrived and sanctioned by Korkin and his deputies, Daragon and Umanskii, from the regional NKVD as well as by Boldin.[155] He explained that the cell was used to pressure arrestees into confession and denied that any of his prisoners died there.[156] He also pointed to the existence of other basement cells (numbers 6, 7, and 9), which were also terrible though not quite as bad as cell number 8.[157] He admitted to beating only one prisoner—and, in fact, there were only one or two accusations against him for beating. He said that if one of his subordinates asked permission to beat, he sent them to Boldin, who then called in Dorov.[158] Basically, Linetskii denied everything, in all probability resenting his role as fall guy.

He continued to deny accusations at the trial. He attempted to have the court call in Vol'skii, Nasonov, and the regional procurator as witnesses, but was denied.[159] He said that he still believed in the guilt of one Kopp, the supposed head of the German counterrevolutionaries. He denied fabricating the German "formation," instead saying that Kopp, an old factory owner, had been a spy since 1902, that he named many names of other enemies under interrogation, and that he, Linetskii, believed his testimony.[160] He also interestingly said that he did not consider the arrests of the Germans incorrect, taking into account Ezhov's order on foreigners. He said Uspenskii confirmed that foreigners must be removed regardless of the existence of compromising material.[161] This last statement seems to belie Linetskii's insistence that he believed in his prisoner's guilt.

Finally, Linetskii was questioned at some length as to precisely when he learned about the 17 November 1938 directive halting mass operations and, in particular, stopping the work of the troikas that adjudicated executions. This was a topic of some importance here and in other cases, as the continuation of executions after 17 November was clearly a violation of law, however cynically deployed in these trials of NKVD operatives, allowing prosecutors to say that the 17 November 1938 directive had been violated.[162] At the February party meeting in Zaporozh'e, Boldin said that the last of the executions occurred at the end of November on the orders of Korkin.[163] In a face-to-face encounter with Boldin, Linetskii said he first heard of the directive only on 5 December 1938, whereas Boldin claimed he received the directive on 22 November 1938.[164] Linetskii's timing was fortuitous; Boldin's was not.

In the course of his court testimony, Linetskii partly echoed Klibanov when he said, "I do not recognize my guilt because I could not not believe the directives of Ezhov and Uspenskii, and everyone believed them." Moreover, he added, "I am 33 years old, in the time of my work in the organs, I was an exemplary worker [*otlichnik*]."[165] He believed, because to do otherwise was unthinkable, whether because of obedience to higher orders or because questioning orders was simply not part of his job. Still, his point was important: He did nothing, or so he claimed, that he had not been ordered to do. Now he was being made responsible for following orders.

Linetskii's defense attorney, Dunaevskii, said in his concluding speech that "it was a pity that Boldin did not sit on the defendant's bench since that would allow the possibility to more correctly weigh the degree of guilt of each of those sitting here on the bench." Further, he stressed the responsibility of Grabar' and his brigade under whom mass arrests and violations of investigative procedures occurred. He said that his clients were guilty only of "blindly trusting them [Grabar's brigade] and the directives and regional leadership." "All this," he concluded, "gives me the right to petition the Tribunal, taking into account the personality of the defendant Linetskii, not to deprive him of life and to give him the opportunity to atone for his guilt through honest labor."[166]

Linetskii continued some of the defense attorney's rationale in his last words to the court:

The defense attorney said that it was a pity that on the defendants' bench did not sit the fourth accused, Boldin, and I would add that it is a pity that there was no fifth defendant, Nasonov, who in fact led investigations. Thanks to the absence of these people all the weight of the accusations fall on me. In the [court's] indictment I am counted as the head of the sector, when, in fact, with the arrival of Grabar's brigade I scarcely had an apparatus. . . . I gave no orders about falsifying cases to anyone, and if here the witness Gorodetskii talks about this, it is on the grounds of his personal prejudice [against me]. I admit that I trusted the leadership and directives of Ezhov and Uspenskii, [I] acted, as [I] understood later, incorrectly, but I had no personal or evil designs. I ask [that the court] take into account all the circumstances to decide the question of my guilt.[167]

All three were found to be guilty. The Military Procurator charged that Klibanov, Linetskii, and Dorov, "who had once been part of the most trusted government institution—the NKVD," and whom the "party and Soviet government had trusted," "had deceived the party, deceived the Soviet government, had taken the position of provocation, the path of falsifying cases, the path of illegal mass arrests of honest Communists, workers, administrative staff, engineering–technical personnel. All this was done exclusively with careerist ends." He went on to say that the accused tried to justify their actions by pointing the finger at Grabar' and Uspenskii, but that these attempts were "erroneous" because the brigade and Uspenskii were in Zaporozh'e for such a short time and the violations took place all throughout 1938. He called for the "physical destruction" of Linetskii as the basic organizer and leader of these crimes and asked for long sentences for Klibanov and Dorov.[168]

In the end, Dorov was sentenced to five years and Klibanov to seven years in the Gulag. Linetskii was sentenced to death.[169] Their defense attorneys appealed the verdict, but the Military Collegium of the Supreme Court of the USSR left the verdicts and sentences in force.[170] Linetskii was executed on 10 September 1940.[171] Klibanov died at the front after his release from the Gulag.[172] A legal review of the case in 1994 by the Ukrainian government confirmed the original sentences.[173]

THE DEFENDANTS' TESTIMONIES, especially Linetskii's, were not without contradictions and, at times, downright lies. Yet their testimony also reflected a number of sometimes undigestible truths. First, the terror and most of its instruments were in place before Grabar's brigade arrived in Zaporozh'e. Second, the terror accelerated in scale and possibly arbitrariness under Grabar'. Third, the defendants were following orders and mainly, at least at that time, thought that they were acting correctly in ways expected of Chekists. Both Klibanov and Linetskii resented the Military Procurator's accusations of careerism, and neither used the defense of fear of superiors, even though evidence of such fear is mentioned a few times in the criminal file.[174]

Klibanov, Linetskii, and their colleagues in Zaporozh'e and elsewhere were caught in a vortex of changeable logic, a discourse of dueling imperatives subject to dramatic and abrupt change.[175] The reigning logic of the Great Terror was to destroy the omnipresent Fifth Column at any cost. This logic contained three interdependent elements. First, arrests occurred according to categories—social, economic, political, and ethnic. Then, NKVD operatives subjected the individuals caught up within these categories to further classification, slotting them into category-appropriate counterrevolutionary formations. Finally, the prisoners so categorized and diagrammed were forced to agree to their placement as counterrevolutionaries, not through polite Marxist dialog, but through grave insult and injury to their bodies. This logic left NKVD operatives like Linetskii resentful, but helpless to see his position other than that of a fall guy, caught in an invisible vortex of nightmarish logic.

The reigning logic of the terror's aftermath, expressed most forcefully in the directive of 17 November 1938, was socialist or revolutionary legality, a rationale mostly latent through 1937 and most of 1938. The logic of the Great Terror evaporated as simplified methods of investigation, the use of torture, and the centrality of the confession were called into question by higher authorities. This change in policy was not difficult, given that so much of the terror's logic had been unwritten, based on varying degrees of NKVD culture, teaching by example through plenipotentiary visits such as Grabar's, and oral communications. Now the center stressed the importance of signalers like Frishko and turned to unjustly arrested but now released Communists to tell the story of the terror from their perspective as supposedly honest Chekists or wronged Communists. References to "mass discontent," especially in the factories, served to further legitimize the center's new course, regardless of whether these references were real and whether some of them may have alarmed higher authorities before they became legitimizing rationalizations.

This new logic (or, more accurately, a return to an earlier logic) meant that men like Klibanov, Linetskii, and Dorov were left on the chopping block despite their testimony highlighting issues of superior orders and the chain of command in the NKVD. The Military Procurator at their trial refused to accept the defendants' and their attorneys' attempts to transfer blame to Grabar' and his brigade. At first glance, this is reasonable given that Grabar' was in Zaporozh'e for such a short time. However, it is, at the same time, curious given that Grabar' would be executed for, among other reasons, his work in Zaporozh'e. In the end, they would all be held responsible, each series of officials scapegoated for orders coming from above, geographic–administrative level by level all the way up to Uspenskii and Ezhov.

7

Uspenskii's Stooge

These are war times now, we are military people and therefore for the slightest violation in work we will be judged by a military field court.
—ATTRIBUTED TO V. R. GRABAR' BY L. I. GORODINSKII, *NKVD operative in Grabar's Sixth Department*

BACK IN KIEV, Grabar' continued to be a target of opprobrium.[1] He was accused of working with enemies of the people Uspenskii and Leplevskii to undermine Soviet rule. Former colleagues called him a careerist, an opportunist, a gossip, and a lickspittle who constantly toadied to his superiors and endlessly boasted of close connections to Uspenskii. At the same time, they spoke of Grabar' as a tyrant to his subordinates, cursing and threatening them with arrest for the smallest trifle. Victims remembered him as cruel, if not sadistic, beating them with anything that came to hand.

At his trial, Grabar' conceded that he perhaps did suffer from "elements of coarseness [*grubost'*] and tactlessness [*netaktichnost'*]," but insisted that he was not an enemy of the people. He admitted only to committing "individual mistakes of an operational character" and even then blamed everything on Uspenskii, who, he said, continually threatened him with arrest.[2] He denied that he was close to Uspenskii, who, he claimed, harassed him repeatedly, calling him, for some reason or another, a Jew.[3] In the final analysis, Grabar' insisted that—despite certain personal failings—he did nothing more than follow orders.

Grabar' was arrested on 4 December 1938 and tried by a Military Tribunal from 7 to 11 October 1940.[4] In spite of their own sentences, Dorov, Klibanov, Linetskii (though less so), and their defense attorneys could rest assured that Grabar' too would answer for what happened in Zaporozh'e. Grabar', in fact, would be charged with the far more serious Ukrainian criminal code Articles 54-1 and 54-7 for counterrevolutionary crimes,[5] although, in the end, the charges would be reduced to Article 206-17 (B) for crimes of office.[6]

GRABAR' WAS A murky character, with all sorts of contradictions in his personal biography. He was born in 1908 in Odessa to a Ukrainian father and a Russian mother. He sometimes listed his nationality as Russian, sometimes as Ukrainian. His father, Roman Iakovlevich, was originally from Moldavia. He only moved to Odessa after his service in the tsarist army. Once in Odessa, he began work in a factory. Grabar's mother was born in a village, but then moved to Odessa as a young person and, at some point, worked as a nurse in the Odessa Jewish hospital. Given the difficult food situation in Odessa at the end of the civil war, Grabar's father moved back to Moldavia in late 1921. There, he joined a collective farm, later serving on its administrative board.[7] His mother's employment was the source for Uspenskii's irritating insistence that Grabar' hid his "Jewish origins."[8] Grabar' alternated between claims of different ethnic backgrounds, just as he cited his social origins, interchangeably, as proletarian and peasant. This made perfect sense in the multiethnic and migratory population of Soviet Ukraine, even if it looked suspicious on paper to those whose job it was to be suspicious.

Although he sometimes claimed a secondary education, Grabar' had no more than seven years of schooling. He began work in Moldavia at the age of 18, serving between 1926 and 1928 in a variety of positions in the Kodyma rural soviet.[9] In his autobiography for his personnel file, he wrote that at the end of 1928, after having been seconded to the OGPU to work in the forced grain requisitioning of that time, his superior recommended him for transfer to work at the Main Administration of Investigations of the Moldavan regular police, where he worked as a clerk. Sometime in 1929, he moved on to work in the Secret Department of Moldavia's Commissariat of Trade. In this capacity, he would have had continuing formal or informal links to the security police.[10] Grabar's earliest work experience, then, was mainly in the sometimes illegally lucrative fields of food and trade, with the security police always in the background.

In 1930, Grabar' went into the Red Army, where he would serve for two years, ending up in Berdichev (Ukraine) as assistant commander in his squadron's Political Department. From the army, Grabar' moved back to the NKVD (at that time, the OGPU), working between 1932 and 1937 in various capacities in the Special Department of the Third Cavalry Division of the Berdichev OGPU–NKVD, and joining the Communist Party in 1932.[11] His time in Berdichev's security police would leave a trail of insinuations, accusations, and deeds that would accompany him to his execution.

In Berdichev, Grabar' developed a reputation as an operator who used his position for gain. Braun, the former head of the Berdichev NKVD, claimed that Grabar' had ties to the town's criminal elements, specifically speculators or traders, and, through them, obtained hard currency and vouchers for use at the local *Torgsin* store.[12] The former deputy head of Grabar's department, Deich, said that Grabar' "used his position" to engage "systematically in swindling, embezzlement, theft, and other crimes."[13] Grabar's personnel file—as a reminder of the danger of negative family ties—also noted that his mother-in-law had supposedly stolen money and goods from the sugar factory where she worked. Perhaps to his credit, Grabar' defended her in 1935, noting that she was a Communist and an excellent worker.[14]

Grabar's Berdichev superiors characterized him, before and after their own arrests, in extremely negative terms. Martyniuk, another former head of the Berdichev NKVD, said Grabar' was an extreme gossip and "not a serious person." Braun called him "unstable," "lazy," and "deceptive."[15] Even in a 1935 certificate [*attestatsiia*], Braun wrote that, although Grabar's general education and political preparation were satisfactory and he was active in Communist Party work, in his relations with others he was arrogant, insincere, and bullying.[16] Some of this testimony may have been obtained under duress, but, all the same, it rings true in light of later charges and accusations against Grabar'.

Grabar' left Berdichev sometime in 1937 to work in Kiev at the republican-level NKVD, this time serving as acting head of the Fourth Sector of the Fifth Department. By the time of his arrest, at the age of 30, he was a senior lieutenant, deputy and acting head of the Special Department, reorganized as the Sixth Department, and de facto head of the Sixth Department's Investigative Section. The Sixth Department formally was in charge of Chekist handling of all militarized organizations, including the various branches of the military, as well as the regular police, defense factories, and border troops. Informally, it could interfere in any organization in which espionage, sabotage, or diversionary activities were suspected.[17]

There were multiple charges against Grabar'. He was accused of responsibility in the fabricated cases against Pavel Kuz'mich Kopaev, from the UkrKabel' Factory, and Serafima Vladimirovna Shibanova, a typist mobilized to work for the Sixth Department. He was broadly implicated in the death under interrogation of the police officer Maiboroda, as well as accused of a rather liberal use of enhanced interrogation methods in numerous cases. The most important charges concerned Grabar's activities in Zaporozh'e and the arrest and torture of Iakov Efimovich Gershkov, the deputy head of the Political Department in the republican apparatus of the Ukrainian (regular) police.[18] Alongside these formal charges, his colleagues and victims alike drew a highly negative portrait of a petty tyrant who at last would receive his just deserts.

HIS FORMER BERDICHEV boss, Martyniuk (himself under arrest at this time), said that Grabar' suffered "from one feature that was particularly intolerable for a Chekist—indiscretion that went beyond all bounds." "When Grabar' came to Berdichev," Martyniuk continued, the NKVD workers would say "the Kiev telephone has arrived."[19] Grabar' was also known for cozying up to his superiors. He socialized with Martyniuk, spending time in restaurants "having intimate conversations."[20] He never failed to boast of his supposedly close connection to Uspenskii.[21] His subordinate from the "storm brigade" in Zaporozhe, David Isaakovich Vaisberg, described Grabar' as "unscrupulous." He also said that, "Grabar' belonged to the kind of people who on the basis of deceit and bootlicking try to create for themselves a halo of glory—all for career."[22]

Mark Mendelevich Tul'skii, an NKVD murderer himself, said that he "saw in Grabar' a crude, uncultured person," who, instead of exercising leadership, ruled by threats, intimidation, and curses.[23] Vaisberg concurred, saying that "for the slightest resistance, Grabar' spat out threats and foul obsceni-ties, threatening [his subordinates] with arrest and reassignment to dis-tant [Gulag] camps." "Grabar' terrorized," he added.[24] At a meeting of the Communist Party cell of the Special Department, one speaker said Grabar's constant refrain was, "[I] will arrest [you], plant [you in prison], report [you] to Aleksandr Ivanovich [Uspenskii]."[25]

Grabar' demanded blind obedience from his subordinates and brooked no opposition.[26] When NKVD worker Mikhail Khaskelevich Khes attempted to ask Grabar' at an operational meeting what to do if he had no corroborating evidence against a prisoner, Grabar' cut him short and shouted at him, "You do not believe in arrests carried out by the organs of the NKVD. Sit down."[27] According to a witness at the meeting, Khes walked around dejected for sev-eral days after the meeting, fully expecting to be arrested.[28] Many colleagues testified to Grabar's imperious behavior at operational meetings, where he demanded, threatened, and cursed.[29] As he said to Lev Isaevich Gorodinskii, a subordinate in the Special Department, "These are war times now, we are military people and therefore for the slightest violation we will be judged by a military field court."[30]

Grabar' made ample use of enhanced interrogation methods. According to Pavel Sidorovich Gal'chenko, who worked under Grabar' in the Special

Department, Grabar' said, "Many interrogators are not necessary. It is enough to have a janitor with a stick to come to beat a prisoner."[31] He instructed his subordinates "to obtain confessions by any means."[32] He taught them how to deceive prisoners by proving to them that it was in their interest to confess.[33] Grabar' was not above bribing the troikas that sentenced prisoners to death. Vaisbarg recalled a conversation in which Grabar' explained to an underling how to get the best results from the troika. He recommended bringing in food, adding "don't skimp [*ne stesniaias'*]."[34]

Even for an officially proclaimed enemy of the people specifically targeted for attack, Grabar' stood out among his peers as an unlikable, indeed disdained, individual. His colleagues' testimony against him was strikingly personal and, even from those also under arrest, contained what was probably a good deal of vengeance as well as more than a hint of *schadenfreude*. Grabar', however, was not being tried for his terrible personality. He in fact shared many of his worst attributes with any number of other Chekists, including, most notably, Uspenskii. Grabar's case was instead built on the basis of a series of concrete crimes and violations of socialist legality.

Grabar' was known within his department as a "master of falsification."[35] In one of the earliest investigations of his activities, Grabar' was charged with making arrests without evidence, "correcting" and falsifying interrogation records, and forcing prisoners to sign confessions they had not read.[36] To use the untrustworthy Uspenskii's words, "Grabar' falsified cases left and right."[37] Grabar' told his subordinates, "If you do not obtain a confession, then you will give one," meaning that they too would be arrested and forced to confess if they failed to fulfill their NKVD duties.[38]

One such falsified case was that against Pavel Kuz'mich Kopaev, who worked at the UkrKabel' Factory. Although it is difficult to take the full measure of this case, it seems that Grabar' forced Kopaev to sign a false confession and to denounce a large number of engineering and technical staff at the factory. They were all arrested and forced to incriminate themselves. Luck was on their side, however, given that these arrests occurred in the fall of 1938 and were not fully processed before the 17 November 1938 directive curtailing the mass operations. As a consequence of a review of their cases, these specialists were set free and soon wrote letters of complaints to the authorities. Their importance and visibility as specialists at an important factory were most probably the reasons that this case was singled out to use against Grabar'.[39]

Another falsified case and one that bears the stamp of Grabar's petty spite was the case against Serafima Vladimirovna Shibanova. A typist who worked in the Department of Technical Control in the NKVD, Shibanova was mobilized to work in Grabar's Special Department on 30 September 1938. She sat if not at the center of the terror, then very close to the center, typing verbatim protocols of interrogations and confessions, working long hours without a break. When Grabar' told her that she was to be appointed as the senior typist in the Special Department, she recoiled, saying that she was not a regular employee at the Special Department and therefore not subject to their decisions. Grabar' then sent her to work for a day and night at the Military Collegium, for which she received a bonus of 200 rubles. After she returned to the Special Department, on 20 October, she pleaded with Grabar' to release her. He agreed, but was not pleased at losing his typist.

At 2:00 a.m. that night, the NKVD came to her home to arrest her. The arrest order was signed by Grabar'. On the next day, she was summoned to interrogation, accused of espionage, and told that there were seventeen confessions "unmasking" her. At the next interrogation, two days later on 23 October, she faced two interrogators who continued to accuse her of spying, with every other word, according to Shibanova, an obscenity. At the same time, they promised to give her cigarettes and a good meal if she would submit a 100-word confession. Her third interrogation came after another two days, on 25 October. This time they planted her in a room from which she could hear the screams of a prisoner being beaten in a nearby room, a fairly common practice of intimidation. She was then surrounded by three or four interrogators, who threatened to beat her with barbed wire. She continued to refuse to admit to any crime and they continued to call her out for interrogations, all the time threatening her and insulting her "as a woman."

Soon, the tone of interrogations began to change. Her interrogator, she said, began to show signs of humanity. He told her that they had a denunciation of her from a colleague who reported her for arguing with and apparently insulting an interrogator about a week before her arrest. She had been exhausted physically, at her wit's end, and when the interrogator ordered her back to work, she broke down in tears and insulted him. Her behavior was then supposedly described as antisoviet. Shibanova, however, was certain that the friend and fellow typist who purportedly wrote the denunciation could not have done so, given their close relationship. The real reason for her arrest, it was clear, was that Grabar' needed a typist and would not accept a resignation from this subordinate, a woman at that. On 3 December, a day before Grabar's own arrest, she was released.[40]

Grabar' was also implicated in a case involving the death while under interrogation of a prisoner, G. I. Maiboroda, an official from the Ukrainian regular police. The actual torturers of Maiboroda were Grabar's apparently sadistic assistant, Vol-Goikhman, and Tul'skii, who used an electric cable and chair legs to beat him. When he died, Tul'skii suddenly became worried about procedure. They called and then sent a car for Dr. Fraiman, who had also serviced Drushliak's (a.k.a. "Vania the Terrible") prisoners in Kiev. When Fraiman arrived, the guard on duty at the prison said, "Too late. He already died. And what happened to him, I do not know." Fraiman was brought to the room where the murdered prisoner still sat at the table, dressed in his uniform, his cap lying nearby. The prison commandant, Nagornyi, was there along with several interrogators. Fraiman removed Maiboroda's shirt and examined him. One of the interrogators, likely Grabar', said, "Why do you need an autopsy? You see that he is dead. Write up a death certificate and, if the Narkom [Uspenskii] finds it necessary to do an autopsy, we will." The doctor wrote the death certificate, indicating that Maiboroda died from a heart attack. According to Tul'skii, it was Grabar' who ordered the case closed without an autopsy. The arrest warrant for Grabar' placed the blame on him as well.[41]

The Maiboroda murder was much discussed in the NKVD and in the regular police. Although it occurred in March 1938, a time when the Ukrainian police was under assault by the NKVD, this case assumed even greater importance in the fall of 1938 when Grabar' and the Sixth Department, which was responsible for monitoring the police, came under attack. To trace developments in the police, it is necessary to turn to two witnesses who not only were able to tell the story of the police's encounter with the NKVD, but who also directly experienced the wrath of Grabar'.

Iakov Efimovich Gershkov was the deputy head of the regular police's Political Department. He spoke at length with Grabar's interrogators and at the trial, proving to be one of the few positive characters in this story. Gershkov claimed—and large parts of his testimony were confirmed by others—that the mass repression of police workers, including the firing of some 1,500 Komsomols and Communist Party members, made a "huge impression" on him. He attributed these actions to the new head of the Ukrainian police, Klochkov, whom Uspenskii brought in in March 1938. Soon Klochkov was joined by another new leader, Sharaburin, who arrived from Moscow to head the police's Political Department and who supposedly consulted with Grabar' about everything. At about that time, Gershkov said, he had a private conversation with colleagues in the police, expressing his disagreement with what was happening there, especially the news of the beating of arrested police officers. Gershkov said that work in the police had become unbearable for him.

Gershkov was personally acquainted with the head of the All-Union police's Political Department, Talalaev. He wrote to him, saying he could no longer work in this cesspit [*kloaka*], but he did not receive an answer from Talalaev. At about the same time, there were plans to convene an All-Union conference of regular police Political Department workers in Moscow. Sharaburin apparently knew about Gershkov's "mood" and told him he could not go to the conference on orders from Uspenskii. In response, Gershkov sent a telegram to Talalaev, requesting an invitation, which Talalaev sent immediately. Once in Moscow, Gershkov reported to Talalaev about what was happening to the police in Kiev. He also brought to Talalaev's attention a report on the political morale of the police that Sharaburin had refused to sign. He told Talalaev that Sharaburin and Uspenskii were close. Then Gershkov spoke at the police Political Department conference. He spoke in detail about the situation in the Ukrainian police and characterized the activities of Uspenskii and Klochkov as hostile. After the conference, Talalaev told him, "Uspenskii is the son of a priest, an upstart bandit, but we will deal with him." Gershkov then met with Chernyshev, one of the deputy heads of the NKVD and the head of the All-Union police, and told him everything he had told Talalaev. Chernyshev, in turn, surprised him with the news that Klochkov had not only been arrested but had just been executed.[42]

When Gershkov returned to Kiev on 9 September 1938, he went to see Sharaburin, but the latter refused to see him. He then confided in a colleague, Efim Korneevich Kichko, who also worked in the police's Political Department in Kiev. Kichko told him that the arrests had continued in his absence. Gershkov then sent Chernyshev a new report based on this conversation. That night, Grabar' summoned Gershkov to the NKVD. Sharaburin approached him first and asked, "What have you been saying about me?" Gershkov reported that Sharaburin could read the text of his speech. Sharaburin replied, "I know it all. You will have to answer for it." At this point, Gershkov said he was prepared to be arrested.

Gershkov saw Grabar' on 11 September. Gershkov reported to Grabar' about his time in Moscow, even sharing the text of his speech. After Grabar' read the text, he left. When he returned, he questioned Gershkov about a list of police workers, ordering several of them arrested in Gershkov's presence—including Kichko. Then Grabar' told Gershkov that his actions were placing the regular police against "Soviet power." With that, Uspenskii barged in. Gershkov stood. Uspenskii came straight at him, slapped him in the face several times, and yelled, "Trotskyite provocateur." He punched Gershkov in the stomach and walked out.

Grabar' then began what Gershkov labeled a "concert," demanding a confession. Because a concert required an orchestra, Tul'skii and another NKVD operative joined them and took turns beating Gershkov brutally. Gershkov finally conceded and wrote a confession "under the dictation" of Grabar'. When he arrived in his cell, Gershkov said his body was covered in bruises, but he was not allowed to see a doctor. Soon he was placed under a different interrogator and immediately retracted his confession. After that, a more senior interrogator took over. While in his office, Uspenskii arrived with the now-arrested Kichko for a face-to-face confrontation with Gershkov. Gershkov said he yelled to Kichko, over the heads of the interrogator, that everything that happened in Moscow was true. They then led Kichko away and began beating Gershkov again. Time was on Gershkov's side, however, and eventually someone in Moscow intervened. He was freed on 17 October 1939.[43]

Kichko was also subjected to brutal torture at the hands of Grabar' and a series of other interrogators, including Tul'skii and Drushliak. It was only in January 1939 that they began to let up on him. Drushliak summoned him for an interrogation on 17 January 1939 and suddenly, perhaps for the first time, behaved "rather correctly," promising Kichko better treatment. That encouraged Kichko to write an appeal in March 1939, in which he essentially told a similar story as Gershkov had, writing about the terror in the police as well as Gershkov's valiant trip to Moscow that ended in their arrests. Both Kichko and Gershkov would testify at Grabar's trial, essentially reiterating their earlier testimony.[44]

Grabar's bloody reign in the Sixth Department was, of course, combined with the special plenipotentiary duties that he fulfilled on Uspenskii's orders. Although his travels were not limited to Zaporozh'e, his excursion there was documented in his criminal file. By now, much of what happened in Zaporozh'e is familiar from the testimony of the Zaporozh'e NKVD. That testimony, as well as parts of their trial, was duplicated in Grabar's criminal file, and a number of Zaporozh'e NKVD workers testified at his trial in Kiev. They basically reiterated the claims of their condemned leadership, pointing out how Grabar's brigade ramped up the terror and introduced the worst of the excesses.[45] NKVD operative P. S. Gal'chenko, who was in Zaporozh'e after Grabar's visit, told the court that the Zaporozh'e NKVD was still reeling from his visit as late as February 1939. He said, "Everyone in Zaporozh'e feared Grabar." Gal'chenko told the court that the night of the mass arrests in the factories of Zaporozh'e had been memorialized as Bartholomew's Night, akin to massacre.[46] Vaisberg, one of Grabar's brigade members, also testified. In addition to his testimony about Grabar's outrages in Kiev, Vaisbarg claimed that Grabar' pressured even the brigade members to increase tempos and numbers of arrest in Zaporozh'e, regardless of whether there was sufficient evidence. He said that Grabar' gave the order to use the same sort of physical pressure with the same instruments in Zaporozh'e as they used in Kiev, thus perhaps substantiating prison commandant Dorov's claims about Grabar's introduction of the rubber truncheon.[47] Although the Military Procurator in Zaporozh'e refused to allow Dorov, Klibanov, and Linetskii to place all blame for their crimes on Grabar', Grabar' was ultimately held responsible in Kiev for what happened in Zaporozh'e.

In the end, Grabar' did not go gently into the night. He fought his interrogators tooth and nail, proving to be a most uncooperative prisoner.[48] At his trial, he intervened and interrupted endlessly, attempting to refute or correct the testimony of witnesses. But he no longer had Uspenskii to protect him. His task, instead, was to convince the court that Uspenskii held him in the lowest regard and to shift all responsibility for his misdeeds on to his former idol.

THE CHARGES AGAINST Grabar' tied him directly to Uspenskii, uniting the two (sometimes with others) into a counterrevolutionary bloc.[49] Grabar', it was charged, "carried out his criminal activities on the direct assignment of enemy of the people Uspenskii."[50] In the 5 September 1939 indictment, "it was established" that "Uspenskii drew Grabar' into an antisoviet conspiratorial organization within the NKVD organs whose assignment was to carry out hostile work by falsifying criminal case files, [carrying out] groundless arrests, and beating prisoners." Further, the indictment read, "Uspenskii, seeing the vast activity of Grabar' in hostile work, sent him to the Zaporozh'e NKVD with the task to carry out not less than 1,000 arrests."[51] Grabar' had made it to the top.

Grabar' himself was partly responsible for this notion of a close association with Uspenskii. Before the latter's flight and his own arrest, Grabar' had bragged about the special relationship he had with Uspenskii. Two of his colleagues in the Special Department testified to Grabar's repeated claims that he was close to Uspenskii. Aleksei Fedorovich Borovkov recalled a meeting in Grabar's office in September 1938 when Grabar' told those in attendance that he was Uspenskii's special emissary and had come to strengthen (and purge) the Special Department based on the trust Uspenskii had for him.[52] Tul'skii, who worked with Grabar' from June 1938, said Grabar' threw around Uspenskii's name, claiming "he could call Uspenskii on the telephone whenever he wanted" and that Uspenskii "always agreed" with him.[53] In Zaporozh'e, Grabar' claimed that he had come on special assignment from Uspenskii and that he acted exclusively in his name.[54]

Grabar's tune began to change after his arrest. In an early interrogation during the night of 11 December 1938, Grabar', though recognizing that he bore a certain responsibility, claimed that everything he did was based on fear. He told his interrogator that "Uspenskii told me that if I did not fulfill everything he said, that he would arrest me."[55] In a face-to-face confrontation with Tul'skii, he denied that he had a close relationship with Uspenskii and said his contacts with him were limited to discussions about work.[56] In his own interrogation, Uspenskii spoke negatively about Grabar'.[57] He said, "nothing existed on the earth [for Grabar'] besides his career." If we are to believe Uspenskii, he took on Grabar' because he was told that "Grabar' was the kind of person for whom nothing was sacred and could be used for any kind of subversive work."[58] In a face-to-face confrontation with Uspenskii in Moscow, Grabar' said that "Uspenskii related to me poorly, and as a result he had bad relations with me." Uspenskii, who was happy to play whatever part his interrogators assigned him, said he had "direct conspiratorial links with Grabar'," but that he soon realized, given Grabar's coarseness, what a mistake that was.[59]

Before his arrest, Grabar' began to tell another story, perhaps influenced by the widespread talk in the Ukrainian NKVD about antisemitism and, in particular, antisemitic acts supposedly ordered by Uspenskii and his minions. Sixth Department operative Lev Isaevich Gorodinskii recalled that Grabar' became suddenly much more "democratic" at this time and told him how Uspenskii constantly harassed him, saying he was Jewish and surrounded by a circle of "Jerusalemites [*ieruslimtsy*]."[60] In a long missive to Khrushchev, Grabar' himself spoke about how Uspenskii "accused" him of being a Jew at a meeting in June 1938 and of hiding his supposed Jewish origins. Grabar' was so upset when Uspenskii did not believe his denials that he brought his 75-year-old Ukrainian father to Kiev to prove his nationality.[61] According to Grabar', Uspenskii nevertheless continued to bait him about his ethnicity, pointing to the time Grabar's mother worked in the Jewish Hospital in Odessa. At one point, Uspenskii accused Grabar' of plotting with his "Jerusalemite circle" against the Politburo.[62] It is impossible to know whether to believe Grabar's story, although Uspenskii's particular kind of cynical sadism, not to mention his antisemitism, could well have been at work here. At his trial, though, Grabar' would instead emphasize his fear of Uspenskii, even suggesting that Uspenskii had been about to arrest him.[63]

The subject of fear was an important thread running through Grabar's twenty-two-page letter to Khrushchev written on 22 November 1938.[64] The letter, composed on the eve of his own arrest, reveals that Grabar' feared that his arrest was imminent.[65] In the very first paragraph of his letter, Grabar' told Khrushchev that "in light of recent events among us in the Narkomat,[66] I have repeatedly called the CC [Central Committee of the Communist Party (b) Ukraine]," but was put off or told that "the leadership is not here."[67] Grabar' was desperately attempting to obtain an audience with Khrushchev in order, in his words, to tell him how Uspenskii was "speculating" on the name of the Politburo and Khrushchev "both at operational meetings and in his reports, which generally ended in threats of arrest, sadism, and humiliation."[68] What followed was a thorough denunciation of Uspenskii, listing a series of falsi-fied cases, which Grabar' claimed he had attempted to correct. These cases, according to Grabar', "did not conform to reality." Moreover, according to Grabar', there were people sitting in prison who must be immediately released! Grabar' documented what he called the "destruction" of the police and expressed his grave doubts on the validity of the case against Gershkov. He argued further that it was only the fear of Uspenskii that motivated him to beat Gershkov. He also documented the several instances when Uspenskii called him a Jew and charged him with being part of a "Jerusalemite circle."[69] His letter to Khrushchev was clearly a desperate attempt to save himself. Two days earlier, he had written similarly to Beriia, pleading for an audience "in light of what was occurring in the Ukrainian NKVD" and how his (Beriia's) and Ezhov's directions were not being fulfilled.[70]

Grabar' saw the writing on the wall, but it was too late. He was arrested less than two weeks after he wrote his desperate and self-serving plea to Khrushchev. After his arrest, Grabar' was subjected to lengthy, repeated inter-rogations that lasted from mid-December 1938 to April 1939. He also had a series of face-to-face encounters, partly at his own request, with a number of his accusers, including Boldin, Tul'skii, Borovkov, Brikker, and Vaisbarg, as well as being transported to Moscow to confront Uspenskii.[71] He accused his interrogators of torturing him; he struggled fiercely with them, signing con-fessions only to retract them later. At his trial, Grabar' admitted to beating prisoners, "but," he said, "it was nothing compared with the torture" he had to endure in these months.[72]

Grabar' was fighting for his life. Perhaps characteristically, he proved to be relatively litigious, at least as far as Soviet justice allowed. He submitted complaints to higher authorities, telling of how his interrogators were acting "nonobjectively" and "deceiving" him with "false promises" in their efforts to extract a confession. He indicated that he had repeatedly begged the prison commandant, Nagornyi, and the guards to call in the procurator and to supply him with paper on which to write complaints.[73] At his trial, he demanded, largely without success, that the court call his witnesses and complained again about failing to obtain face-to-face encounters with some of his accusers.[74] During the trial, he constantly interrupted witnesses, "correcting" them, denying their allegations, and blaming others for his purported crimes.

In his opening statement to the court, Grabar' said, "I understand the charges. I do not admit guilt to the totality of the charges against me. I admit guilt only insofar as, for the period in which I fulfilled the duties of head of the Sixth Department of the Ukrainian [republican] NKVD, I committed individual mistakes of an operational character, and on Uspenskii's orders and under the threat of my own arrest, [I] applied physical measures of influence on Gershkov." He then blamed his erstwhile storm brigade partner and Special Department worker, Vaisbarg, for his arrest, telling the court that there was bad blood between them.[75] His primary defense, however, was that he was following orders, motivated by his fear of enemy of the people Uspenskii.

Grabar' tried desperately to explain and to justify his actions, offering detailed testimony on the key charges. He discussed the Kopaev case and UkrKabel' at some length, concluding that, in his opinion, "Kopaev is an enemy and he was freed only to bury me."[76] He was frankly injured by the accusations about the typist, Shibanova, claiming several times that he tried to help her and even tried to free her.[77] As for Maiboroda, who had died under interrogation, Grabar' said he had not known anything about the use of physical measures on him.[78]

Grabar' blamed the destructive assault on the Ukrainian regular police on Uspenskii: "I had nothing to do with this." He did, however, admit to beating Gershkov. He claimed that he had hurried to see what was happing to Gershkov after he arrested him. In the Narkom's office, Uspenskii fell upon him with cries of "why don't you beat [him]. . . . You arrest him and leave."[79] Grabar' said that "I beat Gershkov only from fear, that otherwise I myself would be arrested."[80] Still, he said that Gershkov's testimony had been "basically correct, although he was embittered toward me and therefore exaggerated."[81] He also claimed that he wrote to Ezhov and the procurator about the groundless arrest of Gershkov.[82]

Finally, Grabar' discussed at length his excursion to Zaporozh'e. He recalled that, in June or July 1938, Uspenskii called to his office all the department heads and told them that the Politburo had taken the decision to purge industrial towns of all antisoviet elements. His task was to lead the brigade to Zaporozh'e and to analyze local lists of agents and people in the NKVD records and, on that basis, to compile arrest lists. He claimed to be surprised when he arrived in Zaporozh'e and saw prisoners subjected to forced standing in the corridors; he said he halted this practice immediately. He knew nothing about cell number 8 and claimed that the use of physical measures began only on 12 July when Uspenskii arrived. He said the new Zaporozh'e NKVD head, Boldin, asked Uspenskii at an operational meeting whether they could use physical pressure on individual prisoners. He said that Uspenskii replied, "[I] permit [this]," and only then did the use of torture become routine.[83]

Grabar' claimed no knowledge that people were arrested in Zaporozh'e without incriminating evidence, apart from the fact of their social or ethnic origin. He maintained further that most of the arrests occurred after his departure from Zaporozh'e, which he claimed was on 14 July, though Boldin said Grabar' left one day later.[84] He continued his testimony, arguing that he did not arrive in Zaporozh'e with a preconceived plan to arrest, but only received his orders when Uspenskii came to Zaporozh'e. He also said there was no control figure to arrest 1,000 people, either from him or from Uspenskii.[85] While he was there, "only" 240 people were arrested, and part of these arrests were, he continued, based on orders from the Dnepropetrovsk regional NKVD. Responding to a telegram in which he had written that 500 people had been arrested, Grabar' claimed that this was a mistake and should have read "to be arrested."[86] He insisted that the responsibility for what happened in Zaporozh'e lay exclusively with the heads of the Zaporozh'e NKVD—Vol'skii-Gitler, until his removal on 12 July, and, after that, Boldin.[87]

Grabar' tried hard. He told the court that he would never have confessed to belonging to Uspenskii's conspiracy had he not been tortured. He wrote only "under the dictation" of his brutal interrogator.[88] He complained that, before his Moscow face-to-face encounter with Uspenskii, he was beaten as well, whereas the cooperative Uspenskii, on the other hand, was treated to tea and cigarettes [papirosy].[89] That was insult added to injury.

In his final statement to the court, Grabar' again went through each charge, presenting his evidence and arguments, as well as asking for a new series of witnesses (which he was denied).[90] He added that he did hold a certain responsibility for the actions of his brigade in Zaporozh'e, but that if innocent people fell into the arrest lists, this was the fault of the members of the brigade who reported to him on arrest lists, thus widening the circle of those at fault beyond Uspenskii and Vaisbarg.[91] He also more or less accepted responsibility for his use of torture, though he carefully framed his admission. He said that he personally never granted anyone a sanction for the use of torture and even asked Ezhov in writing if force was permitted. Ezhov apparently said it was, but Grabar' accepted that, all the same, he must bear the responsibility for this.[92]

Grabar' also sought to explain his problematic personality. He admitted:

> I have elements of coarseness and tactlessness, which were inculcated under the impression of the foul language used by the leadership. I must admit that on these grounds the party organization warned me and after that I settled down a bit. I admit that I cursed at my subordinates in the apparatus, but I did this as a duty and am certain that if I had used the truncheon, which was used on prisoners, on my workers, then I would not sit at the bar now.

He then said, "I am a young worker. It always seemed to me that we could work better and therefore I harassed [my] apparatus as was said here."[93]

He concluded his final words by calling Uspenskii a liar and pleading with the court for mercy:

> I was not and will not be an enemy of the people. I loved my motherland and will continue to love it. I did not change and will not change. I am still young, have only begun to live and therefore I ask you to see me as a living human being, and to take into account the circumstances in which [I] committed crimes. I ask you for a just decision.[94]

It is a testament to his character that Grabar's last words were so long that the Military Procurator was forced to order a brief adjournment partway through.[95]

In the end, Grabar' was accused of blindly fulfilling Uspenskii's orders, motivated by extreme careerism. He was charged not with the criminal code Articles 54-1,7 for counterrevolutionary crimes, but with Article 206-17 (B) for "systematically and crudely violating socialist legality," and sentenced to death.[96] He immediately appealed the sentence, sending petitions for clemency to the Supreme Court of the USSR and the Supreme Soviet of the USSR. He "implored" these bodies "to believe that he had no hostile intentions," placing all the blame once again on "enemy of the people Uspenskii." He explained that he had "honestly" declared from the first day of his arrest that he had supported "petty criminals and, for that, had to face a harsh punishment, [leaving] a stain on his children and family." But "on his knees," he declared that he only tortured people under the threat of his own arrest. He

concluded his appeal by writing, "Is it possible that you, as the representatives of the people, will permit me to be the victim of a harsh, undeserved
sentence?"[97]

The answer came the next day. Both the Military Collegium of the
Supreme Court of the USSR and the Presidium of the Supreme Soviet of the
USSR rejected Grabar's plea for mercy.[98] Grabar' was executed by shooting
on 25 December 1940.[99] He left behind a wife and three small children.[100] The
last document in his criminal file is a letter written by his grandson in June
1994, asking about Grabar's place of burial.[101] The response stated that there
was no information about where Grabar' was buried and he would not be
rehabilitated.[102]

GRABAR'S CASE OFFERS less a straightforward story than a characterization
of a man. It is a characterization, moreover, that stands on somewhat ques-
tionable grounds, relying largely on the statements (however many, however
diverse) of other NKVD operatives, some already under arrest themselves. Yet
paired with his own words and deeds, the overall characterization of Grabar'
constructed here seems reasonable and in accord with a certain type of Soviet
official active in the 1930s.

Like Dolgushev and many of Uspenskii's minions in the Ukrainian
NKVD, Grabar' was a *vydvizhenets*, a product of a Stalinist state-orchestrated
social mobility, who had climbed the rungs of Soviet power from very humble
beginnings. Born in 1908, he was a child of the Revolution, living through the
violence, hardships, and ruptures of revolution and civil war and receiving no
more than a basic education. As a teenager, Grabar' experienced his first real
taste of power. He participated in the violent grain-requisitioning campaigns
of the late 1920s, riding roughshod over a peasantry that had been robbed of
its humanity and fleeced of its grain. At the same time, Grabar' had his own
unique particularities. He was an operator, who exploited his positions and
connections in the food and trade sectors of 1920s Berdichev for gain. He also
cultivated ties to the security police that would serve him well when in 1932
he left the army for a position in the security police. It was the Great Terror
and the rapid turnover it exacted among NKVD operatives that catapulted
him close to the very top of the Ukrainian NKVD.

By 1938, Grabar' had acquired enormous power over the minds and bodies of large numbers of people labeled as enemies. Grabar' was in his element,
throwing around his power among victims and subordinates alike; and he was
intoxicated by associations with his ill-fated superiors. Nadezhda Mandelstam
captured the essence of Grabar's personality type, writing that "anybody who

had the slightest power down to the humblest police official or doorkeeper, was also a dictator. We had not previously understood what a temptation power can be. . . . People cling desperately to what little power they have and will do their best to get all they can out of it."[103] Alexander Solzhenitsyn similarly wrote that "every little chief declares himself to be Soviet power," meaning, in short, that the "little chiefs" exercised vast power that could not be questioned, however arbitrary their rule.[104] Although Grabar's position was rather far above that of a "little chief," in his own domains, he too was "Soviet power," with an imperious and dictatorial style leavened by coarseness and obscenity. Grabar' was both a force of Soviet power and its emanation.

This portrait of Grabar' does not necessarily negate his defense that he was motivated to act as he did out of fear. He trembled before his superiors, most especially before Uspenskii, though it is likely that such fear and trembling increased as the reality of his own arrest came nearer. After all, he had been enthralled by Uspenskii and made a point to tell his subordinates how close the two were. This portrait also need not negate Grabar's defense of following orders. Although his Berdichev past may suggest otherwise, as a Chekist, Grabar' was a military man and it was his duty, if not his nature, to follow orders. At the same time, his pretensions and self-importance made it highly likely that he would follow orders "creatively," inserting his own overly large personality into the shape of things. And he was not simply a blind follower of Uspenskii. He believed that there were enemies and that he was fighting a war. It was his duty to obey, but it is very likely that he did so less out of blind faith and fear than a genuine determination to wield power and to play his part in the struggle.

In the end, Grabar' paid for such power with his life. Although there is little doubt that he, like many of his arrested colleagues, was a scapegoat for Stalin's Great Terror, he was neither an automaton nor simply one among hundreds of conforming Chekists playing their part in the state's mass repression. Grabar' was, instead, a "master of falsification," a talented liar, and a master in the practice of terror, with all its allowances for "creativity," personality, and ambition.

Postscript

AT 9:10 ON the evening of 14 November 1938, Ukrainian NKVD Commissar Uspenskii left his apartment for the last time. Dressed in civilian clothes, he told his bodyguard not to accompany him. He showed him his sidearm and said, "I'm a Chekist. I can defend myself."[1] The following day, Uspenskii's suicide note surfaced. It read:

> Farewell to all true comrades. Look for my body in the Dnepr [River] if you need it. To be sure [of my death], I will shoot myself [as I go] into the water . . . without misfiring. [I] was never a Liushkov.[2]

Uspenskii, Ezhov's man in Ukraine during the final terrible months of the Great Terror and the patron of the NKVD operatives in these pages, feared correctly that his own arrest was imminent.

Nikolai Fedorovich Zakharov, head of the Ukrainian NKVD secretariat, described later, during his own interrogation of 15 November, what happened next at the commissariat. About ten minutes after Uspenskii reportedly left his apartment, none other than Khrushchev called the NKVD to talk to him. Zakharov received the call and told Khrushchev that Uspenskii had just gone out somewhere. Zakharov then immediately contacted Uspenskii's deputy, A. A. Iaraliants, to tell him that Khrushchev had phoned. Iaraliants told Zakharov that he would call Uspenskii at home; he also told Zakharov that he knew where Uspenskii was. In the meantime, following Uspenskii's earlier orders from that day that he would return later to work, Zakharov waited several hours for Uspenskii before clearing his desk and moving his papers into the safe, as per standard procedure.

The next day, November 15, panic began to set in. Early in the morning, Uspenskii's wife called Zakharov at the commissariat to find out why

Uspenskii was not answering his office telephone. She told Zakharov that her husband had not been home all night. Zakharov immediately reported this phone call to Iaraliants and asked him where Uspenskii was. Iaraliants responded, "I said that I knew where Uspenskii is insofar as he warned me that he was leaving his home on personal business." He further told Zakharov not to take any measures. At 1:00 p.m. that same day, Ezhov called Zakharov, reassured him, and told him not to take any measures just yet as they could "compromise" Uspenskii.

It was at this point that Zakharov recalled that Uspenskii had asked him for two envelopes the morning of the 14th, yet had not given him anything to send. Zakharov went to Uspenskii's office and found in a folder labeled "To c[omrade] Khrushchev" one of the envelopes he had given Uspenskii, unsealed with a thin sheet of paper inside. He brought the envelope to Iaraliants who read what was written and immediately phoned M. A. Burmistenko, the second secretary of the Central Committee of the Ukrainian Communist Party. Iaraliants then hurriedly left for the Central Committee office.[3]

Interrogated on 16 November, Iaraliants took up the story from here. He said that 14 November had been a day like any other at the Commissariat. Uspenskii had given him materials to send to Ezhov and had participated in ongoing interrogations of suspects. Later in the early afternoon, Uspenskii told Iaraliants that he had a backache and planned to go to the countryside with his son. Iaraliants only became worried the next day when Uspenskii's wife called in alarm. Iaraliants told his interrogator that he was afraid to report Uspenskii's disappearance to Moscow, lest Uspenskii return. He therefore called Khrushchev, who ordered him to take all measures to find Uspenskii. Soon thereafter, perhaps in response to a call from Khrushchev, Beriia called and also ordered Iaraliants to find Uspenskii. At that point, Burmistenko sent someone to Uspenskii's apartment to question his wife and Iaraliants, on a second phone call, shared the content of the suicide note that Zakharov had found with Beriia. Soon after, the search for Uspenskii's corpse began in the morgues and hospitals of Kiev.[4]

Uspenskii, however, had not killed himself, though suicides did occur among some NKVD leaders and operatives who feared arrest at this time. Uspenskii had good reason to fear and seems to have planned his escape, possibly as early as August 1938. At that time, Uspenskii was in Moscow for a session of the Supreme Soviet of the USSR. Ezhov invited him and M. I. Litvin, the Leningrad regional NKVD boss, to his dacha. Pale, drunk, and fearful, Ezhov reportedly told Uspenskii and Litvin that, with the appointment of Beriia as Ezhov's deputy that month, he feared his own demise and the destruction of the "new people" in the NKVD as "unnecessary witnesses." Uspenskii later claimed that, after this meeting, he decided to flee.[5]

Iaraliants remembered that Uspenskii had been unnerved by the June 1938 flight of the Far Eastern NKVD boss, G. S. Liushkov, which he believed had motivated Molotov to criticize Soviet intelligence in his 7 November speech.[6] That evening, Uspenskii had called Iaraliants in a drunken state. When Iaraliants went over to Uspenskii's apartment, he was told by his boss about "problems" at the Central Committee and Khrushchev's supposed dissatisfaction with him (Uspenskii), saying, "you can't know from what side they'll take you."[7] Soon after Liushkov's flight, the NKVD resident in Spain, Aleksandr Orlov, also fled.[8] Two days before Uspenskii's flight, Litvin killed himself.[9] Word was clearly out, at least among top NKVD leaders, that they were not safe.

Two stories later circulated about Ezhov's warnings to Uspenskii. Uspenskii later claimed in his own interrogation that he had called Ezhov on the morning of 14 November. Ezhov warned him at that time that he was to be summoned to Moscow and "to decide himself what to do."[10] Another version of the story, circulated in part by Khrushchev, claimed that Stalin called Khrushchev on 14 November with an order to arrest Uspenskii, only to call again a short time later to rescind the order and to tell Khrushchev that Uspenskii would be summoned to Moscow instead and arrested there. According to this version of the story, Ezhov then called Uspenskii to warn him.[11] Although it is not possible to verify who called whom, it is clear that Uspenskii had good reason to run on the 14th of November.

It did not take long for Stalin to conclude that Uspenskii had faked his suicide and to launch an all-out manhunt. He ordered the creation of special search groups under all NKVD organs. Uspenskii's photo was to be circulated to all police offices. The search was extended to include all ports and railroad stations.[12]

Reports later said that Uspenskii's wife bought his train ticket to Voronezh. Whether or not this was true, she would be executed for supposedly assisting him.[13] Uspenskii never reached Voronezh; instead he left the train at Kaluga, where he rented an apartment, changed his appearance, and, at some point, assumed the passport of one "Ivan Shmakovskii." After four days in Kaluga, Uspenskii headed for Arkhangel'sk in the far north of European Russia and worked for a time, under his assumed name, in a forestry firm. Then he went back to Kaluga to stay with relatives, and after five to six days, traveled to Moscow to track down his lover, Marisa Matson. The two then left for Murom, moving from apartment to apartment. Their relationship eventually broke down, and she returned to Moscow on 14 March 1939. Uspenskii then traveled to Kazan, Sverdlovsk, and finally Cheliabinsk, where, on 14 April, he was arrested following the discovery of "Ivan Shmakovskii's" luggage in the station's storage room at a small railroad station outside the city.[14]

Uspenskii was arrested and brought to Moscow. He was condemned to death on 27 January 1940. In the interval, he willingly cooperated with his former colleagues—after all, he knew the game—immediately "confessing" to a plot to bring down the Soviet Union, offering extensive information on his former subordinates in Ukraine's NKVD, and taking part in numerous face-to-face confrontations at the Lubianka prison with arrested NKVD operatives, while, if we are to believe Grabar', drinking tea and smoking cigarettes [*papirosy*].[15] Arrested on 10 April 1939, Ezhov was executed one month after Uspenskii, in February 1940.

Conclusion

THE PURGE OF the NKVD at the end of the 1930s and the beginning of the 1940s was an important, perhaps essential, coda to the Great Terror. The 17 November 1938 directive, "On arrests, procurator supervision, and carrying out investigations," brought to a halt the mass operations, resulting in a steep, though certainly not complete, decline in the magnitude of mass repression in the final prewar years. The ending of the terror demonstrated Stalin's power over the NKVD. The trials of NKVD operatives that ensued were both revelatory and dramatic as NKVD officials confronted grave accusations of criminal violations.

Yet Stalin publicly proclaimed the mass operations to be a great success. At the 18th Party Congress in March 1939, he claimed that the nation's purge had resulted in the "final liquidation of the exploiting classes." He forcefully contested what he called the foreign press's contention that the terror had weakened the Soviet state, labeling that kind of talk "banal gossip." Instead, he claimed that the terror had created a new "internal unity" of the Soviet people that made the Red Army stronger than any other nation's army.[1] Stalin did not renounce the Great Terror.

Stalin instead renounced those Soviet officials, mainly in the NKVD, who had violated socialist or revolutionary legality in the conduct of mass operations. His renunciation led to the destruction of important clientele or patronage networks within the NKVD. In Ukraine, Uspenskii's fall cleared the way for the arrest of his subordinates, just as Ezhov's downfall prompted the destruction of Ezhov's clientele network throughout the Soviet Union. Although the NKVD had been subject to purges earlier in 1937 and 1938 as new NKVD leaders brought in their "tails" and destroyed preexisting clientele networks, this particular purge was different for it featured not accusations of Trotskyism or counterrevolution, as in earlier NKVD purges, but served instead to scapegoat the NKVD—or, publicly, elements within the NKVD—for the "violations" of the Great Terror. The NKVD purge also resulted in what some historians call a cadre revolution in the NKVD that effectively purged almost 23% of its operational staff and resulted in the recruitment of some 14,506 new cadres (who would constitute around 45% of all operative workers), mostly with a new clientele network—Beriia's—that would more or less remain in office until Stalin's death in 1953.[2]

The trials of NKVD operatives proceeded under the aegis of Soviet justice, an often oxymoronic designation especially under Stalin. In the Soviet Union, there was no independent judicial system. During the Great Terror, the NKVD carried out both arrests and the subsequent investigations, which resulted in the indictments for the military tribunals and troikas. Moreover, a perverse legal and administrative fetishism demanded that NKVD interrogators beat false confessions out of "enemies" and collect the fictive statements of official witnesses—or, at the least, forge the necessary paperwork to push cases through to their deadly completion. Politics and ideology determined the contours of Soviet justice, or socialist legality as it was labeled. Yet the trials of NKVD operatives were different, and despite clear limitations, are extremely valuable sources of information.[3]

These trials had little in common with the staged, show trials of the 1930s and nothing in common with the assembly-line troika processing of the victims of the mass operations. Instead, these trials resemble more the wartime and postwar trials of World War II collaborators and war criminals within the Soviet Union. Scholars who have studied these later trials have concluded, as Alexander Prusin writes, that, "within the bounds of the Soviet legal system, the trials accorded fully with juridical norms" providing "relatively accurate descriptions" of the war in the Soviet Union. In spite of their political and ideological imprimatur, the wartime and postwar trials contained important pedagogical messages that, according to Ilya Bourtman, aimed "to unify a diverse people in the midst of [and after] a devastating war" by "exacting revenge and extracting retribution; deterring future collaboration; cleansing Soviet society of 'enemies of the state': and garnering evidence for reparation claims." According to Tanja Penter, these trials "served the Stalinist regime for its own legitimation inside Soviet society and abroad." The trials of NKVD cadres at the end of the 1930s also served symbolic and pedagogical purposes, in spite of the fact that, unlike at least some of the later trials, these were closed trials with scant mention in the press.[4]

The NKVD trials were meant to have a disciplinary impact on the NKVD. The relatively wide participation of NKVD operatives in these trials made it highly likely that the substance of the trials was known among NKVD cadres. Their participation as witnesses and signalers meant that they knew what was occurring at these trials locally; certainly they discussed these events with other NKVD colleagues at the late 1938–early 1939 NKVD party meetings and likely elsewhere outside of the trials, given the frequent violations of their secrecy agreements. The trials made it clear, above all, that the NKVD, whether because of "institutional interests," "clans" (i.e., clientele networks), or a few "bad apples," must be brought under the control of Stalin and the Communist Party. Above all, the trials were used to demonstrate that Stalin was not to blame.

Equally important, the trials sent a message to the Communist Party. Stalin cast the Communist Party as the main victim of the malfeasance of the NKVD in the Great Terror. Party members and other elites played a prominent role in the trials, mainly as victims, sometimes as victimized witnesses as in the case of Skvira's official witnesses and some Communist factory workers in Zaporozh'e. The Communist Party was also given a key role to play in "correcting" the violations and seeking out the transgressors in the NKVD.[5] It would hereafter serve, along with its youth wing, the Komsomol, as the main recruitment pool for the new NKVD cadres brought in to replace their disgraced predecessors.[6] The trials were part of an emerging narrative of Communist victimization in the terror followed by the "restoration" of party control, a narrative traditionally associated with Khrushchev and his 20th Party Congress "secret speech" in 1956. The narrative pitted the NKVD against the Communist Party, airbrushing away the majority of the Great Terror's victims, who were neither Communist nor elite, and, importantly, ignoring the central role of the leadership of the Party in the Great Terror. The trials were Stalin's gift to the Party, serving to relegitimize its authority and its power following two years of terror.

Stalin was well aware of the devastating impact of the Great Terror. He certainly knew about its legion of victims as well as the extent to which the terror was undermining local, especially Communist, authority. The victims were not silent, during or after the mass operations. They and their relatives inundated higher authorities with literally hundreds of thousands of letters of complaint. On 22 February 1938, USSR Procurator Vyshinskii complained to Molotov that the USSR Procurator's office was unable to handle the volume of complaints, noting that in the first twenty days of February alone, it had received 40,000 complaints.[7] In 1938, as a whole, the Procurator's office received some 600,000 complaints related to the terror.[8] The Russian Republic Procurator's office was also overwhelmed, receiving 700 to 800 complaints daily, and from February 1938, 50,000 to 60,000 complaints monthly.[9] The Ukrainian Republic Procurator's office received some 170,855 complaints between 1 January 1939 and 1 January 1940, of which 46,695 went to the republican offices of the Procurator and 124,160 to their regional offices. The Kiev regional Procurator received 21,278 complaints in the same period.[10] These complaints represented the tip of the proverbial iceberg as victims and their relatives also besieged the offices of Stalin, Ezhov, and a large range of other individuals and institutions at all geographical–administrative levels. Needless to say, not all these complaints came from Communists. Stalin, however, was fully aware of the push-back against the mass operations.

The 17 November 1938 directive also opened up a second floodgate of complaints. News of the directive very quickly reached the prison cells of the NKVD. Many prisoners, whose cases had not yet been completed, rescinded their confessions at this time. This phenomenon was fairly widespread, according to NKVD complaints, and continued into 1939. As a result of the November directive, unfinished cases were transferred to the courts and possibly as many as 110,000 people were freed.[11] In addition, some 77,000 purged Communists were reinstated into the Party.[12] At the least, these transfers of cases and releases relieved the deadly prison overcrowding of 1938 and the huge backlog of unfinished cases. At the most, they may have served to cover up old wounds and to strengthen further the narrative of victimized Communists.

Stalin may also have been troubled by reports that news of the mass operations had breached the information security perimeters of the NKVD. Although the evidence is far from conclusive and much research is still needed, it is clear that there was considerable leakage of the terror into the public domain. The trials have demonstrated the ways in which the sheer noise of terror reached the streets from the NKVD prisons; Dolgushev was especially concerned with this leakage. Another type of leakage came with the appearance of executed victims' clothing at local markets as the wives of NKVD execution squad members tried to benefit from their self-proclaimed hard and dirty work. NKVD operatives also lived at least for a time in the same general areas as their victims, often leading lonely bachelor lives and living in shoddy Soviet hotels because of local housing shortages and frequent transfers. In Uman, the hotel became a center for NKVD carousing and drunkenness. Here, there were also reports of NKVD interrogators sleeping with prisoners' wives in exchange for the privilege of access to a loved one. In Moscow, according to the Russian historian A. Iu. Vatlin, the solution to the housing shortage was for NKVD operatives to move into the victims' former dwellings; outside of Moscow, this may have been a less attractive prospect, given the dismal state of the housing stock.[13] Occasional reports of demonstrations by prisoners' wives also surface in the Ukrainian documents, providing further possible evidence of leakage and suggesting that some brave souls may have attempted to protest more publicly.[14]

The precise dimensions of public knowledge about the terror cannot be demarcated. Still, it is clear that there was leakage. News of the terror had also leaked out abroad. In the republican NKVD offices in Kiev, there was near panic when the Munich agreement was reached in the fall of 1938.[15] That agreement raised grave doubts in Stalin's mind about the willingness of the West to fight Hitler. Hedging his bets, Stalin may have realized that ending the national operations, especially the repression of Soviet Germans, might be useful in future diplomatic dialog with Germany. Ironically, Stalin's war against a supposed Fifth Column may in fact have strengthened his sense of international danger, as well as planting seeds for new Fifth Column forces during the war.

In any case, it is likely that Stalin utilized these trials to address the grievances of selected audiences, mainly but not only elite audiences, while transferring the blame for their grievances away from himself and on to designated groups and individuals within the NKVD. Perhaps he recognized that in pursuit of the destruction of the much-touted Fifth Column, the terror had begun to create seedlings for new columns. Perhaps he cared only about the damage done to the Communist Party's credibility. Initially, Stalin had asked Vyshinskii to organize an open trial of leading NKVD workers before evidently reconsidering.[16] The open and extremely revelatory reactions of provincial and local NKVD workers at their trials may have influenced him in this reconsideration. Ultimately, though, Ezhov, Uspenskii, and the past leadership of the NKVD would be condemned for treason, for an attempt to undermine the Soviet government and crush the Communist Party, whereas middle- and lower-level personnel were condemned for their violations of socialist legality.

Stalin's scapegoating of officials of various stripes for violations in policy implementation removed the blame from him. It permitted him to explain away "violations" and "excesses" in policy implementation as the work of a relatively few bad apples. It was a face-saving measure for Stalin, and not unlike similar practices used by other governments to avoid blame. The same bad-apples approach to punishment was apparent in the US government's actions in My Lai during the Vietnam War and at Abu Ghraib during the Iraq war.[17] These policies allowed Stalin to distance himself from the worst of policy practices once a radical breakthrough in policy was achieved. It also served a disciplinary, though highly symbolic, purpose for both the NKVD and the Communist Party. Stalin was not interested in justice per se; his goal to purge Soviet society of its Fifth Column, if not exactly fulfilled, had gone as far as it could.

BY TAKING READERS into the interrogation rooms and execution chambers of the Great Terror, the investigative files of NKVD interrogators offer important information on the terror at the local level and in a variety of institutional settings, ranging from the Ukrainian Republic and Kiev regional offices of the NKVD to the workings of an interdistrict operational group in Uman to the rural setting of Skvira and the industrial factories of Zaporozh'e. The chief importance of these sources resides in their depictions of how the terror was implemented, what happened, and who was responsible. The trials demonstrate that orders from above worked in conjunction with a series of situational factors to shape the contours of the Great Terror. These, in turn, formed the context in which individual NKVD interrogators operated.

Orders, administrative rules, and legislation came down from above, from Stalin, creating the overall system of the Great Terror. The dictator, moreover, steered the ship. At the same time, the system created the specific situational factors that shaped the actions and behaviors of NKVD interrogators. Social psychologists who have studied episodes of mass violence and mass murder have tended to downplay the actions of individuals in specific settings of state violence. Instead, they stress the importance of system and situation within the context of institutional settings operating under extraordinary pressures of, for example, war, fear of war, or fear of terrorism. Philip Zimbardo writes:

> The System consists of the agents and agencies whose ideology, values, and power create situations and dictate the roles and expectations for approved behavior of actors within its spheres of influence.... The Situation is the behavioral context that has the power, through its reward and normative functions, to give meaning and identity to the actors' roles and status within its spheres of influence.[18]

In attempting to understand perpetrator behavior, it is important to avoid exaggerating the role of individual or dispositional factors in settings of extreme violence. In the case of the Great Terror, Stalin and the NKVD represented the system, whereas ideology, rules and procedures (written and oral), pressure and force, and the logic of the terror's master plot and the way in which it was implemented shaped the conduct of individual perpetrator behavior, resulting in the dehumanization of victims, torture, and murder.

The trials highlight that the very scope and scale of the Great Terror shaped the contours of its realization. Orders came down from Moscow, from the center to the republics and provinces, with a suddenness and a fury that resembled war. War or, to be more precise, the fear of war and the activization of a Fifth Column, in fact, was the chief animating factor in determining the terror's urgency, speed, and compression. This should not surprise, given the ubiquity of the scholarly consensus that episodes of mass killing generally occur in times of war and civil war, often in connection to state building.[19] Equally important, the experience of the Russian civil war determined the terror's field of enemies as well as its dominant rhetoric. Although in reality, many victims of the terror were arbitrarily chosen to fulfill norms, especially in 1938 when the NKVD files had thinned, the goal of the Great Terror was to complete the civil war with the final elimination of all remaining members of the old prerevolutionary elites, members of prerevolutionary political parties and movements, the kulak (again), recidivist criminals, and foreign elements who could possibly engage in espionage (the national operations). These were Stalin's Fifth Column. In fact, there was no real current danger; these forces had long been depleted.

Within this ideologized martial setting, the huge numbers of people to be arrested in compressed revolutionary time combined with the most fantastical charges of enemy activity and behavior. Because confessions were the centerpiece of the work of the NKVD interrogators, their primary goal, because group cases and the necessary "naming of names" became a key goal in 1938, because the charges to which victims were forced to confess were largely in the realm of civil war nightmare or the absurd, because the time pressures were unremitting, torture assumed a logic of its own as the only means to extract confessions, and it was ubiquitous. Petrov from Uman was absolutely right when he admitted, "No one ordered me to beat the arrested, but they said that I had to provide 100 confessions a day." And the confessions generally followed scripts coming from above that were shouted at and pummeled into the victim's face until he or she confessed.

The head of the Kievan regional NKVD, Dolgushev, claimed that torture had become systemic. He was echoed by multiple other NKVD workers. Those on trial discussed this practice endlessly. The young and sadistic Drushliak admitted quite willingly to the use of torture. At the same time, he argued with all his might that he never applied torture without the sanction of his superiors. Dolgushev confirmed that these sanctions were a necessity.

Yet everyone, everywhere, made extensive use of torture. Moreover, as Stalin made clear in his coded letter of January 1939, the use of torture had been allowed from the summer of 1937.[20] According to Oleg Khlevniuk, he even feared that it might be necessary to arrest the entire NKVD if torture was the main criteria.[21] That is why he wrote this letter and left the issue of the violation of socialist legality for others to clarify—the party committees that reviewed NKVD cadres at this time and the Military Tribunals that tried them.

There were, however, no written orders on the use of torture. That is part of the reason why NKVD operatives like Drushliak kept insisting on permission from his superiors. The trials, though, demonstrate the ways in which torture as a permitted method of the terror was disseminated through the ranks of the NKVD. All discussion on the use of torture was oral. Plenipotentiaries— or *gastrolery*, as Borisov in Uman put it—descended through the entirety of the NKVD territorial-administrative apparatus to expound on the use of torture. They "taught" torture during NKVD operational meetings, threatening and cajoling their subordinates to get tough. They also taught torture during interrogations, interfering in local operations and ongoing interrogations. Every level of the NKVD administration continually pressured the agencies below them, sending plenipotentiaries, making telephone calls, arresting individual NKVD leaders. The military culture of the NKVD, moreover, meant that obedience to superior orders was a given. If torture was the primary lubricant of the terror, it was the unremitting pressure from above, the continual visits of the plenipotentiaries that served to disseminate and accelerate the terror, leading to more and more arrests and larger and larger group cases.

Individual NKVD actors also operated within a political and ideological setting that dehumanized victims, enabling the worst kind of atrocities. Apocalyptic thinking and a conspiratorial view of the world growing out of war, revolution, and civil war likely played a more important role than Marxist ideology per se in the atmosphere of the times. The Communist Party and the NKVD saw themselves as locked in an endless and inevitable war with internal and external enemies. It was a world without neutrality, a world of simple binaries—good vs. evil, proletarian vs. bourgeois—that dictated force in dealing with enemies.

The NKVD trials also break the silence of the execution chambers. Victims became aware of their fate only at the tragic, penultimate moment. Their bodies were subjected to violation and pillage as NKVD executioners competed for the money, clothing, and meager possessions of the dead. This venality, if not sadism, was apparent both in Uman and Zaporozh'e, and, in all likelihood, in many, many other places. From the convoluted discussions of execution-site looting at the Uman trial, it is likely that much of what went on during executions was either sanctioned from above earlier, developed in the course of work, or was part of a longer NKVD culture of executions.[22] The execution shooting squads were made up of the most motley crews of NKVD auxiliaries, including NKVD guards, couriers, chauffeurs, and regular policemen, generally under the direction of the prison commandant. They believed that they carried out the hardest and dirtiest work of the mass operations. They felt entitled to the windfall of clothing and other goods as well as the drinks and food that were served at the end of a hard night of shooting, removing bodies, and transporting them to the cemeteries. In essence, this was the immoral economy of the execution squads, but that economy was shaped by both system and situation.

The terror came down from on high; its scope, scale, time compression, and ideological imprimatur shaped its implementation locally. This discussion of situation and system is not meant to absolve individual NKVD officials of guilt or responsibility. Nor is it to deny an element of agency in their actions. The question that arises is the contribution made by individual perpetrators of the terror, the regional and district NKVD interrogators in the dock. To what extent did these actors influence the course of events?

THE REASONS FOR the Great Terror do not lie in the actions of individual middle- and lower-level NKVD perpetrators, although as a collective they were indispensible, until they were not. However, they did not directly influence the larger course of events. Rather, their primary importance resides in the light that their testimony sheds on the dynamics of the terror at lower levels. Their words and actions not only illuminate the illogical logic of the terror's trajectory, but also the dehumanization of their victims. Martial language, the language of enemies omnipresent, and, in particular, the panoply of euphemisms deployed to cloak, sanitize, or normalize the worst of their activities turned their victims into objects and categories. The biological approach used in their work to excise people with social, political, or economically alien backgrounds, including Jewish NKVD workers, demonstrated the ways in which the Revolution and incomplete civil war endured in defining the fate of the Soviet Union's population. The testimony of these NKVD workers also illustrates other aspects of the terror that often lie beneath the surface of secrecy—the workings of the troika, the use of official witnesses, the work of an interdistrict operational group, the circulation of the master plot of the terror, and the interactions between multiple territorial-administrative levels of the NKVD with higher NKVD offices. At the same time, the NKVD workers' testimony on torture and falsification of cases should be a clear warning to historians to use the interrogation materials of the actual victims of the 1937–1938 terror with extreme caution.[23]

The materials under investigation also demonstrate some of the Ukrainian specificities of the terror. Ukraine's status as borderland with a diverse ethnic population and the heritage—real and imagined—of Ukrainian nationalism made it an especially dangerous zone of terror, placing Ukraine with the capitals and key areas of internal exile like Siberia among the places hit hardest, especially in 1938. The mass operations in Ukraine were extended and enlarged with the arrival of Uspenskii and his minions from the Russian Republic. Along with the targeting of supposed Ukrainian nationalists, Poles, Germans, and Jews figured in large numbers among the victims of the terror. Poles and Germans were, of course, Soviet citizens, but they were also members of so-called diaspora nations, therefore presenting in Stalin's mind the threat of divided loyalties.[24] Both Germans and Jews may have been targets of a more local prejudice as traditional economic elites; moreover, both groups had been labeled suspicious populations and subject to forced deportations during the First World War by the Tsarist military.[25]

Officially, Jews were targeted for excision for exclusively political reasons. Former Zionists and Bundists, though in fact no longer active politically, fell in sufficiently large numbers in Ukraine during the terror. Other Jews, including those in the NKVD, fell victim to the particular and traditional occupational trajectories forced on the Jewish population in the prerevolutionary Pale of Settlement. Dolgushev, the head of the Kievan regional NKVD, strenuously denied antisemitism in the repression of Jews for so-called biological factors; Jewish NKVD men disagreed vigorously at the late 1938–early 1939 Communist Party meetings of the NKVD; and antisemitic torture and harassment of Jewish prisoners occurred. Although it is only possible to speculate about prewar antisemitism, it should be noted that its official manifestation, if indeed that is what it was, arrived with Uspenskii and his clan from Russia with the apparent endorsement of Ezhov—that is, from the very top, perhaps thereby adding a new dimension to the terrible legacy of antisemitism in Russia and Ukraine.

These sources also document the instability within the NKVD itself in Ukraine as it underwent a seemingly endless internal purge combined with changing clientele networks, constant rotations of employees, and large mobilizations of new and untested cadres. The NKVD Communist Party meetings demonstrate not only the complaints of Jewish NKVD men about antisemitism, but also grievances about the NKVD's hard lot during the mass operations and sharp criticism from its newest employees. Younger and newer NKVD workers often claimed naivete and inexperience, criticizing their elders for either failing to teach them correct procedure or for their violations of socialist legality. One young NKVD worker, for example, claimed, "Enemies of the people taught us younger cadres and said 'everything that happens in the NKVD' should be kept secret, 'even from the CC [Central Committee]' of the Communist Party."[26] Another young NKVD worker, who also claimed that "no one taught us younger workers," said:

> Before working in the NKVD organs, [I considered that] the most dedicated, the most honorable people work in the organs and that they work impartially and honestly on all matters, but when I entered into the work of the Dnepropetrovsk NKVD, I saw dishonest people among NKVD workers. In the beginning, I had a wish to leave work since conditions were so terrible.[27]

The sincerity of these words may well be doubtful, given context and the fact that, as one Maksimov admitted, "we were all guilty in this vile work."[28] Nonetheless, it is clear that the NKVD of the period of mass operations was anything but monolithic. Further, its very instability increased not only the fear that drove some NKVD interrogators and the increasingly radical contours of the terror, but may also have facilitated the NKVD's vulnerability to outside intervention and purge.

Finally, these trials hint at a broader complicity in the terror beyond its official agents. Not only did the execution squads consist of a motley crew of NKVD auxiliaries, but the regular police also played a key, if still not entirely documented, role in the terror. NKVD and prison housekeepers, janitors, guards, and cemetery workers were privy to the mass violence, as were civilian typists and typists from nonoperational sectors of the NKVD, who were recruited in large numbers to type up the endless paperwork of terror.[29] NKVD and prison doctors witnessed the direct aftermath of torture and death in the stifling prison cells with a mixture of indifference, frustration, or regret. In places like Skvira, the rural *aktiv* played vital roles, whether willingly or not, as state witnesses. In factories, NKVD plants in hiring committees and special committees, along with Communist Party secretaries, were essential to the compilation of arrest lists of their fellow workers.

The NKVD interrogators on trial were of course the most "complicit" of all. Although their actions may not unravel the central mysteries of the Great Terror, they have thrown open a window on its workings. They played an indispensable role at this time, serving to shape some of the contours of the terror's dynamics at regional and district levels. It is useful, at this point, to return to the main actors of the story in order to attempt to assess questions of agency and the range of defense rationales, which they offered in denying their guilt.

SOCIAL PSYCHOLOGISTS AND historians who study mass violence have generally concluded that most perpetrators were "ordinary men," to use the term popularized by the historian of the Holocaust Christopher Browning.[30] They were, as a rule, neither sadists nor monsters, despite their sadistic and monstrous actions. Circumstances or situational factors combined with the directing role of the state (or, in other societies, elites) are considered far more compelling explanations for mass violence than the dispositional traits of individual perpetrators.[31]

Although Drushliak may well have been a sadist—his colleagues said he was—the other NKVD actors in this story were in all probability not pathological personalities, in spite of the hideous nature of their "violations" of socialist legality. Yet the term ordinary man is not entirely apt either. After all, these were members of the NKVD, an elite and highly politicized organization defined by rules of hierarchy, subordination, and discipline.[32] They were trained in the ways of violence both historically through their participation in the Russian civil war or the collectivization campaigns and in the course of the mass operations. Those who had not served in earlier repressive campaigns were the products of Soviet education. They were also "ideologized," but less in the sense of Marxist–Leninist–Stalinist dogma than in the sense of ideology in practice, or praxis. They followed orders from above, but creatively and savagely, with just enough suggestion that venality, sometimes sadism, and local conditions colored their actions along with the usual elements of obedience to higher orders, fear, and personal ambition. The occasional personal grudge, as in Skvira and Uman, also played a role, though that kind of conflict remains largely opaque in the documents. It is within this context that they exercised a constrained or limited agency exercised within temporal and functional parameters that made them masters (as it were, little dictators) of their own domain and anything but ordinary men in the eyes of their victims.

They were the guardians of Kafka's Castle, replete with constantly changing orders, each more radical than the last, some in simple contradiction to one another, and frequent alternations of the guard. They followed procedures in circumstances that depended on their abrogation and were participants and victims of an administrative-legal fetishism startling in its contradictions, hypocrisy, pervasiveness, and, all too often, its redundancy. They had unlimited powers for a limited time. They certainly did not make the rules, but they interpreted them, at times in their own way, improvising when necessity dictated and taking any and all measures to satisfy their superiors' demands. On the whole, the perpetrators of these pages were young men, in their twenties and thirties, whose baptism by fire came either in the Russian civil war or during the repressive campaigns of the collectivization era in the early 1930s. Most were recruited directly from the military, a practice that would change after the Great Terror.

At their trials, they defended and justified their actions in spite of being tortured during their interrogations. For some, like Drushliak, Fleishman, Tomin, Klibanov, and Linetskii, they "believed and continued to believe," to paraphrase Drushliak, in the world of enemies omnipresent in league with the forces of the capitalist encirclement to destroy the Soviet Union. Others, like Abramovich in Uman or Dorov in Zaporozh'e, acted out of venality, committing atrocities in the special torture rooms and execution chambers. Ambition and careerism played a role in the cases of Drushliak, Grabar', and the celebrated "chopper" Petrov. Combinations of fear and ignorance also factored into the actions of perpetrators like the militia man Krivtsov or the chauffeur Zudin who could not wait for the distribution of murdered victims' clothing that accompanied the end of executions in Uman and elsewhere. Although some expressed doubts and a degree of self-reflection, like Dolgushev and Borisov, all subscribed to what Holocaust historian Raul Hilberg dubbed "the doctrine of superior orders."[33] Without exception, they demonstrated the crucial characteristics required of their profession: brutality, disregard for individual life, and the military discipline that underlay their long working hours in the pursuit of enemies. They operated within the conditions of simulated civil war in a society not yet recovered from the profound dislocations and ruptures of world war, revolution, civil war, and the violent campaigns against the countryside of the late 1920s and early 1930s. Moreover, they operated within an extremely fluid situation, in which policy could shift suddenly, orders frequently changed or were contradictory, and jurisdictional responsibilities were murky and changeable.

The constrained agency of these perpetrators does not absolve them of guilt or responsibility even if they were far from the sole authors of their actions. They played an indispensable role in the implementation of the terror even if individual dispositional character traits may be of decidedly secondary significance in assessing their role vis-à-vis situational factors and Stalin's dictatorial sway. They were more than cogs in a machine; they literally held the power of life and death over the victims of the Great Terror.

Perhaps the clearest sense of their limited agency was on display at their trials. Despite the fact that some of them had been tortured themselves during their own interrogations, they fairly consistently admitted to committing the most hideous and destructive acts, while at the same time fairly consistently denying their guilt. Each blamed higher authorities, though generally casting the blame no further than one NKVD office above them and almost always stopping with Uspenskii. Dolgushev may have been the exception if the informer in his prison cell is to be believed that Dolgushev directly blamed the Central Committee of the Communist Party, stopping short, naturally, of any mention of Stalin.

Dolgushev and the others reveal the usually opaque world of the Stalinist terror, cracking open what James C. Scott has called in other contexts the "hidden transcripts" of the powerful, meaning "discourse that takes place 'offstage.'"[34] It is decidedly not the case, as some historians have argued, that "the Bolsheviks' [*sic*] 'public' and 'private' materials actually differ[ed] little from each other."[35] Materials from the trials of NKVD cadres do not remotely resemble other available published or archival materials. Instead, they raise a set of new questions around issues of the regional and local specificities of the terror, antisemitism, the instability within the NKVD, broader societal complicity, and Stalin's gift to the party—that is, the emerging narrative of Communist victimization he authored. They also provide a certain background for the war of destruction that would follow the German invasion of the Soviet Union on 22 June 1941. A similar cast of seemingly indestructible enemies who were targets in the Russian civil war, the collectivization campaigns, and the Great Terror would resurface as categories in lists of wartime traitors and collaborators.[36] The civil war remained incomplete.

Acknowledgments

THIS BOOK IS the result of serendipity in the archives. When I began the current study, I had planned to explore Soviet perpetrators within three different "theatres" of repression: the collectivization of agriculture, the gulag, and the mass operations of 1937–1938. I had an enormous amount of materials on collectivization and the gulag. The difficult area was the mass repression of the late 1930s—in particular, I wanted entry into the interrogation room, which, up to now, was only fleetingly possible through memoirs, largely by members of the Soviet intelligentsia. I was therefore a historian without sources, all the more so given the near total inaccessibility of the FSB (former KGB) archives in Moscow. In 2010, however, at a conference hosted by James Harris at Leeds University, I had the good fortune to discuss my source problems with Marc Junge, an expert archival researcher and historian of the Great Terror. Marc generously proposed that we go together to the Ukrainian SBU archives in Kyiv. He mentioned a particular type of document—the criminal investigative files of arrested NKVD officials—which he had seen in the archives but had not yet explored in any depth. So in 2011, we traveled together to Kyiv. We were astounded by these sources and, given their volume, quickly decided to put together a larger international collaborative research project, under the heading of "The Practice of Stalin's Terror: A Documentary History of Soviet Perpetrators" and based in Kyiv.

I am enormously grateful to the members of our research team, which includes scholars from six different countries: first and foremost, the indefatigable Marc Junge, along with my colleagues Timothy Blauvelt, Igor Casu, Olga Dovbnia, Sergei Kokin, Roman Podkur, Jeffery Rossman, Andrei Savin, Aleksei Tepliakov (expert of experts), Valerii Vasil'ev (my friend of many years), and Vadym Zolotorov. Together we are in the process of publishing four volumes of essays and documents in Ukrainian and Russian, under the title of *Echo of the Great Terror*; most of us are writing individual monographs as well. I am also happy to express my gratitude to a number of colleagues at the archives, without whom our project would have been impossible: current director and deputy director, Andrei Kogut and Vladimir Birchak, former directors Sergei Kokin and Igor Kulik, and archivists Georgii Smirnov and Maria Panova. My book and the larger research project have received generous research funding from the American Council of Learned Societies, the Social Science and Humanities Research Council of Canada, and the Harry Frank Guggenheim Foundation. I thank Elisa Lee at the History Department of the University of Toronto, who has been tireless in managing my grants.

Many colleagues and students have read all or portions of this book. For their most welcome feedback, I thank Veronica Banaru-Bohantov, Wilson Bell, Doris Bergen, Seth Bernstein, Olga Bertelson, Kate Brown, Marilyn Campeau, Andrei Cusco, Diana Dumitru, Hilary Earl, Sheila Fitzpatrick, Svitlana Frunchak, J. Arch Getty, Wendy Goldman, Mariana Goina, Anna Hajkova, Dan Healey, Page Herlinger, Fran Hirsch, Peter Holquist, Marina Khazanova, Oleg Khlevniuk, Ksenya Kiebyzinski, Eric Kulavig, Wendy Lower, Steve Maddox, Ben McVickers, Vojin Majstorovic, David McDonald, Tracy McDonald, Oleksandr Mel'nyk, Octavian Munteanu, Petro Negura, Doug Northrop (and the Ann Arbor kruzhok), Judith Pallot, Aleksandra Pomiecko, Mark Roseman, Maris Rowe-McCulloch, Roxane Samson-Paquet, Francesca Silano, Pam Shime, Anna Shternshis, Alison Smith, Ron Suny, Pam Thomson-Verrico, Lilia Topouzova, Kathryn Verdery, Alex Voronovici, Lucan Way, and Amir Weiner. Although I was unable to attend, I am very happy to have the opportunity to thank the members of the 14th Conference of the Polish Colloquium of 2016 (Recovering Forgotten History) for their discussion of my book manuscript. For research assistance at various times, I thank Anastassia Kostrioukova and especially Oleksandr Mel'nyk. Needless to say, only I can be incriminated for this work.

Special thanks are owed to my colleague Peter Solomon, who has served as an invaluable source of advice and knowledge throughout this project; Elena Osokina for generous assistance, always with good humor, in dealing with thorny Russian language or Soviet history problems; Serhy Yekelchyk for his expertise in Ukrainian history and his assistance and goodwill at several key moments; David Shearer for sharing his vast knowledge of the NKVD and, indeed, the 1930s with me in the most kind and generous fashion; my former PhD students Max Bergholz and Denis Kozlov, for their detailed and insightful critiques of my work; and Susan Ferber and her editorial team at Oxford University Press, Maya Bringe, and Victoria

Danahy for their fine work in making this book a reality. The critiques offered by the anonymous readers were invaluable and went beyond the call of professional duty.

Finally, I would like to express my gratitude to Colleen Craig, who has been by my side for twenty-five years, and without whom this work would never have been completed.

Notes

INTRODUCTION

1. The epigraph, attributed to Stalin, is cited in Oleg V. Khlevniuk, *Stalin: New Biography of a Dictator* (New Haven, CT: Yale University Press, 2015), p. 41. Khlevniuk writes that "Ignatiev [Minister of State Security in the early 1950s] related this statement during testimony given on 27 March 1953, after Stalin's death." The original conversation took place sometime in the fall of 1951, according to Khlevniuk (email communication of 23 September 2016).

2. See Sheila Fitzpatrick, *Education and Social Mobility in the Soviet Union, 1921–1934* (Cambridge: Cambridge University Press, 1979) for a full discussion of Stalin's First Five-Year Plan promotion of workers in education and industry.

3. For full information on Dolgushev and the other three NKVD officers described here, see Chapters 2, 3, 5, and 7.

4. NKVD is *Narodnyi komissariat vnutrennykh del* or People's Commissariat of Internal Affairs. The NKVD replaced the OGPU [*Ob"edinennoe gosudarstvennoe politicheskoe upravlenie*, or Unified State Political Administration] in 1934.

5. The estimates vary according to source. See V. P. Popov, "Gosudarstvennyi terror v Sovetskoi Rossii, 1923–1953 gg. (istochniki i ikh interpretatsiia)," *Otechestvennye arkhivy*, no. 2 (1992), p. 28; and the discussion in Stephen G. Wheatcroft, "The Great Terror in Historical Perspective: The Records of the Statistical Department of the Investigative Organs of OGPU/NKVD," in James Harris, ed., *The Anatomy of Terror: Political Violence Under Stalin* (Oxford: Oxford University Press, 2013), pp. 287–305. Also see Stephen G. Wheatcroft, "Victims of Stalinism and the Soviet Secret Police," *Europe-Asia Studies*, 51(2)(1999), 337–338. Oleg V. Khlevniuk provides statistics for 1937 and 1938, which indicate that approximately 1.6 million people were arrested in these years, 700,000 of them executed. He estimates that 1,500 people were executed per day, on average, during the Great Terror. See Khlevniuk, *Stalin*, p. 151.

6. The classic works are Robert Conquest (who coined the term "Great Terror"), *The Great Terror* (New York: Collier, 1973); and Roy Medvedev, *Let History Judge*, trans. George Shriver (New York: Columbia University Press, 1989).

7. Order 00447 was first published in *Trud*, 4 June 1992. It is republished in V. P. Danilov, R. T. Manning, and L. Viola, eds., *Tragediia Sovetskoi derevni: Kollektivizatsiia i raskulachivanie. Dokumenty i materialy. 1927–1939*, 5 vols. (Moscow: Rosspen, 1999–2006), Vol. 5, Book 2, pp. 330–337. (This work will be cited further as *TSD*.)

8. See bibliography for a selection of monographs and archival document collections that have been published since the fall of the Soviet Union.

9. For example, J. Arch Getty, "Excesses Are Not Permitted: Mass Terror and Stalinist Governance in the Late 1930s," *Russian Review* 61(1) (2002), 113–138; Oleg Khlevniuk, "Top Down vs. Bottom-Up: Regarding the Potential of Contemporary 'Revisionism,'" *Cahiers du monde Russe*, 56(4) (2015), 837–857; and idem., *Politburo* (Moscow: Rosspen, 1996), pp. 207–208. For a careful and considered discussion of this debate see Marc Iunge, Gennadii Bordiugov, and Rol'f Binner, *Vertikal' bol'shogo terrora* (Moscow: Novyi Khronograf, 2008).

10. See David R. Shearer, *Policing Stalin's Socialism: Repression and Social Order in the Soviet Union, 1924–1953* (New Haven, CT, and London: Yale University Press, 2009), p. 320, for an actual example of the head of the Penza NKVD asking, "Isn't it time Stalin wrote another 'Dizzy from Success' article?," though he asked the question too early, in September 1937.

11. In both the collectivization and Great Terror campaigns, there were a series of warnings (in directives and decrees) discussing problems before the more radical pronouncements of March 1930 and November 1938. For the prehistory of Stalin's "Dizziness from Success," see Lynne Viola, "The Campaign to Eliminate the Kulak as a Class, Winter 1929–1930: A Reevaluation of the Legislation," *Slavic Review*, 45(3) (fall 1986), 504–524. For a rare press report, see *Kommunist* (Ukraine), 30 December 1938, p. 4; 31 December 1938, p. 4; and 1 January 1939, p. 4, for reports on the NKVD trial in the Moldavskaia Autonomous Soviet Socialist Republic.

12. Aleksandr Kokurin and Nikita Petrov, "NKVD: Struktura, funktsii, kadry, stat'ia vtoraia," *Svobodnaia mysl'*, no. 7 (1997), 111–112; and S. V. Mironenko and N. Werth, eds., *Istoriia Stalinskogo Gulaga: Konets 1920-kh—pervaia polovina 1950-kh godov*, 7 vols. (Moscow: Rosspen, 2004–2005), vol. 2, p. 173, for the original document on NKVD operative arrests in 1939. The data on Moscow Province is from A. Iu. Vatlin, *Terror raionnogo masshtaba* (Moscow: Rosspen, 2004), p. 109.

13. Mironenko and Werth, eds., *Istoriia Stalinskogo Gulaga*, vol. 2, p. 173. In a communique to Stalin from Beriia in December 1941, the latter requested permission to release some 1,610 NKVD cadres arrested earlier for "violations of socialist legality" to the front. See V. N. Khaustov, V. P. Naumov, and N. S. Plotnikova, eds., *Lubianka: Stalin i NKVD-NKGB-GUKR "Smersh," 1939–mart 1946* (Moscow: Materik, 2006), p. 563, n. 7.

14. On NKVD clans, see, for examples, J. Arch Getty, *Practicing Stalinism: Bolsheviks, Boyars, and the Persistence of Tradition* (New Haven, CT: Yale University Press, 2013), pp. 170–179; Leonid Naumov, *Bor'ba v rukovodstve NKVD v 1936–1938 gg.* (Moscow: Modern-A, 2006); and M. Tumshis, *VChK: Voina klanov* (Moscow: Eksmo, 2004).

15. The relevant article in the criminal code was 193-17 in Russia and 206-17 in Ukraine. (Point A carried a less severe punishment of imprisonment, whereas point B carried the death penalty.) For the Ukrainian article, see *Uholovnyi kodeks URSR* (Kyiv, 1938), p. 132. The exceptions to this rule were the top NKVD leaders, like Ezhov and Uspenskii, who were charged with treason.

16. For critical discussions of the Nuremberg trials as a historical source, see Donald Bloxham, *Genocide on Trial* (Oxford: Oxford University Press, 2001); Hilary Earl, *The Nuremberg SS-Einsatzgruppen Trial, 1945–1958* (Cambridge: Cambridge University Press, 2009); and Lawrence Douglas, *The Memory of Judgment: Making Law and History in the Trials of the Holocaust* (New Haven, CT: Yale University Press, 2001).

17. Vadym Zolotar'ov, *Oleksandr Uspens'kyi: Osoba, chas, otochennia* (Kharkiv: Folio, 2004), p. 163. See also Vadym Zolotar'ov, "Sotrudniki NKVD Ukrainskoi SSR, osuzhdennye za narushenie sotsialisticheskoi zakonnosti vo vremia raboty v organakh gosudarstvennoi bezopasnosti v 1937–1938 gg.," unpublished paper presented at the conference "Echoes of the Great Terror" at the University of Virginia, 30 September–1 October 2016. (The arrest figures for Ukraine do not include those who were fired or transferred.) Thanks to Vadym Zolotar'ov for clarifying this data.

18. For a detailed discussion of the jurisdictions and functions of the Military Tribunals, see Harold J. Berman and Miroslav Kerner, *Soviet Military Law and Administration* (Cambridge, MA: Harvard University Press, 1955), pp. 101–127.

19. It is important to note that these same cases would be revisited in the Khrushchev years, when victims, real ones, petitioned for rehabilitation. In that period, these cases were used to demonstrate the innocence of victims subject to "violations of socialist legality."

20. Researchers had some access to similar files in the Central Archives of the FSB in Moscow, as well as in a few regional archives, in the 1990s and early years of this century, but it was far from comprehensive. For examples, see Vatlin, *Terror raionnogo masshtaba*; Marc Jansen and Nikita Petrov, *Stalin's Loyal Executioner: People's Commissar Nikolai Ezhov, 1895–1940* (Stanford, CA: Hoover Institution Press, 2002); and especially the fine work of A. G. Tepliakov, *Mashina terrora: OGPU–NKVD Sibiri v 1929–1941 gg.* (Moscow: Novyi Khronograf, 2008). My book has emerged from an international research project centered at the archives of the SBU. The project will result in the publication of a series of document collections based specifically on these sources.

21. For a critical discussion of these sources, see Roman Podkur and Viktor Chentsov, *Dokumenty organov bezopasnosti U[kr.]SSR. 1920–1930-kh godov. Istochnikovedcheskii analiz* (Ternopol', Ukraine: Zbruch, 2010).

22. It is often clear in the documents when NKVD defendants have been tortured. First, the nature of the *dopros* or interrogation becomes stilted, sometimes mono-syllabic (on the part of the defendants' responses). Second, the context is key: If the defendant is disagreeing with his interrogator, objecting to accusations of guilt, then it is more than likely that torture, if used, was ineffective and therefore does not skew the evidence. In some cases, the NKVD defendants speak openly about their torture and its effect on what they consider their false confessions. This can occur at a time of retraction of testimony. However, it is important to note that in this time period, torture was by no means an automatic response on the part of interrogators.

23. I have translated *obvinitel'noe zakliuchenie* as indictment. Peter Solomon writes "that the Russian 'indictment' represents the culmination of the preliminary investigation and is based on the written evidence contained in the case file." He therefore notes that *obvinitel'noe zakliuchenie* might best be rendered as "accusatory act" (email communication of 4 May 2015). For an excellent discussion of the lingering "inquisi-torial" aspects of post-Soviet criminal justice, including the police-generated "indict-ment," see Peter H. Solomon, Jr., "Post-Soviet Criminal Justice: The Persistence of Distorted Neo-Inquisitorialism," *Theoretical Criminology*, 19(2) (2015), 7–8.

24. See, for examples, works on Siberia (Tepliakov, *Mashina terrora*), Moscow (Vatlin, *Terror raionnogo masshtaba*), Tatarstan (A. F. Stepanov, *Rasstrel po limitu. Iz istorii politicheskikh repressii v TASSR v gody "ezhovshchiny"* {Kazan, Russia: Novoe Znanie, 1999}; and Ural (O. Leibovich, A. Koldushko, and A. Kazenkov, eds., *"Vkliuchen v operatsiiu": Massovyi terror v Prikam'e v 1937–1938 gg.* {Moscow: Rosspen, 2009}.)

25. The phrasing is from the "confession" of Andrei Ivanovich Egorov, the former head of the Chernigov regional NKVD in Ukraine. This document and the files used in the pages that follow are from the Ukrainian State Archives of the Security Police, *Haluzevyi derzhavnyi arkhiv Sluzhbyi bezpeky Ukrainy* and will be hereafter cited as "SBU." For Egorov's testimony, see *SBU*, f. 12, d. 107 (Georgii Matveevich Kretov), ll. 77–111 ("Sobstvennoruchnye pokazaniia obviniaemogo Egorova Andreia Ivanovicha ot 15–16 dekabria 1938 goda"), l. 92.

26. Cited in Annette Wieviorka, *The Era of the Witness*, trans. Jared Stark (Ithaca, NY: Cornell University Press, 2006), p. 94.

27. Christopher R. Browning, *Ordinary Men: Reserve Police Battalion 101 and the Final Solution in Poland* (New York: Harper Perennial, 1992), p. xx.

28. For a broader approach to the topic of perpetrators and the historiography, see Lynne Viola, "The Question of the Perpetrator in Soviet History," *Slavic Review*, 72(1) (spring 2013), 1–23.

CHAPTER 1

1. The citations are from Nadezhda Mandelstam, trans. Max Hayward, *Hope Against Hope: A Memoir* (New York: Atheneum, 1976), p. 28; and Felix Chuev, ed., *Molotov*

Remembers: Inside Kremlin Politics (Chicago: Ivan R. Dee, 1993), p. 254 ("Who whom," or *kto kogo*, may be translated, roughly, as "Who will beat whom?").

2. Compare the OGPU directive (no. 44/21) of 2 February 1930 on dekulakization with NKVD directive 00447 of 30 July 1937 on the kulak mass operation in *TSD*, vol. 2, pp. 163–167; vol. 5, book 1, pp. 330–337.

3. I. Stalin, *Sochineniia*, 13 vols. (Moscow: Gospolizdat, 1946–1952), vol. 13, pp. 211–212.

4. On dekulakization as a preemptive strike, see Chapter 1 ("The Preemptive Strike") in Lynne Viola, *The Unknown Gulag: The Lost World of Stalin's Special Settlements* (New York: Oxford University Press, 2007).

5. See, for example, Khlevniuk, *Stalin: New Biography*, pp. 141, 153 (where he also discusses the origins of the phrase "Fifth Column" in the Spanish Civil War). Also see James Harris, *The Great Fear: Stalin's Terror of the 1930s* (Oxford: Oxford University Press, 2016), which seeks to explain how and why Stalin's fears of counterrevolution and threat from abroad persisted through the first two decades of power, coming to a head in 1937–1938.

6. See the argument of David Shearer in his "Stalin at War, 1918–1953: Patterns of Violence and Foreign Threat," *Jahrbücher für Geschichte Osteuropas* (forthcoming). He writes that "The waves of repression that Stalin launched inside the country coincided with periods of intense military-industrial buildup, and neither can be understood or fully explained without reference to Stalin's expectations of foreign intervention." And it should be noted that Stalin's expectations came to pass in 1941 when Hitler launched Operation Barbarossa.

7. J. Arch Getty and Oleg V. Naumov, eds., *The Road to Terror: Stalin and the Self-Destruction of the Bolsheviks, 1932–1939*, trans. Benjamin Sher (New Haven, CT and London: Yale University Press, 1999), p. 557 (italics in original).

8. Conquest, *The Great Terror*, p. 11. The Communist regime never used the term terror for the mass repression of 1937–1938. Conquest derived the term from the French Revolution and the Bolshevik civil war–era "Red Terror," both of which were quite different in form and function from the mass repression of the late 1930s. Nonetheless, the term "Great Terror" has become the standard label for the mass repression of this period and I use it throughout this book as shorthand for what were a series of repressive campaigns that lacked the revolutionary symbolism and public nature of the French and earlier Red Terror.

9. Conquest, p. 11.

10. *Trud*, 4 June 1992. The directive is republished in *TSD*, vol. 5, book 1, pp. 330–337.

11. See the excellent collection of articles on the mass operations in Barry McLoughlin and Kevin McDermott, eds., *Stalin's Terror: High Politics and Mass Repression in the Soviet Union* (New York: Palgrave, 2003), p. 6. Among other recent, pioneering works on the mass operations, see Wendy Goldman, *Terror and Democracy in the Age of Stalin: The Social Dynamics of Repression* (Cambridge: Cambridge University Press, 2007); *idem., Inventing the Enemy: Denunciation and Terror in*

Stalin's Russia (Cambridge: Cambridge University Press, 2011); Paul Hagenloh, *Stalin's Police: Public Order and Mass Repression in the USSR, 1926–1941* (Baltimore: Johns Hopkins Press, 2009); Marc Iunge and Rol'f Binner, *Kak terror stal "bol'shim"* (Moscow: AIRO-XX, 2003); Marc Iunge et al., *Vertikal bol'shogo terrora*; Vladimir Khaustov and Lennart Samuel'son, *Stalin, NKVD i repressii 1936–1938 gg.* (Moscow: Rosspen, 2009); O. L. Leibovich, ed., *"Vkliuchen v operatsiiu:" Massovyi terror v Prikam'e v 1937–1938 gg.* (Moscow: Rosspen, 2009); Shearer, *Policing Stalin's Socialism*; Tepliakov, *Mashina terrora*; Vatlin, *Terror raionnogo masshtaba*; and Nikolai Vert [Nicholas Werth], *Terror i besporiadok: Stalinizm kak sistema* (Moscow: Rosspen, 2010).

12. On the role of the regular police and the continuities between these two massive campaigns of repression in police practice and mentalite, see Hagenloh, *Stalin's Police*; Shearer, *Policing Stalin's Socialism*; Lynne Viola, *The Unknown Gulag: The Lost World of Stalin's Special Settlements* (New York: Oxford University Press, 2007); and *idem., Peasant Rebels Under Stalin: Collectivization and the Culture of Peasant Resistance* (New York: Oxford University Press, 1996).

13. *TSD*, vol. 5, book 1, pp. 330–337. At the 18th Congress of the Communist Party in March 1939, the Central Committee noted the widespread use of the "biological approach" in 1937–1938, and condemned it as having nothing in common with Marxism. See *XVIII s'ezd vsesoiuznoi kommunisticheskoi partii (b). 10–21 marta 1939 g. Stenograficheskii otchet* (Moscow: OGIZ, 1939), p. 523. Also see Iunge et al., *Vertikal' bol'shego terrora*, pp. 128–130, on arrest lists in Vinnytsa, including those who had been involved in the collective farm disturbances of 1930.

14. *TSD*, vol. 5, book 1, pp. 330–337.

15. On the 16 July meeting, see Iunge et al., *Vertikal' bol'shego terrora*, pp. 19–26; for other preparations behind the directive, see *TSD*, vol. 5, book 1, pp. 319–327.

16. *TSD*, vol. 5, book 1, pp. 331–333.

17. *TSD*, vol. 5, book 1, pp. 331–334.

18. *TSD*, vol. 5, book 1, pp. 334–335.

19. *TSD*, vol. 5, book 1, p. 335.

20. On the *troika*s, see *TSD*, vol. 5, book 1, pp. 335–336; and Getty and Naumov, *The Road to Terror*, p. 470

21. *TSD*, vol. 5, book 1, pp. 335–336.

22. *TSD*, vol. 5, book 1, p. 340. On 7 July 1937, Frinovskii had issued an earlier order to this effect, on 9 July 1937. See A. G. Tepliakov, *Protsedura: ispolnenie smertnykh prigovorov v 1920–1930-kh godakh* (Moscow: Vozvrashchenie, 2007).

23. Iunge et al., *Vertikal' bol'shego terrora*, pp. 52–53; A .G. Tepliakov, "Organy NKVD Zapadnoi Sibiri v 'kulatskoi operatsii' 1937–1938 gg.," in M. Iunge and R. Binner, eds., *Stalinizm v Sovetskoi provintsii, 1937–1938 gg. Massovaia operatsiia na osnove prikaza No. 00447* (Moscow: Rosspen, 2009), p. 560.

24. Iunge et al., *Vertikal' bol'shego terrora*, p. 162; and *TSD*, vol. 5, book 1, pp. 387–393.

25. On orders not to increase regional control figures independently, see *TSD*, vol. 5, book 1, p. 333; on the center seldom refusing, see Iunge et al., *Vertikal' bol'shego terrora*, pp. 141–142. In the historiography, there has been controversy over the exact meaning of *limity*, translated variously as "quotas" or "limits," with scope for regional initiative. See, for examples, Getty, *Practicing Stalinism*, chap. 7; *idem.*, "'Excesses are not permitted,'" pp. 112–137; Oleg V. Khlevniuk, *The History of the Gulag: From Collectivization to the Great Terror*, trans. Vadim A. Staklo (New Haven, CT, and London: Yale University Press, 2004), pp. 148–149.

26. Iunge et al., *Vertikal' bol'shego terrora*, pp. 150, 277.

27. Iunge et al., *Vertikal' bol'shego terrora*, p. 285; Iunge et al., eds., *"Cherez trupy vraga na blago naroda": "Kulatskaia operatsiia" v Ukrainskoi SSR, 1937–1941 gg.: 1938–1941 gg. Vtoroi etap repressii. Zavershenie Bol'shogo terrora i vosstanovelnie "sotsialisticheskoi zakonnosti,"* 2 vols. (Moscow: Rosspen, 2010), vol. 2, pp. 23–25.

28. See Nikita Petrov and Arsenii Roginskii, "The 'Polish Operation' of the NKVD, 1937–8," in McLoughlin and McDermott, eds., *Stalin's Terror*, p. 154; and subsequent chapters. For a copy of the directive on the Polish Operation, see V. N. Khaustov, V. P. Naumov, and N. S. Plotnikova, eds., *Lubianka: Stalin i glavnoe upravlenie gosbezopasnosti NKVD, 1937–1938: Dokumenty* (Moscow: Materik, 2004), pp. 301–303, and, for the official view on "Polish enemies" in the Soviet Union, pp. 303–321. The German "national operation" was not a part of the national operations, per se, but began earlier, from 25 July 1937. See Mark Iunge and Bernd Bonvech, eds., *Bol'shevistskii poriadok v Gruzii*, 2 vols. (Moscow: AIRO-XXI, 2015), vol. 1, p. 205, n. 21.

29. Petrov and Roginskii, "The 'Polish Operation,'" in McLoughlin and McDermott, eds., *Stalin's Terror*, pp. 154–155. See Timothy Snyder, *Sketches from a Secret War* (New Haven, CT: Yale University Press, 2005) for information on the POV and Polish attempts, largely unsuccessful, to infiltrate Soviet Ukraine with a spy network.

30. *TSD*, vol. 5, book 2, p. 163 (data for the period from 1 January 1936 to 1 July 1938).

31. Terry Martin, "The Origins of Soviet Ethnic Cleansing," *Journal of Modern History*, 70(4) (December 1998), 837.

32. Peter Holquist, "State Violence as Technique: The Logic of Violence in Soviet Totalitarianism," in Amir Weiner, ed., *Landscaping the Human Garden: Twentieth-Century Population Management in a Comparative Framework* (Stanford, CA: Stanford University Press, 2003), pp. 29, 44.

33. This was the so-called album method. Petrov and Roginskii, "The 'Polish Operation,'" p. 159; and Iunge et al., eds., *"Cherez trupy vraga na blago naroda,"* vol. 2, p. 175. Also see Hagenloh, *Stalin's Police*, pp. 279–287 for a discussion about the ultimate failure of the album method that would result in their cancellation in September 1938 (partly because of a huge overload of cases), after which, like operation 00447, no outside confirmation would be needed to make arrests in the national operations.

34. Barry McLoughlin, "Mass Operations of the NVKD, 1937–8: A Survey," in McLoughlin and McDermott, eds., *Stalin's Terror*, p. 141.

35. Petrov and Roginskii, "The 'Polish Operation,'" p. 161.

36. *TSD*, vol. 5, book 2, pp. 156–163.

37. McLoughlin, "Mass Operations of the NVKD," p. 141. For sentencing statistics, see Oleg V. Khlevniuk, ed., *The History of the Gulag from Collectivization to the Great Terror*, trans. Vadim A. Staklo (New Haven, CT: Yale University Press, 2004), p. 290.

38. George O. Liber, *Total Wars and the Making of Modern Ukraine, 1914–1954* (Toronto: University of Toronto Press, 2016), p. 187.

39. "*Gde les rubiat, tam shchepki letiat.*" See this phrase as used by an NKVD operative, quoting Bel'skii, in Iunge et al., eds., "*Cherez trupy vraga na blago naroda,*" p. 471.

40. For a discussion of *kolunstvo* [choppping], see Iunge et al., *Vertikal' bol'shego terrora*, p. 456.

41. See Chapter 7.

42. *TSD*, vol. 5, book 1, p. 335.

43. Peter H. Solomon, Jr., *Soviet Criminal Justice Under Stalin* (New York: Cambridge University Press, 1996), pp. 236–237.

44. Solomon, *Soviet Criminal Justice*, p. 236.

45. See Iunge and Binner, *Kak terror stal "bol'shim,"* pp. 98–99, for Vyshinskii's coded telegram; and Tepliakov, *Mashina terrora*, p. 353. See also Solomon, *Soviet Criminal Justice*, p. 238.

46. Solomon, *Soviet Criminal Justice*, p. 237.

47. On *uchet*, see Iunge and Binner, *Kak terror stal "bol'shim,"* p. 279; Shearer, *Policing Stalin's Socialism*, chapter 5; Tepliakov, *Mashina terrora*, p. 220.

48. Hagenloh, *Stalin's Police*, pp. 273–279; Shearer, *Policing Stalin's Socialism*, pp. 350–352; and *Istoriia Stalinskogo Gulaga. Konets 1920-kh—pervaia polovina 1950-kh godov. Sobranie dokumentov*, 7 vols. (Moscow: Rosspen, 2004), vol. 1, pp. 313–325. See also the discussion of this phenomenon by Communist NKVD workers at the 3–4 February 1939 meeting of the Dneprodzerzhinsk city NKVD party collective *SBU*, f. 5, d. 64858 Daragona, vol. 8, ll. 97, 117.

49. On repression against agents, see Tepliakov, *Mashina terrora*, pp. 183–185. Many NKVD agents and informers were chosen for their usefulness specifically from suspect populations; hence they were targeted in the same way their "objects" of observation were. On *shtatnye* witnesses, see M. Iunge and R. Binner, "Spravki sel'soveta kak faktor v osuzhdenii krest'ian," in Iunge and Binner, eds., *Stalinizm v sovetskoi provintsii*, pp. 613–623; and A. N. Kabatskov, "Shtatnyi svidetel': istochniki rekrutirovaniia i sotsial'naia rol' v repressiiakh po prikazu no. 00447," in A. Sorokin, A. Kobak, and O. Kuvaldina, eds., *Istoriia Stalinizma: zhizn' v terrore. Sotsial'nye aspekty repressii. Materialy mezhdunarodnoi nauchnoi konferentsii Sankt-Peterburg, 18–20 oktiabria 2012 g.* (Moscow: Rosspen, 2013), pp. 444–452.

50. Tepliakov, *Mashina terrora*, p. 450.

51. V. N. Khaustov, et al., eds., *Lubianka: Stalin i NKVD-NKGB-GUKR "Smersh," 1939–mart 1946*, pp. 14–15; also see p. 19 (for Vyshinskii's note informing Procuracy workers of Stalin's 10 January 1939 coded telegram). Some historians speculate that Stalin wrote this telegram not only to justify torture but to prevent a wholesale purge of NKVD operatives on the basis of their use of torture alone. See, for examples, the documents in Iunge et al., eds., *"Cherez trupy vraga na blago naroda,"* vol. 2, pp. 462–463; and "Zapiska komissii prezidiuma TsK KPSS v presidium TsK KPSS o rezul'tatakh raboty po rassledovaniiu prichin repressii i obstoiatel'stv politicheskikh protsessov 30-kh godov," *Istochnik*, no. 1 (1995), 88–89.

52. On transmission of orders in the NKVD, orally at operational meetings or by telephone, see O. L. Leibovich, "'Kulatskaia operatsiia' na territorii Prikam'ia v 1937–1938 gg.," in Iunge and Binner, eds., *Stalinizm v Sovetskoi provintsii*, p. 595. According to the former NKVD resident in Spain and defector Alexander Orlov, "teaching by example" through late-night visits to interrogators' offices had been a practice in the NKVD under Iagoda and Ezhov. See his *The Secret History of Stalin's Crimes* (New York: Random House, 1953), p. 82.

53. See A. I. Kokurin and N. V. Petrov, eds., *Lubianka: Organy VChK–OGPU–NKVD–NKGB–MGB–MVD–KGB, 1917–1991: Spravochnik* (Moscow: Materik, 2003), for the 7 June 1937 NKVD directive sending Frinovskii and Leplevskii to Ukraine. See Tepliakov, *Mashina terrora*, pp. 264–265 on these practices.

54. Iunge et al., ed., *Vertikal' bol'shego terrora*, p. 48.

55. Iunge et al., ed., *Vertikal' bol'shego terrora*, p. 25; Iunge and Binner, *Kak terror stal "bol'shim,"* pp. 233–240; and Iunge, et al., eds., *Stalinizm v Sovetskoi provintsii*, p. 44. See also Michael Ellman, "Regional Influences on the Formulation and Implementation of NKVD Order 00447," *Europe-Asia Studies*, 62(6) (2010), 915–931. (Note that "recidivist criminals" were among the listed "enemies" in NKVD Order 00447.)

56. On Cheka "culture," see Julie Fedor, *Russia and the Cult of State Security: The Chekist Tradition, from Lenin to Putin* (New York: Routledge, 2011); Iain Lauchlan, "Chekist *Mentalite* and the Origins of the Great Terror," in Harris, ed., *The Anatomy of Terror*, pp. 13–28; and the masterful Tepliakov, *Mashina terrora*, chapter 5.

57. My thanks to David Shearer for clarification of this point.

58. For examples, see *Pravda*, 3 December 1937, p. 2, for a poem to Ezhov by the poet Dzhambul. See also the *Pravda* coverage for the December 1937 Cheka anniversary celebrations (16 December 1937, p. 2; 17 December 1937, p. 6; 18 December 1937, pp. 6, 19 December 1937, p. 6; 20 December 1937, p. 1; and 21 December 1937, p. 1).

59. This figure is cited in Sheila Fitzpatrick and Robert Gellately, eds., *Accusatory Practices: Denunciation in Modern European History, 1789–1989* (Chicago: University of Chicago Press, 1997), p. 9.

60. N. G. Okhotin and A. B. Roginskii, eds., *Kto rukovodil NKVD, 1934–1941: Spravochnik* (Moscow: Zven'ia, 1999), p. 501.

61. Email communication with Aleksei Tepliakov from 25 September 2015.

62. The use of plenipotentiaries from the Communist Party Central Committee or the NKVD in the provinces was a common practice to spur on policy. For examples, see Mikhail Shreider, *NKVD iznutri: Zapiska chekista* (Moscow: Vozvrashchenie, 1995), pp. 64–65. For the practice of using plenipotentiaries in the collectivization campaigns, see Lynne Viola, *The Best Sons of the Fatherland: Workers in the Vanguard of Soviet Collectivization* (New York: Oxford University Press, 1987), pp. 28–30. For further information on NKVD central and territorial organs and personnel, see Okhotin and Roginskii, eds., *Kto rukovodil NKVD*, pp. 45–79.

63. Iunge et al., *Vertikal' bol'shego terrora*, pp. 128, 132.

64. Tepliakov, "Organy NKVD Zapadnoi Sibiri," in Iunge and Binner, eds., *Stalinizm v Sovetskii provintsii*, pp. 551.

65. This was the case for Ezhov, Uspenskii, and a series of other key NKVD leaders.

66. Okhotin and Roginskii, eds., *Kto rukovodil NKVD*, pp. 493–497; Vadym Zolotar'ov, "Kerivnyi sklad NKVS URSR pid chas 'velykoho teroru' (1936–1938 rr.): Sotsial'no-statystychnyi analiz," in *Z arkhiviv VUChK–GPU–NKVD–KGB*, no. 2(33) (2009), 100–109. Also see Iu. I. Shapoval and Vadym Zolotar'ov, "Ievrei v kerivnytstvi orhaniv DPU–NKVD USRR–URSR u 1920–1930-kh rr.," *Z arkhiviv VUChK–GPU–NKVD–KGB*, no. 1(34) (2010), 53–93.

67. See subsequent chapters for more information on these "everyday" problems.

68. Mandelstam, *Hope Against Hope*, p. 14. See also Richard A. Leo, *Police Interrogation and American Justice* (Cambridge, MA: Harvard University Press, 2008), on the universality of the police tendency to assume that those they arrest are guilty.

69. See Chapter 6.

70. See Chapter 5.

71. The Procurator of the USSR received 600,000 complaints in 1938. See "Zapiska komissii prezidiuma TsK KPSS v presidium TsK KPSS o rezul'tatakh raboty po rassledovaniiu prichin repressii i obstoiatel'stv politicheskikh protsessov 30-kh godov," *Istochnik*, no. 1 (1995), 84. According to another report, the Procurator of the RSFSR received between 50,000 and 60,000 complaints monthly, with 700 to 800 complaints coming in each day. *Istoriia Stalinskogo Gulaga*, vol. 1, pp. 327–328. In Ukraine, the Procurator (at both republican and regional levels) received 170,855 complaints between 1 January 1939 and 1 March 1940 alone. (Iunge et al., eds., "*Cherez trupy vraga na blago naroda*," p. 489). See also Iunge et al., *Vertikal' bol'shego terrora*, pp. 299, 323–324. On the Procuracy, see Gabor T. Rittersporn, "Terror and Soviet Legality: Police vs. Judiciary, 1933–1940," in Harris, ed., *Anatomy of Terror*, pp. 184–188; and Solomon, *Soviet Criminal Justice*, pp. 252–257.

72. This topic is worth further exploration. For examples, see *SBU*, f. 16, d. 322. Also see Vatlin, *Terror raionnogo masshtaba*, pp. 156–157.

73. Mandelstam, *Hope Against Hope*, p. 296.

74. Khaustov et al., eds., *Lubianka: Stalin i glavnoe upravlenie gosbezopasnotsi NKVD, 1937–1938*, pp. 604–606.

75. Iunge et al., *Vertikal' bol'shego terrora*, pp. 426–429. The decree is published in Danilov, Manning, and Viola, eds., *TSD*, vol. 5, book 2, pp. 307–311. The regional *troiki* were composed of the first secretary of the regional party organization, the head of the regional NKVD, and the regional procurator. See also Khaustov, et al., eds., *Lubianka: Stalin i glavnoe upravlenie gosbezopasnosti NKVD, 1937–1938*, p. 562 (for the Politburo decree to organize a commission to work out the 17 November 1938 directive), 607–611 (Postanovlenie Politbiuro TsK VKP (b) "Ob arestakh, prokurorskom nadzore i vedenii sledstviia").

76. I. A. Serov took over as head of the NKVD in Ukraine in the fall of 1939.

77. Shearer, "Stalin at War," p. 18.

78. *TSD*, vol. 5, book 2, pp. 161–163. See Liber, *Total Wars*, p. 187, previously cited, for slightly higher figures extending through the end of 1938.

79. *TSD*, vol. 5, book 2, pp. 161–163. The ethnic data on victims represent the Soviet Union as a whole. In Ukraine, Jews made up the third-largest population group after Russians and Ukrainians, estimated at about 900,000 in the 1926 census and about 800,000 in the 1937 census. Estimates of the numbers of Poles and Germans living in Ukraine are roughly 500,000 and 156,000, respectively, in 1926. See Liber, *Total Wars*, pp. 161, 186; and Paul Robert Magocsi, *Historical Atlas of Central Europe*, rev. ed. (Toronto: University of Toronto Press, 2002), p. 139.

80. Viola, *Unknown Gulag*, pp. 195–196; and Hiroaki Kuromiya, *Stalin* (Harlow, UK: Pearson, 2005), p. 103.

81. Peter Holquist has explored in the most depth Tsarist military practices of mass expulsion of suspect nationalities before and during the First World War. See, for example, his "Forms of Violence During the Russian Occupation of Ottoman Territory and in Northern Persia (Urmia and Astrabad), October 1914–December 1917," in Omer Bartov and Eric D. Weitz, eds., *Shatterzone of Empires: Coexistence and Violence in the German, Hapsburg, Russian, and Ottoman Borderlands* (Bloomington: Indiana University Press, 2013), pp. 343–345; "'In Accord with State Interests and the People's Wishes': The Technocratic Ideology of Imperial Russia's Resettlement Administration," *Slavic Review*, 69(1) (Spring 2010); and "To Count, To Extract, and to Exterminate: Population Statistics and Population Politics in Late Imperial and Soviet Russia," in Ronald Grigor Suny and Terry Martin, eds., *A State of Nations: Empire and Nation-Making in the Age of Lenin and Stalin* (New York: Oxford University Press, 2001). See also Jonathan Dekel-Chen, David Gaunt, Natan M. Meir, and Israel Bartal, eds., *Anti-Jewish Violence: Rethinking the Pogrom in East European History* (Bloomington: Indiana University Press, 2011), pp. 43, 48–49, 61; Joshua A. Sanborn, *Imperial Apocalypse: The Great War and the Destruction of the Russian Empire* (Oxford: Oxford University Press, 2014), p. 97; Peter Gatrell, *A Whole Empire Walking: Refugees in Russia During World War I* (Bloomington and Indianapolis: Indiana University Press, 1999); Willard Sutherland, *The*

Baron's Cloak: A History of the Russian Empire in War and Revolution (Ithaca, NY: Cornell University Press, 2014); and especially Eric Lohr, *Nationalizing the Russian Empire: The Campaign Against Enemy Aliens During World War I* (Cambridge, MA: Harvard University Press, 2003).

82. *XVIII s'ezd vsesoiuznoi kommunisticheskoi partii (b). 10-21 marta 1939 g. Stenograficheskii otchet* (Moscow: OGIZ, 1939), p. 523.

83. The list is even more expansive than what I present here. See *TSD*, vol. 5, book 2, pp. 55–56.

84. Vadym Zolotar'ov, "Favoryt Iezhova: Storinky biohrafii narkoma vnutrishnikh sprav URSR O.I. Uspens'koho," in Oleh Bazhan and Roman Podkur, eds., *Politychni represii v Ukrain'skii RSR: doslidnyts'ki refleksii ta interpretatsii. Do 75-richchia "Velykoho teroru" v SRSR. Materialy vseukrains'koi naukovoi konferentsii* (Kiev: Instytut istorii Ukrainy NAN Ukrainy, 2013), pp. 181–182; Jansen and Petrov, *Stalin's Loyal Executioner*, p. 134.

85. Cited in Zolotar'ov, "Favoryt Iezhova," p. 182.

86. *TSD*, vol. 5, book 2, pp. 49, 550–551, n. 22.

87. *TSD*, vol. 5, book 2, p. 51.

88. B. I. Ivkin, ed., *Gosudarstvennaia vlast' SSSR. Vysshie organy vlasti i upravleniia i ikh rukovoditeli. 1923–1991. Istoriko-biograficheskii spravochnik* (Moscow: Rosspen, 1999), pp. 360–361.

89. Okhotin and Roginskii, eds., *Kto rukovodil NKVD*, pp. 416–417.

90. Okhotin and Roginskii, eds., *Kto rukovodil NKVD*, pp. 270–271.

91. These dates are from Jansen and Petrov, *Stalin's Loyal Executioner*, p. 133.

92. Zolotar'ov, *Oleksandr Uspens'kyi*, chapter 6, p. 119.

93. Vadym Zolotar'ov, "Kolyshni spivrobitnyky NKVS URSR na kerivnii roboti u systemi HUTAB SRSR (1936–1939 rr.)," *Z arkhiviv VUChK–GPU–NKVD–KGB*, nos. 1–2 (2013), 51–79.

94. On *vydvizhentsy*, see Fitzpatrick, *Education and Social Mobility in the Soviet Union*.

95. On the civil war as a "defining influence," see V. N. Khaustov, "Mentalitet sotrudnikov organov gosudarstvennoi bezopasnosti NKVD SSSR v period massovykh repressii," in A. Sorokin et al., eds., *Istoriia Stalinizma: Zhizn' v terrore*, p. 428. My sample of personnel in the pages that follow are divided roughly evenly between those who fought in the civil war and those who came into the NKVD later.

96. For an example, see Vadim Rogovin, *Partiia rasstreliannykh* (Moscow: RAN, 1997).

97. See Iunge et al., *Vertikal*, pp. 55–56; Vatlin, *Terror raionnogo masshtaba*, p. 72; Jansen and Petrov, *Stalin's Loyal Executioner*, p. 91; and Hagenloh, *Stalin's Police*, for arguments against the thesis that the NKVD was at war with the Communist Party, the latter simply a victim of Stalin and the NKVD.

98. See A. I. Savin and A. G. Tepliakov, "'Partiia mozhet oshibat'sia, a NKVD nikogda': Sotrudniki UNKVD po Odesskoi oblasti na skam'e podsudimykh (1939–1943 gg.)," in Mark Junge, Lynne Viola, and Jeffrey Rossman, eds., *Chekisty na skam'e podsudimykh*, 4 vols. (Moscow: Probel, 2017). The question of how prisoners found out about the transformations in the leadership of the NKVD is partly addressed in Eugenia Ginzburg, *Journey Into the Whirlwind*, trans. Paul Stevenson and Max Hayward (New York: Harcourt Brace Jovanovich, 1967), pp. 254–258, where she describes warders coming into the cells to replace signage on prison regulations, whiting out Ezhov's name. In general, the rumor mill in the prisons worked very effectively and was certainly facilitated by the institution of cell elders, prisoners who were direct (and often nefarious) liaisons between the prisoners in their cells and the interrogators.

99. Oleg Khlevniuk, "Party and NKVD: Power Relationships in the Years of the Great Terror," in McLoughlin and McDermott, eds., *Stalin's Terror*, pp. 26–27. *TSD*, vol. 5, book 2, p. 304, presents the figure of 12,903 people freed as of 1 November 1938. Khaustov, Naumov, and Plotnikova, eds., *Lubianka. Stalin i NKVD–NKGB–GUKR "Smersh,"* p. 564, n. 11, present the figure of 110,000 people liberated in 1939 from among those who had been arrested in 1937–1938.

100. Oleg V. Khlevniuk, *Master of the House: Stalin and His Inner Circle*, trans. by Nora Seligman Favorov (New Haven, CT: Yale University Press, 2009), p. 185. It is important to note that Khlevniuk adds that "such elemental factors and initiatives by local authorities were the inevitable results of incentives inherent in orders from Moscow."

101. Scholars Vladimir Khaustov and Lennart Samuelson agree, concluding that Stalin "managed" the terror but entrusted the mass operations to Communist Party and NKVD leaders locally [*na mestakh*]. Khaustov and Samuel'son, *Stalin, NKVD i repressii*, p. 328.

CHAPTER 2

1. *SBU*, f. 5, d. 38237 (Sledstvennoe delo A. R. Dolgusheva, 4 vols.), vol. 1, l. 5 (Order No. 43 na arest Dolgusheva). The epigraphs are from (in order of placement): M. Iunge et al., eds., *Cherez trupy vraga na blago naroda*, vol. 2, p. 458; and *SBU*, f. 16, d. 95, l. 177 (Stenogramma zakrytogo partsobraniia kollektiva NKVD po Kievskoi obl. za 14–16 dekabria 1938 g.) Unless otherwise noted, all archival references will be from this *fond* (5) and delo (38237), and identified further only by volume number, page number, and document title.

2. Vol. 4, ll. 143–144 (Protokol sudebnogo zasedaniia, 24–27 February 1941). All subsequent references to the trial proceedings, Protokol sudebnogo zasedaniia, will be cited as PSZ with date.

3. *SBU*, f. 12, d. 2999, vol. 1, part 3, ll. 1–3. (Lichnoe delo Dolgusheva).

4. The first trial took place in August 1940 and is in vol. 3, ll. 31–47 (PSZ 10–13 August 1940). The second trial was in February 1941 and is in vol. 4, ll. 118–144 (PSZ 24–27 February 1941). The third trial was in May 1942 and is in vol. 4, ll. 188–199 (PSZ 20–21 May 1942). The first two trials were held under the jurisdiction of the Military Tribunal of the NKVD, Kiev county [*okrug*]; the third trial was held under the jurisdiction of the Military Tribunal of the NKVD, Urals county [*okrug*].

5. Vol. 3, ll. 31–47 (PSZ 10–13 August 1940).

6. Vol. 3, ll. 52–53 (Prigovor, not before 13 August 1940). Article 206 of the Ukrainian criminal code dealt with crimes of office. "Point A" of the article dealt with minor offenses and could result in imprisonment for a period of no fewer than six months; "Point B" was more serious and could result in the death sentence.

7. Vol. 3, ll. 73–73 ob. (Opredelenie, 14 August 1940).

8. Vol. 4, ll. 160–163 (Prigovor, not before 27 February 1941).

9. Vol. 4, l. 182 (Postanovlenie verkh. sud SSSR, 12 August 1941).

10. Vol. 4, ll. 188–199 (PSZ 20–21 May 1942), ll. 202-3 (Prigovor, 21 May 1942).

11. Vol. 1, l. 276 (Sobstvennoruchnye pokazaniia obviniamogo Dolgusheva A. R. ot 16 oktiabria 1939 g.), vol. 2, ll. 9 (Vypiska iz protokola doprosa arestovannogo Reikhmana L'va Iosifovicha. 25 April 1939), l. 303 (Vypiska iz protokola obshchego zakrytogo partiinogo sobraniia partorganizatsii UGB Kievskogo oblastnogo Upr. NKVD. 14 December 1938), vol. 3, l. 33 (PSZ 10–13 August 1940).

12. For biographical information on Kobyzev, see Okhotin and Roginskii, eds., *Kto rukovodil NKVD*, pp. 235–236.

13. For biographical information on Frinovskii, see Okhotin and Roginskii, eds., *Kto rukovodil NKVD*, pp. 425–426.

14. Vol. 2, ll. 362–363 (Vypiska iz protkola doprosa obvin. Kobyzeva, G. N. 1 April 1939).

15. Ibid.

16. Cited in Zolotar'ov, *Oleksandr Uspens'kyi*, p. 196.

17. Vol. 2, ll. 362–363 (Vypiska iz protkola doprosa obvin. Kobyzeva, G. N. 1 April 1939).

18. Zolotar'ov, *Oleksandr Uspens'kyi*, p. 196.

19. Ibid., pp. 196–197.

20. See *SBU*, f. 16, d. 95 (Stenogramma zakrytogo partsobraniia kollektiva NKVD po Kievskoi obl. (14–16 December 1938).

21. *SBU*, f. 12, d. 107 (Georgii Matveevich Kretov), ll. 89, 91–92, 108 ("Sobstvennoruchnye pokazaniia obviniaemogo Egorova Andreia Ivanovicha ot 15–16 dekabria 1938 goda").

22. Valerii Vasil'iev, "Mekhanizmy 'velykoho teroru': Mistsevyi zriz (diial'nist' oblasnykh UNKVS URSR u liutomu-lystopadi 1938 r.," *Z arkhiviv VUChK–GPU–NKVD–KGB*, no. 1/28 (2007), pp. 137–138.

23. Vadym Zolotar'ov, "Favoryt Iezhova: Storinky biohrafii narkoma vnutrishnikh sprav URSR O. I. Uspens'koho," in Oleh Bazhan and Roman Podkur, eds., *Politychni represii v Ukrain'skii RSR: Doslidnyts'ki refleksii ta interpretatsii. Do 75-richchia "Velykoho teroru" v SRSR. Materialy vseukrains'koi naukovoi konferentsii* (Kiev: Instytut istorii Ukrainy NAN Ukrainy, 2013), p. 177.

24. Ibid.

25. This is a reference to a remark made at the Kiev regional NKVD party collective meeting, in *SBU,* f. 16, d. 95, l. 297 (Stenogramma zakrytogo partsobraniia kollektiva NKVD po Kievskoi obl. za 14–16 dekabria 1938 g.).

26. *Kto rukovodil NKVD,* p. 495.

27. Zolotar'ov, *Oleksandr Uspens'kyi,* p. 163. According to Ukrainian historian Iuri Shapoval, in 1938, under Uspenskii, 261 people were arrested in the central republican NKVD administration, and in all about 994 NKVD cadres throughout the Ukrainian territorial apparatus. These numbers include both those who fell in the purge of "Leplevskii's men" as well as early arrests of "Uspenskii's men." Iu. I. Shapoval, "Iezhovshchyna," *Politychnyi teror i teroryzm v Ukraini XIX-XX st: Istorychni narysy* (Kiev: Naukova dumka, 2002), p. 470.

28. Valerii Vasil'ev and Roman Podkhur, "Organizatory i ispoliniteli massovogo ubiistva liudei v 1937–1938 gg. Sud'by sotrudnikov Vinnitskogo i Kamenets-Podol'skogo oblastnykh upravlenii NKVD," in Junge, Viola, and Rossman, eds., *Chekisty na skam'e podsudimykh.*

29. Iunge et al., eds., *"Cherez trupy vraga na blago naroda,"* vol. 2, p. 300.

30. Vol. 1 (Sledstvennoe delo A. R. Dolgusheva), l. 74 (Protokol doprosa Dolgusheva, 9 June 1939) and vol. 3, l. 33 (PSZ 10–13 August 1940).

31. Vol. 2, ll. 362–363 (Vypiska iz protkola doprosa obvin. Kobyzeva, G. N., 1 April 1939).

32. Vol 2, ll. 362–363 (Vypiska iz protkola doprosa obvin. Kobyzeva, G. N., 1 April 1939). Italics are mine.

33. Jansen and Petrov, *Stalin's Loyal Executioner,* pp. 133–134.

34. Zolotar'ov, *Uspens'kyi,* pp. 167–168, and idem., "Kolyshni spivrobitnyky NKVS URSR na kerivnii roboti u systemi HUTAB SRSR (1936–1939rr.)," *Z arkhiviv VUChK–GPU–NKVD–KGB,* nos. 1–2 (2013), pp. 51–79.

35. Jansen and Petrov, pp. 134–135; Zolotar'ov, "Favoryt Iezhova," pp. 181–182.

36. Zolotar'ov, *Oleksandr Uspens'kyi,* p. 119.

37. Vasil'iev, "Mekhanizmy," p. 147. See, for example, *Velykyi teror: Pol'ska operatsiia, 1937–1938,* 2 vols. (Warsaw: Instytut Pamieci Narodowej, 2010), back inside cover, for a diagram of the Polish "organization."

38. Vol. 1, l. 75 (Protokol doprosa Dolgusheva, 9 June 1939); vol. 3, l. 34 (PSZ 10–13 August 1940). Ivan Koroblev, the new appointment to lead the Vinnitsa NKVD, also demurred when Ezhov first asked him to serve in this post. (This response was likely a fairly typical response of new appointees, perhaps because of the genuine pressure of the office, but, more probably, as a customary response to promotions at this time.)

39. Vol. 3, l. 34 (PSZ 10–13 August 1940) and vol. 4, l. 126 (PSZ 24–27 February 1941).

40. Vol. 1, l. 99 (Protokol doprosa Dolgusheva, 15 June 1939).

41. Iunge et al., eds., *"Cherez trupy vraga na blago naroda,"* vol. 2, p. 374.

42. Ibid., vol. 1, p. 82.

43. Vol. 1, l. 47 (Protokol doprosa Dolgusheva, 20 January 1939).

44. Vol. 1, l. 97 (Protokol doprosa Dolgusheva, 15 June 1939).

45. Zolotar'ov writes that Uspenskii, "knowing the game," immediately "confessed" to whatever he was asked to confess. See Zolotar'ov, "Favoryt Iezhova," p. 186.

46. Vol. 1, ll. 207–208 (Protokol doprosa Uspenskogo, 10 May 1939), ll. 209–211 (Vypiska iz pokazanii Uspenskogo, 20 May 1939).

47. Vol. 1, ll. 197–206 (Protokol ochnoi stavki mezhdu arestovannymi Uspenskim Aleksandrom Ivanovichem i Dolgushevym Alekseem Romanovichem, 20 July 1939).

48. Vol. 1, ll. 151–153 (Protokol doprosa Dolgusheva, 19 August 1939).

49. Vol. 1, ll. 273–274 (Sobstvennoruchnye pokazaniia obviniamogo Dolgusheva, 16 October 1939).

50. Vol. 2, l. 5 (Protokol doprosa Ezhova Nikolaia Ivanovicha, 31 January 1940).

51. Vol. 2, ll. 6–8 (Protokol doprosa obviniaemogo Radzilovskogo A. P., 11 January 1940). For biographical information on Radzilovskii, see Okhotin and Roginskii, eds., *Kto rukovodil NKVD*, p. 352.

52. Vol. 1, l. 48 (Protokol doprosa Dolgusheva, 20 January 1939); vol. 2, ll. 38–54 (Protokol doprosa Dolgusheva, 21 March 1940). As early as February 1937, a Central Committee coded telegram to all party secretaries and NKVD bosses ordered that arrests of specialists required the agreement of the corresponding People's Commissar in which the specialist worked; in cases of conflict, the Central Committee had the final say. These categories of people, along with NKVD officials, were normally tried by the Military Collegium of the Soviet Supreme Court. In fact, throughout the period of the Great Terror, there was considerable confusion in practice in the use of the troika and Military Collegia. See, for example, Junge and Bonvech, eds., *Bol'shevistskii poriadok v Gruzii*, vol. 1, pp. 128, 146, 159–160, n. 16. Beriia's circular from 21 September 1938 is published in ibid., vol. 2, pp. 167–169, referring mainly to the national operations.

53. Vol. 1, ll. 48–49 (Protokol doprosa Dolgusheva, 20 January 1939); vol. 2, ll. 38–54 (Protokol doprosa Dolgusheva, 21 March 1940).

54. Vol. 3, ll. 33–34 (PSZ 10–13 August 1940). Dolgushev told his interrogator earlier that "for me, the instructions of the former Narkom Uspenskii were sufficient since I considered that he had a directive on this issue from NKVD SSSR." See Vol. 1, l. 59 (Protokol doprosa Dolgusheva, 13 February 1939). Dolgushev's interrogator also noted that Slavin had told him that he did not give permission to Dolgushev to arrest NKVD officers in Vol. 1, ll. 65–68 (Protokol doprosa Dolgusheva, 19 March 1939).

55. Vol. 4, l. 121 (PSZ 24–27 February 1941).

56. Vol. 4, l. 196 (PSZ 20–21 May 1942).

57. Vol. 2, ll. 38–54 (Protokol doprosa Dolgusheva, 21 March 1940), 55–62 (Protokol doprosa Dolgusheva, 7 April 1940).

58. Vol. 3, l. 43–43 ob. (PSZ 10–13 August 1940). In the end, if official statistics are to be trusted, from June to August 1938, nine operatives and sixty-two members of the nonoperative staff were fired; thirty-three operatives and three members of the nonoperative staff were transferred. Vol. 4, l. 64 (Svedeniia o kolichestvo

sotrudnikov NKVD po Kievskoi obl. ovolennykh i otkomandirovannykh za vremia 2/VI–2 VIII 1938). A document from 12 January 1939 claimed that the Kiev regional troika convicted to death eleven NKVD workers. Vol. 1, ll. 28–29 (Postanovlenie, 17 January 1939). Another, slightly later document claimed that twenty-four NKVD workers and forty specialists of high rank were sentenced to death through Dolgushev's troika. Vol 1, ll. 39–40 (Postanovlenie, 21 June 1939).

59. Vol. 2, ll. 294–313 (Vypiska iz protokola obshchego zakrytogo partiinogo sobraniia partorganizatsii UGB Kievskogo obl. Upr. NKVD, 14 December 1938); and *SBU*, f. 16, d. 95 (Stenogramma zakrytogo partsobraniia kollektiva NKVD po Kievskoi obl., 14–16 December 1938). Also see Iunge et al., eds., *"Cherez trupy vraga na blago naroda*," vol. 2, pp. 447–459.

60. *SBU*, f. 16, d. 95, ll. 54–55, 103, 111, 131, 172, 174–175, 182, 198 (Stenogramma zakrytogo partsobraniia kollektiva NKVD po Kievskoi obl., 14–16 December 1938).

61. *SBU*, f. 16, d. 95, ll. 111, 117 (Stenogramma zakrytogo partsobraniia kollektiva NKVD po Kievskoi obl., 14–16 December 1938).

62. *SBU*, f. 16, d. 95, l. 165 (Stenogramma zakrytogo partsobraniia kollektiva NKVD po Kievskoi obl., 14–16 December1938).

63. Zolotar'ov, *Uspens'kyi*, p. 196.

64. *SBU*, f. 16, d. 95, ll. 16–17 (Stenogramma zakrytogo partsobraniia kollektiva NKVD po Kievskoi obl., 14–16 December 1938).

65. *SBU*, f. 16, d. 95, ll. 174–175 (Stenogramma zakrytogo partsobraniia kollektiva NKVD po Kievskoi obl., 14–16 December 1938).

66. *SBU*, f. 16, d. 95, ll. 279, 285 (Stenogramma zakrytogo partsobraniia kollektiva NKVD po Kievskoi obl., 14–16 December 1938).

67. Vol. 2, l. 300 (Vypiska iz protokola obshchego zakrytogo partiinogo sobraniia partorganizatsii UGB Kievskogo obl. Upr. NKVD, 14 December 1938).

68. Vol. 2, l. 299 (Vypiska iz protokola obshchego zakrytogo partiinogo sobraniia partorganizatsii UGB Kievskogo obl. Upr. NKVD, 14 December 1938).

69. Vol. 2, l. 299 (Vypiska iz protokola obshchego zakrytogo partiinogo sobraniia partorganizatsii UGB Kievskogo obl. Upr. NKVD, 14 December 1938).

70. Vol. 2, l. 299 (Vypiska iz protokola obshchego zakrytogo partiinogo sobraniia partorganizatsii UGB Kievskogo obl. Upr. NKVD, 14 December 1938).

71. Vol. 2, l. 300 (Vypiska iz protokola obshchego zakrytogo partiinogo sobraniia partorganizatsii UGB Kievskogo obl. Upr. NKVD, 14 December 1938).

72. Vol. 2, l. 300 (Vypiska iz protokola obshchego zakrytogo partiinogo sobraniia partorganizatsii UGB Kievskogo obl. Upr. NKVD, 14 December 1938).

73. Vol. 2, ll. 301–303 (Vypiska iz protokola obshchego zakrytogo partiinogo sobraniia partorganizatsii UGB Kievskogo obl. Upr. NKVD, 14 December 1938).

74. Vol. 4, ll. 128 ob.-129 (PSZ 24–27 February 1941).

75. See, for example, Olga Bertelsen, "New Archival Documentation on Soviet Jewish Policy in Interwar Ukraine. Part Two: GPU Repression of Jews and Jewish Groups in 1937–1940," *On the Jewish Street: A Journal of Russian-Jewish History and Culture*, 1(2) (2011), 165–206.

76. *SBU*, f. 16, d. 95, ll. 3–4, 240 (Stenogramma zakrytogo partsobraniia kollektiva NKVD po Kievskoi obl., 14–16 December 1938).

77. Vol. 2, l. 305 (Vypiska iz protokola obshchego zakrytogo partiinogo sobraniia partorganizatsii UGB Kievskogo obl. Upr. NKVD, 14 December 1938).

78. Vol. 2, ll. 303–304 (Vypiska iz protokola obshchego zakrytogo partiinogo sobraniia partorganizatsii UGB Kievskogo obl. Upr. NKVD, 14 December 1938).

79. *TSD*, vol. 5, book 2, p. 543; Khaustov et al., ed., *Lubianka. Stalin i NKVD–NKGB–GUKR "Smersh,"* pp. 14–15.

80. Vol. 4, ll. 129–129 ob. (PSZ 24–27 February 1941).

81. Vol. 3, ll. 33–33 ob. (PSZ 10–13 August 1939); vol. 4, 129–131 (PSZ 24–27 February 1941).

82. Vol. 4, l. 129 ob. (PSZ 24–27 February 1941).

83. *SBU*, f. 16, d. 95, l. 49 Stenogramma zakrytogo partsobraniia kollektiva NKVD po Kievskoi obl., 14–16 December 1938). The factory special sections were under the dual jurisdiction of the factory administration and the NKVD; the deputy head of the special section was typically an NKVD employee.

84. Iunge et al., eds., *"Cherez trupy vraga na blago naroda,"* vol. 2, pp. 458–459.

85. *SBU*, f. 16, d. 95, l. 177 (Stenogramma zakrytogo partsobraniia kollektiva NKVD po Kievskoi obl. za 14–16 dekabria 1938 g.)

86. Vol. 3, l. 34 ob. (PSZ 10–13 August 1940).

87. Vol. 3, l. 37 (PSZ 10–13 August 1940).

88. Vol. 3, l. 37 ob. (PSZ 10–13 August 1940).

89. Vol. 4, l. 141 (PSZ 24–27 February 1941).

90. Vol. 2, l. 5 (Protokol doprosa Ezhova Nikolaia Ivanovicha, 31 January 1940); Vol. 2, ll. 6–8 (Protokol doprosa obviniaemogo Radzilovskogo A. P., 11 January 1940).

91. Vol. 3, l. 38 ob. (PSZ 10–13 August 1940).

92. Vol. 3, ll. 38–38 ob. (PSZ 10–13 August 1940).

93. Vol. 3, l. 34 ob. (PSZ 10–13 August 1940).

94. Vol. 3, l. 37 ob. (PSZ. 10–13 August 1940).

95. Vol. 4, l. 133 (PSZ 24–27 February 1941).

96. See n. 52 in this chapter.

97. Vol. 1, l. 36 (PSZ 10–13 August 1940).

98. Vol. 4, l. 128 ob. (PSZ 24–27 February 1941).

99. Vol. 3, l. 43 (PSZ 10–13 August 1940).

100. Vol. 4, l. 141 (PSZ 24–27 February 1941).

101. On 7 August 1937, USSR Procurator Andrei Vyshinskii issued the following instruction to his procurators, "simplifying" legal procedure: "The observance of legal procedure and the preliminary approval of arrests are not demanded" in relation to Order 00447. See Jansen and Petrov, *Stalin's Loyal Executioner*, p. 88.

102. Vol. 3, l. 41 (PSZ 10–13 August 1940).

103. Pavlychev's name appears in many NKVD investigative files. In 1938, he moved around through the regional and republic NKVD as a kind of troubleshooter. He

was eventually arrested and tried along with A. D. Balychev, the former deputy head of the Voroshilovogradskaia regional NKVD. The trial records are in SBU, f. 5, d. 38810, vol. 8, ll. 62–83 (Protokol sudebnogo zasedaniia Voennogo Tribunala Voisk NKVD Kievskogo okruga, 12–14 avgusta 1941). Pavlychev received ten years, was released to fight in WWII, and was killed in Kiev during the war. See f. 5, d. 67462 (Spravka po arkh. ugolovym delam na Korkunova, Balycheva, Sokolova, Voiskoboinikova, Pavlycheva, Tarasovskogo), l. 17 (Obzornaia spravka), and f. 12, d. 265, ll. 39–45 (Protokol doprosa Drushliaka ot 26 aprelia 1954).

104. Vol. 3, l. 41 (PSZ 10–13 August 1940). Also see Pavlychev's personnel file in f. 12, d. 3186, 2 vols.

105. Vol. 3, ll. 40, 44 (PSZ 10–13 August 1940).

106. Vol. 3, l. 43 (PSZ 10–13 August 1940).

107. Vol. 3, l. 36 (PSZ 10–13 August 1940).

108. Vol. 4, l. 128 ob. (PSZ 24–27 February 1941).

109. Vol. 3, l. 37 (PSZ 10–13 August 1940).

110. Vol. 3, l. 39 ob. (PSZ 10–13 August 1940).

111. Vol. 3, l. 37 (PSZ 10–13 August 1940).

112. Vol. 3, l. 35 (PSZ 10–13 August 1940).

113. Vol. 1, ll. 185–187 (Protokol doprosa Neimana).

114. Vol. 4, l. 129 (PSZ 24–27 February 1941).

115. Vol. 3, l. 42 (PSZ 10–13 August 1940).

116. Vol. 4, ll. 129–129 ob. (PSZ 24–27 February 1941).

117. Vol. 1, l. 243 (Postanovlenie, 3 June 1940).

118. Vol. 3, l. 36 (PSZ 10–13 August 1940).

119. *SBU*, f. 16, d. 95, ll. 118–124 (Stenogramma zakrytogo partsobraniia kollektiva NKVD po Kievskoi ob. za 14–16 dekabria 1938 g.).

120. Vol. 3, l. 40 ob., 41 ob. (PSZ 10–13 August 1940); vol. 4, l. 134 (PSZ 24–27 February 1941).

121. Vol. 4, l. 143 (PSZ 24–27 February 1941). See *SBU*, f. 6, d. 43975 for Mozheiko's sledstvennoe delo, in particular l. 24 (Nachal'niku NKVD Kievsk. oblasti, Kapitana Dolughevu) and l. 25 (Protokol vskrytiia Mozheiko Kazimira Kazimirovicha).

122. Vol. 4, pp. 202–203 (Prigovor 20–21 May 1942).

123. Vol. 3, l. 35 ob. (PSZ 10–13 August 1940).

124. Vol. 2, ll. 294–295 (Vypiska iz protokola obshchego zakrytogo partiinogo sobraniia partorganizatsii UGB Kievskogo oblastnogo Upr. NKVD ot 13 dekabria 1938).

125. Vol. 2, ll. 303–304 (Vypiska iz protokola obshchego zakrytogo partiinogo sobraniia partorganizatsii UGB Kievskogo oblastnogo Upr. NKVD ot 13 dekabria 1938).

126. Vol. 3, l. 38 ob. (PSZ 10–13 August 1940).

127. See Vadym Zolotar'ov, "Diial'nist' orhaniv radians'koi derzhbezpeky zi zdiisnennia kurkul's'koi operatsii u Kharkivs'kii oblasti (1937–1938 rr.)," *Z arkhiviv VChK–GPU–NKVD–KGB*, No. 1 (2007), 165; and Iunge et al., eds., *"Cherez trupy vraga na blago naroda,"* vol. 2, p. 457.

128. Iunge et al., eds., *"Cherez trupy vraga na blago naroda,"* vol. 2, p. 458. See *Kto ruko-vodil NKVD*, p. 104, on Bel'skii.

129. Iunge et al., eds., *"Cherez trupy vraga na blago naroda,"* vol. 2, p. 458.

130. Ibid.

131. Iunge, et al., eds., *"Cherez trupy vraga na blago naroda,"* vol. 2, p. 458.

132. Vol. 1, l. 197 (Protokol ochnoi stavki mezhdu arestovannymi Uspenskim Aleksandrom Ivanovichem i Dolgushevym Alekseem Romanovichem, 20 July 1939); vol. 2, ll. 295–296 (Vypiska iz protokola obshchego zakrytogo partiinogo sobraniia partorganizatsii UGB Kievskogo oblastnogo Upr. NKVD ot 13 dekabria 1938). Also see Vol. 3, l. 33 (PSZ 10–13 August 1940), where he talks about disci-plining several NKVD workers for beating people under arrest. See Max Bergholz, *Violence as a Generative Force: Identity, Nationalism, and Memory in a Balkan Community* (Ithaca, NY: Cornell University Press, 2016), whose concept of vio-lence as a "generative force" is highly relevant to the development of the "taste for terror."

133. Iunge et al., eds., *"Cherez trupy vraga na blago naroda,"* vol. 2, p. 410.

134. *SBU*, f. 16, d. 95, ll. 25, 55, 178, 182, for examples (Stenogramma zakrytogo partso-braniia kollektiva NKVD po Kievskoi obl., 14–16 December 1938).

135. *SBU*, f. 16, d. 95, ll. 25–29 (Stenogramma zakrytogo partsobraniia kollektiva NKVD po Kievskoi obl., 14–16 December 1938).

136. Vol. 3, ll. 46 ob.–47 (PSZ 10–13 August 1940); vol. 4, l. 192 (PSZ 20–21 May 1942).

137. Vol. 2, ll. 21–37 (Protokol doprosa Dolgusheva, 14 March 1940), 38–54 (Protokol doprosa Dolgusheva, 21 March 1940).

138. Vol. 1, ll. 221–222 (Zaiavlenie Tverdokhlebenko, osobouponomoch. NKVD Ukraine, ot Kozlova, Iakova Aleseekvicha, 9 May 1939); Vol. 1, ll. 224–227 (Zaiavlenie ot arestovannogo Ia. Kozlova Tverdokhlebenko, 15 June 1939); vol. 1, ll. 1–4 of envelope content inserted at end of file (Protokol doprosa arestovannogo Kozlova Iakova Alekseevicha ot 13 maia 1939 goda).

139. Vol. 1, l. 2 of envelope content (Protokol doprosa arestovannogo Kozlova Iakova Alekseevicha ot 13 maia 1939 goda); vol. 1, l. 2 of envelope content (Protokol doprosa arestovannogo Kozlova Iakova Alekseevicha ot 13 maia 1939 goda). For biographical information on Kobulev, see Okhotin and Roginskii, eds., *Kto ruko-vodil NKVD*, pp. 233–234.

140. Vol. 1, ll. 221–222 (Zaiavlenie Tverdokhlebenko, osobouponomoch. NKVD Ukraine, ot Kozlova, Iakova Aleseekvicha, 9 May 1939).

141. Vol. 1, l. 224 (Zaiavlenie ot arestovannogo Ia. Kozlova Tverdokhlebenko, 15 June 1939).

142. Vol. 1, ll. 224–227 (Zaiavlenie ot arestovannogo Ia. Kozlova Tverdokhlebenko, 15 June 1939).

143. Vol. 1, ll. 2–3 of envelope content (Protokol doprosa arestovannogo Kozlova Iakova Alekseevicha ot 13 maia 1939 goda).

144. Vol. 1, l. 4 of envelope content (Protokol doprosa arestovannogo Kozlova Iakova Alekseevicha ot 13 maia 1939 goda).
145. Vol. 4, ll. 126–128 (PSZ 24–27 February 1941).
146. Vol. 4, l. 11 (Protokol doprosa Doglusheva, 11 December 1940).
147. Vol. 4, ll. 143–144 (PSZ 24–27 February 1941).
148. Vol. 4, l. 144 (PSZ 24–27 February 1941).
149. Vol. 4, ll. 198–199 (PSZ 20–21 May 1942).
150. Vol. 4, ll. 202–203 (Prigovor, 20–21 May 1942).
151. Vol. 4, ll. 202–203 (Prigovor, 20–21 May 1942).
152. Vol. 4, l. 210 (Spravka. 4 June 1997). On Dolgushev's fate, see Oleg Bazhan and Vadym Zolotar'ov, "Visuvanets' Mikoli Ezhova abo Traektoriia zletu ta padinnia kapitana derzhavnoi bezpeki Oleksiia Dolgusheva," *Kraieznavstvo*, no. 3 (2013). My thanks to Vadim Zolotar'ov for alerting me to this source.

CHAPTER 3

1. The epigraph is from *SBU*, f. 5, d. 45704 (Sledstvennoe delo I. S. Drushliaka), vol. 2, ll. 749 ob.–750 (Protokol sudebnogo zasedaniia, 14–15 January 1940). Unless otherwise specified, all archival citations will be from this *delo* and identified by volume and page number, as well as document title and date. All references from the trial proceedings, Protokoly sudebnogo zasedaniia, will be cited as PSZ.
2. Vol. 2, ll. 751–754 (Prigovor, 14–15 January 1940).
3. Vol. 1, l. 4 (Postanovlenie, 9 June 1939); *SBU*, f. 12, d. 3042, vol. 1, ch. 3, l. 14 (Lichnoe delo Drushliaka). The Fourth Department was the Secret-Political, later Special [*Osobyi*] Department. It is not entirely clear whether Drushliak's work in Khar'kov was in the Second Department (operative work) or the Fourth Department.
4. *SBU*, f. 12, d. 3042 (Lichnoe delo Drushliaka), part III, ll. 8, 14–17.
5. Vol. 1, ll. 1–3 (Postanovlenie, 4 June 1939), 7 (Protokol obyska v kvartire); and *SBU*, f. 12, d. 3042, ll. 1–13, vol. 1 (part 1), l. 7 (part 2), l. 8 (part 3), tom 2, ll. 10–11 (Lichnoe delo I. S. Drushliaka).
6. Vol. 2, l. 325 (Protokol doprosa Rotshteina Iakova Efimovicha, 29 August 1939).
7. Vol. 2, ll. 355–356 (Protokol doprosa svidetelia Kriukova Nikolaia Nesterovicha, 8 September 1939); l. 749 (PSZ). NKVD cadres moved around the Republic, and the officials listed here are no exception. For further and more detailed career data, see *Velykyi teror: Pol'ska operatsiia, 1937–1938*, 2 vols. (Warsaw: Instytut Pamieci Narodowej, 2010), vol. 1, p. 1674, nn. 6–7; Iurii Shapoval et al., eds., *Ukraina v dobu '"Velykoho teroru," 1936–1938 roky* (Kiev: Lybid', 2009); and Iurii Shapoval and Vadym Zolotar'ov, "Ievrei v kerivnytstvi orhaniv DPU–NKVD USRR–URSR u 1920–1930-kh rr.," *Z arkhiviv VUChK-GPU-NKVD-KGB*, no. 1 (34) (2010), 53–93.

8. Vol. 2, ll. 344–347 (Protokol doprosa svidetelia Gokhberga, Moiseia Evseevicha, 8 September 1939).

9. Vol. 2, ll. 386–387 (Vypiska iz zaiavleniia byv. arestovannogo-st. leitenanta gosbezopasnosti Polishchuka Borisa Aleksandrovicha, nd).

10. Vol. 2, ll. 739 ob.-740 (PSZ). (Gokhberg also testified that Drushliak interfered in other investigators' cases [ll. 344–347]).

11. Vol. 2, ll. 359–361 (Protokol doprosa svidetelia Gol'dshteina Semena Il'icha, 10 September 1939).

12. Vol. 2, l. 325 (Protokol doprosa Rotshteina Iakova Efimovicha, 29 August 1939).

13. Vol. 2, l. 587 (Vypiska iz protokola zakrytogo sobraniia partorganizatsii UGB UNKVD po Khar'kovskoi oblaste ot 26–7 ianvaria 1939 g.).

14. Ibid.

15. Vol. 2, ll. 350–353 (Protokol doprosa svidetelia Frei Borisa Konstantinovicha, 8 September 1939).

16. Vol. 2, l. 325 (Protokol doprosa Rotshteina Iakova Efimovicha, 29 August 1939).

17. Vol. 2, ll. 344–347 (Protokol doprosa svidetelia Gokhberga, Moiseia Evseevicha, 8 September 1939).

18. Vol. 2, ll. 386–387 (Vypiska iz zaiavleniia byv. arestovannogo-st. leitenanta gosbezopasnosti Polishchuka Borisa Aleksandrovicha, nd).

19. Vol. 1, ll. 266–269 (Protokol doprosa Egupova Aleksia Konstantinovicha, 15 August 1939); vol. 1, l. 198 (Dopolnitel'nye pokazaniia Drushliaka, 2 September 1939); l. 746 (PSZ).

20. Vol. 2, l. 743 ob. (PSZ).

21. Vol. 2, ll. 580–586 (Protokol doprosa svidetalia Shatnogo Semena Shaevicha); vol. 2, ll. 741–741 ob. (PSZ).

22. Vol. 2, l. 740 ob. (PSZ).

23. Vol. 2, ll. 386–387 (Vypiska iz zaiavleniia byv. arestovannogo-st. leitenanta gosbezopasnosti Polishchuka Borisa Aleksandrovicha, nd).

24. Vol. 1, ll. 277–279 (Protokol doprosa Bessmertnogo Tikhona Kuz'micha, 15 August 1939).

25. Vol. 2, l. 737 ob. (PSZ).

26. The victims who testified were invited by the Military Tribunal. It is impossible to say how many victims Drushliak had in all or whether there were far worse cases than what surfaced in court.

27. Vol. 1, l. 201 (Vypiska iz protokola doprosa obviniaemoi Bodanskoi Lidii Iosifovnu, 19 January 1939); vol. 2, l. 740 ob. (PSZ).

28. Vol. 2, ll. 739 ob.-740 (PSZ).

29. Vol. 1, l. 212 (Protokol doprosa svidetelia Nechaevoi Evgenii Nikolaevny, 2 March 1939).

30. Vol. 2, ll. 350–353 (Protokol doprosa svidetelia Frei Borisa Konstaninovicha, 8 September 1939).

31. Vol. 2, l. 740 ob. (PSZ).

32. Vol. 1, l. 117 (Dopol'nitelnye pokazaniia Drushliaka, 13 August 1939). When his interrogator asked him to explain the meaning of "ne korrektirovan" [not corrected] on the printed confession of Tarasov, Drushliak answered, "The word 'not corrected' can be explained in this way: In that period of time almost all declarations of the accused and their subsequent handwritten confessions were corrected by the heads of departments or their deputies. As far as I know, Tarasov's confession was not corrected, therefore I wrote on it 'uncorrected.'"

33. Vol. 2, ll. 744–745 (PSZ). See also l. 745 ob.

34. Vol. 2, ll. 616–620 (Protokol doprosa svidetelia Rokhlina L. L. 25 October 1939).

35. SBU, f. 12, d. 265, ll. 2–8 (Vypiska iz zhaloby Liudmirskogo Evseia L'vovicha na imia Ministra Vuntrennykh Del Soiuza SSR tov. Kruglova ot 25 noiabria 1953 g.). For another reference to Drushliak, see the memoirs of M. S. Rotfort in "Vospominaniia o Gulage i ikh avtory," www.sakharov-center.ru

36. Vol. 1, ll. 23 (Ob"iasnenie); 69 (Po delu Vitkovskogo, nd). Petliura was a Ukrainian nationalist and civil war leader who led Ukraine's struggle for independence after the 1917 Revolution.

37. Vol. 2, ll. 739, 743 ob. (PSZ); vol. 1, l. 208 (Osobupolnomochennomu Khar'kovskogo UNKVD tov. Modukhovichu ot Fedorova-Berkova F. S., nd). See also Nechaeva's protokol doprosa from 2 March 1939 (vol. 1, l. 212).

38. Vol. 2, ll. 738 ob.–739 ob. (PSZ); vol. 2, ll. 325 (Protokol doprosa Rotshteina Iakova Efimovicha, 29 August 1939), 395–397 (Protokol ochnoi stavki mezhdu obviniaemym Drushliakom i svidetelem (Iakovlevoi Lidiei Andriianovnoi, 27 August 1939). See also Iakovleva's protokol doprosa from 25 April 1939 (vol. 1, l. 215) and Boiko's protokol doprosa from 22 February 1939 (vol. 1, l. 205).

39. Vol. 2, l. 803 (Akt sudebno-meditsinskogo vskrytiia trup gg. Bandura, 22 February 1938).

40. Vol. 1, l. 83 (Protokol doprosa obviniamogo Drushliaka Ivana Stepanovicha, 17 July 1939).

41. Vol. 1, l. 234 (Protokol doprosa Benderskogo Vasiliia Filimonovicha, 21 June 1939).

42. Vol. 2, l. 741 ob. (PSZ).

43. Vol. 2, l. 742 (PSZ). The precise term was "kniga ucheta vyzovov arestovannykh," according to the Military Tribunal.

44. Vol. 2, l. 742 (PSZ).

45. Vol. 2, ll. 748 ob.–749 (PSZ).

46. Vol. 1, ll. 228–229 (Protokol doprosa Kobeniuka Davida Dmitrievicha, 16 July 1939).

47. Vol. 1, ll. 238–239 (Osobupolnomochennomu NKVD Ukraina Vracha tiur'my UGB NKVD Ukaina Fraimana E. E. "Ob"iasnenie," nd); ll. 742 ob-743 (PSZ).

48. Vol. 2, ll. 746 ob.-749 ob. (PSZ).

49. Vol. 1, ll. 228–229 (Protokol doprosa Kobeniuka Davida Dmitrievicha, 16 July 1939), 293–294 (Protokol doprosa Fraimana Efima Evseevicha, 23 August 1939).

50. Vol. 2, ll. 512–513 (Dopolnitel'nye pokazaniia obviniaemogo Drushliaka I. S., 2 October 1939), 736 (and elsewhere).

51. See Chapter 2.

52. Vol. 2, l. 737 (PSZ).

53. Vol. 2 (Protokol doprosa svidetelia Gokhberga Moiseia Evseevicha, 8 September 1939), ll. 344–347.

54. Vol. 1, l. 208 (Osobupolnomochennomu Khar'kovskogo UNKVD tov. Modukhovichu ot Fedorova-Berkova F. S., nd), vol. 2, 645–649 (Protokol doprosa obviniaemogo Fedorova-Berkova Fedora Semenovicha, 23 September 1939).

55. Vol. 1, l. 65 (Sobstvennoruchnye pokazaniia arestovannogo Drushliaka, nd); vol. 2, ll. 608–614 (Dopolnitel'nye pokazaniia Drushliaka, 20 October 1939).

56. Vol. 1, ll. 45–46 (Osobupolnomochennomu NKVD UNKVD Tverdokhlebenko ot Drushliaka, nd).

57. Vol. 1 (Po delu Vitkovskogo, nd), l. 68.

58. See Eugenia Ginzburg, *Journey Into the Whirlwind*, trans. Paul Stevenson and Max Hayward (New York: Harcourt Brace Jovanovich, 1967), pp. 254–258, for information on one way in which prisoners discovered the change in NKVD leadership.

59. Vol. 1, l. 65 (Sobstvennoruchnye pokazaniia arestovannogo Drushliaka, nd).

60. Vol. 1, ll. 64 (Sobstvennoruchnye pokazaniia arestovannogo Drushliaka, nd), vol. 2, l. 737 ob. (PSZ).

61. Vol. 1, ll. 23 (Ob"iasnenie); 69 (Po delu Vitkovskogo, nd).

62. Vol. 1, ll. 124–125 (Dopolnitel'nye pokazaniia Drushliaka, 15 August 1939).

63. Vol. 2, l. 737 (PSZ).

64. Vol. 2, l. 736 (PSZ).

65. Vol. 1, l. 96 (Pokazaniia obviniaemogo Drushliaka Ivana Stepanovicha, 19 July 1939).

66. Vol. 1 Pokazaniia obviniaemogo Drushliaka I. S., 19 July 1939), l. 97.

67. Vol. 2, ll. 737, 747 (PSZ).

68. Vol. 1, ll. 109–110 (Dopolnitel'nye pokazaniia Drushliaka, 22 July 1939), 116–117 (Dopolnitel'nye pokazaniia Drushliaka, 13 August 1939).

69. Vol. 2, ll. 748 ob.–749 (PSZ).

70. Vol. 2, ll. 749–750 (PSZ).

71. Vol. 1, l. 3 (Postanovlenie, 4 June 1939).

72. Vol. 1, ll. 162–163 (Dopolnitel'nye pokazaniia Drushliaka, 2 September 1939).

73. Vol. 1, l. 194 (Dopolnitel'nye pokazaniia Drushliaka, 18 September 1939).

74. Vol. 2, l. 736 ob. (PSZ).

75. Vol. 2, ll. 608–614 (Dopolnitel'nye pokazaniia Drushliaka, 20 October 1939).

76. Vol. 2, l. 736 ob. (PSZ).

77. Vol. 2, l. 737 ob. (PSZ).

78. Vol. 2, l. 737 ob. (PSZ).

79. Vol. 2, l. 749 ob. (PSZ).

80. *SBU*, f. 12, d. 3042, vol. 1, ch. 1, l. 1. (Lichnoe delo Drushliaka). Also see f. 12, d. 265, ll. 39–45 (Protokol doprosa Drushliaka ot 26 aprelia 1954).

CHAPTER 4

1. *SBU,* f. 5, d. 57637 (Sledstvennoe delo Fleishmana, O. S. i Krivtsova, M. M.), l. 50. Unless otherwise noted, all archival references will be from this *fond* and *delo,* and identified further only by the volume and page numbers. The epigraphs are from (in order of placement) vol. 3, l. 61 (Protokol sudebnogo zasedaniia, 3–8 August 1940) and vol. 3, l. 56 (Protokol sudebnogo zasedaniia, 3–8 August 1940). All subsequent references from the trial proceedings, the Protokol sudebnogo zasedaniia, will be cited as PSZ.

2. Vol. 3, ll. 50, 52 (PSZ). See Chapter 2, note 6, for a description of these criminal articles.

3. Vol. 1, l. 2 (Postanovlenie na arrest, 1 February 1940); vol. 3, l. 50 ob. (PSZ).

4. Vol. 3, l. 50 ob. (PSZ).

5. Vol. 3, ll. 52–53, 67 (PSZ).

6. Vol. 1, l. 33 (Zakliuchenie, 16 January 1940).

7. Vol. 1, l. 34 (Zakliuchenie, 16 January 1940).

8. Vol. 1, l. 35 (Zakliuchenie, 16 January 1940); vol. 2, ll. 227–236 (Obvinitel'noe zakliuchenie, 27 June 1940).

9. Vol. 1, l. 33 (Zakliuchenie, 16 January 1940).

10. Vol. 2, ll. 198–199 (Obvinitel'noe zakliuchenie po obvineniu zhitelei sela Kalennaia Skvirskogo raiona Kievskoi oblasti, November 1938); ll. 205–206; ll. 227–228 (Obvinitel'noe zakliuchenie, 27 June 1940); vol. 3, l. 107 (PSZ).

11. Vol. 2, ll. 112–113 (Spravka po sledstvennomu delu no 146430, nd); ll. 114–152 (Povestka zasedaniia Osoboi troiki Kievskogo oblastnogo upravleniia NKVD Ukraine. Belotserkovskaia opergruppa. Raion Skvirskii, nd); ll. 153–170 (Obvinitel'noe zakliuchenie, July 1938).

12. Vol. 2, ll. 27–28 (Protokol dopros Sverinenko, Z. E., January 1940); vol. 3, ll. 76–78 (PSZ).

13. Vol. 2, ll. 112–113 (Spravka po sledstvennomu delu no 146430, nd).

14. Vol. 2, ll. 112–113 (Spravka po sledstvennomu delu no 146430, nd); ll. 114–152 (Povestka zasedaniia Osoboi troiki Kievskogo oblastnogo upravleniia NKVD Ukraine. Belotserkovskaia opergruppa. Raion Skvirskii, nd).

15. Vol. 2, ll. 112–113 (Spravka po sledstvennomu delu no 146430, nd).

16. Vol. 2, ll. 227–236 (Obvinitel'noe zakliuchenie, 27 June 1940).

17. Vol. 2, l. 124 (Povestka zasedaniia Osoboi troiki Kievskogo oblastnogo upravleniia NKVD Ukraine. Belotserkovskaia opergruppa. Raion Skvirskii, nd).

18. Vol. 3, ll. 81, 107 (PSZ). (He had not sought witnesses before the case was returned by the troika.)

19. Vol. 2, ll. 228–229 (Obvinitel'noe zakliuchenie, 27 June 1940).

20. Vol. 2, ll. 174–179 (Postanovlenie o prekreshchenii sledstviia, 29 November 1939); 181–185 (Zaiavlenie Zalevskogo, 19 August 1939); 188 (Zaiavlenie Chetverika, 16 January 1940).

21. Vol. 1, l. 39 (Zakliuchenie, 16 January 1940); vol. 2, ll. 174–179 (Postanovlenie o prekreshchenii sledstviia, 29 November 1939).
22. Vol. 1, l. 43 (Zakliuchenie, 16 January 1940).
23. Vol. 1, l. 32 (Postanovlenie, 1 June 1940); vol. 3, ll. 2, 32 (PSZ). Fleishman was arrested on 1 February 1940—vol. 1, l. 2 (Postanovlenie na arrest); and Krivtsov on 29 March 1940—vol. 1, l. 17 (Postanovlenie na arrest).
24. Vol. 1, l. 30 (Postanovlenie, 25 March 1940); vol. 3, l. 52 (PSZ).
25. Vol. 1, ll. 2–3 (Postanovlenie na arrest. 1 February 1940); vol. 3, l. 50 ob. (PSZ).
26. Vol. 3, l. 52 (PSZ).
27. It is not clear who ran the group in October. Vol. 1, l. 152 (Dopolnitel'noe-ob"iasnenie o metodakh vedeniia sledstviia v 1937–38 gg, 14 January 1940, from Krivtsov); vol. 2, ll. 78–79 (Protokol doprosa Tsirul'nitskogo, 16 December 1939); vol. 3, ll. 152, 161–162 (PSZ). My thanks to Vadym Zolotar'ov for information on Pivchikov. Note also that there were *two* NKVD officers named Babich—Ivan Ignat'evich (who is noted here) and Isai Iakovlevich (who figures in the Uman case).
28. In Dolgushev's *sledstvennoe delo* (d. 38237, vol. 3, l. 42). (Protokol sudebnogo zasedaniia, 10–13 August 1940), NKVD operative L. M. Pavlychev, who worked as deputy head of the Kiev NKVD, said that Dolgushev went to Belaia Tserkov' several times to deal with the *lipa* (falsification, forgery) and as a result several prisoners were freed.
29. Vol. 3, l. 61 (PSZ).
30. Vol. 3, l. 63 (PSZ).
31. Vol. 3, l. 156 (Vypiska iz protokola doprosa Fleishmana, 18 June 1940).
32. Vol. 3, ll. 52–53 (PSZ); vol. 3, l. 155 (Vypiska. Sobstvennoruchnye pokazaniia Fleishman).
33. Vol. 2, ll. 114–152 (Povestka zasedaniia osoboi troiki Kievskogo oblastnogo Upravleniia NKVD Ukraine. Belotserkovskaia opergruppa. Raion Skvirskii).
34. Vol. 3, l. 54 (PSZ).
35. Vol. 3, l. 64 (PSZ). Babich denied this and also said Dolgushev did not give such an order.
36. Vol. 3, l. 54 (PSZ).
37. Vol. 3, ll. 54–55 (PSZ).
38. Vol. 3, ll. 53, 56 (PSZ).
39. Vol. 1, ll. 72–73 (Protokol doprosa, 9 March 1940).
40. Vol. 3, l. 153 (Protokol doprosa. 2 March 1940); vol. 3, l. 154 (Vypiska iz protokola doprosa Fleishmana, 9 March 1940).
41. Vol. 1, l. 17 (Postanovlenie na arrest, 29 March 1940), l. 18 (Postanovlenie, 29 March 1940). 121 (Protokol doprosa, 10 December 1939); vol. 3, l. 50 ob. (PSZ).
42. Vol. 3, ll. 56–59 (PSZ).
43. Vol. 3, ll. 56–59 (PSZ, 3–8 August 1940); on Pivchikov, see vol. 3, l. 61 (PSZ).
44. Vol. 1, ll. 121–123 (Protokol doprosa, 10 December 1939); ll. 139–141 (Ob"iasnital'naia zapiska po voprosu metodov vedeniia sledstviia v 1937–1938 gg. ot byvshego sotrudnika militsiia Krivtsova M. M., 13 January 1940.)

45. Vol. 1, ll. 139 (Ob"iasnital'naia zapiska . . .).

46. Vol. 1, l. 122 (Protokol doprosa, 10 December 1939).

47. Vol. 1, l. 123 (Protokol doprosa, 10 December 1939).

48. Vol. 1, l. 121 (Protokol doprosa, 10 December 1939), l. 141 (Ob"iasnitel'naia zapiska . . .).

49. Vol. 1, ll. 139–141 (Ob"iasnitel'naia zapiska . . .).

50. Vol. 1, ll. 146–152 (Dopolnitel'noe-ob"iasnenie o metodakh vedeniia sledstviia v 1937–38 gg. ot Krivtsova, 14 January 1940).

51. Vol. 1, l. 32 (Postanovlenie, 1 June 1940); vol. 1, ll. 49–51 (Zakliuchenie, 14 June 1940).

52. Vol. 3, l. 67 (PSZ).

53. Vol. 2, l. 3 (Protokol doprosa Romanova, 13 January 1940); vol. 3, l. 75 (PSZ).

54. Vol. 3, l. 75 (PSZ).

55. Vol. 2, l. 1 (Protokol doprosa Romanova, 13 January 1940).

56. Vol. 2, ll. 9a–11 (Protokol doprosa Beregovogo, 13 January 1940).

57. Vol. 3, l. 78 (PSZ). Antonets and Romanov said nothing about Krivtsov beating anyone.

58. Vol. 3, l. 77 (PSZ).

59. Vol. 3, l. 68 (PSZ).

60. Vol. 2, l. 25 (Protokol doprosa Adamchuka); vol. 3, l. 79 (PSZ). Also see the testimony of a policeman, Z. E. Sverinenko, in vol. 2, ll. 27–8 (Protokol doprosa), where he describes the torment unleashed on a series of teachers during *stoiki*.

61. Vol. 2, ll. 60–61 (Protokol doprosa Gutsalo, 13 January 1940); vol. 3, l. 85 (PSZ).

62. Vol. 2, ll. 56–57 (Protokol doprosa Korinnogo, 13 January 1940); vol. 3, ll. 84–85 (PSZ).

63. Vol. 3, ll. 72–74 (PSZ).

64. Vol. 2, l. 2 (Protokol doprosa Romanova, 13 January 1940); vol. 3, l. 75 (PSZ).

65. Vol. 3, l. 75 (PSZ).

66. Vol. 2, ll. 9–11 (Protokol doprosa Romanova, 11 January 1940).

67. Vol. 2, ll. 16–17 (Ob"iasnitel'naia zapiska from Beregovoi to the deputy of the *oblast'* procurator, 12 January 1940).

68. Vol. 3, l. 67 (PSZ).

69. Vol. 3, l. 61 (PSZ).

70. Vol. 3, l. 65 (PSZ).

71. On this type of evidence, see Iunge and Binner, "Spravki sel'soveta kak faktor v osuzhdenii krest'ian," *Stalinizm v sovetskoi provintsii*, pp. 613–623. On the use of village "geneology" to purge collective farmers (or to settle scores), see Lynne Viola, "The Second Coming: Class Enemies in the Soviet Countryside, 1927–1935," in J. Arch Getty and Roberta T. Manning, eds., *Stalinist Terror: New Perspectives* (New York: Cambridge University Press, 1993), pp. 65–98.

72. Vol. 2, l. 11 (Protokol doprosa Beregovogo, 13 January 1940).

73. Vol. 2, l. 10 (Protokol doprosa Beregovogo, 13 January 1940).

74. Vol. 3, ll. 68–69, 75 (PSZ).

75. Vol. 2, l. 11 (Protokol doprosa Beregovogo, 13 January 1940); vol. 3, l. 80 (PSZ).

76. Vol. 3, ll. 76–77 (PSZ).

77. Vol. 2, l. 3 (Protokol doprosa Romanova, 13 January 1940); vol. 3, l. 77 (PSZ).

78. Vol. 2, l. 10 (Protokol doprosa Beregovogo, 13 January 1940).

79. Vol. 3, l. 69 (PSZ).

80. Vol. 2, l. 48 (Protokol doprosa Nikolaichuk, 13 January 1940).

81. Vol. 3, ll. 80–81 (PSZ).

82. Vol. 2, ll. 89–90 (Protokol doprosa Antonika, 13 January 1940). Ianchuk had been exiled for three years for "sabotage" in the collective farm in 1933, certainly a famine-related "crime" (vol. 2, l. 147, Povestka Zasedaniia Osoboi Troiki Kievskogo oblastnogo Upravleniia NKVD Ukraine. Belotserkovskaia opergruppa. Raion Skvirskii, approx. July 1938).

83. Vol. 2, l. 87 (Protokol doprosa Orlovy, 13 January 1940).

84. Vol. 3, l. 102 (PSZ).

85. Vol. 3, ll. 100–107 (PSZ).

86. On this point, see Junge and Binner, "Spravki sel'soveta," p. 622.

87. For example, see vol. 3, ll. 97–99 (PSZ), where one witness went so far as to accuse another witness of being a gendarme under the tsar.

88. Vol. 3, l. 72 (PSZ).

89. Vol. 3, l. 63 (PSZ). Also see Fleishman's testimony to this in vol. 3, l. 155 (Vypiska. Sobstvennoruchnye pokazaniia Fleishman).

90. Vol. 3, l. 107 (PSZ).

91. Vol. 3, ll. 64, 76 (PSZ).

92. Vol. 3, l. 96 (PSZ).

93. Vol. 3, l. 96 (PSZ).

94. Vol. 3, l. 93 (PSZ).

95. Vol. 3, l. 108 (PSZ).

96. Vol. 3, l. 110 (PSZ).

97. Vol. 3, ll. 83, 109 (PSZ).

98. Vol. 3, l. 111 (PSZ).

99. Vol. 3, ll. 169–172 (Zaiavlenie to Vorshilov from Krivtsov, 20 December 1958), l. 173 (Zaiavlenie to Voroshilov from Krivtsov, 15 August 1959), ll. 218–233 (Postanovlenie, 23 November 1959, with detailed investigation into the case); l. 324 (decision of the Ukrainian courts from 1998).

100. See *SBU*, f. 5, d. 38237, ll. 31–47 (Protokol sudebnogo zasedaniia, 10–13 August 1940).

101. Oleg Khlevniuk is correct when he postulates that Stalin launched mass operations in order to eliminate a potential Fifth Column in the event of war. See his *Master of the House*, p. 173.

CHAPTER 5

1. The epigraphs are from *SBU*, f. 5, d. 38195 (Sledstvennoe delo Abramovicha, S. M. et al.), vol. 6, l. 143 (Protokol sudebnogo zasedaniia 5–10 May 1940) and

ll. 315–315 ob. (Protokol sudebnogo zasedaniia, 31 January–6 February 1941). All archival references will be from this *fond* and *delo*, and identified further by the volume, page numbers, title, and date of document. References to the trials, Protokol sudebnogo zasedaniia, will be cited as "PSZ" followed by the date.

2. Vol. 6, ll. 148 (PSZ, 5–10 May 1940), 312, 337 ob., 340 ob. (PSZ, 31 January– 6 February 1941). On l. 331, the head of the prison sanitary department, Gol'denshtein claimed that 4,000 people were under guard in Uman. (PSZ, 31 January–6 February 1941).

3. This section is based on a compilation of the two main indictments in the case. Vol. 5, ll. 1–8 (Zakliuchenie, 13 August 1939) and ll. 277–302 (Obvinitel'noe zakliuchenie, 20 February 1940).

4. Vol. 5, ll. 1–2 (Zakliuchenie, 13 August 1939), 277–278 (Obvinitel'noe zakliuchenie, 20 February 1940). [In Vol. 6, l. 339 ob.–340 ob. (PSZ, 31 January–6 February 1941), Borisov says there were eighteen districts in the group).] (There was another defendant originally mentioned, one Vasili Korneevich Kozachenko {or Kazachenko} who followed Tomin as head of the Uman NKVD. He disappears in the documents after the first reference {which preceded the second trial}). It is important to note that both Borisov and Tomin were caught up in the spring 1938 cadres' shuffles, with Borisov sent to a position in the Gulag tantamount to a serious demotion and Tomin sent to work in Tiraspol in Moldavia (present-day Moldova).

5. Vol. 5, ll. 1–4 (Zakliuchenie, 13 August 1939).

6. Vol. 5, ll. 4–5 (Zakliuchenie, 13 August 1939).

7. See Vol. 5, l. 300 (Obvinitel'noe zakliuchenie, 20 February 1940) for the charges against Abramovich concerning secrecy. See the Prigovor following the second trial, for the other charges: Vol. 6, ll. 172–176 (Prigovor, 5–10 May 1940).

8. Vol. 5, l. 292 (Obvinitel'noe zakliuchenie, 20 February 1940).

9. Vol. 1, ll. 180–216 (PSZ, 26–27 July 1939).

10. Vol. 1, l. 219 (Opredelenie, 27 July 1939), l. 231 (Postanovlenie, 10 September 1939); l. 233 (Postanovlenie, 22 September 1939).

11. Vol. 6, 96–161 (PSZ, 5–10 May 1940), ll. 172–176 (Prigovor, 5–10 May 1940), l. 225 (Opredelenie, 22 November 1940). Noncustodial compulsory labor generally entailed a deduction in wages.

12. Vol. 6, l. 476 (Zakliuchenie, 21 January 1943).

13. Vol. 5, ll. 1–8 (Zakliuchenie, 13 August 1939); Vol. 6, ll. 96, 141–144 (PSZ, 5–10 May 1940), 308–308 ob. (PSZ, 31 January–6 February 1941).

14. For biographical information on Babich, see Okhotin and Roginskii, eds., *Kto rukovodil NKVD*, pp. 95–96.

15. Vol. 6, ll. 141–144 (PSZ, 5–10 May 1940).

16. Vol. 6, ll. 313–313 ob. (PSZ, 31 January–6 February 1941).

17. For biographical information on Sharov, see Okhotin and Roginskii, eds., *Kto rukovodil NKVD*, pp. 444–445.

18. For biographical information on Reikhman, see Okhotin and Roginskii, eds., *Kto rukovodil NKVD*, pp. 358–359.

19. Vol. 6, ll. 96, 141–144 (PSZ, 5–10 May 1940), 308–308 ob., 320–320 ob. (PSZ, 31 January–6 February 1941)—testimony of Neiman on ll. 320–320 ob. regarding students).

20. Vol. 6, ll. 141–144 (PSZ, 5–10 May 1940).

21. Vol. 4, ll. 6–11 (Protokol doprosa Borisova, 26 November 1939); Vol. 6, ll. 97, 141–144, 146 (PSZ, 5–10 May 1940), 308–308 ob. (PSZ, 31 January–6 February 1941).

22. Vol. 4, ll. 6–11, 27–31 (Protokol doprosa Borisova, 26 November 1939 and 4 January 1940); vol. 5, l. 170 (Protokol doprosa na ochnoi stavke mezhdu Tominom i Borisovom, 8 February 1940); vol. 6, l. 146 (PSZ, 5–10 May 1940).

23. Leplevskii was at this time the head of the Ukrainian Republic NKVD and Frinovskii was the first deputy [*zam*] commissar of the All-Union NKVD. For biographical information on Leplevskii and Frinovskii, see Okhotin and Roginskii, eds., *Kto rukovodil NKVD,* pp. 270–271, 425–426. For the 7 June 1937 NKVD order on sending Frinovskii and Leplevskii, as well as Deribas, to Ukraine, see *Lubianka. Organy VChK–OGPU–NKVD–NKGB–MGB–MVD–KGB, 1917–1991. Spravochnik,* A. I. Kokurin, N. V. Petrov, eds. (Moscow: Materik, 2003), p. 586. For an analysis of Leplevskii's and Frinovskii's activities in Ukraine at this time, see Iurii Shapoval et al., eds., *Ukraina v dobu "Velykoho teroru," 1936–1938 roky* (Kiev: Lybid', 2009), pp. 12–37.

24. Tom 6, ll. 339 ob.–340 ob. (PSZ, 31 January–6 February 1941).

25. Tom 6, ll. 340 (PSZ, 31 January–6 February 1941); also see Danilov's testimony on l. 311 (PSZ, 31 January–6 February 1941).

26. Tom 6, ll. 339–340 ob. (PSZ, 31 January–6 February 1941).

27. Tom 6, ll. 113–114, 116, 118, 145–151 (PSZ, 5–10 May 1940), 334 ob., 348 (PSZ, 31 January–6 February 1941); and vol. 4, ll. 51–57 (Protokol doprosa Tomina, 19 October 1939).

28. Vol. 6, l. 340 (PSZ, 31 January–6 February 1941).

29. Vol. 4, ll. 27–31 (Protokol doprosa Borisova, 4 January 1940).

30. Vol. 3, ll. 142–145 (Raport nachal'nika Kirovskogo GORRO NKVD U[krainsk] SSR g. Kieva—leitenanta Gosbezopasnosti t. Ustinova V. P. t. Kobulovu, 26 January 1939).

31. Vol. 6, ll. 142–144, 145, 147–148 (PSZ, 5–10 May 1940); Vol. 5, l. 170 (Protokol doprosa na ochnoi stavke mezhdu Tominom i Borisovom, 8 February 1940).

32. Vol. 6, ll. 97 (PSZ, 5–10 May 1940), 308 ob. (PSZ, 31 January–6 February 1941).

33. Vol. 6, ll. 141–144 (PSZ, 5–10 May 1940), 340–340 ob. (PSZ, 31 January–6 February 1941).

34. Vol. 6, ll. 145, 150 (PSZ, 5–10 May 1940).

35. Vol. 4, ll. 27–31 (Protokol doprosa Borisova, 4 January 1940).

36. Vol. 6, ll. 141–142 (PSZ, 5–10 May 1940).

37. Vol. 1, ll. 45–53 (Protokol doprosa Neimana, 21 May 1939), 180–216 (PSZ, 26–27 July 1939); Vol. 4, ll. 6–11 (Protokol doprosa Borisova, 26 November 1939).

38. Vol. 6, ll. 97, 151–153 (PSZ, 5–10 May 1940), 308 ob., 336 ob. (PSZ, 31 January–6 February 1941).

39. Vol. 6, ll. 151–153 (PSZ, 5–10 May 1940).

40. Vol. 6, ll. 320–320 ob. (PSZ, 31 January–6 February 1941—testimony of Neiman).

41. Vol. 4, ll. 39–47 (Protokol doprosa Tomina, 21 September 1939); Vol. 6, ll. 320–320 ob. (PSZ, 31 January–6 February 1941—testimony of Neiman). Frinovskii had issued an NKVD memorandum on 8 August 1937 ordering all UNKVD nachal'niki *not* to announce in advance sentences of execution to prisoners in cases of category 1 executions. See Marc Junge et al., eds., *"Cherez trupy vraga na blago naroda,"* vol. 1, p. 163.

42. Vol. 6, l. 332 (PSZ, 31 January–6 February 1941—testimony of Zudin). See also the valuable contribution by Karel C. Berkhoff, "Bykivnia: How Grave Robbers, Activists, and Foreigners Ended Official Silence About Stalin's Mass Graves Near Kiev," in Elisabeth Anstett and Jean-Marc Dreyfus, eds., *Human Remains and Identification: Mass Violence, Genocide, and the "Forensic Turn,"* (Manchester: Manchester University Press, 2015), pp. 59–82.

43. Vol. 6, l. 143 (PSZ, 5–10 May 1940).

44. Vol. 4, ll. 6–11 (Protokol doprosa Borisova, 26 November 1939); Vol. 6, l. 143 (PSZ, 5–10 May 1940).

45. Vol. 6, l. 143 (PSZ, 5–10 May 1940).

46. Vol. 6, l. 144 (PSZ, 5–10 May 1940).

47. Vadym Zolotar'ov, "Kolyshni spivrobitnyky NKVS URSR na kerivnii roboti u systemi HUTAB SRSR (1936–1939 rr.)," *Z arkhiviv VUChK–GPU–NKVD–KGB,* nos. 1–2 (2013), p. 71.

48. Vol. 6, ll. 313–313 ob. (PSZ, 31 January–6 February 1941).

49. Vol. 6, l. 311 (PSZ, 31 January–6 February 1941).

50. Vol. 6, l. 311 (PSZ, 31 January–6 February 1941). Interrogator M. I. Belov also told the court that there was a general opinion that Tomin did not listen to Borisov and that differences between the two were generally decided in Tomin's favor. Vol. 6, ll. 116–117 (PSZ. 5–10 May 1940).

51. Vol. 6, l. 312 (PSZ, 31 January–6 February 1941).

52. Vol. 6, l. 312 (PSZ, 31 January–6 February 1941).

53. Vol. 6, ll. 311–312 (PSZ, 31 January–6 February 1941).

54. Vol. 6, l. 311 (PSZ, 31 January–6 February 1941).

55. Vol. 6, ll. 113–115 (PSZ, 5–10 May 1940).

56. Vol. 6, ll. 124–128 (PSZ, 5–10 May 1940).

57. For biographical information on Mark Pavlovich Rogol' (1905–1941), see Okhotin and Roginskii, eds., *Kto rukovodil NKVD,* pp. 363–364.

58. Vol. 6, ll. 124–126 (PSZ, 5–10 May 1940).

59. Vol. 6, l. 322 (PSZ, 31 January–6 February 1941).

60. Vol. 6, ll. 124–125 (PSZ, 5–10 May 1940).

61. Vol. 1, ll. 42–45 (Protokol doprosa Neimana, 8 April 1939); ll. 45–53 (Protokol doprosa Neimana, 21 May 1939); ll. 106–111 (Protokol ochnoi stavki mezhdu Abramovichom i Neimanem. 23 May 1939); Vol. 6, ll. 124–128 (PSZ, 5–10 May 1940), 320–323 (PSZ, 31 January–6 February 1941).

62. Vol. 1, ll. 180–216 (PSZ, 26–27 July 1939); Vol. 6, ll. 128 (PSZ, 5–10 May 1940), 326–327, 337–337 ob. (PSZ, 31 January–6 February 1941).

63. Vol. 6, ll. 322–322 ob. (PSZ, 31 January–6 February 1941).

64. Vol. 6, l. 104 (PSZ, 5–10 May 1940). See also Vol. 1, ll. 106a–110a (Protokol doprosa Kravchenko, nd), where Kravchenko claims that his wife was selling his own clothes. Kravchenko also said that he received from Abramovich two pairs of boots, one suit, three shirts, two jackets, and several pairs of underwear.

65. Vol. 6, ll. 337–337 ob. (PSZ, 31 January–6 February 1941).

66. Vol. 6, ll. 129–131 (PSZ, 5–10 May 1940).

67. Vol. 1, ll. 180–216 (PSZ, 26–27 July 1939).

68. Vol. 1, ll. 54–61 (Protokol doprosa Zudina, nd).

69. Vol. 6, ll. 155 (PSZ, 5–10 May 1940), 332 (PSZ, 31 January–6 February 1941).

70. Vol. 6, l. 333 (PSZ, 31 January–6 February 1941).

71. Thanks to Ron Suny for suggesting that "moral economy," a term from peasant studies, should more correctly be "immoral economy." In peasant studies, moral economy refers to the ways in which peasants justified their actions, including resistance, according to fairness in economic relations. The Uman executioners did the same, but their justification was hardly moral.

72. Vol. 3, ll. 129–131 (Protokol doprosa svidetelia Kalachevskogo, Tikhona Semenovicha, 1 July 1939).

73. See the amazing work by Tepliakov, *Protsedura*, pp. 33–59, on practices in execution work.

74. Vol. 1, ll. 45–53 (Protokol doprosa Neimana, 21 May 1939). On the issue of money (as opposed to possessions), the prison bookkeeper and the prison cashier served as witnesses, providing "expert" testimony about how prisoners' money was returned to them before a transport—or, in this case, before execution. Viktor Grigor'evich Gol'dguber, the bookkeeper [*bukhgalter*], kept very precise records, was able to tell the court how much pocket money prisoners were allowed to take with them on transport, and Abramovich's orders to allow prisoners to take more than the standard 100 rubles. Vol. 6, ll. 131–132 (PSZ, 5–10 May 1940), 331–331 ob. (PSZ, 31 January–6 February 1941).

75. Vol. 4, ll. 41–42 (Protokol doprosa Tomina, 21 September 1939).

76. Vol. 4, l. 47 (Protokol doprosa Tomina, 21 September 1939).

77. Vol. 4, ll. 43–44 (Protokol doprosa Tomina, 21 September 1939).

78. Vol. 1, ll. 54–56 (Protokol doprosa Zudina, nd).

79. Vol. 1, ll. 106–111 (Protokol ochnoi stavki mezhdu Abramovichem i Neimanem, 23 May 1939).

80. Vol. 1, ll. 128–131 (Protokol ochnoi stavki Abramovichem i Zudinym, 23 May 1939); Vol. 6, l. 153 (PSZ, 5–10 May 1940).

81. Vol. 1, l. 154 (Postanovlenie, 20 June 1939), l. 219 (Opredelenie, 27 July 1939), 231 (Postanovlenie, 10 September 1939), 233 (Postanovlenie, 22 September 1939).

82. Vol. 6, 172–176 (Prigovor, 5–10 May 1940).

83. Vol. 6, l. 99 (PSZ, 5–10 May 1940).

84. See note 2 of this chapter.

85. Vol. 6, ll. 103, 109, 144 (PSZ, 5–10 May 1940).

86. Vol. 6, ll. 112–113 (PSZ, 5–10 May 1940).

87. Vol. 6, ll. 110–112 (PSZ, 5–10 May 1940).

88. Vol. 6, ll. 328–329 ob. (PSZ, 31 January–6 February 1941).

89. Vol. 3, ll. 227–228 (Zaiavlenie, nd).

90. Specifically, the student made several allegations regarding sexual molestation at the site of execution. Interrogators asked witnesses about these events repeatedly, but without result.

91. Vol. 3, ll. 231–235 (Pis'mo, 24 May 1939).

92. Vol. 3, ll. 237–239 (Pis'mo, 21 January 1939), 243–244 (Pis'mo, 12 January 1939), 247 (Zaiavlenie, nd).

93. Vol. 3, ll. 251–255 (Pis'mo, nd).

94. Vol. 3, l. 256 (Pis'mo, nd).

95. Vol. 3, ll. 263–270 (Pis'mo, nd).

96. Vol. 6, ll. 128–129 (PSZ, 5–10 May 1940), 323–323 ob. (PSZ, 31 January–6 February 1941).

97. Vol. 3, ll. 57–58 (Protokol doprosa M. I. Smerchinskogo, 15 June 1939).

98. Vol. 3, ll. 1–8 (Vypiska iz protokola sudebnogo zasedaniia Voennogo Tribunala Pogranichnykh vnutrennykh voisk Kievskogo okruga v g. Kieve, 9 February 1939), 45–48 (Protokol doprosa svidetelia Dubiniaka Dmitriia Efimovicha, 10 April 1939).

99. Their protokoly doprosa (from November and December 1939) are in vol. 3, ll. 188–209, followed by the protokol doprosa ochnoi stavki mezhdu Tomin i Statsenko. 27 December 1939, ll. 210–214. Their testimony is in Vol. 6, ll. 118–122 (PSZ, 5–10 May 1940), 324–325 (PSZ, 31 January–6 February 1941).

100. Vol. 6, l. 149 (PSZ, 5–10 May 1940).

101. Vol. 6, ll. 132–133 (PSZ, 5–10 May 1940), 325 (PSZ, 31 January–6 February 1941).

102. Vol. 6, ll. 133 (PSZ, 5–10 May 1940), 325 (PSZ, 31 January–6 February 1941).

103. Vol. 6, ll. 315–315 ob. (PSZ, 31 January–6 February 1941).

104. Raul Hilberg, *The Destruction of the European Jews* (New York: Holmes and Meier, 1985), p. 288.

105. Vol. 4, ll. 27–31 (Protokol doprosa Borisova, 4 January 1940).

106. Vol. 6, l. 349 ob. (PSZ, 31 January–6 February 1941).

107. Vol. 6, ll. 158–159 (PSZ, 5–10 May 1940).

108. Vol. 6, ll. 158–159 (PSZ, 5–10 May 1940).

109. Vol. 5, ll. 32–33 (Spravka na nachal'nika Umanskogo raiotdelenii NKVD Borisova-Lendermana Solomona Isaevicha, nd).

110. A. N. Zhukov, *Kadrovyi sostav organov gosudarstvennoi bezopasnosti SSSR, 1935–1939* (Moscow: Elektronnoe izdanie Mezhdunarodnyi Memorial, 2016).

111. Vol. 4, ll. 36–37, 39–47, 48–50, 62–64, 76, 110–116 (Protokoly doprosa Tomina, from September 1939 to January 1940).

112. Vol. 6, l. 146 (PSZ, 5–10 May 1940).

113. Vol. 6, ll. 147 (PSZ, 5–10 May 1940), 346 (PSZ, 31 January–6 February 1941).

114. Vol. 6, ll. 148 (PSZ, 5–10 May 1940), 343 ob. (PSZ, 31 January–6 February 1941).

115. Vol. 6, ll. 343 ob.–344 (PSZ, 31 January–6 February 1941).

116. Vol. 6, ll. 146–147 (PSZ, 5–10 May 1940), 346 (PSZ, 31 January–6 February 1941).

117. Vol. 6, l. 147 (PSZ, 5–10 May 1940).

118. Vol. 6, l. 149 (PSZ, 5–10 May 1940).

119. Vol. 6, l. 149 (PSZ, 5–10 May 1940).

120. Vol. 6, l. 103 (PSZ, 5–10 May 1940).

121. Vol. 6, l. 159 (PSZ, 5–10 May 1940).

122. Vol. 6, l. 159 (PSZ, 5–10 May 1940).

123. Vol. 3, l. 145 (Raport nachal'nika Kirovskogo GORRO NKVD U[krainsk]SSR g. Kieva—leitenanta Gosbezopasnosti t. Ustinova V. P. t. Kobulovu, 26 January 1939) ll. 155–157 (Ob"iasnitel'naia zapiska, 11 February 1939).

124. Vol. 6, l. 309 ob. (PSZ, 31 January–6 February 1941).

125. Vol. 6, ll. 476 (Postanovlenie ob otkaze v peresmotr dela, 21 January 1943), 488 (Zhaloba).

126. Vol. 6, ll. 488–491 (Zhaloba "ob ustanovlenii Alibi," 20 October 1977).

127. Vol. 4, l. 122 (Protokol doprosa Petrova, 25 February 1939).

128. Vol. 4, l. 131 (Protokol doprosa Petrova,19 June 1939).

129. Vol. 6, l. 99 (PSZ, 5–10 May 1940).

130. Vol. 6, l. 145 (PSZ, 5–10 May 1940).

131. Vol. 3, ll. 165–166 (Ob"iasnenie tov. Polishchuku, 16 February 1939). The term "chopper" was widely in use among Chekists at this time and referred to effective interrogators.

132. Vol. 6, l. 319 (PSZ, 31 January–6 February 1941).

133. Vol. 4, ll. 130–133 (Protokol doprosa Petrova, 19 June 1939).

134. Vol. 6, l. 160 (PSZ, 5–10 May 1940).

135. Vol. 6, l. 335–335 ob. (PSZ, 31 January–6 February 1941).

136. This was actually a rather large size apartment, given that the average size of Moscow apartments in 1930 was 5.5 meters and 4 square meters in 1940. Apartment sizes, however, may have been larger in small towns. See Sheila Fitzpatrick, *Everyday Stalinism: Ordinary Life in Extraordinary Times: Soviet Russia in the 1930s* (New York: Oxford University Press, 1999), p. 46.

137. Vol. 6, ll. 335–336 (PSZ, 31 January–6 February 1941).

138. Vol. 6, ll. 137, 160 (PSZ, 5–10 May 1940), 335–337 ob. (PSZ, 31 January–6 February 1941); Vol. 7, l. 10 ob. (Zaiavlenie, nd).

139. Vol. 1, ll. 2–3 (Postanovlenie, between 20 and 22 May 1939), 180–216; Vol. 6, ll. 110, 130, 151–153, 160 (PSZ, 5–10 May 1940), 335–337 ob. (PSZ, 31 January–6 February 1941).

140. Vol. 4, l. 131 (Protokol doprosa Petrova, 19 June 1939). The inventory of Abramovich's property in Vol. 1, l. 7, lists a scant six items (mainly documents).

141. Vol. 6, ll. 172–176 (Prigovor, 5–10 May 1940).

142. Vol. 6, l. 321 ob. (PSZ, 31 January–6 February 1941).

143. Vol. 6, ll. 132–133 (PSZ, 5–10 May 1940), 325–325 ob. (PSZ, 31 January–6 February 1941).

144. Vol. 6, l. 154 (PSZ, 5–10 May 1940).

145. Vol. 7, ll. 49–50 (Spravka na nachal'nika tiurm'y gor. Umani Abramovicha Samuila Moseevicha, nd).

146. Vol. 6, ll. 97 (PSZ, 5–10 May 1940), 308 ob. (PSZ, 31 January–6 February 1941).

147. Vol. 6, l. 332 (PSZ, 31 January–6 February 1941).

148. Vol. 6, ll. 137–138, 155–156 (PSZ, 5–10 May 1940), 332.

149. Vol. 1, ll. 129–131 (Protokol doprosa svidetelia Kalachevskogo, 1 July 1939); Vol. 4, ll. 41–43 (Protokol doprosa Tomina, 21 September 1939).

150. Vol. 5, l. 292 (Obvinitel'noe zakliuchenie, 20 February 1940).

151. Vol. 6, l. 156 (PSZ, 5–10 May 1940).

152. Vol. 6, ll. 172–176 (Prigovor, 5–10 May 1940).

153. Vol. 6, ll. 97 (PSZ, 5–10 May 1940), 308 ob. (PSZ, 31 January–6 February 1941).

154. Vol. 4, ll. 12–22 (Protokol doprosa Borisova, 10 December 1939).

155. Vol. 6, ll. 132–133 (PSZ, 5–10 May 1940), 325 (PSZ, 31 January–6 February 1941).

156. Vol. 6, ll. 338–339 (PSZ, 31 January–6 February 1941).

157. Vol. 6, ll. 156 (PSZ, 5–10 May 1940), 350 (PSZ, 31 January–6 February 1941).

158. See the interesting work, Sonke Neitzel and Harald Welzer, *Soldaten: On Fighting, Killing, and Dying. The Secret World War II Transcripts of German POWs* (Toronto: McClelland and Stewart, 2011), pp. 8–10, for a discussion of what they see as various "orders" of frames of reference with the aim "to understand the preconditions for psychologically normal people to do things they would not otherwise do."

159. Jan Tomasz Gross, with Irena Grudzinska Gross, *Golden Harvest* (New York: Oxford University Press, 2012), pp. 65, 67.

CHAPTER 6

1. The epigraph is from *SBU*, f. 5, d. 68219 (Sledstvennoe delo Klibanova, Linetskogo, i Dorova, 6 vols.), vol. 3, l. 175 (Narodnomu komissaru vnutrennyky del SSSR General'nomu komissaru gosudarstvennoi bezopasnosti tov. Ezhovu). Unless otherwise noted, all archival references will be from this *fond* and *delo*, and identified further only by volume number, page number, and document title (abbreviated after first reference). All subsequent references to the trial proceedings, Protokoly sudebnogo zasedaniia, will be cited as PSZ. For Grabar's reference to Uspenskii's announcement of a Politburo order to purge industrial towns, see Grabar's *Sledstvennoe delo* in *SBU*, f. 5, d. 43626, vol. 5, l. 579 ob (Protokoly sudebnoi zasedaniia, 7–11 October 1940).

2. Vol 2, ll. 56–59 (Protokol pokazanii Darova [*sic*], Grigoriia Iakovlevicha ot 28 ianvaria 1939 goda), 82 (Protokol doprosa obviniaemogo Dorova-Piontashko, Grigoriia Iakovlevicha ot 22 maia 1939 goda). Boldin, the head of the Zaporozh'e NKVD at this time, said there were 4,500 prisoners in the jail. See vol. 1, l. 80 (Osobupolnomochennomu NKVD Ukraina ot arestovannogo Boldina).

3. Vol. 2, l. 83 (Protokol doprosa obviniaemogo Dorova–Piontashko); vol. 5, l. 214 (Sobstvennoruchnye pokazaniia arestovannogo Dorova Grigoriia Iakovlevicha ot 21 dekabria 1939).

4. Vol. 1, ll. 42–43 (Postanovlenie).

5. Vol. 5, l. 246 (Postanovlenie).

6. Vol. 1, ll. 1–7 (Postanovleniia); 42–43 (Postanovlenie); vol. 5, ll. 330–359 (PSZ). The term "sector" within the city NKVD is the same as "department" in higher levels of the NKVD.

7. A. I. Savin and A. G. Tepliakov, in " 'Partiia mozhet oshibat'sia, a NKVD nikogda': Sotrudniki UNKVD po Odesskoi oblasti na skam'e podsudimykh (1939–1943 gg.)," in Junge, Viola, and Rossman, eds., *Chekisty na skam'e podsudimykh* first made this point in reference to cases in Odessa.

8. For the extension of the deadline of the national operations, see Khaustov et al., eds., *Lubianka: Stalin i Glavnoe Upravlenie Gosbezopasnosti NKVD, 1937–1938*, p. 538. The "kulak operation" (00447) continued past January 1938 in Ukraine (and in several other selected areas in the Russian Republic), with an increase in the limits on numbers to 30,000. In most places, the kulak operation was over by mid-May 1938, but in some parts of Ukraine continued into the fall of 1938. See Iunge et al., eds., *"Cherez trupy vraga na blago naroda,"* vol. 1, pp. 123, 147–148, 151–152; vol. 2, ll. 23–24.

9. For more information on industrial development and Dneprostroi in this region, see Anne D. Rassweiler, *The Generation of Power: The History of Dneprostroi* (New York: Oxford University Press, 1988).

10. Volodymyr Nikol's'kyi, "Statystyka politychnykh represii 1937 r. v Ukrainsk'ii RSR," *Z arkhiviv VUChK–GPU–NKVD–KGB*, nos. 3–4 (2000), pp. 104, 106.

11. Iunge et al., eds., *"Cherez trupy vraga na blago naroda*, vol. 2, pp. 17, 39–41, 57–60; for the extension of the deadline of the national operations, see Khaustov et al., eds., *Lubianka: Stalin i Glavnoe Upravlenie Gosbezopasnosti NKVD, 1937–1938*, p. 538

12. *SBU*, f. 16, op. 32, d. 31, l. 40 (Protokol zakrytogo partiinogo sobraniia UGB Upravleniia NKVD po Dnepropetrovskoi oblasti, 9–10 January 1939).

13. For example, vol. 1, ll. 2 (Postanovlenie), 26–31 (Postanovleniia), 42–43 (Postanovleniia), 64 (Postanovlenie).

14. Vol. 5, ll. 37–43 (Obvinitel'noe zakliuchenie po delu no. 147011 po obvineniiu Boldina Borisa Pavlochiva, Klibanova Davida Iakovlevicha, Linetskogo Borisa L'vovicha i Dorova-Piontashko Grigoriia Iakovlevicha).

15. For an example of such a diagram from Dnepropetrovsk, see *SBU*, f. 5, d. 64858 (Daragon), vol. 6, l. 90 (skema).

16. Vol. 3, ll. 170–175 (Narodnomu komissaru vnutrennyky del SSSR General'nomu komissaru gosudarstvennoi bezopasnosti tov. Ezhovu).

17. See the discussion in Jansen and Petrov, *Stalin's Loyal Executioner,* pp. 159–180.

18. Vol. 3, ll. 167–169 (Sekretariu TsK KP/b/U[kraina] tov. Khrushchevu).

19. Vol. 2, ll. 115–125 (Protokol pokazanii tov. Frishko ot 26 ianvaria 1939), 133–137 (Dopolnitel'nye pokazaniia t. Frishko ot 27 ianvaria 1939), 142–147 (Dopolnitel'nye pokazaniia t. Frishko ot 27 ianvaria 1939 goda).

20. Vol. 5, ll. 341–342 (PSZ).

21. See Savin and Tepliakov, " 'Partiia mozhet oshibat'sia, a NKVD nikogda.' "

22. The information about the hidden corpses is from Oleh Bazhan and Vadym Zolotar'ov, "Konveier smerti v chasy o vremena 'Velykoho teroru' v Ukraini," *Kraieznavstvo*, 1/86 (2014), 191–194.

23. For the July 1939 indictment, see vol. 5, ll. 37–43 (Obvinitel'noe zakliuchenie).

24. Boldin said that the "gorotdel did not have the right to make independent arrests and all arrests had to receive preliminary sanction from the [regional] NKVD" and its corresponding departments (Department Three or Four in most cases). Vol. 1, l. 72 (Osobupolnomochennomu NKVD Ukraina ot arestovannogo Boldina). It also may be that Boldin and others were referring exclusively to the national operations for which the "album method," requiring confirmation from the regional NKVD and Moscow, was in use.

25. Vol. 2, ll. 183–184 (Vypiska iz pokazanii arestovannogo Babaseva, Mikhaila Grigor'evicha, ot 8–11 marta 1939 goda). Also see *SBU*, f. 5, d. 43626 (Sledstvennoe delo Grabaria), vol. 2, ll. 428–447 (Pokazaniia arestovannogo Babaseva, Mikhaila Grigor'evicha, ot 8–11 marta 1939 goda). Vol'skii's hyphenated surname was "Vol'skii-Gitler," according to Iurii Shapoval et al., eds., *Ukraina v dobu "Velykoho teroru," 1936–1938 roky* (Kiev: Lybid', 2009), p. 136. Gitler is the Russian spelling for Hitler.

26. Vol. 2, ll. 183–184 (Vypiska iz pokazanii arestovannogo Babaseva, Mikhaila Grigor'evicha, ot 8–11 marta 1939 goda).

27. Ibid. In his testimony to Grabar's interrogators, Babasev said that in Kiev, his cellmates, former interrogators, told him that "Moscow doesn't know about the local arbitrariness [*proizvol*] of the Ukrainian NKVD leadership and the only way to save oneself was to get Moscow to investigate the case." When Babasev asked how to get word to Moscow, they told him "that the only way out was to agree to give a confession to someone among the leaders in the center." *SBU*, f. 5, d. 43626 (Sledstvennoe delo Grabaria), l. 436 (Pokazaniia arestovannogo Babaseva, Mikhaila Grigor'evicha, ot 8-11 marta 1939 goda). Babasev's case was officially dismissed on 17 December 1939. See SBU, f. 12, d. 163, ll. 57–59 (Postanovlenie).

28. Vol. 1, vol. 2, ll. 176–182 (Protokol doprosa svidetelia Brikkera Konstantina Alekseevicha ot 20 fevralia 1939 goda).

29. Ibid. Brikker was called to testify at the trial of Grabar' in October 1940. At the trial, he explained why Uspenskii called him a *barakhol'shchik*. He said that since his family lived in Kiev, he had nothing in Zaporozh'e and slept on the floor of the Zaporozh'e NKVD. When he asked Vol'skii, then the head of the Zaporozh'e NKVD, to help him get some things or to let him return to Kiev for this purpose, according to Brikker, the director of Factory No. 29, who happened to be present, offered him a table and chairs, which Vol'skii agreed he could have. See *SBU*, f. 5, d. 43626 (Sledstvennoe delo Grabaria), ll. 599–599 ob (Protokoly sudebnoi zasedaniia 7–11 oktiabria 1940). Brikker was freed on 1 December 1939, according to *SBU*, f. 5, d. 38153 (Sledstvennoe delo Nazarenko), vol. 3, l. 184 (Protokol sudebnogo zasedaniia. 8–9 maia 1940).

30. Vol. 1, ll. 92–93 (Protokol pokazanii obviniaemogo Boldina Borisa Pavlovicha ot 13 aprilia 1939 goda). It is likely that he worked in the Ukrainian Republican NKVD as an interrogator for a short time directly before his assignment to Dnepropetrovsk and Zaporozhe. See f. 6, d. 49855 (Sledstvennoe delo Frenkelia, Mikhaila Veniaminovicha), l. 67 (Vypiska iz protokola doprosa svietelia).

31. Vol. 3, l. 265 (Protokol obshchego zakrytogo partiinogo sobraniia chlenov i kandidatov VKP(b) partiinoi organizatsii UGB UNKVD po Zaporozhskoi oblasti ot 9–10 fevralia 1939 g.).

32. Vol. 1, l. 94 (Protokol doprosa Boldina Borisa Pavlovicha ot 13 aprelia 1939 goda).

33. Vol. 1, ll. 72–73 (Osobupolnomochennomu NKVD Ukraina ot arestovannogo Boldina).

34. Ibid., ll. 73–75.

35. Ibid., ll. 82–83. He also shifted some blame to Vol'skii, who preceded him in his position.

36. Ibid., l. 66.

37. Ibid., l. 83.

38. Ibid., l. 66.

39. Ibid., ll. 70–72.

40. Ibid., ll. 73–74.

41. Ibid., ll. 67–69, 74–75.

42. Ibid., ll. 77.

43. Vol. 2, ll. 102–107 (Protokol ochnoi stavki mezhdu obviniamymi Grabarem Vasiliem Romanovichem i Boldinym Borisom Pavlovichem ot 23 aprelia 1939 goda).

44. Vol. 5, ll. 246 (Postanovlenie), 404–405 (Spravka po arkhivnym ugolovnym delam No. 7148).

45. Vol 3, ll. 72–72 ob. (Vitiag z protokolu No. 75. Zasidannia biura Zaporiz'koho miskkomu KP(b)U, 5 marta 1939), 257–295 (Protokol obshchego zakrytogo partiinogo sobraniia chlenov i kandidatov VKP(b) partiinoi organizatsii UGB UNKVD po Zaporozhskoi oblasti ot 9–10 fevralia 1939 g.).

46. The villages outside of Zaporozh'e were also targeted, mainly by Klibanov's Fourth Sector. See Vol. 5, l. 347 (PSZ).

47. O. Leibovich, A. Koldushko, and A. Kazankov, eds., *"Vkliuchen v operatsiiu": Massovyi terror v Prikam'e v 1937–1938 gg.* (Moscow: Rosspen, 2009), pp. 117, 125, 128; and A. V. Chashchukhin, "Uchastie sovetskikh organov vlasti v provedenii massovoi operatsii," in M. Iunge et al., eds., *Stalinizm v sovetskoi provinitsii: 1937– 1938 gg.*, pp. 638–44.

48. Vol. 5, ll. 335–335 ob. (PSZ).

49. Vol. 5, l. 333 (PSZ).

50. Vol. 6, ll. 1–2 (Nachal'niku gorotdela NKVD, nachal'niku III otdela UGB UNKVD, nachal'niku IV otdela UGB NKVD Ukraine. Ot Bogdanova).

51. Ibid.

52. Vol. 6, ll. 16–26 (Protokol No. 1 zasidaniia Biuro Voroshilovskogo raikomu KP(b) U m. Zaporizhzhia, zavod no. 29, 7 July 1938).

53. Vol. 6, ll. 27–29 (Postanovlenie biuro Voroshilovskogo RKP KP/b/U po dokladu komissii obsledovaniia sostoianiia raboty po ONU Zavoda no. 29, ot 7/VII-1938).

54. Vol. 6, ll. 1–2 (Nachal'niku gorotdela NKVD . . .), 45–46 (Nachal'niku gorotdela NKVD tov. Boldinu, ot Bogdanova D. P., 27 August 1938), 47–49 (Nachal'niku gorotdela NKVD tov. Boldinu, ot Bogdanova, 31 August 1938).

55. Vol. 6, l. 50 (2 sentiabria 1938 ot Boldina i Linetskogo).

56. Vol. 6, ll. 51–53 (ot Bogdanova. 3 sentiabria 1938).

57. Vol. 6, ll. 56–58 (Spravka o partorge TsK VKP(b) zavoda No. 29).

58. Vol. 6, ll. 67–68 (Spravka o sostoianii zavoda No. 29 . . .).

59. Vol. 6, l. 69 (ot Svirskogo).

60. Vol. 1, l. 68 (Osobupolnomochennomu NKVD Ukraina ot arestovannogo Boldina).

61. Vol. 5, l. 346 ob. (PSZ).

62. Vol. 5, ll. 348 ob.–349 (PSZ).

63. Vol. 5, l. 340 (PSZ).

64. Vol. 5, ll. 339–340, 342–342 ob. (PSZ).

65. Vol. 3, l. 104 (Akt 1939 goda).

66. Vol. 3, l. 260 (Protokol obshchego zakrytogo partiinogo sobraniia chlenov i kandidatov VKP(b) partiinoi organizatsii UGB UNKVD po Zaporozhskoi oblasti ot 9–10 fevralia 1939 g.).

67. Ibid.

68. Vol. 1, ll. 42–43 (Postanovleniia); vol. 2, ll. 185–186 (Protokol doprosa svidetelia Savicheva Zinoviia Prokof'evicha ot 31 marta 1939 goda); vol. 5, l. 349 ob. (PSZ).

69. Vol. 5, l. 37 (Obvinitel'noe zakliuchenie).

70. See Chapter 2.

71. Vol. 5, l. 334 ob. (PSZ). Earlier, Gorodetskii claimed that Linetskii threatened him with arrest, when he "refused to write fake protocols." Vol. 3, l. 272 (Protokol obshchego zakrytogo partiinogo sobraniia . . . ot 9–10 fevralia 1939 g.).

72. Vol. 5, l. 336 (PSZ).

73. Vol. 5, l. 344 (PSZ).

74. Vol. 5, l. 346 (PSZ).
75. Vol. 5, ll. 337–338 (PSZ).
76. Vol. 5, l. 333 ob. (PSZ).
77. Vol. 5, ll. 346 ob. –347 (PSZ).
78. Vol. 5, ll. 337–338 (PSZ).
79. Vol. 5, ll. 338 ob., 343 ob. (PSZ).
80. Vol. 3, ll. 286–287 (Protokol obshchego zakrytogo partiinogo sobraniia . . . ot 9–10 fevralia 1939 g.).
81. Vol. 5, ll. 334–335 (PSZ).
82. Vol. 5, l. 337 (PSZ); also see l. 339 (PSZ).
83. Vol. 2, l. 57 (Protokol pokazanii Darova . . . ot ianvaria 1939 g.).
84. Vol. 2, l. 82 (Protokol doprosa obviniamogo Dorova-Piontashko Grigoriia Iakovlevicha ot 22 maia 1939 g.).
85. Vol. 5, ll. 166–168 (Spravka. 21 noiabria 1939; Spravka. 25 noibria 1939; Protokol osmotra pomeshcheniia, 20–21 noiabria 1939.)
86. Vol. 1, ll. 181–182 (Osobupolnomochennomu NKVD Ukraina ot arestovannogo Boldina). Jailer N. A. Mashchenko (b. 1910) confirmed Boldin's testimony regarding who had the right to place prisoners in cell number 8. Vol. 2, l. 154 (Protokol pokazanii Mashchenko, Nikolaia Alekseevicha . . . ot 28 ianvaria 1939 g.).
87. Vol. 1, ll. 168–170 (Protokol doprosa Klibanova ot 2 aprelia 1939 g.); Vol. 2, ll. 1–5 (Protokol pokazanii Linetskogo Borisa L'vovicha ot 8 aprelia 1939 g.); ll. 57–58 (Protokol pokazanii Darova . . . ot 28 ianvaria 1939 g.).
88. Vol. 3, l. 272 (Protokol obshchego zakrytogo partiinogo sobraniia . . . ot 9–10 fevralia 1939 g.).
89. Vol. 5, l. 339 (PSZ). "Vse ee nazyvali 'salotopka' tak kak chelovek v nei talal, poryvalas' sliz'iu."
90. Vol. 5, ll. 340 ob.–341 (PSZ).
91. Vol. 5, l. 335 (PSZ).
92. Vol. 5, l. 336 ob. (PSZ).
93. Vol. 2, l. 155 (Protokol pokazanii Mashchenko . . . ot 28 ianvaria 1939 g.); vol. 5, l. 332 ob. (PSZ).
94. Vol. 5, ll. 344 ob.–345 (PSZ).
95. Vol. 5, l. 355 (PSZ).
96. Vol. 5, l. 259 (Protokol ochnoi stavka mezhdu Klibanovym i Gol'dvugem), l. 339 ob. (PSZ). Two different spellings are used for this former prisoner—Gol'dbug and Gol'dvug.
97. Vol. 5, ll. 340–340 ob. (PSZ).
98. Vol. 5, ll. 343–343 ob. (PSZ).
99. Vol. 1, ll. 42–43 (Postanovleniia). "Etap," in this instance, was a euphemism for the executions of category 1 prisoners.
100. Vol. 2, l. 80 (Protokol doprosa obviniaemogo Dorova-Piontashko . . . ot 22 maia 1939 g.).

101. Ibid., ll. 80–81.
102. Vol 2, ll. 185–186 (Protokol doprosa svidetelia Savicheva Zinoviia Prokof'evicha ot 31 marta 1939 g.); vol. 5, l. 349 ob. (PSZ).
103. Vol. 5, ll. 77–78 (Protokol doprosa svidetelia Fil, M. D.); 335 ob. (PSZ).
104. Vol. 5, l. 347 ob. (PSZ).
105. Vol. 5, ll. 348, 349 (PSZ).
106. Vol. 5, ll. 68–70 (Protokol doprosa obviniaemogo Felosenko Ili Ivanovicha), 71–72 (Protokol doprosa svidetelia Iavorskogo Mikhaila Sergeevicha), 73–74 (Protokol doprosa Radzionova Mikhaila Ill'icha), 337 (PSZ).
107. Vol. 5, ll. 68–70 (Protokol doprosa obviniaemogo Felosenko). Felosenko said that thirty to forty people were executed nightly in August 1938, but he added, "I told no one about this."
108. Vol. 5, l. 210 (Sobstvennoruchnye pokazaniia arestovannogo Dorova Grigoriia Iakovlevicha ot 21 dekabria 1939 g.).
109. Vol. 3, ll. 175 (Narodnomu komissaru vnutrennyky del SSSR General'nomu komissaru gosudarstvennoi bezopasnosti tov. Ezhovu).
110. Vol. 1, l. 82 (Osobupolnomochennomu NKVD Ukraina ot arestovannogo Boldina).
111. Vol. 1, ll. 105–106 (Dopolnitel'nye pokazaniia Boldina Borisa Pavlovicha ot 16 aprelia 1939 g.).
112. Vol. 1, l. 83 (Osobupolnomochennomu NKVD Ukraina ot arestovannogo Boldina).
113. Ibid., l. 83; vol. 1, l. 105 (Dopolnitel'nye pokazaniia Boldina Borisa Pavlovicha ot 16 aprelia 1939 g.).
114. Ibid., ll. 65–71; vol. 2, ll. 102–107 (Protokol ochnoi stavki mezhdu Grabarem i Boldinym).
115. Vol. 5, ll. 246 (Postanovlenie), 404–405 (Spravka po arkhivnym ugolovnym delam No. 7148).
116. Vol. 5, ll. 330–359 (PSZ).
117. Vol. 5, l. 331 (PSZ). See vol. 5, l. 59, for a document on "Narodnyi Konsultant" stationery asking if it is admissible for relatives to hire an attorney; also see vol. 5, ll. 328–329, for NKIust Ukraine document calling the defense attorneys to court.
118. Vol. 5, ll. 331 ob.–332 (PSZ).
119. Vol. 2, ll. 56–59 (Protokol pokazanie Darova [sic] . . . ot 28 ianvaria 1939 goda), 64–70 (Protokol doprosa Dorova . . . ot 22 maia 1939); vol. 5, l. 330 ob. (PSZ).
120. Vol. 5, l. 332 (PSZ)—this was testimony from Mashchenko, on Dunaevskii's prompting.
121. Vol. 5, l. 358 ob. (PSZ).
122. Vol. 5, ll. 358 (PSZ).
123. Vol. 2, ll. 17–18 (Protokol doprosa obviniaemogo Linetskogo . . . ot 25 maia 1939 g.); vol. 5, ll. 351–353 (PSZ).

124. Vol. 1, ll. 120–129 (Raport); vol. 5, ll. 330–330 ob. (PSZ).

125. Vol. 1, l. 158 (Protokol doprosa obviniaemogo Klibanova Davida Iakovlevicha ot 29 marta 1939 goda).

126. Ibid., ll. 155–156.

127. Vol. 1, ll. 168–169 (Protokol doprosa Klibanova ot 2 aprelia 1939 goda), 172 (Protokol doprosa Klibanova ot 4 aprelia 1939 goda).

128. Vol. 1, ll. 180–181 (Dopolnitel'nye pokazaniia Klibanova ot 5 aprelia 1939 goda).

129. Ibid., l. 182, l. 185 (Prodolzhenie pokazaniia Klibanova ot 8.IV–1939 g.).

130. Vol. 1, l. 179 (Dopolnitel'nye pokazaniia Klibanova ot 5 aprelia 1939 goda).

131. Vol. 1, l. 187 (Prodolzhenie pokazaniia Klibanova ot 8/IV–1939 g.).

132. Ibid., l. 186.

133. Vol. 1, l. 160 (Protokol doprosa obviniaemogo Klibanova Davida Iakovlevicha ot 29 marta 1939 goda), 169 (Protokol doprosa Klibanova ot 1 aprelia 1939 goda); vol. 5, l. 351 (PSZ).

134. Vol. 1, ll. 159–160 (Protokol doprosa Klibanova ot 29 marta 1939 goda), 172–173 (Protokol doprosa Klibanova ot 4 aprelia 1939 goda).

135. Vol. 5, l. 351 (PSZ).

136. Vol. 1, l. 215 (Protokol doprosa Klibanova ot 5 iiunia 1939 g.); vol. 5, l. 351 (PSZ).

137. Vol. 1, l. 215 (Protokol doprosa Klibanova ot 5 iiunia 1939 g.).

138. Ibid.

139. Vol. 1, ll. 207–208 (Dopolnitel'nye pokazaniia Klibanova ot 23 aprelia 1939 g.). On this point, see Junge et al., eds., *"Cherez trupy vraga na blago naroda,"* vol. 2, pp. 565–566, for an NKVD Circular of 22 August 1937, which indicated that the "majority of foreigners living in the USSR are organizers of espionage and diversion" ("Ustanovleno, chto podavliaiushchee bol'shinstvo inostrantsev, zhivushchikh v SSSR, iavliaetsia organiziuiushchim nachalom shpionazha i diversii").

140. Vol. 1, ll. 169 (Protokol doprosa Klibanova ot 2 aprelia 1939 g.), 172–173 (Protokol doprosa Klibanova ot 4 aprelia 1939 goda), 198 (Dopolnitel'nye pokazaniia Klibanova ot 15 aprelia 1939 g.).

141. Vol. 5, l. 351 (PSZ).

142. Vol. 5, ll. 358–358 ob. (PSZ). The court temporarily adjourned earlier in the proceedings because Klibanov was feeling weak and asked for a break (l. 336).

143. Vol. 2, ll. 1–5 (Protokol pokazanii Linetskogo Borisa L'vovoicha ot 8 aprelia 1939 g.); vol. 3, l. 72 (Vitiag z protokolu No. 75. Zasidannia biura Zaporiz'koho miskkom KP(b)U ot 5 marta 1939 r.); vol. 5, l. 330 ob. (PSZ).

144. Vol. 1, l. 73 (Osobupolnomochennomu NKVD Ukraina ot arestovannogo Boldina).

145. Ibid., l. 75.

146. Ibid., ll. 71–72.

147. Vol. 5, l. 353 (PSZ).

148. Vol. 2, ll. 1–2 (Protokol pokazanii Linetskogo ot 8 aprelia 1939 g.).

149. Vol. 3, l. 262, 291 (Protokol obshchego zakrytogo partiinogo sobraniia . . . ot 9–10 fevralia 1939 g.).

150. Ibid., ll. 263, 291.

151. Ibid., l. 291.

152. Ibid., l. 294.

153. Vol. 2, ll. 9 (Dopolnitel'nye pokazaniia Linetskogo ot 11 aprelia 1939 g.), 20 (Protokol doprosa obviniaemogo Linetskogo ot 25 maia 1939 goda).

154. Ibid., ll. 2, 10, 20.

155. Ibid., ll. 4, 10, 17–18.

156. Ibid., ll. 17, 19.

157. Ibid., l. 3.

158. Ibid., ll. 2–3, l. 33 (Protokol doprosa Linetskogo ot 26 maia 1939 goda).

159. Vol. 5, l. 356 (PSZ).

160. Vol. 5, ll. 353, 355 (PSZ).

161. Vol. 5, l. 353 (PSZ).

162. Vol. 3, ll. 72 (Vitiag z protokolu No. 75. Zasidannia biura Zaporiz'koho miskkom KP(b)U ot 5 marta 1939 r.); 260, 262 (Protokol obshchego zakrytogo partiinogo sobraniia . . . ot 9–10 fevralia 1939 g.).

163. Ibid., l. 262.

164. Vol. 2, ll. 108–111 (Protokol doprosa mezhdu obviniamymi Linetskim i Boldonym ot 2 iiunia 1939 goda—ochnaia stavka).

165. Vol. 5, l. 353 (PSZ).

166. Vol. 5, l. 358 (PSZ).

167. Vol. 5, l. 358 ob. In vol. 3, l. 291 (Protokol obshchego zakrytogo partiinogo sobraniia . . . ot 9-10 fevralia 1939 g.), Linetskii said that Gorodetskii had cohabited with the wife of a prisoner, promising her to help free her husband; that may have been the source of the dispute with Linetskii.

168. Vol. 5, ll. 357 ob–358 (PSZ).

169. Vol. 5, ll. 367–369 (Prigovor, 21 April 1940).

170. Vol. 5, ll. 380 (Zaveduvaiushchemu iuridicheskoi konsul'tatsiei, 5 May 1940), 393 (Opredelenie, 8 May 1940).

171. Vol. 5, l. 403 (Spravka, 7 May 1940).

172. Vadym Zolotar'ov, "Sotrudniki NKVD Ukrainskoi SSR, osuzhdennye za narushenie sotsialisticheskoi zakonnosti vo vremia raboty v organakh gosudarstvennoi bezopasnosti v 1937–1938 gg.," unpublished paper presented at the conference, "Echoes of the Great Terror," at the University of Virginia, 30 September–1 October 2016.

173. Vol. 5, ll. 404–405 (Spravka 23 August 1994).

174. For example, vol. 2, ll. 135–136 (Dopolnitel'nye pokazaniia t. Frishko S. A. ot 27 ianvaria 1939 g.); vol. 3, l. 262 (Protokol obshchego zakrytogo partiinogo sobraniia . . . ot 9–10 fevralia 1939 g.).

175. Thanks to Petru Negura for this insight.

CHAPTER 7

1. The epigraph is from *SBU*, f. 5, d. 43626 (Sledstvennoe delo Grabaria), vol. 5, l. 296 (Protokoly sudebnoi zasedaniia 7–11 oktiabria 1940—further, "PSZ"). Unless otherwise noted, all archival references will be from this *fond* and *delo*, and identified further only by volume number, page number, and document title (abbreviated after first reference).

2. Vol. 5, ll. 269, 304 ob. (PSZ).

3. Vol. 2, l. 193 (Protokol ochnoi stavki mezhdu obviniaemym Grabarem Vasiliem Romanovichem i svid. Tul'skim Markom Mendelevichem ot 3 marta 1939 g.); vol. 3, ll. 34–35, 39–40 (Sekretariu TsK KP(b) Ukrainy tov. Khrushchevu, N. S.).

4. Vol. 5, ll. 268–305 (PSZ).

5. Vol. 1, l. 6 (Postanovlenie, 3 December 1938).

6. Vol. 5, ll. 330–334 (Prigovor).

7. *SBU*, f. 12, d. 3061 (Lichnoe delo Grabaria), vol. 1, part 1, l. 14.

8. Vol. 3, ll. 34–35, 39–40 (Sekretariu TsK KP(b) Ukrainy tov. Khrushchevu).

9. Kodyma is now part of Ukraine in the Odessa area.

10. *SBU*, f. 12, d. 3061 (Lichnoe delo Grabaria), vol. 1, part 1, l. 14.

11. *SBU*, f. 12, d. 3061 (Lichnoe delo Grabaria), vol. 1, part 1, l. 1.

12. These were stores that sold food and goods to foreigners and Soviet citizens (from June 1931) in exchange for foreign currency, gold, silver, platinum, diamonds, and other precious stones and metals.

13. *SBU*, f. 12, d. 3061 (Lichnoe delo Grabaria), vol. 1, part 1, ll. 2–4; vol. 3, l. 294 (Vypiska iz protokola zakrytogo partsobraniia ob"edinenykh partorganizatsii OO v/ch No. 5395 i G/O NKVD ot 29 aprelia 1939 g.). Also see Vol. 1, ll. 209–217, for a series of *vypiski* with information about Grabar's shady activities in Berdichev.

14. *SBU*, f. 12, d. 3061 (Lichnoe delo Grabaria), vol. 1, part 1, l. 4.

15. *SBU*, f. 12, d. 3061 (Lichnoe delo Grabaria), vol. 1, part 1, ll. 2–4.

16. *SBU*, f. 12, d. 3061 (Lichnoe delo Grabaria), vol. 1, part 1, l. 13.

17. *SBU*, f. 12, d. 3061 (Lichnoe delo Grabaria), vol. 1, part 1, l. 1; vol. 1, l. 5 (Spravka); vol. 5, l. 268 (PSZ). At times, Grabar' was listed as head of the Sixth Department. For further information on these departments, see Okhotin and Roginskii, eds., *Kto rukovodil NKVD*, pp. 20–22, 43–44; A. I. Kokurin and N. V. Petrov, eds., *Lubianka. VChK–OGPU–NKVD–NKGB–MGB–MVD–KGB, 1917–1960. Spravochnik* (Moscow: MFD, 1997), pp. 17–21. At the All-Union level of the NKVD, from November 1936 to June 1938, the Special Department was the Fifth Department. Between June and September 1938, the Sixth Department took over the responsibilities of the Special Department, which was responsible for work with the police, fire department, and military organization. The Special Department became the Fourth Department from September 1938, whereas the Sixth Department was charged with more limited work with "militarized organizations." In Grabar's criminal file, "Sixth Department" and "Special Department" are used interchangeably.

18. See vol. 2, ll. 275–280 (Obvinitel'noe zakliuchenie, 5 September 1939).

19. Vol. 1, ll. 207–208 (Vypiska iz zaiavleniia byvsh. Nach. Berdichevskogo gorotdela NKVD Martyniuka, n.d.).

20. Vol. 3, ll. 294–295 (Vypiska iz protokola zakrytogo partsobraniia . . . 29 aprelia 1939 g.).

21. For example, vol. 1, l. 311 (Protokol doprosa svidetelia Borovkova Alekseia Fedorovicha, 13 January 1939); vol. 2, l. 60 (Protokol doprosa Boldina Borisa Pavlovicha ot 28 fevralia 1939 g.), 192 (Protokol ochnoi stavki mezhdu Grabarem i Tul'skim).

22. Vol. 2, l. 48 (Protokol doprosa Vaisbarga); vol. 5, l. 293 ob. (PSZ).

23. Vol. 1, l. 325 (Protokol doprosa svidetelia Tul'skogo Marka Mendelevicha, 14 January 1939). For further information on Tul'skii, see his *Sledstvennoe delo* in *SBU*, f. 5, d. 38902, and his *lichnoe delo* in f. 12, d. 3201.

24. Vol. 2, ll. 43–44 (Protokol doprosa Vaisbarga).

25. Vol. 3, ll. 324–325 (Protokol zakrytogo partiinogo sobraniia partorganizatsii osobogo otdela KOVO). In Russian, this phrase is far more threatening: "Arestuiu, posazhu, dolozhu Aleksandru Ivanovichu."

26. Vol. 5, l. 293 ob. (PSZ).

27. Vol. 5, l. 290 (PSZ).

28. Vol. 5, l. 296 (PSZ).

29. Vol. 1, ll. 293–295 (Protokol doprosa Khesa), 310–314 (Protokol doprosa Borovkova), 326 (Protokol doprosa Tul'skogo); vol. 2, l. 53 (Protokol doprosa Vaisbarga).

30. Vol. 5, l. 296 (PSZ).

31. Vol. 5, l. 290 ob. (PSZ).

32. Vol. 1, l. 326 (Protokol doprosa Tul'skogo).

33. Vol. 2, ll. 48–49 (Protokol doprosa Vaisbarga).

34. Vol. 2, l. 50 (Protokol doprosa Vaisbarga).

35. Vol. 1, ll. 280–281 (Raport tov. Osokinu, 21 November 1938).

36. Ibid.

37. Vol. 1, l. 229 (Vypiska iz protokola doprosa Uspenskogo A .I., 20 May 1939).

38. Vol. 1, l. 326 (Protokol doprosa Tul'skogo).

39. Vol. 2, l. 276 (Obvinitel'noe zakliuchenie); vol. 5, ll. 280–280 ob. (PSZ). See Chapter 2 for the central decrees noted here. Grabar' claimed in an encounter with A. I. Maiskii, during the former's trial, that UkrKabel in fact had no relation to the Sixth Department and should have been investigated by the NKVD Economic Department. If this was indeed the case, Grabar' could have been correct to claim that this case was used "to bury" him. See vol. 5, l. 286 ob. (PSZ); and *SBU*, f. 5, d. 51645 (Sledstvennoe delo A. I. Maiskogo), vol. 1, l. 214.

40. Vol. 4, ll. 297–299 (Protokol dopros svidetelia Shibanovoi Serafimy Vladimirovny ot19 fevralia 1940 g.); vol. 5, l. 1 (Postanovlenie, 23 February 1940 g.).

41. Vol. 3, ll. 85–88 (Spravka po sledstvennomu delu No. 148019 po obvineniiu Maiborodu Georgiia Il'icha, 22 March 1939); vol. 4, ll. 284 (Protokol doprosa

svidetelia Fraimana Efima Evseevicha, 4 February 1940; vol. 5, ll. 3–4 (Vypiska iz pokazanii svidetelia Tul'skogo M.M. ot 20 fevralia 1940 g.), 170 (Obvinitel'nyi akt, 4 December 1938), 285 ob., 289, 297 ob. (PSZ).

42. For more information on Klochkov, see his criminal file in *SBU*, f. 5, d. 38868.

43. Vol. 5, ll. 287–288 ob. (PSZ). Also see vol. 4, ll. 247 (Protokol dopros svidetelia Gershkova, Iakova Efimovicha ot 24 ianvaria 1940 g.).

44. Vol. 5, ll. 6 (Protokol doprosa svidetelia Kichko, E. K. ot 2 marta 1940 g.), 9–17 (Zaiavlenie Kichko, April 1939), 298 ob. –299 (PSZ). See Chapter 3 for information on Drushliak.

45. Vol. 5, ll. 291–291 ob. (PSZ, Brikker), 292 (PSZ, Zalevskii), 292 ob. (PSZ, Gontarenko), 293–293 ob. (PSZ, Gal'chenko).

46. Vol. 5, ll. 293–293 ob. (PSZ). The phrase "Bartholomew's Night" was used in Russian popularly to describe acts of violence or rebellion.

47. See Chapter 6, and vol. 5, ll. 294 ob. –295 (PSZ).

48. See vol. 3, ll. 56–57, 66–82, for a series of documents from Grabar' and responses from NKVD Ukraine, concerning Grabar's complaints about his arrest.

49. Vol. 1, ll. 1–3 (Motivirovannoe postanovlenie na arest, 29 November 1938), 6 (Postanovlenie, 3 December 1938), 8 (Order no. 18 na arest Grabaria), 29 (Postanovlenie, 16 July 1939).

50. Vol. 3, l. 82 (Akt, 14–17 January 1939).

51. Vol. 2, ll. 275–280 (Obvinitel'noe zakliuchenie).

52. Vol. 1, ll. 310–314 (Protokol doprosa Borovkova); vol. 2, l. 209 (Protokol ochnoi stavki mezhdu obviniaemym Grabarem V. R. i svid. Borovkovym A. F. ot 3 marta 1939 g.).

53. Vol. 2, l. 192 (Protokol ochnoi stavki mezhdu Grabarem i Tul'skim).

54. Vol. 2, l. 59 (Protokol doprosa Boldina).

55. Vol. 1, ll. 32–39 (Protokol doprosa Grabaria, 11 December 1938).

56. Vol. 2, l. 191 (Protokol ochnoi stavki mezhdu Grabarem i Tul'skim).

57. Vol. 1, ll. 228–229 (Vypiska iz protokola doprosa Uspenskogo).

58. Ibid.

59. Vol. 1, ll. 232–241 (Protokol ochnoi stavki mezhdu arestovannymi Uspenskim, A. I. i Grabarem. V. R., 22 July 1939.) The confrontation lasted for 4.5 hours.

60. Vol. 5, ll. 296–296 ob. (PSZ).

61. Vol. 3, l. 34 (Sekretariu TsK KP(b) Ukraine tov. Khrushchevu).

62. Ibid., ll. 34–35, 39–40.

63. Vol. 5, ll. 270–270 ob. (PSZ).

64. It is possible that the date of the letter was 20 November; the print of the document is blurred. See vol. 3, l. 55 (Sekretariu TsK KP(b) Ukraine tov. Khrushchevu).

65. In his letter to Khrushchev, Grabar' noted that he "was removed from the position of [acting] head of the Sixth Department" shortly after Gershkov's arrest. Grabar' claimed that Upsenskii ordered him to write a report on the purge of the police. After reading Grabar's report, Uspenskii then, according to Grabar', had "doubts"

about Grabar', removed him from his current position, and purportedly asked Grabar', "where will we send you?" Grabar' requested a transfer to the cadre department, but Uspenskii sent him instead to serve in the Special Department in the Dnepropetrovsk regional NKVD. Vol. 3, ll. 41–42 (Sekretariu TsK KP(b) Ukraine tov. Khrushchevu).

66. It is likely that Grabar' is referring to the recent 17 November 1938 Central Committee Sovnarkom decree scaling back the terror; alternatively he may have been referring to Uspenskii's flight on 14 November.

67. Vol. 3, l. 33 (Sekretariu TsK KP(b) Ukraine tov. Khrushchevu).

68. Ibid.

69. Ibid., ll. 34–35.

70. Vol. 3, ll. 56–57 (Zaiavlenia to Beriia, 20 November 1938).

71. See the preceding notes for the confrontations with Tul'skii, Borovkov, Vaisbarg, and Uspenskii. Also see Vol. 2, ll. 150–156 (Protokol ochnoi stavki mezhdu oviniaemym Grabarem V. R. i Brikkerom K. V. ot 20 febralia 1939 g.) and *SBU*, f. 5, d. 68219 (sledstvennoe delo Dorova, Klibanova, Linetskogo), vol. 2, ll. 102–107 (Protokol ochnoi stavki mezhdu obviniamymi Grabarem V. R. i Boldinym B. P. ot 23 aprelia 1939 g.).

72. Vol. 5, l. 269 ob. (PSZ).

73. Vol. 4, l. 2 (Protokol doprosa Grabaria ot 3 noiabria 1939 g.). Grabar' also complained that he was not allowed face-to-face confrontations with Kopaev and several others.

74. Vol. 5, ll. 268 ob. –269 (PSZ).

75. Vol. 5, l. 269 (PSZ). Grabar' claimed that Vaisbarg was resentful because Grabar' refused to give him (most likely complimentary) theatre tickets, as well as other issues. Vol. 5, l. 288 ob. (PSZ).

76. Vol. 5, l. 288 ob. (PSZ).

77. Vol. 5, ll. 271 ob., 273 (PSZ).

78. Vol. 5, l. 272 (PSZ).

79. Vol. 5, l. 271 ob. (PSZ).

80. Vol. 5, l. 288 ob. (PSZ).

81. Vol. 5, l. 288 (PSZ).

82. Vol. 5, l. 272 (PSZ).

83. Vol. 5, ll. 270 ob. –271 (PSZ).

84. Vol. 5, l. 271 (PSZ). See Chapter 6 for Boldin's assertion that Grabar' left Zaporozh'e on 15 July.

85. Grabar' claimed that this figure of 1,000 arrests came from the former head of the Zaporozh'e NKVD, Vol'skii, who had claimed that they had 1,000 people in NKVD records [*na uchete*]. Vol. 5, l. 271 (PSZ).

86. Vol. 5, l. 271 (PSZ).

87. Vol. 5, l. 272 ob. (PSZ).

88. Vol. 5, l. 272 (PSZ).

89. Vol. 5, l. 272 (PSZ).

90. Vol. 5, ll. 302–305 (PSZ).

91. Vol. 5, l. 304 ob. (PSZ).

92. Vol. 5, ll. 304 ob. –305 (PSZ).

93. Vol. 5, l. 304 ob. (PSZ).

94. Vol. 5, l. 305 (PSZ).

95. Vol. 5, l. 304 ob. (PSZ). The adjournment was brief.

96. Vol. 5, ll. 330–334 (Prigovor).

97. Vol. 5, ll. 352–353 (Vypiska Prezidiuma Verkhovnogo soveta soiuza SSR ot osuzh-
dennogo pos. t. 206–18 p b UK Ukraine, sotrudnikov NKVD Ukraine Grabar' V.
R.: "Khodaistvo o pomilovanii," 25 October 1940).

98. Vol. 5, ll. 365 (Opredelenie voennaia kollegiia verkhovnogo suda SSSR [Ul'rikh],
26 October 1940), 366 (Vypiska iz protokola zasedaniia preziduma verkhovnogo
soveta SSSR, 21 December 1940).

99. Vol. 5, l. 372 (Spravka. Prigovor voennogo tribunala voisk NKVD Kievskogo
okruga).

100. Vol. 5, l. 368 (PSZ).

101. Vol. 5, l. 374.

102. Vol. 5, l. 376.

103. Mandelstam, *Hope Against Hope*, p. 266.

104. Aleksandr I. Solzhenitsyn, *The Gulag Archipelago*, trans. Thomas P. Whitney
(New York: Harper and Row, 1973), vol. 1, p. 509.

POSTSCRIPT

1. *SBU*, f. 13, d. 409, ll. 4–20 (Protokol dopros Zakharova N. F. ot 15-ogo noiabria
1938 goda).

2. *SBU*, f. 13, d. 409, l. 3 (Uspenskii's suicide note). Liushkov was the head of the Far
Eastern NKVD who fled to Japan. (See subsequent discussion.)

3. *SBU*, f. 13, d. 409, ll. 4–20 (Protokol doprosa Zakharova N. F. ot 15-ogo noiabria
1938 goda).

4. *SBU*, f. 13, d. 409, ll. 21–38 (Na postavlennyi mne Komdivom Osokinym vopros
ob izlozhenii vsekh obstoiatel'st predshestvovavshikh i sviazannykh s ischeznove-
niem Uspenskogo dokladuvaiu," from Iaraliants, 16 November 1938).

5. I. Ie. Nikolaiev, "Chystky kerivnoi verkhivky NKVS Ukrainy (II polovyna 30-kh
rr. XX stolittia)," *Istoriia Ukrainy: Malovidomi imena, podii, fakty*, no. 34 (2007),
pp. 252–253.

6. *SBU*, f. 13, d. 409, ll. 31–32. On Liushkov, see Jansen and Petrov, *Stalin's Loyal
Executioner*, pp. 143–146.

7. *SBU*, f. 13, d. 409, ll. 21–38 (Na postavlennyi mne Komdivom Osokinym vopros
ob izlozhenii vsekh obstoiatel'st predshestvovavshikh i sviazannykh s ischeznove-
niem Uspenskogo dokladuvaiu," from Iaraliants, 16 November 1938).

8. On Orlov, see Jansen and Petrov, *Stalin's Loyal Executioner*, p. 147.
9. On Litvin, see V. I. Berezhkov, *Piterskie prokuratory* (St. Petersburg: BLITS/ Russko-Baltiiskii informatsionnyi tsentr, 1998), pp. 164, 172–173.
10. Nikolaiev, "Chystky kerivnoi verkhivky NKVS Ukrainy," p. 252.
11. See, e.g., Jansen and Petrov, *Stalin's Loyal Executioner*, pp. 163–164; and Zolotar'ov, "Favoryt Iezhova," pp. 183–186.
12. Nikolaiev, "Chystky kerivnoi verkhivky NKVS Ukrainy," p. 253.
13. Zolotar'ov, "Favoryt Iezhova," pp. 184–185.
14. Nikolaiev, "Chystky kerivnoi verkhivky NKVS Ukrainy," p. 253.
15. *SBU,* f. 5, d. 43626 (sledstvennoe delo Grabaria), vol. 5, ll. 302–305 (PSZ); on Uspenskii "knowing the game," see Zolotar'ov, "Favoryt Iezhova," p. 186.

CONCLUSION

1. *XVIII s"ezd vsesoiuznoi kommunisticheskoi partii (b). 10–21 marta 1939 g. Stenograficheskii otchet*, pp. 16, 26–27.
2. Kokurin and Petrov, "NKVD: Struktura, funktsii, kadry," *Svobodnaia mysl'*, no. 7 (1997), 111; and Khlevniuk, "Party and NKVD: Power Relationships in the Years of the Great Terror," in Barry McLoughlin and Kevin McDermott, eds., *Stalin's Terror*, p. 30.
3. These trials were subsequently utilized by Communist Party and Soviet legal officials in the 1950s, the 1970s, and the 1990s to address rehabilitation petitions of both actual victims and the rehabilitation petitions of the NKVD perpetrators or their surviving family members.
4. For mention of the trials against NKVD workers in Moldova, see *Kommunist* (Ukraine), 30 December 1938; 31 December 1938; and 1 January 1930. On the war and postwar trials, see Alexander Victor Prusin, "'Fascist Criminals to the Gallows!': The Holocaust and Soviet War Crimes Trials, December 1945–February 1946," *Holocaust and Genocide Studies*, 17(1) (2003), 17, 21; Ilya Bourtman, "'Blood for Blood, Death for Death': The Soviet Military Tribunal in Krasnodar, 1943," *Holocaust and Genocide Studies*, 22(2) (2008), pp. 258–259; Tanya Penter, "Local Collaborators on Trial: Soviet War Crimes Trials Under Stalin (1943–1953)," *Cahiers du monde Russe*, 49(2) (2008), 361.
5. Khaustov et al., eds., *Lubianka: Stalin i glavnoe upravlenie gosbezopasnosti NKVD 1937–1938*, pp. 663–664, n. 92.
6. See Khlevniuk, "Party and NKVD," p. 30, indicating that of 14,500 new NKVD workers in 1939, over 11,000 were recruited from the Communist Party and Komsomol.
7. Mark Iunge et al., *Vertikal bol'shogo terrora*, p. 299.
8. "Zapiska komissii prezidiuma TsK KPSS v prezidium TsK KPSS o rezul'takh raboty po rassledovaniiu prichin repressii i obstoiatel'stv politicheskikh protsessov 30-kh godov," *Istochnik*, no. 1 (1995), 84.

9. *Istoriia Stalinskogo gulaga,* vol. 1, pp. 327–328.

10. Iunge et al., eds., "*Cherez trupy vraga na blago naroda,* vol. 2, pp. 489, 511–513.

11. V. N. Khaustov et al., *Lubianka: Stalin i NKVD–NKGB–GUKR "Smersh" 1939–mart 1946,* p. 564, n. 11.

12. Khlevniuk, "Party and NKVD," p. 27.

13. Vatlin, *Terror raionnogo masshtaba,* pp. 85–87.

14. E.g., *SBU,* f. 16, d. 322, ll. 248-52.

15. *SBU,* f. 5, d. 43626 (Sledstvennoe delo Grabaria), vol. 3, ll. 297–298 (Protokol zakrytogo partiinogo sobraniia partorganizatsii osobovo otdela KOVO, sostoia-vshegosia 2 dekabria 1938 g.), vol. 5, ll. 585, 595 (PSZ). See also *SBU,* f. 12, d. 107 (Kretov, Georgii Matveevich), ll. 105–108.

16. Khaustov et al., eds., *Lubianka: Stalin i NKVD–NKGB–GUKR "Smersh" 1939–mart 1946,* p. 9; David R. Shearer and Vladimir Khaustov, eds., *Stalin and the Lubianka: A Documentary History of the Political Police and Security Organs in the Soviet Union, 1922–1953* (New Haven, CT: Yale University Press, 2015), pp. 228–229.

17. See, e.g., Seymour M. Hersh, *Cover-Up* (New York: Random House, 1972); Douglas Valentine, *The Phoenix Program: America's Use of Terror in Vietnam* (New York: Open Road, 1990); Eric Fair, *Consequence: A Memoir* (New York: Holt, 2016); Philip Gourevitch and Errol Morris, *The Ballad of Abu Ghraib* (New York: Penguin, 2009); and, especially, *The Torture Papers: The Road to Abu Ghraib,* Karen J. Greenberg and Joshua L. Dratel, eds. (New York: Cambridge University Press, 2005).

18. Philip Zimbardo, *The Lucifer Effect: Understanding How Good People Turn Evil* (New York: Random House, 2007), pp. 438, 445–446.

19. See, for example, Christian Gerlach, *Extremely Violent Societies: Mass Violence in the Twentieth-Century World* (Cambridge: Cambridge University Press, 2010), pp. 273–274.

20. Khaustov et al., eds., *Lubianka: Stalin i NKVD–NKGB–GUKR "Smersh" 1939–mart 1946,* pp. 14–15.

21. Khlevniuk, "Party and NKVD," p. 31.

22. See Tepliakov, *Protsedura,* for a rare scholarly treatment of the topic.

23. See, for examples, Igal Halfin, *Stalinist Confessions* (Pittsburgh: University of Pittsburgh Press, 2009); and Hiroaki Kuromiya, *The Voices of the Dead* (New Haven, CT: Yale University Press, 2007).

24. On diaspora nations and repression in the Soviet Union, see Terry Martin, *The Affirmative Action Empire: Nations and Nationalism in the Soviet Union, 1923–1939* (Ithaca, NY: Cornell University Press, 2001), pp. 342–343.

25. Eric Lohr, "1915 and the War Pogrom Paradigm in the Russian Empire," in Jonathan Dekel-Chen, David Gaunt, Natan M. Meir, Israel Bartal, eds., *Anti-Jewish Violence: Rethinking the Pogrom in East European History* (Bloomington: Indiana University Press, 2011), pp. 41, 43, 48; Peter Holquist, "The Role of Personality in the First (1914–1915) Russian Occupation of Galicia and Bukovina," *ibid.,* p. 61;

Joshua A. Sanborn, *Imperial Apocalypse: The Great War and the Destruction of the Russian Empire* (Oxford: Oxford University Press, 2014), p. 97; Oleg Budnitskii, *Russian Jews Between the Reds and the Whites, 1917–1920*, trans. Timothy J. Portice (Philadelphia: University of Pennsylvania Press, 2012), p. 116.

26. *SBU*, f. 5, d. 68219 (Sledstvennoe delo Klibanova et al.), vol. 3, l. 282 (Protokol obshchego zakrytogo partiinogo sobraniia chlenov i kandidatov VKP (b) partiinoi organizatsii UGB UNKVD po Zaporozhskoi oblasti ot 9–10 fevralia 1939 g.).

27. Ibid., l. 277.

28. Ibid., l. 280.

29. Vatlin, *Terror raionnogo masshtaba*, p. 52. See also Chapter 6.

30. Browning, *Ordinary Men*.

31. See, e.g., Zimbardo, *The Lucifer Effect*, vii–viii, 32–33, 445–446; Martha K. Huggins, Mika Haritos-Fatouros, and Philip G. Zimbardo, *Violence Workers: Police Torturers and Murderers Reconstruct Brazilian Atrocities* (Berkeley: University of California Press, 2002), pp. 137, 167–168. My thanks to Max Bergholz for introducing me to this literature. See also the very fine studies of James Waller, *Becoming Evil: How Ordinary People Commit Genocide and Mass Killing* (New York: Oxford University Press, 2002); and Roy T. Baumeister, *Evil: Inside Human Violence and Cruelty* (New York: Holt, 2001).

32. For a critique of the notion of "ordinary men" in the Holocaust, see Michael Mann, "Were the Perpetrators of Genocide 'Ordinary Men' or 'Real Nazis'? Results from Fifteen Hundred Biographies," *Holocaust and Genocide Studies*, 14(3) (Winter 2000), 331–366; and Jurgen Matthaus, "Historiography and the Perpetrators of the Holocaust," in Dan Stone, ed., *The Historiography of the Holocaust* (London: Palgrave-Macmillan, 2005).

33. Raul Hilberg, *The Destruction of the European Jews* (New York: Holmes and Meier, 1985), p. 288.

34. James C. Scott, *Domination and the Arts of Resistance: Hidden Transcripts* (New Haven, CT: Yale University Press, 1990), pp. 4–5.

35. Sarah Davies and James Harris, *Stalin's World: Dictating the Soviet Order* (New Haven, CT: Yale University Press, 2014), p. 3.

36. On collaboration and categories of collaborators, see Oleg Budnitskii, "The Great Patriotic War and Soviet Society: Defeatism, 1941–42," *Kritika*, 15(4) (2014), 767–797; and Oleksandr Melnyk, "Historical Politics, Legitimacy Contests, and the (Re)-Construction of Political Communities in Ukraine During the Second World War," PhD dissertation (University of Toronto, 2016).

Bibliography

ARCHIVAL SOURCES

Haluzevyi derzhavnyi arkhiv Sluzhbyi bezpeky Ukrainy (SBU).

Published Archival Documents and Other Primary Sources

Artizov, A., et al., eds. *Reabilitatsiia: Kak eto bylo. Dokumenty.* 3 vols. Moscow: Demokratiia, 2000–2004.

Belenkin, Boris. *Malotirazhnye izdaniia po istorii politicheskikh repressii v SSSR v biblioteke Obshchestva "Memorial."* Moscow: Zven'ia, 2014.

Berelovich, A., and V. Danilov, eds. *Sovetskaia derevnia glazami VKP-OGPU-NKVD, 1918–1939. Dokumenty i materialy.* 4 vols. Moscow: Rosspen, 2000–2006.

Chuev, Felix, ed. *Molotov Remembers: Inside Kremlin Politics.* Chicago: Ivan R. Dee, 1993.

Danilov, V. P., R. T. Manning, and L. Viola, eds. *Tragediia Sovetskoi derevni. Kollektivizatsiia i raskulachivanie. Dokumenty i materialy, 1927–1939.* 5 vols. Moscow: Rosspen, 1999–2006.

Fair, Eric. *Consequences. A Memoir.* New York: Holt, 2016.

Genrikh Iagoda: Narkom vnutrennikh del SSSR. General'nyi komissar gosbezopasnosti. Sbornik dokumentov. Kazan': Krista, 1997.

Ginzburg, Eugeniia S. *Journey Into the Whirlwind.* Trans. Paul Stevenson and Max Hayward. New York: Harcourt Brace Jovanovich, 1967.

Greenberg, Karen, and Joshua L. Dratel, eds. *The Torture Papers: The Road to Abu Ghraib.* New York: Cambridge University Press, 2005.

Ivkin, B. I., ed. *Gosudarstvennaia vlast' SSSR. Vysshie organy vlasti i upravleniia i ikh rukovoditeli. 1923–1991. Istoriko-biograficheskii spravochnik.* Moscow: Rosspen, 1999.

Junge, Marc, et al., eds., *Bol'shevistskii poriadok v Gruzii.* 2 vols. Moscow: AIRO-XXI, 2015.

Junge, Marc, et al., eds. *Cherez trupy vraga na blago naroda: Kulatskaia operatsiia v Ukrainskoi SSR, 1937–1941 gg.* 2 Vols. Moscow: Rosspen, 2010

Junge, Marc, et al., eds. *Massovye repressii v Altaiskom krae, 1937-1938. Prikaz No. 00447.* Moscow: Rosspen, 2010.

Khaustov, V. N., V. P. Naumov, and N. S. Plotnikova, eds. *Lubianka: Stalin i NKVD–NKGB–GUKR "Smersh." 1939–mart 1946.* Moscow: Demokratiia, 2006.

Khaustov, V. N., V. P. Naumov, and N. S. Plotnikova, eds. *Lubianka: Stalin i glavnoe upravlenie gosbezopasnosti NKVD, 1937–1938: Dokumenty.* Moscow: Materik, 2004.

Khaustov, V. N., V. P. Naumov, and N. S. Plotnikova, eds. *Lubianka: Stalin i VChK–GPU–OGPU–NKVD. Ianvar' 1922–dekabr' 1936.* Moscow: Demokratiia, 2003.

Khlevniuk, Oleg V. *The History of the Gulag: From Collectivization to the Great Terror.* Trans. Vadim A. Staklo. New Haven, CT: Yale University Press, 2004.

Klee, Ernst, Willi Dressen, and Volker Riess, eds. *"The Good Old Days": The Holocaust as Seen by Its Perpetrators and Bystanders.* Trans. Deborah Burnstone. Old Saybrook, CT: Konecky and Konecky, 1991.

Kokurin, A. I., and N. V. Petrov, eds. *Lubianka. VChK-OGPU-NKVD-NKGB-MGB-MVD-KGB, 1917-1991. Spravochnik.* Moscow: Demokratiia, 2003.

Kokurin, A. I., and N. V. Petrov, eds. *GULAG, 1917–1960: Dokumenty.* Moscow: Materik, 2000.

Kosheleva, L. P., O. V. Naumov, and L. A. Rogovaia, "Materialy fevral'sko-martovskogo plenuma TsK VKP (b) 1937 goda." *Voprosy istorii.* Nos. 4–5 (1992).

Magocsi, Paul Robert. *Historical Atlas of Central Europe.* Rev. ed. Toronto: University of Toronto Press, 2002.

Mandelstam, Nadezhda. *Hope Against Hope.* Trans. Max Hayward. New York: Atheneum, 1976.

Mironenko, S. V., and N. Werth, eds. *Istoriia Stalinskogo gulaga: konets 1920-kh—pervaia polovina 1950-kh godov.* 7 vols. Moscow: Rosspen, 2004–2005.

Okhotin, N. G., and A. B. Roginskii, eds. *Kto rukovodil NKVD, 1934-1941. Spravochnik.* Moscow: Zven'ia, 1999.

Orlov, Alexander. *The Secret History of Stalin's Crimes.* New York: Random House, 1953.

Petrov, N. V., ed. *Kto rukovodil organami gosbezopasnosti, 1941–1954.* Moscow: Zven'ia, 2010.

Podkur, Roman, and Viktor Cherntsov. *Dokumenty organov bezopasnosti U[kr]SSR. 1920-1930-kh godov. Istochnikovedcheskii analiz.* Ternopol': Zbruch, 2010.

Pokaianie. Komi Republikanskii martirolog zhertv massovykh politicheskikh repressii. 9 Vols. Syktyvkar: Fond "Pokaianie," 1999-2009.

Rasstrel'nye spiski. Moskva, 1935–1953. Donskoe kladbishche. Moscow: Zven'ia, 2005.

Rasstrel'nye spiski. Moskva, 1937–1941. "Kommunarka," Butovo. Moscow: Zven'ia, 2002.

Roginskii, A. B., S. V. Mironenko, N. G. Okhotin, A. K. Sorokin, and V. S. Khristoforov, eds. *Kto rukovodil organami gosbezopasnosti, 1941–1954. Spravochnik.* Moscow: Zven'ia, 2010.

Shapoval, Iurii, et al., eds. *Ukraina v dobu velykoho teroru, 1936–1938 roky*. Kiev: Lybid', 2009.

Shearer, David R., and Vladimir Khaustov, eds. *Stalin and the Lubianka: A Documentary History of the Political Police and Security Organs in the Soviet Union, 1922–1953*. New Haven, CT: Yale University Press, 2015.

Shreider, Mikhail. *NKVD iznutri: Zapiska chekista*. Moscow: Vozvrashchenie, 1995.

Solzhenitsyn, Aleksandr I. *The Gulag Archipelago*. Trans. Thomas P. Whitney. New York: Harper and Row, 1973. Vol. 1.

Stalin, I. *Sochineniia*. 13 vols. Moscow: Gospolizdat, 1946–1952.

Trenin, B. P., ed. *1937–1938 gg. Operatsii NKVD. Iz khroniki bol'shogo terrora na Tomskoi zemle*. Tomsk-Moscow: Volodei Publishers, 2006.

Trenin, B. P., ed. *1936–1937. Konveier NKVD. Iz khroniki bol'shogo terrora na Tomskoi zemle*. Tomsk-Moscow: Vodolei Publishers, 2004.

Uholovnyi kodeks URSR. Kiev, 1938.

Vasil'ev, V. Iu. et al., eds. *Politychni represii na Podilli*. Vinnytsia: Logos, 1999.

Velykyi teror: Pol'ska operatsiia, 1937–1938. 2 vols. Warsaw: Instytut Pamieci Narodowej, 2010.

XVIII s"ezd vsesoiuznoi kommunisticheskoi partii (b). 10–21 marta 1939 g. Stenograficheskii otchet. Moscow: OGIZ, 1939.

Zaitsev, E. A., ed. *Sbornik zakonodatel'nykh i normativnykh aktov o repressiiakh i reabili-tatsii zhertv politicheskikh repressii*. Moscow: Respublika, 1993.

"Zapiska komissii prezidiuma TsK KPSS v presidium TsK KPSS o rezul'tatakh raboty po rassledovaniiu prichin repressii i obstoiatel'stv politicheskikh protsessov 30-kh godov." *Istochnik*. No. 1. 1995.

Zhukov, A. N. *Kadrovyi sostav organov gosudarstvennoi bezopasnosti SSSR, 1935–1939*. Moscow: Mezhdunarodnyi Memorial (Elektronnoe izdanie), 2016.

SECONDARY SOURCES

Alexopoulos, Golfo. "Stalin and the Politics of Kinship: Practices of Collective Punishment, 1920s–1940s." *Comparative Studies in Society and History*. 50(1) (January 2008).

Alexopoulos, Golfo. *Stalin's Outcasts: Aliens, Citizens, and the Soviet State, 1926–36*. Ithaca, NY: Cornell University Press, 2003.

Aly, Gotz. *Hitler's Beneficiaries: Plunder, Racial War, and the Nazi Welfare State*. Trans. Jefferson Chase. New York: Holt, 2006.

Aly, Gotz. *Final Solution: Nazi Population Policy and the Murder of the European Jews*. Trans. Belinda Cooper and Allison Brown. London: Arnold, 1999.

Aly, Gotz, and Susanne Heim. *Architects of Annihilation: Auschwitz and the Logic of Destruction*. Trans A.G. Blunden. Princeton, NJ: Princeton University Press, 2002.

Arendt, Hannah. *Eichmann in Jerusalem: A Report on the Banality of Evil*. Rev. ed. New York: Penguin, 1985.

Arendt, Hannah. *The Origins of Totalitarianism*. New ed. New York: Harcourt, Brace, Jovanovich, 1973.

Arendt, Hannah. *On Violence*. New York: Harcourt Brace, 1970.

Bartov, Omer, and Eric D. Weitz, eds. *Shatterzone of Empires: Coexistence and Violence in the German, Hapsburg, Russian, and Ottoman Borderlands*. Bloomington, IN: Indiana University Press, 2013.

Bauman, Zygmunt. *Modernity and the Holocaust*. Ithaca, NY: Cornell University Press, 1992.

Baumeister, Roy F. *Evil: Inside Human Violence and Cruelty*. New York: Holt, 1999.

Bazhan, Oleg. "The Rehabilitation of Stalin's Victims in Ukraine, 1953–64: A Socio-Legal Perspective." In *De-Stalinising Eastern Europe: The Rehabilitation of Stalin's Victims After 1953*. Kevin McDermott and Matthew Stibbe, eds. London: Palgrave-Macmillan, 2015.

Bazhan, Oleh, and Vadym Zolotar'ov. "Konveier smerti v chasy 'Velykoho teroru' v Ukraini: tekhnolohiia rozstriliv, vykonavtsi, mistsia pokhovan." *Kraieznavstvo*. No. 1/86 (2014).

Belkovets, L. P. *Bol'shoi terror i sud'by nemetskoi derevni v Sibiri*. Moscow: IVDK, 1995.

Berezhkov, V. I. *Piterskie prokuratory*. St. Petersburg: BLITS/Russko-Baltiiskii informatsionnyi tsentr, 1998.

Bergen, Doris. *War and Genocide*. New York: Rowman and Littlefield, 2009.

Bergholz, Max. *Violence as a Generative Force: Identity, Nationalism, and Memory in a Balkan Community*. Ithaca, NY: Cornell University Press, 2016.

Berkhoff, Karel C. "Bykivnia: How Grave Robbers, Activists, and Foreigners Ended Official Silence about Stalin's Mass Graves near Kiev." In *Human Remains and Identification: Mass Violence, Genocide, and the "Forensic Turn."* Elisabeth Anstett and Jean-Marc Dreyfus, eds. Manchester: Manchester University Press, 2015.

Berman, Harold J., and Miroslav Kerner. *Soviet Military Law and Administration*. Cambridge, MA: Harvard University Press, 1955.

Bertelsen, Olga. "New Archival Documentation on Soviet Jewish Policy in Interwar Ukraine. Part Two: GPU Repression of Jews and Jewish Groups in 1937–1940." *On the Jewish Street: A Journal of Russian-Jewish History and Culture*. 1(2) (2011).

Bloxham, Donald. *Genocide on Trial: War Crimes, Trials and the Formation of Holocaust History and Memory*. Oxford: Oxford University Press, 2001.

Bloxham, Donald, and Robert Gerwarth, eds. *Political Violence in Twentieth-Century Europe*. Cambridge: Cambridge University Press, 2011.

Bourke, Joanna. *An Intimate History of Killing: Face to Face Killing in the 20th Century*. New York: Basic Books, 1999.

Bourtman, Ilya. "'Blood for Blood, Death for Death': The Soviet Military Tribunal in Krasnodar, 1943." *Holocaust and Genocide Studies*. 22(2) (2008).

Briukhanov, B. B., and E. N. Shoshkov. *Opravdaniiu ne podlezhit: Ezhov i Ezhovshchina, 1936–1938*. St. Petersburg: OOO PF, 1998.

Browning, Christopher R. *Ordinary Men: Reserve Police Battalion 101 and the Final Solution in Poland*. New York: Harper Perennial, 1992.

Browning, Christopher R. With contributions by Jurgen Matthaus. *The Origins of the Final Solution: The Evolution of Nazi Jewish Policy, September 1939–March 1942*. Lincoln, NE, and Jerusalem: University of Nebraska Press and Yad Vashem, 2004.

Budnitskii, Oleg. "The Great Patriotic War and Soviet Society: Defeatism, 1941–42." *Kritika*. 15(4) (2014).

Budnitskii, Oleg. *Russian Jews Between the Reds and the Whites, 1917–1920*. Trans. Timothy J. Portice. Philadelphia: University of Pennsylvania Press, 2012.

Cesarani, David. *Becoming Eichmann*. Cambridge, UK: Da Capo, 2004.

Conquest, Robert. *The Great Terror*. New York: Collier, 1973.

Davies, Sarah, and James Harris. *Stalin's World: Dictating the Soviet Order*. New Haven, CT: Yale University Press, 2014.

Dekel-Chen, Jonathan et al., eds. *Anti-Jewish Violence: Rethinking the Pogrom in East European History*. Bloomington and Indianapolis: Indiana University Press, 2011.

Douglas, Lawrence. *The Memory of Judgment: Making Law and History in the Trials of the Holocaust*. New Haven, CT: Yale University Press, 2001.

Earl, Hilary. *The Nuremberg SS-Einsatzgruppen Trial, 1945–1958*. Cambridge: Cambridge University Press, 2009.

Ellman, Michael. "Regional Influences on the Formulation and Implementation of NKVD Order 00447." *Europe-Asia Studies*. 62(6) (2010).

Fedor, Julie. *Russia and the Cult of State Security: The Chekist Tradition, from Lenin to Putin*. New York: Routledge, 2011.

Fitzpatrick, Sheila. *Everyday Stalinism: Ordinary Life in Extraordinary Times: Soviet Russia in the 1930s*. New York: Oxford University Press, 1999.

Fitzpatrick, Sheila. *Education and Social Mobility in the Soviet Union, 1921–1934*. Cambridge: Cambridge University Press, 1979.

Fitzpatrick, Sheila, and Robert Gellately, eds. *Accusatory Practices: Denunciation in Modern European History, 1789–1989*. Chicago: University of Chicago Press, 1997.

Friedlander, Saul. *Nazi Germany and the Jews*. 2 Vols. New York: Harper, 1997, 2007.

Fujii, Lee Ann. *Killing Neighbors: Webs of Violence in Rwanda*. Ithaca, NY: Cornell University Press, 2009.

Gatrell, Peter. *A Whole Empire Walking: Refugees in Russia During World War I*. Bloomington and Indianapolis: Indiana University Press, 1999.

Gellately, Robert. *The Gestapo and German Society: Enforcing Racial Policy, 1933–1945*. Oxford: Clarendon, 1990.

Gellately, Robert, and Ben Kiernan, ed. *The Specter of Genocide: Mass Murder in Historical Perspective*. New York: Cambridge University Press, 2003.

Gerlach, Christian. *Extremely Violent Societies: Mass Violence in the Twentieth-Century World*. Cambridge: Cambridge University Press, 2010.

Getty, J. Arch. *Practicing Stalinism: Bolsheviks, Boyars, and the Persistence of Tradition.* New Haven: Yale University Press, 2013.

Getty, J. Arch. "Excesses are not Permitted: Mass Terror and Stalinist Governance in the late 1930s." *Russian Review.* 61(1) (2002).

Getty, J. Arch, and Oleg V. Naumov, eds. *The Road to Terror.* New Haven, CT: Yale University Press, 1999.

Getty, J. Arch, and Oleg V. Naumov, *Yezhov: The Rise of Stalin's "Iron Fist."* New Haven, CT: Yale University Press, 2008.

Geyer, Michael, and Sheila Fitzpatrick, eds. *Beyond Totalitarianism: Stalinism and Nazism Compared.* New York: Cambridge University Press, 2009.

Goldhagen, Daniel Jonah. *Hitler's Willing Executioners: Ordinary Germans and the Holocaust.* New York: Vintage, 1997.

Goldman, Wendy Z. *Inventing the Enemy: Denunciation and Terror in Stalin's Russia.* Cambridge: Cambridge University Press, 2011.

Goldman, Wendy Z. *Terror and Democracy in the Age of Stalin.* Cambridge: Cambridge University Press, 2007.

Gourevitch, Philip, and Errol Morris. *The Ballad of Abu Ghraib.* New York: Penguin, 2009.

Gross, Jan Tomasz, and Irena Grudzinska Gross. *Golden Harvest.* New York: Oxford University Press, 2012.

Hagenloh, Paul. *Stalin's Police.* Baltimore: Johns Hopkins Press, 2009.

Halfin, Igal. *Stalinist Confessions: Messianism and Terror at the Leningrad Communist University.* Pittsburgh: Pittsburgh University Press, 2009.

Halfin, Igal. *Intimate Enemies: Demonizing the Bolshevik Opposition, 1918–1928.* Pittsburgh: Pittsburgh University Press, 2007.

Halfin, Igal. *Terror in My Soul: Communist Autobiographies on Trial.* Cambridge, MA: Harvard University Press, 2003.

Halfin, Igal. *From Darkness to Light: Class, Consciousness, and Salvation in Revolutionary Russia.* Pittsburgh: Pittsburgh University Press, 2000.

Harris, James, *The Great Fear: Stalin's Terror of the 1930s.* Oxford: Oxford University Press, 2016.

Harris, James, ed. *The Anatomy of Terror: Political Violence Under Stalin.* Oxford: Oxford University Press, 2013.

Hatzfeld, Jean. *Machete Season: The Killers in Rwanda Speak.* New York: Picador, 2003.

Hellbeck, Jochen. *Revolution on My Mind: Writing a Diary Under Stalin.* Cambridge, MA: Harvard University Press, 2006.

Herbert, Ulrich, ed. *National Socialist Extermination Policies: Contemporary German Perspectives and Controversies.* New York: Berghahn Books, 2004.

Hersh, Seymour M. *Cover-Up.* New York: Random House, 1972.

Hilberg, Raul. *The Destruction of the European Jews.* New York: Holmes and Meier, 1985.

Hoffmann, David L. *Cultivating the Masses: Modern State Practices and Soviet Socialism, 1914–1939*. Ithaca, NY: Cornell University Press, 2011.

Hoffmann, David L. *Stalinist Values: The Cultural Norms of Soviet Modernity, 1917–1941*. Ithaca, NY, and London: Cornell University Press, 2003.

Holquist, Peter. "'In Accord with State Interests and the People's Wishes': The Technocratic Ideology of Imperial Russia's Resettlement Administration." *Slavic Review* 69(1) (Spring 2010).

Holquist, Peter. "State Violence as Technique: The Logic of Violence in Soviet Totalitarianism." In *Landscaping the Human Garden: Twentieth-Century Population Management in a Comparative Framework*. Amir Weiner, ed. Stanford, CA: Stanford University Press, 2003.

Holquist, Peter. *Making War, Forging Revolution: Russia's Continuum of Crisis, 1914–1921* (Cambridge, MA: Harvard University Press, 2002).

Holquist, Peter. "To Count, to Extract, and to Exterminate: Population Statistics and Population Politics in Late Imperial and Soviet Russia." In *A State of Nations: Empire and Nation-Making in the Age of Lenin and Stalin*. Ronald Grigor Suny and Terry Martin eds. New York: Oxford University Press, 2001.

Holquist, Peter. "'Conduct Merciless Mass Terror': Decossackization on the Don, 1919," *Cahiers du Monde Russe*. Nos. 1–2 (1997).

Huggins, Martha K., Mika Haritos-Fatouros, and Philip G. Zimbardo. *Violence Workers: Police Torturers and Murderers Reconstruct Brazilian Atrocities*. Berkeley: University of California Press, 2002.

Il'inskii, Mikhail. *Narkom Iagoda*. Moscow: Veche, 2002.

Ismailov, El'dar. *Istoriia "Bol'shogo terrora" v Azerbaidzhane*. Moscow: Rosspen, 2015.

Jansen, Marc, and Nikita Petrov. *Stalin's Loyal Executioner: People's Commissar Nikolai Ezhov, 1895–1940*. Stanford, CA: Hoover Press, 2002.

Jensen, Olaf, and Claus-Christian W. Szejnmann, eds. *Ordinary People as Mass Murderers: Perpetrators in Comparative Perspective*. New York: Palgrave, 2008.

Junge, Marc, and Rol'f Binner. *Kak terror stal "bol'shim."* Moscow: AIRO-XX, 2003.

Junge, Marc, B. Bonvech, and R. Binner, eds. *Stalinizm v sovetskoi provintsii: 1937–1938 gg. Massovaia operatsiia na osnove prikaza No. 00447*. Moscow: Rosspen, 2009.

Junge, Marc, Gennadii Bordiugov, and Rol'f Binner, *Vertikal' bol'shogo terrora*. Moscow: Novyi Khronograf, 2008.

Kalyvas, Stathis N. *The Logic of Violence in Civil War*. Cambridge: Cambridge University Press, 2006.

Kalyvas, Stathis N, Ian Shapiro, and Tarek Masoud. *Order, Conflict, and Violence*. Cambridge: Cambridge University Press, 2008.

Kershaw, Ian. *Hitler, the Germans, and the Final Solution*. New Haven, CT: Yale University Press, 2008.

Kharkhordin, Oleg. *The Collective and the Individual in Russia*. Berkeley: University of California Press, 1999.

Khaustov, Vladimir, and Lennart Samuel'son. *Stalin, NKVD i repressii 1936–1938 gg.* Moscow: Rosspen, 2009.

Khlevniuk, O. V. *Master of the House: Stalin and His Inner Circle.* Trans. Nora Seligman Favorov. New Haven, CT: Yale University Press, 2009.

Khlevniuk, O. V. "The Objectives of the Great Terror, 1938–1938." In *Stalinism.* David L. Hoffmann, ed. Oxford: Blackwell, 2003.

Khlevniuk, O. V. *Politburo.* Moscow: Rosspen, 1996.

Khlevniuk, O. V. *Stalin: New Biography of a Dictator.* Trans. Nora Seligman Favorov. New Haven, CT: Yale University Press, 2015.

Khlevniuk, O. V. "Top Down vs. Bottom-Up: Regarding the Potential of Contemporary 'Revisionism.'" *Cahiers du monde Russe.* 56(4) (2015).

Kiernan, Ben. *The Pol Pot Regime: Race, Power, and Genocide in Cambodia under the Khmer Rouge.* 3rd. ed. New Haven, CT: Yale University Press, 2008.

Kiernan, Ben. *Blood and Soil: A History of Genocide and Extermination from Sparta to Darfur.* New Haven, CT: Yale University Press, 2007.

Knight, Amy. *Beria: Stalin's First Lieutenant.* Princeton, NJ: Princeton University Press, 1993.

Kokurin, Aleksandr, and Nikita Petrov. "NKVD: Struktura, funktsii, kadry, stat'ia vtoraia." *Svobodnaia mysl'.* No. 7 (1997).

Koonz, Claudia. *The Nazi Conscience.* Cambridge, MA: Belknap, 2003.

Kotkin, Stephen. *Stalin: Paradoxes of Power, 1878–1928.* New York: Penguin Press, 2014, Vol. 1.

Krasil'nikov, S. A. *Sovetskie sudebnye politicheskie protsessy v 1920–1930-e gg.* Novosibirsk: RITs NGU, 2014.

Kuromiya, Hiroaki. *The Voices of the Dead: Stalin's Great Terror in the 1930s.* New Haven, CT: Yale University Press, 2007.

Kuromiya, Hiroaki. *Stalin.* Harlow, UK: Pearson, 2005.

Lawrence, Bruce B., and Aisha Karim, eds. *On Violence: A Reader.* Durham, NC: Duke University Press, 2007.

Leibovich, O., A. Koldushko, and A. Kazankov, eds. *"Vkliuchen v operatsii:" Massovyi terror v Prikam'e v 1937–1938 gg.*, 2nd ed. Moscow: Rosspen, 2009.

Leo, Richard A. *Police Interrogation and American Justice.* Cambridge, MA: Harvard University Press, 2008.

Levene, Mark. *Genocide in the Age of the Nation State.* 2 Vols. London: Tauris, 2005.

Liber, George O. *Total Wars and the Making of Modern Ukraine, 1914–1954.* Toronto: University of Toronto Press, 2016.

Lohr, Eric. *Nationalizing the Russian Empire: The Campaign Against Enemy Aliens During World War I.* Cambridge, MA: Harvard University Press, 2003.

Lower, Wendy. *Hitler's Furies: German Women in the Nazi Killing Fields.* Boston and New York: Houghton Mifflin Harcourt, 2013.

Lower, Wendy. *Nazi Empire-Building and the Holocaust in Ukraine.* Chapel Hill: University of North Carolina Press, 2005.

Lyons, Robert, and Scott Straus. *Intimate Enemy: Images and Voices of the Rwandan Genocide*. New York: Zone Books, 2006.

Makarov, A. A. *Repressii v Krasnoiarskom krae*. Abakan: Khakasskoe knizhnoe izdatel'stvo, 2008.

Mann, Michael. "Were the Perpetrators of Genocide 'Ordinary Men' or 'Real Nazis'? Results from Fifteen Hundred Biographies." *Holocaust and Genocide Studies*. 14(3) (Winter 2000).

Martin, Terry. *The Affirmative Action Empire: Nations and Nationalism in the Soviet Union, 1923–1939*. Ithaca, NY: Cornell University Press, 2001.

Martin, Terry. "The Origins of Soviet Ethnic Cleansing." *Journal of Modern History*. 70(4) (December 1998).

Matthaus, Jurgen. "Historiography and the Perpetrators of the Holocaust." In *The Historiography of the Holocaust*. Dan Stone, ed. London: Palgrave, 2004.

Mazower, Mark. *Hitler's Empire: How the Nazis Ruled Europe*. New York: Penguin, 2008.

Mazower, Mark. *Dark Continent: Europe's Twentieth Century*. New York: Penguin, 1998.

McCoy, Alfred W. *A Question of Torture: CIA Interrogation From the Cold War to the War on Terror*. New York: Holt, 2007.

McDonald, Tracy. "The Process of Collectivisation Violence." *Europe-Asia Studies*. 65(9) (November 2013).

McLoughlin, Barry, and Kevin McDermott, eds. *Stalin's Terror*. New York: Palgrave Macmillan, 2003.

Medvedev, Roy. *Let History Judge*. Trans George Shriver. New York: Columbia University Press, 1989.

Melnyk, Oleksandr. "Historical Politics, Legitimacy Contests, and the (Re)-Construction of Political Communities in Ukraine During the Second World War." PhD dissertation. University of Toronto, 2016.

Mil'bakh, V. S. *Politicheskie repressii komandno-nachal'stvuiushchego sostava, 1937–1938*. St. Petersburg: S. Peterburgskii universitet, 2007.

Mozokhin, O. B. *Pravo na repressii. Vnesudebnye polnomochiia organov gosudarstvennoi bezopasnosti*. Moscow: Kuchkovo pole, 2011.

Naumov, Leonid. *Stalin i NKVD*. Moscow: EKSMO, 2007.

Naumov, Leonid. *Bor'ba v rukovodstve NKVD v 1936–1938 gg*. Moscow: Modern-A, 2006.

Neitzel, Sonke, and Harald Welzer. *Soldaten: On Fighting, Killing, and Dying. The Secret World War II Transcripts of German POWs*. Toronto: McClelland and Stewart, 2011.

Nikolaiev, I. Ie. "Chystky kerivnoi verkhivky NKVS Ukrainy (II polovyna 30-kh rr. XX stolittia)." *Istoriia Ukrainy: Malovidomi imena, podii, fakty*. No. 34 (2007).

Nikol's'kyĭ, Volodymyr. "Statystyka politychnykh represii 1937 r. v Ukrainsk'ii RSR." *Z arkhiviv VUChK-GPU-NKVD-KGB*. Nos. 3-4 (2000).

Papkov, S., and K. Teraiam, eds., *Politicheskie i sotsial'nye aspekty istorii Stalinizma*. Moscow: Rosspen, 2015.

Pendas, Devin O. "Seeking Justice, Finding Law: Nazi Trials in Postwar Europe" *Journal of Modern History*. 81(2) (June 2009).

Penter, Tanya. "Local Collaborators on Trial: Soviet War Crimes Trials under Stalin (1943–1953)." *Cahiers du monde Russe*. 49(2) (2008).

Petrov, Nikita. *Palachi: Oni vypolniali zakazy Stalina*. Moscow: Novaia gazeta, 2011.

Polianskii, Aleksei. *Ezhov: Istoriia "zheleznogo" stalinskogo narkoma*. Moscow: Veche, 2001.

Popov, V. P. "Gosudarstvennyi terror v Sovetskoi Rossii, 1923–1953 gg. (istochnik i ikh interpretatsiia)," *Otechestvennye arkhivy*. No. 2 (1992).

Prusin, Alexander Victor. *The Lands Between: Conflict in the East European Borderlands*. Oxford: Oxford University Press, 2010.

Prusin, Alexander Victor. *Nationalizing a Borderland: War, Ethnicity, and Anti-Jewish Violence in East Galicia, 1914–1920*. Tuscaloosa: University of Alabama Press, 2005.

Prusin, Alexander Victor. "'Fascist Criminals to the Gallows!': The Holocaust and Soviet War Crimes Trials, December 1945–February 1946." *Holocaust and Genocide Studies*. 17(1) (2003).

Rassweiler, Anne D. *The Generation of Power: The History of Dneprostroi*. New York: Oxford University Press, 1988.

Rittersporn, Gabor T. *Anguish, Anger and Folkways*. Pittsburgh: University of Pittsburgh Press, 2014.

Robin, Corey. *Fear: The History of a Political Idea*. New York: Oxford University Press, 2004.

Robin, Corey. "The Language of Fear: Security and Modern Politics." In *Fear Across the Disciplines*. Jan Plamper and Benjamin Lazier, eds. Pittsburgh: University of Pittsburgh Press, 2012.

Rogovin, Vadim. *Partiia rasstreliannykh*. Moscow: RAN, 1997.

Roseman, Mark. "Beyond Conviction? Perpetrators, Ideas, and Actions in the Holocaust in Historiographical Perspective." In *Conflict, Catastrophe and Continuity: Essays on Modern German History*. Frank Biess, Mark Roseman, and Hanna Schissler, eds. New York: Berghahn Press, 2007.

Samosudov, V. M. *O repressiiakh v Omskom priirtysh'e*. Omsk: OMGPU, 1998.

Sanborn, Joshua A. *Imperial Apocalypse: The Great War and the Destruction of the Russian Empire*. Oxford: Oxford University Press, 2014.

Savin, A. I., and A. G. Tepliakov. "'Partiia mozhet oshibat'sia, a NKVD nikogda': Sotrudniki UNKVD po Odesskoi oblasti na skam'e podsudimykh (1939–1943 gg.)" In *Chekisty na skam'e podsudimykh*. Lynne Viola, Marc Junge, and Jeffery Rossman, eds. Moscow: Probel, 2017.

Scott, James C. *Domination and the Arts of Resistance: Hidden Transcripts*. New Haven, CT: Yale University Press, 1990.

Sereny, Gitta. *Into that Darkness: From Mercy Killing to Mass Murder*. London: Pimlico, 1995.

Shapoval, Iu. I. et al., eds. "Iezhovshchyna." *Politychnyi teror i teroryzm v Ukraini XIX-XX st: Istorychni narysy*. Kiev: Naukova dumka, 2002.

Shapoval, Iu. I. et al., eds. *Vsevold Balytsk'yi: osoba, chas, otochennia*. Kiev: Stylos, 2002.

Shapoval, Iu. I. et al., eds. *ChK-HPU-NKVD v Ukraini*. Kiev: Abrys, 1997.

Shapoval, Iu. I. et al., and Vadym Zolotar'ov. "Ievrei v kerivnytstvi orhaniv DPU-NKVD USRR-URSR u 1920–1930-kh rr." *Z arkhiviv VUChK-GPU-NKVD-KGB*. No. 1 (34) (2010).

Shearer, David R. "Stalin at War, 1918–1953: Patterns of Violence and Foreign Threat." *Jahrbucher fur Geschichte Osteuropas*, forthcoming.

Shearer, David R. *Policing Stalin's Socialism*. New Haven, CT: Yale University Press, 2009.

Smirnov, N. G. *Rapava, Bagirov i drugie: Antistalinskie protsessy 1950-kh. gg*. Moscow: AIRO-XXI, 2014.

Sofsky, Wolfgang. *The Order of Terror: The Concentration Camp*. Trans. William Templer. Princeton, NJ: Princeton University Press, 1997.

Solomon, Peter H., Jr. "Post-Soviet Criminal Justice: The Persistence of Distorted Neo-Inquisitorialism," *Theoretical Criminology*. 19(2) (2015).

Solomon, Peter H., Jr. *Soviet Criminal Justice Under Stalin*. Cambridge: Cambridge University Press, 1996.

Sorokin, A., A. Kobak, and O. Kuvaldina, eds. *Istoriia Stalinizma: zhizn' v terrore. Sotsial'nye aspekty repressii. Materialy mezhdunarodnoi nauchnoi konferentsii Sankt-Peterburg, 18–20 oktiabria 2012 g.* Moscow: Rosspen, 2013.

Staub, Ervin. *The Roots of Evil: The Origins of Genocide and Other Group Violence*. Cambridge: Cambridge University Press, 1989.

Stepanov, A. F. *Rasstrel po limitu*. Kazan: Novoe Znanie, 1999.

Straus, Scott. *The Order of Genocide: Race, Power, and War in Rwanda*. Ithaca, NY: Cornell University Press, 2006.

Sutherland, Willard. *The Baron's Cloak: A History of the Russian Empire in War and Revolution*. Ithaca, NY: Cornell University Press, 2014.

Tepliakov, A. G. *Oprichniki Stalina*. Moscow: EKSMO, 2009.

Tepliakov, A. G. *Mashina terrora: OGPU-NKVD Sibiri v 1929-1941 gg*. Moscow: Novyi Khronograf, 2008.

Tepliakov, A. G. *"Nepronitsaemye nedra." VChK-OGPU v Sibiri, 1918–1929 gg*. Moscow: AIRO, 2007.

Tepliakov, A. G. *Protsedura: Ispolnenie smertnykh prigovorov v 1920–1930 kh. godov*. Moscow: Vozvrashchenie, 2007.

Traverso, Enzo. *The Origins of Nazi Violence*. Trans. Janet Lloyd. New York: New Press, 2003.

Tumshis, M. *VChK: Voina klanov*. Moscow: Eksmo, 2004.

Valentine, Douglas. *The Phoenix Program: America's Use of Terror in Vietnam*. New York: Open Road, 1990.

Vasil'iev, Valerii. "Mekhanizmy 'velykoho teroru': mistsevyi zriz (diial'nist' oblasnykh UNKVS URSR u liutomu-lystopadi 1938 r." *Z arkhiviv VUChK-GPU-NKVD-KGB.* No. 1(28) (2007).

Vasil'iev, Valerii, and Roman Podkhur, "Organizatory i ispoliniteli massovogo ubiistva liudei v 1937-1938 gg. Sud'by sotrudnikov Vinnitskogo i Kamenets-Podol'skogo oblastnykh upravlenii NKVD." In *Chekisty na skam'e podsudimykh.* Lynne Viola, Marc Junge, Jeffery Rossman, eds. Moscow: Probel.

Vatlin, Alexander. *Agents of Terror: Ordinary Men and Extraordinary Violence in Stalin's Secret Police.* Trans. Seth Bernstein. Madison: University of Wisconsin Press, 2016.

Vatlin, A. Iu. *"Nu i nechist'": Nemetskaia operatsiia NKVD v Moskve i Moskovskoi oblasti, 1936–1941 gg.* Moscow: Rosspen, 2012.

Vatlin, A. Iu. *Terror raionnogo masshtaba.* Moscow: Rosspen, 2004.

Vert, Nikolia. *Terror v besporiadok. Stalinizm kak sistema.* Moscow: Rosspen, 2010.

Viola, Lynne. "The Question of the Perpetrator in Soviet History." *Slavic Review.* 72(1) (Spring 2013).

Viola, Lynne. *The Unknown Gulag: The Lost World of Stalin's Special Settlements.* New York: Oxford University Press, 2007.

Viola, Lynne. *Peasant Rebels Under Stalin: Collectivization and the Culture of Peasant Resistance.* Oxford: Oxford University Press, 1996.

Viola, Lynne. "The Second Coming: Class Enemies in the Soviet Countryside, 1927–1935." In *Stalinist Terror: New Perspectives.* J. Arch Getty and Roberta T. Manning, eds. New York: Cambridge University Press, 1993.

Viola, Lynne. *The Best Sons of the Fatherland: Workers in the Vanguard of Soviet Collectivization.* New York: Oxford University Press, 1987.

Viola, Lynne. "The Campaign to Eliminate the Kulak as a Class, Winter 1929–1930: A Reevaluation of the Legislation." *Slavic Review.* 45(3) (Fall 1986).

Waller, James. *Becoming Evil: How Ordinary People Commit Genocide and Mass Killing.* New York: Oxford University Press, 2002.

Weiner, Amir, ed. *Landscaping the Human Garden: Twentieth-Century Population Management in a Comparative Framework.* Stanford, CA: Stanford University Press, 2003.

Weiner, Amir. "Nature, Nurture, and Memory in a Socialist Utopia: Delineating the Soviet Socio-Ethnic Body in the Age of Socialism." *American Historical Review.* 104(4), (October 1999).

Wheatcroft, Stephen G. "Victims of Stalinism and the Soviet Secret Police." *Europe-Asia Studies.* 51(2) (1999).

Wildt, Michael. *An Uncompromising Generation: The Nazi Leadership of the Reich Security Main Office.* Trans. Tom Lampert. Madison: University of Wisconsin Press, 2009.

Wieviorka, Annette. *The Era of the Witness.* Trans Jared Stark. Ithaca, NY: Cornell University Press, 2006.

Zimbardo, Philip. *The Lucifer Effect: Understanding How Good People Turn Evil.* New York: Random House, 2008.

Zolotar'ov, Vadym. "Favoryt Iezhova: storinky biohrafii narkoma vnutrishnikh sprav URSR O. I. Uspens'koho." In *Politychni represii v Ukran'skii RSR: Doslidnyts'ki refleksii ta interpretatsii. Do 75-richchia "Velykoho teroru" v SRSR. Materialy vseukrains'koi naukovii konferentsii.* Oleh Bazhan and Roman Podkur, eds. Kiev: Instytut istorii Ukrainy NAN Ukrainy, 2013.

Zolotar'ov, Vadym. "Kolyshni spivrobitnyky NKVS URSR na kerivnii roboti u systemi HUTAB SRSR (1936-1939rr.)." *Z arkhiviv VUChK-GPU-NKVD-KGB.* Nos. 1–2 (2013).

Zolotar'ov, Vadym. "Kerivnyi sklad NKVS URSR pid chas 'velykoho teroru' (1936–1938 rr.): sotsial'no-statystychnyi analiz." *Z arkhiviv VUChK-GPU-NKVD-KGB.* No. 2(33) (2009).

Zolotar'ov, Vadym. "Diial'nist' orhaniv radians'koi derzhbezpeky zi zdiisnennia kurkul's'koi operatsii u Kharkivs'kii oblasti (1937–1938rr.)." *Z arkhiviv VChK-GPU-NKVD-KGB.* No. 1. (2007).

Zolotar'ov, Vadym. *Oleksandr Uspens'kyi: osoba, chas, otochennia.* Kharkiv: Folio, 2004.

Index